EAGLE ON THE STREET

ALSO BY STEVE COLL

The Deal of the Century
The Taking of Getty Oil

EAGLE ON THE STREET

BASED ON THE PULITZER PRIZE—WINNING ACCOUNT OF THE SEC'S BATTLE WITH WALL STREET

DAVID A. VISE
STEVE COLL

Charles Scribner's Sons
New York

Maxwell Macmillan Canada
Toronto
Maxwell Macmillan International
New York   Oxford   Singapore   Sydney

Charles Scribner's Sons
Macmillan Publishing Company
866 Third Avenue, New York, NY 10022

Maxwell Macmillan Canada, Inc.
1200 Eglinton Avenue East, Suite 200
Don Mills, Ontario M3C 3N1

Macmillan Publishing Company is part of the Maxwell Communication Group of Companies.

Library of Congress Cataloging-in-Publication Data
Vise, David A.
Eagle on the Street: based on the Pulitzer Prize–winning account of the SEC's battle with Wall Street
David A. Vise and Steve Coll.
p.   cm.
Includes bibliographical references and index.
ISBN 0-684-19314-0
1. United States.   Securities and Exchange Commission—Officials and employees.   2. Securities industry—United States—Corrupt practices.   3. Securities fraud—United States.   I. Coll, Steve.   II. Title.
KF1444.C65   1991
345.73'0268—dc20
[347.305268]   91-9529

Macmillan books are available at special discounts for bulk purchases for sales promotions, premiums, fund-raising, or educational use. For details, contact:

Special Sales Director
Macmillan Publishing Company
866 Third Avenue
New York, NY 10022

10 9 8 7 6 5 4 3 2 1
Designed by Nancy Sugihara
Printed in the United States of America

To Lori and Susan

Contents

1 A Great New Beginning 1

2 The Man from Wall Street 21

3 A Giant of the Opera 43

4 Closed Meeting 59

5 The Hunted 73

6 Trick or Treat 89

7 The Chicago School 111

8 High Yield, High Risk 131

9 Naked Options 153

10 The Leveraging of America 171

11 Leaking 191

12 Dr Pepper 207

13   Confrontation   225

14   Testing a Friendship   249

15   A Tale of Two Buildings   259

16   The Manipulation   275

17   A Big Fish   291

18   The Fall   309

19   A Generation of Giants   329

20   A Form of Service   353

Epilogue   373

A Note on Sources   383

Acknowledgments   387

Index   389

Illustrations

(following page 184)

SEC meeting room where John Shad and his colleagues deliberated

SEC Chairman John S. R. Shad

SEC enforcement director Stanley Sporkin introducing his successor, John Fedders

SEC San Francisco office director Bobby Lawyer

Gary Lynch, who succeeded John Fedders

John Shad testifying before Congress

Ivan Boesky

Ivan Boesky on furlough from prison

Michael Milken

Hobnail boots presented to Chairman John Shad during his campaign to clean up Wall Street

EAGLE ON THE STREET

1

A Great New Beginning

On that last day, May 14, 1981, Stanley Sporkin wanted to avoid all the "sentimental junk," as he called it, so he worked straight through, hard and fast. After almost twenty years at the Securities and Exchange Commission, there was no easy way for him to go. How could there be, after all they had done together, all that history? They had built the toughest, most creative law enforcement machine in the country, Sporkin thought, a machine nobody could ever duplicate. And now he was leaving it behind.

There would be a going-away party later, and that seemed the right time to reminisce and toast and joke. Until then, it seemed to Sporkin that there was still so much to worry about. There were two big, controversial enforcement cases on his desk that day, one involving giant Mobil Oil Corporation, the other involving Citicorp, New York's biggest bank. Sporkin wanted to talk with David Doherty, one of his key deputies, about how to handle them when he was gone. That evening, he was scheduled to have dinner with some longtime colleagues from the SEC and with John Shad, the Wall Street financier picked by President Reagan to be the new SEC chairman.

And there were the files—boxes, folders, and discarded papers all over his office. It was a big corner room on the fourth floor of the SEC's Washington headquarters, with a view of the Capitol. The room had all the amenities decreed appropriate for a bu-

1

reaucrat of Stanley Sporkin's rank: carpeting, a couch, a rectangular table for meetings, and a desk. The office was large but somewhat disheveled, like Sporkin himself. There were records about past SEC investigations—corporate bribery cases from the 1970s, bank fraud probes, embezzlement cases, investigations of Wall Street. Ira Pearce, one of Sporkin's investigators, kept other files nearby, as well as old newspapers he intended to read and boxes jammed with documents only he could find. The boxes were everywhere; they had grown like moss around an ancient oak. One day, Pearce said, he would go through and sort it all properly. But that day never came, and new boxes had piled up on the old ones.

That Thursday, however, Sporkin called for help. Personal materials were hauled away to his house in suburban Maryland. Sporkin dumped many of his old SEC files in Pearce's office. He didn't want just to throw them away, so he thought he'd have a little fun by depositing them anonymously with Pearce, who wasn't around that day. Sporkin figured Pearce would probably never notice new mounds of clutter loaded into his office.

In the enforcement division files, there were a thousand secrets: confidential Securities and Exchange Commission memos, testimony taken from the targets of Sporkin's investigations, private corporate records handed over to the SEC with the assurance that they wouldn't be made public. The SEC's enforcement division, which Sporkin had headed since 1974, did most of its work in secret, as did the rest of the SEC. The commission was the federal agency responsible for policing the nation's financial markets and regulating 9,000 publicly owned corporations, 3,500 brokerage houses, 3,700 investment advisers, and 1,300 investment companies. The job of Sporkin's enforcement division was to oversee a litany of laws proscribing what was popularly called "white collar crime." Under Sporkin, the division had gained a worldwide reputation.

But now the feared and celebrated enforcement chief was on his way out. A month earlier, in April 1981, the newly elected Reagan administration had announced that Sporkin was to become the Central Intelligence Agency's general counsel, its chief lawyer. In the wake of his announced departure, there was talk of major changes at the SEC. Exactly what Shad wanted, whom he would select as Sporkin's replacement, and what kind of institution the SEC would become after Sporkin left was very difficult that May to predict.

It was Stanley Sporkin, himself, who had become a key issue for members of the ascendant Reagan team. Their transition report said outright that he should be replaced. He was only a civil servant, equal in rank to four other division directors at the SEC, none of whom could make policy or file lawsuits on their own. A division director such as Sporkin needed a majority vote from the five presidentially appointed SEC commissioners to bring an enforcement action or even issue a subpoena as part of an investigation. By the spring of 1981, however, Sporkin's power belied the commission's organization chart. Between 1977 and early 1981, Harold Williams, a Democrat and former corporate executive, had been the SEC's chairman. He had battled with Sporkin for control of the SEC's agenda, and to shape its priorities. Still, it was Sporkin's ideas about corporate morality and the SEC's public service mission that often defined the commissioners' debate at their regular closed meetings on the seventh floor. To the public, and to the corporations and Wall Street firms the SEC regulated, Sporkin *was* the commission.

If you had a problem with the SEC, it was Sporkin who could take care of it. If you were the target of an SEC fraud investigation, you made a pilgrimage to Sporkin's corner office, sometimes to sit on his seventy dollar, tufted, ugly, one-armed couch and negotiate your peace. Sporkin greeted you with his jacket off and tie loosened, a picture of wrinkled agitation, like a newspaper editor on some perpetual deadline. As you made your defense, Sporkin would often lean back and shut his aqua-colored eyes, as if he had fallen asleep. Then, as voices lulled and you were certain that he had nodded off, he would spring from his seat and pace like a cat, firing off a list of conditions and settlement terms. He was tough, the lawyers who battled him generally agreed, and they said, too, that it would be foolish to underestimate Stanley Sporkin's authority or zeal.

It was the zeal, the sense of mission, that so attracted and re-
pulsed people when they dealt with Sporkin. The young staff
lawyers he recruited to the SEC from top law schools and prestigious corporate firms considered Sporkin to be the consummate
public servant, the Ralph Nader of the federal government. Like
Nader, Sporkin had his rumpled peculiarities, and he projected
an air of righteousness. He was an activist who defined the SEC's
purpose broadly and possessed the talent to extend its reach.

Goaded by Sporkin, the SEC chased big corporations for paying bribes in far-off countries of the Third World. At home, it
cracked down on illegal political contributions. And Sporkin's
cases grabbed headlines and generated fear. Even before the SEC
formally went after New York–based United Brands for paying
bribes in the mid-1970s, its top executive Eli Black took his life by
jumping out a window in the Chrysler Building. When the SEC
later sued United Brands for paying bribes to members of the
Honduran government to lower the Central American country's
banana-export tax, the resulting publicity toppled the Honduran
president within a month. Scandal rocked the Japanese government when Sporkin prosecuted the aircraft manufacturer Lockheed for making overseas payoffs. Reformers in Congress enacted
sweeping domestic campaign law revisions because of cases he
filed against U.S. corporations that maintained slush funds for
national political candidates. Working for Sporkin, jetting around
the country, negotiating with top defense lawyers and their powerful clients, investigators in the SEC's enforcement division felt
with good reason that they made a difference in the world. It was
a far cry from the work at other bureaucracies around the capital,
where the institutions seemed too often stagnant, captured by the
industries they regulated. At the SEC, Sporkin's lawyers felt they
wore the white hats.

As his power had grown, as his policies had become more effective and more creative, Sporkin had met with increasing resis-
tance from the commissioners on the seventh floor and from his
rivals within the commission. At the table in the hearing room
where closed SEC meetings were held, the tone of debate had
grown increasingly heated in recent years. All the fighting literally

made Sporkin sick. He attributed a gall bladder problem that required surgery in 1980 in part to tension from his battles inside the SEC.

There were two layers to the debate about Sporkin. One had to do with the issues, whether Sporkin's approach to enforcement was correct under the law. The other layer was less polite and had to do with power. "What frightened me most about Sporkin's power at the time I became a commissioner was the fear he aroused of both him and the SEC," wrote Roberta Karmel, an SEC commissioner from 1977 to 1980, not long after Sporkin left the commission. "No unelected government official should wield that kind of power too long."

Before he left his office for the last time that Thursday, and headed off to dinner with John Shad and the others, Sporkin met with David Doherty to talk about Mobil and Citicorp, two cases that exemplified the ambitious prosecutions Sporkin had inspired at the commission. If it was no longer possible for him to wield the power opponents such as Karmel found so threatening, then perhaps he could bequeath his clout to handpicked successors. Doherty was typical of the lawyers who worked closely with Sporkin. It was a tightly knit group. Many of them intended to stay after Sporkin was gone and they were concerned about how the new chairman, Shad, a Reagan campaign fund-raiser from Wall Street, would treat them. Doherty was an associate director of the enforcement division, one notch below Sporkin, and he was intensely loyal to his boss. So were others like Ted Levine, another associate director, and a leading candidate to take Sporkin's job.

There were other investigations pending in the enforcement division that May, of course, but Mobil and Citicorp were the most important. Each was a model of how Sporkin approached law enforcement and how he thought the SEC should fulfill its regulatory mission. In each, Sporkin had considered filing public charges against a major corporation for failing to disclose questionable conduct to its shareholders. In Citicorp, the alleged misdeeds involved foreign currency transactions the bank had engaged in to avoid overseas taxes. That case was less pressing; it would be months before it was presented at a closed meeting to the five SEC commissioners for final action. The Mobil matter, however, was in its final stages. It was Sporkin's legacy on the seventh floor, and he wanted to be sure that Doherty shepherded the case successfully through the SEC.

They discussed strategy, legal details, office politics, the upcoming closed hearing—the bread and butter of Stanley Sporkin's life for nearly two decades. Finally, there was nothing more that Sporkin could do. It was Doherty's case now.

That evening Stanley Sporkin collected the last of his things and left the building.

It was a different Washington into which he stepped.

That May of 1981, the capital was undergoing one of its quadrennial postelection renewals. It was part calculated politics, part cultural theatrics. Washington, for more than a century, had been used as a kind of canvas on which politicians sketched symbolic pictures of the country's mood. This was especially true following presidential elections, when the members of a new administration came pouring into town, beaming with energy and ambition, wearing the styles that had carried them to victory. Beginning with Andrew Jackson, who stomped through the White House in muddy boots to show that he was a man of the people, the "political arrival" grew into a capital art form. With the advent of television, the presidential inauguration and its aftermath became a carefully crafted extravaganza handled by specialists in pomp. It was a chance for a newly elected president to set the tone of his administration, to remind the voters why they had entrusted him with power. Flanked by his beautiful and well-dressed wife, John F. Kennedy, the youngest president in history, went hatless in the cold in 1960 to emphasize his youth and vigor. Jimmy Carter eschewed a car during his inaugural parade and walked smiling and waving down Pennsylvania Avenue, reminding his television audience that he was a casual, informal man "as good as the American people," as his campaign had put it.

Like everybody else in the capital, and as they had several times before, the senior lawyers and investigators at the SEC in Washington were now watching with interest a new drama: the arrival of Ronald Reagan's administration, in early 1981. For those in the business of regulating the nation's finance, it was in some ways an unnerving spectacle.

It wasn't just the money, although there was plenty of that. It was the character of the people who came to the capital that winter and spring, their style. Beginning almost immediately after Reagan's crushing victory over Carter, the private jets began to arrive at Washington's National Airport. From the cabins stepped silver-haired businessmen and industrialists and lawyers, men who by and large had never spent much time in Washington before, whose fortunes had been earned and not inherited, who considered themselves deserving of their wealth, and whose radically conservative ideas about government were in many cases untempered by any experience working for the public good. Dressed in double-breasted pinstripe suits with handkerchiefs neatly folded in their lapel pockets, many of these men looked like the kind of financial sharpshooters whom the SEC had often prosecuted. As officers at the country's largest corporations and Wall Street banks, or as partners in the biggest law firms in New York, these Reagan loyalists knew the SEC as a powerful and self-satisfied agency prone to moralizing. Some of them despised the commission.

They came to Washington seeking jobs in Ronald Reagan's government, or to become advisers to the president without portfolio, in part because they sensed the change that was in the air. Nobody in the capital that winter and spring could have missed it. Radically conservative intellectuals who had flocked to Reagan's campaign trumpeted that a revolution was at hand, one in which the capital's sprawling federal bureaucracies—with the exception of the Pentagon—would be pared to the bone. Taxes would be slashed, defense spending raised, and somehow, the federal budget balanced. Reagan would get government off the backs of the American people and, free from burdensome interference, business would flourish. AMERICA, said the sign in the lobby of Washington's L'Enfant Plaza Hotel, A GREAT NEW BEGINNING.

What seemed a political fantasy was complemented by an air of Hollywood escapism. The story began with a happy ending: after

444 days in captivity, the fifty-two Americans held hostage in Iran were freed just as Reagan was sworn in. The new tone was set perhaps most conspicuously by Nancy Reagan, the former actress and new First Lady. Unabashedly, she raised a quarter of a million dollars from friends in California to pay for new White House china and interior decoration, and then badgered the Carters to leave the place early so she could get to work. During a difficult winter, when inflation was soaring and small businesses around the country were closing because of high interest rates, Nancy Reagan spent $25,000—more than the country's annual per capita income—on clothes to wear to the inaugural balls. One inaugural gala was so extravagant that it had to be staged at a sports arena with 19,000 seats. There, men in shining tuxedos and women wearing full-length minks and sables over their designer gowns partied into the night, led by a cavalcade of singers and stars from Reagan's Hollywood.

Reagan's men considered the display a service to the nation. Charles Wick, the businessman and financier who was cochairman of the festivities, said that for those in the country who were suffering economically, watching the Reagan inaugural on television would have the same uplifting effect as Hollywood movies did on the nation's poor during the Great Depression. Greed, as one of Reagan's financial backers would later tell a group of college students, was good.

The Securities and Exchange Commission—as a law enforcement institution and as a national symbol—stood in opposition to such bold ostentation in May of 1981.

On the surface, it looked like a modest place, though its appearance understated its power and influence. Sequestered in the shadows cast by Capitol Hill, boxed in by crumbling homes and offices, the commission's headquarters was as dull a building as existed in Washington, no small distinction in a city that often confused drabness with virtue. With its poured concrete, plate glass, and straight lines, and durable coats of pallid paint, the headquarters seemed a consummate expression of utility. It was the architectural equivalent of wash-and-wear.

The building's facade suited well many of those who strode

through the front door each morning, purposeful and confident, briefcases gripped firmly, pens clipped in breast pockets. Not for them the pomp and fashion of the capital's great political buildings nearby—the loud power of the domed Capitol, for instance, or the self-conscious authority of the Supreme Court, where granite steps rose to tall marble columns, forcing visitors to climb like supplicants seeking wisdom from an oracle. At the SEC, power wore an unobtrusive face. For nearly fifty years, the agency had ruled over the economy, creating and supervising trillion-dollar financial markets, chasing crooks, closing wayward businesses, and at times playing God on Wall Street by deciding who would keep his fortune and who would give it back. Far beyond the size of its budget, the number of its employees, or its congressional mandate, the SEC had grown to become one of the mightiest agencies of the federal government. By the end of the 1970s, the SEC was the institution in Washington that Wall Street and Corporate America feared most.

Many of the lawyers and investigators who worked for the commission had come to cherish both their unusual power and their anonymity. They liked to be feared—among other things, it was a way to keep their adversaries off balance. And so, to protect their growing authority and feed the guilty imaginations of those who dreaded them, the commission staff revealed as little of themselves as possible. SEC lawyers conducted their investigations in secret. Commissioners made far-reaching policy decisions at closed-door meetings from which the public and even the Congress were excluded. Staff interpreted the law without consulting other agencies of the federal government. They considered themselves independent, protected if not altogether isolated from the emotional tides of electoral politics that swept through Washington every four years.

Increasingly at the commission, the staff thought of itself as a permanent and elite corps of policemen and policymakers whose mission was to define and enforce morality on the byways of American capitalism. In the hallways of their headquarters they talked about it like that—the SEC staffers were the good guys, the cops, and the economy they supervised was populated by legions of avaricious outlaws and bandits. The agency's symbol was a bald federal eagle with an olive branch in one claw and arrows in the other; its efforts to keep a sharp eye on Wall Street had prompted some to refer to the commission as "Eagle on the Street." Only through vigilance and discretion and discipline, the SEC staffers thought, could the commission save Wall Street and the nation from itself.

The sin most often denounced by the commission was greed, but what distinguished the SEC from, for example, the Catholic Church was the commission's deep and historical ambivalence about this manifestation of moral weakness. The sum and effect of all the SEC's rules and regulations, and of its fifty years of law enforcement, was that the commission believed a strong desire to make money and profit was good, but that unchecked greed was evil. The profit motive played an essential role in healthy and efficient financial markets, but rampant greed could throw the country's economic machine out of whack, enriching a few at the expense of many or at the cost of collective imperatives such as breathable air or stable prices or even something as intangible as social equity. Ever since it was created in response to the country's populist disgust over the scams and scandals of the 1920s—and over the 1929 market crash and depression that followed—the commission's lawyers and investigators had struggled to decide how much greed in America was too much.

The commission was created by Congress in 1934 to attack the corruption and greed on Wall Street exposed in the 1929 stock market crash. When Joseph P. Kennedy—patriarch of what would become the nation's greatest political family and a Wall Street titan who profited handsomely and fraudulently during the crash—was named to be the SEC's first chairman, there were those who sounded warnings about the fox and the chicken coop. But Kennedy appeared to prosecute Wall Street fraud to the hilt during his year-long tenure and the agency acquired a reputation for strength and integrity early on.

Much of the SEC's charter was defined in its early years by such legal minds as James M. Landis, William O. Douglas, and Felix Frankfurter, fixtures of the New Deal intellectual landscape.

When the New Deal was overtaken by war and the commission's founding fathers moved on to the Supreme Court, the agency began to drift in the manner of most federal bureaucracies, often reflecting the prevailing political mood in Washington in its own prosecutorial priorities. During World War II, the SEC's headquarters was moved to the Pennsylvania Athletic Club in Philadelphia, and its influence waned in favor of more pressing national security concerns. Still, the agency pursued a fundamental restructuring of the once-badly corrupt public utility industry. But the agency's budget was cut so severely by the Eisenhower administration in the mid-1950s that it had resources to prosecute a few blatant fraud and financial-market-manipulation cases but little else.

In the early 1960s, swept along in Kennedy's wake, intellectuals arrived again at the commission to reawaken the place, bringing with them high ideals and equally lofty pretensions. Slowly the power of the bureaucracy was centralized, just as the power of other federal agencies grew during eight consecutive years of Democratic reign in the capital. It was during this Great Society era of expansion and growth that the SEC established itself as the policeman of Wall Street and the guardian of the small investor. In 1968, Congress passed the Williams Act, which put the SEC in charge of administering and developing rules of conduct for the multimillion-dollar corporate takeover game. Under Nixon, keeping up with the times, the SEC had a minor political scandal—its first—when G. Bradford Cook resigned after only two months as chairman amid allegations that he took part in a scheme to protect a major Nixon contributor from SEC charges. It was a challenge to the SEC's reputation for uncompromising integrity and independence. But the agency rebounded strongly during the 1970s, spurred by Stanley Sporkin's cabal of committed prosecutors in the enforcement division.

With Sporkin, it wasn't so much whether something was illegal; what mattered was whether it was wrong. Overseas bribery and political payoffs—crimes that catapulted the SEC to international renown during the 1970s—had little relevance to the nation's securities laws, which the SEC was supposed to enforce. Those laws had been enacted mainly during the 1930s, in the aftermath of the 1929 crash, and were designed to rid the stock market of fraud and give public shareholders a fair shake.

During the 1970s, the SEC's enforcement division stretched the law to suit its needs. The crusade against corporate corruption began in the fall of 1974, shortly before Sporkin was promoted to enforcement chief, when the rumpled prosecutor would go home to his wife and family in the suburbs and turn on the local public TV station, channel 26, to watch nightly replays of the last round of the congressional Watergate hearings. By then the nation's fascination with the hearings was on the wane. Nixon had resigned; the drama was finished. But the Watergate committee still had witnesses to hear from. Among them were executives from the Northrop Corporation, American Airlines, the Gulf Oil Corporation, and other giant companies. They testified about large, secret cash payments made to Nixon's 1972 Committee to Re-Elect the President, or CREEP.

As he watched, Sporkin was outraged. Somehow, this has to be a securities law violation, he thought. A trained accountant, he wondered how the companies had reflected their illegal campaign contributions on the financial reports they filed every three months at the SEC's headquarters in Washington. When he ordered his investigators to dig into it, Sporkin found that the companies hadn't listed their domestic and foreign bribes at all. Why would they? The payments had been against the law. Were the companies supposed to confess to felonies in their SEC financial statements?

Sporkin decreed they should. If companies stopped paying bribes, the SEC began to assert, their earnings would decline because they would lose business. Therefore, the bribes themselves needed to be disclosed when paid. When the country's multinational corporations argued that the bribes were so small they need not be reported, Sporkin answered that it was the millions of dollars in revenue and profits that flowed from the bribes, rather than the small bribes themselves, that mattered in making the judgment.

It was a novel, creative, but disingenuous theory. The SEC

served notice under Stanley Sporkin that it would sue any company or anybody who failed to disclose illegal acts promptly and publicly at the commission.

In the years of upheaval following Watergate, it was easy to see Sporkin's crusade in partisan terms, and many did. Conservatives denounced his zealotry as thinly disguised liberal politicking. Liberals cheered his pursuit of Republican moneymen. But such assessments were too pat. Sporkin was a lifelong Republican who late in his career registered as an independent, and he maintained close friendships with Republican leaders such as William Casey, Ronald Reagan's 1980 campaign chairman and Central Intelligence Agency director. It was Casey, himself a former chairman of the SEC under Nixon, who had persuaded Sporkin to leave the commission for the CIA after Reagan's victory. It was legend at the SEC that Casey had once followed Sporkin's advice by resisting political pressure from Nixon aides who wanted to block an SEC probe on the eve of the 1972 presidential election. "Some day you'll thank me" for the advice, Sporkin had told Casey. Now Casey was taking him to the CIA.

The theories Sporkin developed at the SEC during the 1970s provided the commission with a virtually unlimited mandate. So sweeping was Sporkin's interpretation of the disclosure requirements of the federal securities law that, by the late 1970s, virtually any improper conduct at a publicly owned corporation fell within the SEC's jurisdiction. The genius of Sporkin's approach was that it shifted the burden of law enforcement from government to industry. No longer was the SEC merely a cop on the Wall Street beat, whistling on the proverbial street corner with its eyes open for suspicious activity. Instead, Sporkin projected an image of the commission as a kind of regulatory confessional. Wrongdoers of every stripe, but especially those at the country's largest corporations, were invited to admit their sins voluntarily in the SEC's public filing room—or else face the commission's wrath.

By the spring of 1981, when Sporkin finally left, that was a choice many of the country's biggest companies had grown tired of making.

*　　*　　*

"I think there have been times when the commission has been unfair," John Shad told Stanley Sporkin.

It was the night of Sporkin's departure from the SEC and they were seated with their wives amid the chime and clank of silver and china in a comfortable Georgetown restaurant, miles from the seedy strip of prewar government buildings where the SEC had its headquarters. Shad was staying at the Georgetown Inn, a clubby, richly appointed hotel on Wisconsin Avenue. He was preparing to move to Washington from his Park Avenue apartment in Manhattan. The new SEC chairman was friendly, pleasant, respectful, a chain-smoking bulldog of a man with drooping jowls and an affable manner. He had invited Sporkin to dinner because he wanted to pick his brain about how the SEC really worked, and about how it might be changed. Shad was candid: He thought Sporkin had taken the enforcement program too far. Now, at the beginning of the Reagan era, it was time to roll back regulation.

"I can understand how people would feel that way," Sporkin answered. By now he was used to the complaints about his aggressive prosecutions; they had grown into a chorus on Wall Street and in corporate boardrooms.

"John," he continued, "you have to understand that we had to keep a tight rein on the marketplace or else it will get out of control. Enforcement is an extraordinarily important program. It has to be in every area and it has to have a presence."

For most of the dinner, Sporkin had been doing the talking. Shad was enormously inquisitive, like a sponge soaking up information. He was unfamiliar with the SEC's inner workings and was still learning. Shad and Sporkin were both self-confident, plain-speaking men, sure of themselves but not combative. And there was an unspoken bond between them; both men admired and respected Bill Casey, the Reagan CIA director, and both considered him a friend. That helped ease their suspicions.

Sporkin summarized his ideas about enforcement for Shad. They boiled down to what Sporkin and his lieutenants sometimes termed the *access theory*. There were thousands of brokerage firms on Wall Street subject to SEC regulation and enforcement, but about a hundred of them were doing 95 percent of the business.

These were the big firms that provided access to the marketplace for all sorts of investors—huge pension funds, university endowments, mutual funds, and millions of individuals across the country. These big firms also provided access to the market for companies that wanted to raise money by selling new issues of stocks and bonds. The key, Sporkin insisted, was to concentrate enforcement on these access points, on the big investment and accounting firms that handled millions of transactions annually. A giant investment house like E. F. Hutton, where Shad had spent the last decade as vice chairman, cherished its SEC license to do business. By disciplining brokerage firms with access to the nation's marketplaces, by holding the institutions responsible for the acts of their employees, the SEC could encourage effective self-policing and make its limited resources go a long way.

Shad listened. He asked questions. But it seemed to Sporkin that the new chairman really didn't know or understand the commission's enforcement program very well. Perhaps that would take time. Or was Sporkin sensing Shad's biases as a man who had spent his entire professional life on Wall Street, who had little experience with or tolerance for the priorities of Washington bureaucrats? Sporkin wondered whether Shad would make the enforcement division weaker as part of President Reagan's deregulation program. But over one dinner it was hard to answer those kinds of questions.

Do you have any suggestions about who should be your successor? Shad asked.

"Ted Levine," Sporkin answered without hesitation.

The bearded, intense Levine was the obvious choice inside the commission. He was a brilliant lawyer, and experienced. The enforcement program's institutional memory was critically important, Sporkin believed. New enforcement directors had always been appointed from inside—and there was a reason. So much of the fraud and abuse the SEC pursued was repetitive. The same con artists appeared in different parts of the country to practice new versions of their old tricks. Corporations and Wall Street firms always tried to test the commission's limits. You had to know what had gone on before.

Shad gave little indication of his feelings about Levine, but Sporkin sensed Shad would hire someone from outside the agency to
replace him. What didn't need to be said was that Levine was a
Sporkin loyalist, a member of the old guard at the commission.
And despite his diplomacy, his respect, Shad had made one thing
clear to Sporkin over dinner. There would be changes at the SEC,
and soon.

"Mobil? Is there someone here from enforcement on Mobil?"
John Shad asked from his high-backed swivel chair at the round
table where the commissioners held their private debates. It was
July 23, 1981, two months after Sporkin's departure. Shad had
been on his new job for only a few weeks and not all the faces were
familiar.

On the side of the table where the staff sat, David Doherty
indicated his presence. There were other lawyers from the enforcement division with him and still other SEC staff sitting in the
chairs toward the back, set up for commission employees to observe proceedings closed to the public. Sporkin, then at the CIA,
was absent from his traditional seat beside the big pillar that separated the commissioner's side from the staff's side. Commission
policy was made at the wooden table where they sat in the closed
meeting room, which actually was two horseshoe-shaped tables
pushed together at the ends, leaving a hollow ring in the center.
Inside the SEC, people spoke of arguing a case "at the table," as
though it were like performing at center stage on the opening
night of a Broadway show. All around the closed meeting room
were signs of the SEC's rich past: an old bookcase in the corner
where the records of the earliest commission decisions from 1934
rested; colorful flags; and on the wall a wooden SEC seal with its
eagle clutching arrows and an olive branch. Across the room hung
a portrait of the late Manuel F. Cohen, considered in his day to be
the consummate agency official and keeper of the SEC's
tradition—the tradition many staff feared was now to be undermined by Shad, one of the vanguard of the Reagan Revolution.
They had come to the closed meeting room to find out if their
suspicions were justified.

The Mobil case symbolized to some at the SEC what was good and right about the Sporkin era at the commission and to others what was wrong with the enforcement program. The case involved Mobil's failure to disclose to its shareholders that Peter Tavoulareas, the son of Mobil's chairman, was part-owner of a shipping company that had close ties to Mobil. There were questions about whether the shipping company had received money and favors because of the family ties. But the case was fraught with political and legal complexities. A key question was whether the shipping company was actually a subsidiary of Mobil—if it was, then Mobil would likely be required to disclose the details of the business and family relationships under SEC rules. The traditional way to determine whether one company was a subsidiary of another was to examine ownership. Was the shipping company owned by Mobil?

The answer was no, which meant the SEC probably did not have a case it could win in court if Mobil wanted to fight. Still, Doherty had written in a confidential memo to the SEC commissioners, "The investigation has disclosed that [Mobil chairman] William Tavoulareas was directly involved in numerous transactions and management affairs relating to the marine management company in which his then 24-year-old son was a principal . . . Mobil has never made any disclosure of these matters in its filings with the commission." The enforcement division's argument was that even though Mobil didn't own the shipping company in question, it was nonetheless a "de facto subsidiary" because of the nature and extent of its business ties with the oil giant. Mobil should have disclosed these ties, the enforcement staff said, rather than trying to paper over the business relationship between father and son.

Not everyone inside the SEC was sure what "de facto subsidiary" meant, or whether it was a legally valid concept. Lawyers in the corporate finance division of the SEC, which was responsible for monitoring the reams of public account statements filed by companies at the commission, worried that Sporkin's brainchild could have unforeseen—and potentially undesirable—consequences. The Mobil lawyers thought the SEC enforcers were way off base, but they were looking for a reasonable way to put the matter behind them. There were other difficulties, too. Tavoulareas had initiated a libel suit against the *Washington Post* over its reporting on the matter; any decision the SEC made could have an impact on that case. And some members of Congress were pressing for action.

In a series of private meetings between SEC enforcement staff and Mobil lawyers, a deal had been cut, or so the SEC side led now by David Doherty believed. Rather than publicly charge Mobil with wrongdoing in an SEC enforcement action, the commission staff accepted a compromise. Doherty would draft a report of the SEC's investigation—a report of the facts only, not of legal conclusions about whether Mobil had violated any laws. Assuming the report was approved by the five SEC commissioners, Mobil would publish it in a public statement at SEC headquarters. The facts would be laid out for all to see.

Now the meeting had arrived to secure the SEC's approval for this deal. Doherty was on his own to face the new Reagan-appointed chairman. Many SEC staff attorneys—the keepers of the bureaucracy's traditions, what Sporkin called its "institutional memory"—were still trying to figure out John Shad. There were the obvious questions about his ideology, his loyalty to Reagan's program of immediate and drastic deregulation. Even more basic at this early date were concerns about his work habits and his personality. There were some commissioners who passed through the SEC whom the staff regarded as less than serious, commissioners who didn't read the staff's memos or study the legal issues to be debated, who enjoyed the trappings of their jobs but paid little attention to the substance. Would Shad be one of those? Would he respect the staff?

That Thursday, Barbara Thomas and Phil Loomis flanked Shad on the commissioners' side of the table—only three of the five SEC commissioners were present. Thomas was not a favorite of the staff; some in the enforcement division considered her more interested in her own self-promotion than in the serious work of the commission. Loomis, on the other hand, was respected for his intelligence and was seen as a friend of the bureaucracy.

Doherty would carry the burden of the meeting for the enforcement division. Here would be the first evidence for the Sporkin loyalists of what was ahead at the SEC.

"David, my question was," Shad began, "when one deals with the absence of violations, why are we, in effect, exercising sanctions against Mobil to file a report . . . ?"

"I have the same, precise question," added Thomas.

"First, I don't think we have necessarily found nothing," Doherty answered. ". . . As we explained in our memo, we had originally received allegations of a possible conflict of interest, which is an area which all of us are significantly concerned about. . . . We think we could take the position that . . . [the shipping company] was, in effect, a subsidiary of Mobil under these circumstances because of the control exercised. And, accordingly, disclosure would have been required."

Shad jumped in.

"On that point, it seems to me that you would not be able to argue that on the basis of equity ownership."

Shad had cut to the heart of the matter. The SEC staff's position was that the shipping company was a "de facto subsidiary," and therefore had to be disclosed by Mobil, even though there was no equity, or stock, ownership.

"No, it wouldn't be equity ownership," Doherty conceded. "It would be a—"

"Under managerial direction," Shad said.

"That's right. It would be under, basically, a control theory but not control by virtue of the equity ownership."

"Have we sustained that argument in the past?" Shad asked.

"Yes, we have, I believe, without—"

"No, I think in fairness, Dave, this would be what you might call a novel interpretation," interjected Lee Spencer, director of the SEC's corporate finance division, with the first attack from another staff member.

And so it went. Argument on argument piled up on Doherty.

"Well, you haven't sold me," Shad declared at one point.

Shad made clear that he thought the case was a stretch by any standard. The enforcement staff had conceded that it was not prepared to file a lawsuit against Mobil. If it wasn't ready to fight Mobil in court, Shad asked, how could the SEC justify a decision that would force the oil company to publish the staff's investigative report?

The answer was that this was Stanley Sporkin's deal, his settlement, just like the others that had come to the commission from his corner office and been approved. Only occasionally in the past seven years had the SEC rejected a recommendation from the enforcement division. And here, in John Shad's first month on the job, it was turning down a modest settlement involving Sporkin's compromise with the second biggest oil company in the world.

"I don't know," said Barbara Thomas when the 3 to o vote in favor of Mobil was over. "All this sympathy to Mobil. It just seems to me that they're—I mean, obviously the vote is taken, but it seems to me that we're doing better by them than they expected."

"I won't guess the answer," Shad said. "I agree with that."

When Sporkin heard what happened, he couldn't understand it. He didn't think the commissioners had acted in bad faith, he said. It must have been some kind of misunderstanding.

There was a deal. Stanley Sporkin had made a deal.

"I had been the architect of this sort of resolution," Sporkin explained afterward. "I had left before it got to the commission. . . . Something gets lost here and I think the unfortunate part here was that everything was aboard, and I just think it was misunderstood. . . . Mobil was on board. . . . Mobil was on board. There would have been no reason why the commission would not have accepted this."

No reason—except that Stanley Sporkin didn't work at the SEC anymore.

Doherty, Levine, and the other lawyers in the celebrated enforcement division were beginning to understand: the Securities and Exchange Commission belonged to John Shad now.

2

The Man from Wall Street

When John Shad met Ronald Reagan for the first time, they had the kind of instant rapport that men of like values often find. They shared a common philosophy about limited government and America's rightful place as a world leader. Though one had been a politician and the other a Wall Street financier, both believed that private enterprise nearly always provided the best solution to problems. They also shared conflicting impulses about government: They wanted Washington off the backs of the people, but they wanted to go to Washington and hold office themselves. Similarly, they believed sincerely that the basic American virtues of hard work and ingenuity could overcome any evil and were the bases of success; yet they were both white, middle-aged men who had prospered at times in their own lives because of connections. They understood that to get ahead in America, it helped to break into the inner circle. The setting for their initial chance meeting, and the profound impact it would have on John Shad's life, reinforced that notion.

The Bohemian Grove, where Shad first met Reagan, seemed as improbable a setting as any in Shad's life.

"Cast your grief to the fires and be strong with the holy trees and the spirit of the Grove," a voice decreed before the altar of the giant owl in the night air by the lake. "The owl is in his leafy temple; let all within the Grove be reverent before him."

21

There Shad stood, one summer's night in the northern California wood, surrounded by similarly pale, flabby businessmen and politicians. Only hours had elapsed since they had been wearing business suits, but the uniform of commerce and governance had no place here. Some of the men wore bizarre costumes and hoods; the public, especially women, was strictly forbidden at Bohemian Grove. Some of the guests had marched through the trees of their encampment bearing torches and a coffin—part of the Grove's "Cremation of Care" ritual.

The Bohemian Grove was an all-male summer camp for the rich and powerful. It thrived on its exclusiveness. It attracted overgrown boy scouts in government and business who relaxed and let loose by regressing in each other's company. To protests about the exclusion of women, the members responded that if the opposite sex were permitted, the men would have to cease urinating on trees, thereby destroying the ambience of the place. Shad wasn't a member, but he was invited to attend during the late 1970s by Hutton executives on the West Coast. It was, among other things, a good place to meet people who could help one's career. The annual Cremation of Care ritual, wherein a high priest sacredly invoked Shakespeare's proscription against intrigue—"Weaving spiders come not here"—was among the Grove's more obvious hypocrisies, since it was precisely their thirst for power and their immersion in worldly cares that drew men to the camp each year. Shad was no exception.

When they met, in the summer of 1978, Reagan was wearing cowboy boots and sat perched on a railing, absorbed in a performance by the ventriloquist Edgar Bergen. In the initial yet important conversation, Reagan was his usual, congenial self. After the show, the two men chatted and took a walk to another campsite within the Grove called the Hillbillies, where Shad ate lunch. (His waiter was a former U.S. ambassador to China named George Bush, who was taking his turn serving tables at the Hillbillies.) The tone of the Shad-Reagan conversation was more important than its substance; it was enough to establish that they were kindred spirits.

Reagan telephoned Shad the following year and asked him for

help in the upcoming Republican presidential primary campaign. But Shad initially deferred; he told the candidate's aides that they should try to recruit Donald Regan, a more prominent executive who ran Merrill Lynch, Wall Street's biggest firm. Regan, it turned out, wasn't interested—he was an early supporter of Bush. Just about everybody on Wall Street supported either Bush or John Connally, Reagan's other main opponent. Though they would later rally around, Reagan's extreme ideological conservatism at first unsettled the titans of business and finance—but not John Shad. When the Reagan staff came back to Shad and told him that he was their first choice, he agreed to be chairman of the New York campaign.

Shad went to work raising money and planning campaign events. He brought Reagan to the bastion of capitalism, the New York Stock Exchange, on March 19, 1980, in the midst of the tough New York State primary—a moment in the campaign when the surge to Reagan was just under way. Shortly before the close of trading that afternoon, Shad escorted the candidate across the boisterous exchange floor, where curious traders and floor brokers crowded around them. The Dow Jones Industrial Average, the most widely followed measure of daily stock market performance, had hardly moved at all that day, losing less than a point to 800.94. The market's performance was a symptom of the sluggish economy that Reagan promised to reverse with his "free market" policies.

They fought their way around the floor and up to the exchange's venerable lunch club, where Shad introduced his candidate to the audience. "Ladies and gentlemen," he intoned, "I present to you the next president of the United States." The visit turned out to be Reagan's second most successful fund-raiser of the month, netting $42,680.

Shad arranged, too, for Reagan to meet privately at the exchange with a group of influential New York business leaders— the sort of men who summered at the Bohemian Grove and now found their establishment-Republican candidates, Bush and Connally, fading from the race. Shad waited outside the conference room, wondering how things were going. When the door opened, financier Laurence A. Tisch emerged and flashed a "thumbs up" sign. The group approved of Shad's candidate.

During the campaign, Shad made it clear that if Reagan were elected, he would be interested in taking a post in Washington. He talked privately with Martin Lipton, a prominent Manhattan takeover lawyer, about how the two of them might go to Washington together to serve under Reagan, with Shad as Treasury Secretary. But after Reagan won, he appointed Merrill Lynch's Donald Regan to head Treasury. Shad's reward didn't come until February 1981, when Reagan personnel chief, E. Pendelton James, called to offer the SEC. James said afterward that Shad was selected because "he was probably the first businessman on Wall Street that came out early for Ronald Reagan."

If confirmed by the Senate, Shad would take a cut in pay from about $500,000 a year at E. F. Hutton to $55,000 a year as chairman of the SEC. He would trade the currency of success in Manhattan, money, for the currency of success in Washington, power.

There were pages and pages of government forms for Shad to fill out—the sort of forms Shad intuitively disliked. And there were decisions to be made about his family's massive stock market holdings, including more than $10 million of E. F. Hutton stock. There were sure to be questions about a conflict of interest for the SEC chairman if Shad tried to hold on to the Hutton stock, even in some sort of blind trust. Then, too, there was much for Shad to learn about how the SEC operated before he went in front of the Senate Banking Committee for confirmation.

Shad studied the Reagan transition team's written report about the SEC in the weeks before his April 6 confirmation hearing. All over Washington, Reagan's transition team was having its influence, calling, in one form or another, for most federal agencies to be trimmed in size by about one-third over three years. The SEC report was even more far-reaching. It not only called for a 30 percent cut in the SEC's budget, but also recommended that the SEC's enforcement division in Washington be dismantled, essentially decentralizing the law enforcement function. In theory, these aspects of the report should have appealed to Shad. He wanted to get government off the backs of the American people and cutting the size of the SEC might be one way to do that. He had seen the benefits of a decentralized management structure at E. F. Hutton and at some of the companies where he served as an investment banker or corporate director.

But Shad was not an ideologue. He thought the SEC's enforcement division had an important job to do and had carried out that mission pretty well in the 1970s, even if he hadn't agreed with all of its cases or priorities. He recognized, too, that decentralizing enforcement would weaken the division. On the issue of the SEC's size, he was a loyal Reagan man and wanted to explore how the agency's growth could be trimmed without hurting its productivity. But on the most controversial proposal in the transition report, he was not persuaded: Shad would not preside over the dismantling of the SEC's vaunted enforcement division. It was a decision he made on the basis of judgment and gut feel.

The immediate problem Shad faced was getting through the Senate confirmation process, and he feared that some senators would be looking to trick him into making a mistake. Such hearings usually constituted a rehearsed endorsement with little substantive questioning, but unpredictable things sometimes happened and Shad was apprehensive. He was a remarkably indistinct and unimpressive public speaker, inclined to mumble words until they were virtually inaudible. Shad planned for the hearing carefully, deciding, for example, not to smoke in front of fellow Utah native Senator Jake Garn, a Mormon.

For Shad, and for the senior SEC staff who came to watch him, there was an air of anticipation as the hearing began. It turned out to be a lark. The senators told bad jokes about each other's states and Shad praised the senators. His prepared statement followed a predictable line—Shad said he wanted to ease certain provisions of the Foreign Corrupt Practices Act, the law Stanley Sporkin had helped to make famous, and to eliminate other regulations that he said placed an undue burden on business. But when he came to the Reagan transition team's report on the SEC, Shad delivered a pleasant surprise to the skeptical SEC staff. He declined to endorse the recommendations.

One of the only tough questions at the hearing concerned the president's budget—that was where warfare was being waged in the early days of the Reagan revolution. Reagan's budget director, David Stockman, was proposing big cuts in the resources of nearly every federal agency. Shad, though, evaded the issue. He said he didn't know whether the SEC's present budget was sufficient.

"I am a total outsider at this point," Shad explained.

Two days later, he was confirmed by a voice vote. On May 6, 1981, Vice President Bush swore in John Sigsbee Rees Shad as the twenty-second chairman of the Securities and Exchange Commission. He was an outsider no more.

When Shad walked into the SEC's headquarters in Washington for the first time, he felt a deeper sense of personal fulfillment than anyone on the wary agency staff realized. The staff feared Shad was nothing more than a rich Reagan campaign fund-raiser from Wall Street who had been rewarded with an agency chairmanship and a meat ax to slash the size of the place. They were right about Shad's wealth but wrong about his political and personal character.

Shad's Mormon grandmother had told him that a person should spend one third of life learning, one third earning, and, if possible, one third serving. He had memorized that aphorism, repeating it over and over. He had devoted himself to learning, graduating from the University of Southern California, the prestigious Harvard Business School, and New York University law school. For more than thirty years, he dressed in dark pinstripe suits and suspenders on Wall Street, rising from his first job as a junior analyst to become a top executive of the giant E. F. Hutton brokerage house. Having amassed a fortune in excess of $15 million, it was time now, he felt, at age fifty-eight, to fulfill his grandmother's credo and turn his attention to government service in Washington.

He was tall and heavyset, broad-shouldered but slightly stooped. His big, floppy ears and droopy eyes conjured the image of a basset hound, though he possessed the drive of a greyhound. He was not a particularly handsome man, but there was something appealing about him—his clear blue eyes could be soft and sincere, and he had a warm smile that could light up a room.

Some among the SEC staff saw him as a caricature of Wall Street greed. It seemed to them that Shad was being asked to regulate his old New York pals, and that it was unlikely that he would really leave the elite social club of Manhattan finance even while working at the commission. Prior SEC chairmen had come from academia or law practice or corporate life. Shad's arrival marked a major turning point: He was the first man from Wall Street nominated to be SEC chairman in more than forty-five years, since President Roosevelt picked Joseph P. Kennedy to be the agency's first chairman.

Shad could remember having been inside the SEC building only once before, but the agency didn't seem completely foreign to him because he had worked with SEC documents and abided by commission regulations on a regular basis. He had never known a Wall Street without the SEC, and in his day-to-day work there, he relied heavily on the documents the commission required companies to file. As a young stock market analyst, he studied corporate account statements filed with the SEC to determine which stocks were good buys. He enjoyed crunching numbers and actually felt, in an indirect sort of way, indebted to the SEC for pushing companies to disclose the information he needed to do financial analysis. Though he had a strong free market bias, Shad also believed that the SEC's presence as a watchdog had made the markets and the economy stronger.

More than anything else, Shad wanted the SEC to protect the interests of stockholders in America's public companies. He was less interested in supporting adventuresome law enforcement work than in determining the impact on stockholders of any new rule, regulation, policy, or enforcement case. Insisting on a high level of corporate morality may have enlivened the SEC enforcement staff, but Shad wondered whether it did any good for shareholders—they were the constituents he worried about. Shad was convinced that broad ownership of stock by the public was what made the American political and economic system work better than any other, and he wanted to make the system stronger. During the 1970s, the SEC had gained an international reputation by defining its mission broadly—Stanley Sporkin's commission was concerned about the public interest, rather than the interests of shareholders. From what Shad read and heard, it seemed the agency had been overzealous and too undisciplined in its enforcement program. He wanted the SEC to start focusing on the impact that its actions had on stock prices and shareholders and the economy.

Shad was impressed by departing SEC chairman Harold Williams, a Carter appointee and a Democrat, who warned him about what a tough time he had had taking charge on arrival in 1976 because of the power then wielded by the SEC's staff, particularly Stanley Sporkin. Williams tried to convince Shad that he should push public companies to have mostly outside experts on their boards of directors to keep top management honest and performing at a high level. Shad listened, but he had other priorities. He thought most businessmen were honest and did a good job for their stockholders, and didn't need more outsiders looking over their shoulders. But one thing Williams told him left an indelible impression. At the conclusion of dinner one night, Williams pulled out his wallet and mentioned that he was paying for the meal out of his own pocket. The SEC had only a small budget for entertaining, even for the chairman, Williams explained. Shad was stunned. This isn't going to be like Wall Street, he thought.

Like anyone starting a new job, Shad had much to learn. As an investment banker on Wall Street who helped corporations raise money to build new factories and make acquisitions, he had a working knowledge of many important SEC rules. But as chairman of the agency, he needed to have a much more detailed understanding. What powers and restrictions were there on the agency? What could the SEC do on its own and what did it need permission from Congress to do? Why did the SEC have a bunch of lawyers running its division of market regulation instead of bringing in people with direct experience in the markets? What were the names of the key SEC staff members and what authority did he have to replace them? What vacancies needed to be filled immediately? Where was the fat in the agency that could be cut? Which members of the staff could he trust to give him objective advice, and which had their own private agendas? Where did people eat lunch around here?

Then there were the lawyers, lawyers, lawyers. To Shad, who had lived in a world of numbers and financial facts on Wall Street, there seemed to be lawyers everywhere he turned at the SEC. Why, he wondered, were there so damn many lawyers making all the decisions in this place—instead of economists who knew how to look at the financial impact of decisions and to assess their costs and benefits for stockholders?

Shad brought intensity to his new job, pushing virtually everything else aside to work the long hours he needed to master the details. Though they didn't know whether they could trust him, staff members found him charming and perplexing initially. His blue eyes and occasional smiles conveyed a sense of warmth that seemed at odds with his gruff, businesslike exterior. This much was clear: He was engaged and committed.

He concentrated and worked as if he were a new recruit at his first job. One night early on, around 10:00 P.M., while Shad, typically, was still at the SEC, an exterminator came to spray his spacious office. Those few aides who were still around evacuated the building. The foul odor was too much and they didn't think it was healthy to be around poison. Shad, though, didn't budge. He had been sitting at his big wooden desk working when the exterminator came in, he remained there while the office was sprayed, and he went right on reading after the exterminator and the others had gone.

Nearly every self-made man traces his fortune to principles allegedly learned in youth, and Jack Shad was no exception. He subscribed as an adult to the usual rhetoric culled from the Horatio Alger stories so popular in the days of his childhood—hard work, fair dealing, and perseverance. It was hard to say where truth yielded to myth, but certainly Shad was exceptionally independent, enterprising, and competitive while growing up. His drive was tempered by a good-natured manner and by a virtuous streak inspired by his grandmother, Sarah Johnson Rees.

He was born in 1923, in the same adobe house in Brigham City, Utah, where his mother, Lillie Mae, was born. The place was just two blocks from the colossal Brigham City Tabernacle, the Gothic landmark church with sixteen pinnacles that overlooks Box Elder

County. It was in the heart of the Mormon colony, and when Shad was a child the place had changed little from the days of its founding decades earlier, when the Mormons fled west to live by the tenets of their God's revelations. The family of Shad's mother played a central role in the building of Brigham City. The Mormons were an austere people—smoking, drinking, and gambling were all proscribed. Yet there was a vitality, too, a sense of community that arose not only from the strict adherence to scripture but also from the colony's isolation.

Shad's lineage was divided—his father, after whom he was named, was a quick-tempered, nonobservant Catholic from Florida who enjoyed drinking, smoking, and playing cards. He was domineering and a boaster, slick by Brigham City standards, and there was tension between him and his only son. His father did things that upset him; one time in his youth, John Shad became infuriated when his father bragged that he had charmed the hostess of a party the family had attended.

When Shad was two, his father took them west from Brigham City to Los Angeles, then a small and dusty place in a basin by the sea. As a lad, Shad often returned to Brigham City, where he found the companionship that he at times lacked as an only child in Los Angeles. They struggled in Los Angeles, first living in the back of a Laundromat his father ran. Through all of it, Shad's mother played the peacemaker. In Brigham they remembered her as a lovely, gentle woman who drew pictures in her spare time. She died after a brief illness in 1942, two days before her forty-sixth birthday, when Shad was only nineteen. It was an enormous shock. In Brigham City, Lillie Mae was buried beneath a pink marble headstone marked SWEETHEART. John Shad the elder later remarried, and by the time he died, he and his son had little to do with one another. In contrast, Jack Shad clung to the memory of his mother and remained deeply sentimental about her throughout his life.

He was determined to be more financially successful than his father—the erstwhile Laundromat owner who lost everything when his business burned down late in the 1930s—and to make a bigger contribution to society as well. John Shad—his friends called him Jack—worked at dozens of jobs: as a caddy, a pinsetter in a bowling alley, an ice cream vendor, a newspaper boy. There were few things he liked better than making money.

There was a tension visible in him that seemed to reflect the contrast between his father and his mother, and there was a playful, mischievous streak. On visits to his relatives' ranch in Utah, Shad stole fruit and drove trucks through the mud with his cousins. Once they shot out the giant bulb lights that illuminated the Brigham City Tabernacle; when someone called the police, they fled. Another time they had to run for cover when an angry farmer caught them stealing pumpkins and fired shots into the air.

Yet Shad worked and pushed and competed to get ahead. The Great Depression taught an unavoidable lesson about hard work, but Shad's competitiveness seemed to run deeper than that. No one could work harder than he did. After graduating from Hollywood High, where his yearbook declared "America Forever," he worked as an aircraft riveter at Lockheed from midnight until 8:00 A.M., and attended college during the day. His education was interrupted when he joined the Navy during World War II, and was sent to the Pacific and China.

There was, however, a pull in him between the spiritual and the material. While serving at sea Shad read books about religion and grappled earnestly with whether he believed in God. He unsuccessfully tried to induce a religious experience by fasting for days. On another occasion he climbed onto the deck of his ship, looked to the heavens, and declared that unless God showed him a sign, he was going to become an agnostic. When no sign was forthcoming he made it official, vowing for the rest of his life never to change his mind again. When the war ended he finished college and then, with the financial aid of the GI bill, went to the Harvard Business School to get a master's degree in business administration.

He had traded make-believe stock portfolios as a boy, and at Harvard his hobby became a profession. The school became enormously important to him, mainly because of the people he met there, but also as a symbol of what he and the country could accomplish. Shad founded the business school's finance club, which later became its most popular student organization. At West Point, the class that graduated the most generals is remembered as "The Class the Stars Fell On." Shad's Harvard Business School class of 1949 accomplished so much in business and finance that it was dubbed "The Class the Dollars Fell On." While many of his classmates went off to work in manufacturing operations as the country revved up its postwar economic engine, Shad borrowed $500 from a school fund and headed for the far less fashionable quarters of Wall Street. Utilizing his exceptional mathematical skills, Shad began working sixteen-hour days analyzing stocks for an investment firm that hired him at $3,500 a year.

In background and inclination, Shad was an outsider to the self-consciously aristocratic culture of Protestant Wall Street. Though he enjoyed analyzing the finances of companies, he grew disillusioned with his first job, especially after attending a conference at a New York hotel where he watched stuffy men wearing frock coats brag about their stock-picking prowess. This was not the future Shad imagined for himself.

A series of events took Shad to the executive suite at E. F. Hutton. In 1952, he married Patricia Pratt, a conservative-minded and well-to-do woman from Arkansas. With his wife's support, Shad changed jobs several times; the third time when he was passed over for a promotion at Shearson, Hamill & Company. He joined E. F. Hutton, well-known for its extensive retail brokerage operation, in 1963. But Shad's job wasn't to sell stocks. He made his career at Hutton by building a corporate-finance department that would provide financial advice and funding to small and medium-sized companies, as well as a few large ones.

As at every Wall Street firm, office politics on Hutton's executive floor was treacherous. But as the head of his own department, one outside the mainstream of the firm's brokerage operations, Shad was able to build his own loyal team—and a base of power.

He recruited almost exclusively from the Harvard Business School. One of his first hires was Fred Joseph, the aggressive son of a Boston cab driver. Joseph was cut from Shad's cloth—he was a former boxer, a climber, a worker. He became Shad's protégé and their relationship lasted decades. Shad was a disciplined, fact-driven, methodical manager, and he tried to instill his approach in Joseph. "Reorganize the form, beef-up the facts and boil down the size to five to eight single-spaced, fact-packed pages that conform to the firm's format," Shad scrawled to Joseph in a 1965 memo that rejected a corporate report Joseph had submitted. "Assume the reader is a well-informed, skeptical investor. Use layman's terminology and explanations. . . . Say the cup is half full, rather than half empty, but do not overstate affirmatives or ignore material negatives." So impressed was Joseph by Shad's precepts that two decades later, when both of them were gone from Hutton, Joseph framed the memo and hung it on his office wall. By then the relationship between them had grown enormously complex and the memo had acquired an ironic resonance: Shad was chairman of the SEC while Joseph was the chief executive officer of Drexel Burnham Lambert, the target during the late 1980s of the most sweeping fraud and corruption investigation in Securities and Exchange Commission history.

On Wall Street, Shad was curious, adventurous, and tenacious. He traveled to the Soviet Union to observe a centrally planned economy firsthand, long before détente made such trips popular among Americans. The trip reinforced his faith in capitalism. He broke ranks with Wall Street by raising money for Caesars World Resorts, the casino company, in the days when organized crime's grip on Las Vegas was just beginning to loosen. The deal was credited with making casino financings acceptable on Wall Street. And Shad made his mark by advising midsized, growing companies whose credit was not as sound and whose banking needs were not as predictable as the giant blue-chip corporations. He distinguished himself as a negotiator with an insatiable, utilitarian thirst for facts and a high level of integrity. He was a little rough around the edges; he won over clients more through logic and persistence than through the Brahmin charm common on Wall Street.

Shad thrived on stress, and he maintained a state of controlled ferment around him. He hated the time it took to get from one place to another, calling it purgatory. He drove his own cars fast and ordered cabdrivers to do the same. Once Shad drove a cab to

La Guardia Airport himself after a cabdriver tired of his orders and relinquished the wheel. He worked long, smoked his Viceroy filter tips unceasingly, grew overweight, and paid little attention to his health. He seasoned his foods heavily, saying he couldn't taste much because of an operation years earlier. He put Tabasco in soup, on grilled-cheese sandwiches, and on just about anything else. Before elegant meals in the Hutton dining room, Shad would sometimes pile butter high between two Triscuits and then add pepper, making a sandwich that ruined the appetites of his guests.

He played with reckless abandon. He shot white water rapids on the Colorado River. At his summer home on a lake in Massachusetts, one of his favorite games was to drive his boat at high speed while friends tried to stay up on water skis. With one friend he bet on his weight and with another he went skydiving. On occasional trips to Las Vegas he played blackjack, where his talent for math helped him count cards. At Hutton, he got on well with many of his colleagues and would join them after work in a back room at Christ Cella, a New York steak house, for dinner and games of Liar's Poker, where bets were made from the serial numbers on dollar bills. It wasn't the money that seemed to excite Shad most of all in such gaming, but rather the risk, the mathematical challenge, and the competition.

Though he worked long hours at Hutton, Shad sometimes got home in time for dinner with Pat and their two children, Leslie Anne and Rees. They would eat in the dining room of their comfortable two-story apartment at 535 Park Avenue, where the family had moved after outgrowing an apartment in Brooklyn Heights. The dining room had old hardwood floors, high ceilings, and brightly colored wallpaper on one wall depicting a scene at West Point. They were living in one of Manhattan's most prestigious locations—61st and Park Avenue across from the Regency Hotel. After dinner, Shad would often go to the small bedroom / office upstairs he called the cockpit. In this crowded room, he had a desk, a small refrigerator, a telephone, a television, extra packs of cigarettes, and a cot. Late into the night, Shad would sit in the cockpit, working and smoking, reading through documents and papers that affected the financing activities of major corporations, or studying the private proposals of companies on whose boards of directors he served. Sometimes, after hours of working, Shad would fall asleep on the cot in the cockpit and spend the night alone. Other times he would walk across the short hallway into the master bedroom and crawl into bed with Pat, where they would talk about many things, including the law; the Shads found time to attend night law school together at New York University, where Pat did most of the schoolwork and prepared her husband for exams since he often missed classes due to his hectic Wall Street schedule.

All this energy and ambition eventually took a direction: Shad wanted to run E. F. Hutton, to win the firm's top job. Though he was not a gifted politician, he took his shot in 1970, in a hectic contest involving many of Hutton's top executives. The firm's chief executive was retiring and the job was thrown open. Shad jumped in, but despite vigorous support from Fred Joseph and others on his team in the corporate-finance department, he ended up in a dead heat with an opposing candidate from another department. After days of deadlock, a compromise candidate from the firm's West Coast office, Robert Fomon, won the job. Shad was given the title of vice chairman, but it was a consolation prize at best. His career seemed to have peaked. He had built Hutton's corporate-finance department into a solid second-tier performer. But there was little chance he would become chief executive at Hutton or any other firm on Wall Street.

Jack and Pat Shad sometimes talked about what it would be like to try something new, to start over fresh. Shad still thought about his grandmother's credo to spend one-third of his life serving, and he could afford to follow through, given the hundreds of thousands of dollars in salary he earned each year at Hutton and the valuable Hutton stock he owned. Shad had been offered several government jobs in Washington over the years, but in each instance the timing had been bad or the offer not attractive enough. The SEC chairmanship was the right job at the right time. They found a Georgian home with high ceilings in northwest Washington's fashionable Kalorama neighborhood, near the embassies and the old estates that would become the nexus of social Washington in the Reagan years, a swirl into which the Shads expected to emerse themselves, at least when Shad wasn't working. For the first time in twenty-nine years of married life, they prepared to move out of Manhattan. After so much struggle, after so much energy, John Shad had what he wanted.

On a Saturday night in July 1981, Jack Shad sat quietly reading in his Georgetown hotel room while the bars and restaurants on Wisconsin Avenue teemed with well-dressed bureaucrats, lawyers, and students hungry for action in the wealthiest quadrant of the nation's capital city. The move to Washington had been a wondrous adventure, a rare opportunity for renewal. Shad was digging into the office, making his mark in cases like the one proposed against Mobil. The house in Kalorama was nearly ready and they were about to buy it.

But that night in Georgetown, everything changed.

Shad had decided to stay in to catch up on some reading. Pat Shad had dined with an old friend. When she got back, she said that she had dropped her fork several times during the meal and couldn't figure out why. She asked him to fix her a drink, and he did.

Then she slumped over in a chair. Thinking she had merely fallen asleep, Shad cradled his wife's body and carried her to bed.

"I can't walk," Pat told him the next morning when she awoke.

The hurried 7:00 A.M. phone call to the family doctor in New York, the call for an ambulance, the ride together to nearby Georgetown University hospital, the CAT scan—all of it was like a nightmare, and cruelly timed. Shad had been at the commission only weeks. They were supposed to close on their new house the next day.

It was a stroke, the doctors said, and a serious one. Pat's recovery from paralysis would be long and slow and would require the most sophisticated rehabilitation facilities. There were no guarantees she would ever walk again.

In general, Shad was not a terribly emotional man. On Wall Street his rationalism had served him well professionally. But this was different. This was Pat. He couldn't believe this was happening to her—it wasn't fair—Pat was so good, everyone liked her. He sat by her bed. She looked frighteningly close to death as she lay there with tubes and wires and electronic beepers attached everywhere. There was something eerily other-worldly about it. He felt himself starting to lose control. He excused himself from the room, leaving his daughter, Leslie, who had come to help, alone with Pat.

He walked down the hall toward a hospital supply closet. The door was open. He stepped inside, closed the door, and sat down on a box. Then the man who had declared himself agnostic on a ship nearly forty years earlier began to pray. He asked God to save Pat's life. He began to cry.

"Cancel everything," Shad told his aides when he called over to the SEC on Monday.

Later he found out that his blanket order derailed an important reception welcoming the Shads to Washington, involving several members of the president's new cabinet. It was to have been the Shads' social and political introduction to Washington. But Shad didn't have time for that now. He worked the phones, trying to be sure Pat was getting the best medical care possible and exploring where she could get the best rehabilitation treatment. How could he balance the demands of his new job at the SEC with the demands of her recovery? He called the real estate agent and killed the plans to buy the Kalorama house. It needed some work, including new air conditioning, and he didn't have time to deal with that. Pat was to have taken care of those things. Anyway, Shad thought, the house had stairs everywhere and she would never be able to get around in a wheelchair.

In the end, Shad decided that the right thing was to get Pat back to New York, where the rehabilitation facilities were more advanced, in his estimation, and where she would be more comfortable. Though the waiting list was long, Shad gained admission for his wife to New York University's Rusk Institute—he did it with the help of his friend Laurence A. Tisch, the wealthy New York financier who would eventually become chief executive of CBS Inc. Shad knew that by moving Pat back to New York he was setting himself up for a two-city commute between Manhattan and the capital that would make him an outsider to the political and social mainstream in Washington. But what mattered most was getting Pat the best care possible.

Shad continued to live at the Georgetown Inn hotel in Washington, returning to New York on weekends and on certain days during the week to spend time with Pat. It was a commute he would continue for six years. SEC aides remembered him as unusually quiet during this early period. Soon after Pat became ill, he began working long hours during the week, sometimes remaining at the SEC past midnight before returning alone in a cab to his hotel room, where his dinner would often consist of a bowl of Campbell's soup heated on a hotplate.

It was during this strained and difficult period, a redoubled transition, that some of the senior staff at the SEC on North Capitol Street learned about their new SEC chairman. Not all of them knew the extent or significance of Pat's illness or how the new chairman felt about it. It was primarily to old friends from Wall Street or the Harvard Business School that Shad opened up. He asked his Harvard classmate James E. Burke, chairman of giant Johnson & Johnson, for advice about what the SEC should be doing. In their talks Shad said he felt torn over how much time he should be spending at his new job in the aftermath of Pat's stroke. "He talked about it enough so I remember how deeply he felt about it and how heavy that burden was," Burke recalled.

There were moments when Pat's stroke made Shad feel as though a heavyweight boxer had just landed a punch to his midsection. Still, he pressed ahead at the SEC. He was determined to carry on, but he was struggling—the SEC bureaucracy at times seemed so large and there was much that was new and strange. . . .

Until the Monocle. That was something the new SEC chairman knew how to do—he knew how to meet a man for lunch and make a deal.

The Monocle was the right setting, too. It was a favorite watering hole for congressmen, lobbyists, and regulatory officials, just a few hundred yards down the north slope of Capitol Hill. It was one of those Washington restaurants that had evolved into oppressive, if casually appointed, citadels of power—where a regular could count on getting his favorite table and a congressman could count on getting his favorite lobbyist to pick up the tab. It was said but never proven that, when certain members of Congress dined alone at the Monocle, their bill was routinely but quietly added to the tab of prominent Washington lobbying groups.

That summer of 1981, Shad and Philip Johnson sat down to lunch in a rear booth at the Monocle. The high-backed booths, rust-colored wallpaper, and red brick arches gave the dimly lit restaurant the feeling of an old-world club. Johnson was a top-flight commodities lawyer who had left his practice in Chicago in part to heed the call of the Reagan Revolution and in part to escape a messy divorce situation. He was named to head the Commodity Futures Trading Commission, or CFTC, a kind of sister agency to the SEC. The CFTC had jurisdiction over the free-wheeling Chicago futures markets, where pork bellies, grains, silver, and other commodities were traded.

During the briefings he received from the SEC staff in preparation for his Senate confirmation hearings, Shad had learned all about Phil Johnson and the CFTC problem. The SEC and the CFTC had been embroiled in an emotional courtroom fight over bureaucratic turf and politics. At the heart of the battle was a proposal for a new kind of financial instrument called a stock index future, a cross between a stock and a commodity. The product had the potential to cause enormous changes in the way the country's stock markets functioned. The problem was that nobody was quite sure what a stock index future was or who should regulate it. The futures product would give investors the opportunity to bet on the future value of broad stock market averages. Shad saw the legal battle as a fight over jurisdiction—which agency would regulate the new futures—rather than a battle over the merits of stock index futures. Though no one understood the new product all that well, Shad believed the futures could help the stock market work more efficiently, in part by increasing the volume of trading. It was up to investors, not regulators, to decide whether they liked these new instruments—that was a tenet of Reagan's conservative ideology. Doubters and Democrats thought the new stock futures would encourage gambling in the stock markets. But rather than dealing with such substantive questions, the debate between the SEC and the CFTC had grown less and less elevated, sinking into an open squabble over regulatory turf. The SEC staff, with a proud fifty-year tradition and powerful sense of self-importance, had been unwilling to allow the upstart CFTC, which it viewed as relatively incompetent, the chance to get its regulatory paws on any product having to do with stocks. While the agencies fought in court, stock index futures remained in limbo—nobody could trade them until Washington decided who would regulate them.

Shad thought he had the answer. Let's cut a deal, he told Phil Johnson that August afternoon at the Monocle.

Both of them thought the turf fight between their staffs was unseemly. They were Reagan men, outsiders to their bureaucracies. They had market experience, Shad in New York, Johnson in Chicago, and they were committed to the administration's free market ideology—here was something they could actually do about it. Over lunch Shad and Johnson agreed to agree, and within weeks they had put their staffs to work drafting the specifics of a peace treaty between the SEC and the CFTC.

To Shad, it was a simple deal. It reminded him of two kids sorting marbles. You take the red ones and I'll take the green ones, he thought. You take the futures and I'll take the options. The peace treaty, which came to be known as the Accord, clarified who should regulate stock futures—the CFTC, and who should regulate stocks and stock options—the SEC. Options were a lot like futures, but the SEC already regulated them and there was no question of giving them over to the CFTC. Whatever the limits of its logic, Shad's deal allowed the new futures to begin trading after years of delay.

What neither Shad nor Johnson realized at lunch, in their haste to get government regulators out of the way of a new financial product, was that the deal they cut would unleash forces that would fundamentally transform the character of the stock market during the 1980s. It was a deal, in some of its aspects, that Shad would later have reason to regret.

The senior staff at the SEC who worked to implement Shad's

deal with Johnson—general counsel Ed Greene, Shad's executive assistant, Dan Goelzer, and others—saw in the Accord the outline of Shad's basic ideas about what the Securities and Exchange Commission should be doing. What Shad cared about more than anything else was the impact of the SEC on shareholders, the people and institutions who bought, sold, and held shares of stock issued by the nation's public corporations. This approach went beyond futures. Shad enthusiastically embraced a major project he believed could save shareholders billions of dollars by eliminating redundant corporate filings with the SEC. And at his first news conference, Shad, when asked about corporate takeovers, said they produced a "net economic gain" because they made stockholders richer.

With stock futures and corporate takeovers, as with virtually every other issue on his desk—enforcement, what disclosures corporations should make to the public, regulation of the stock market—Shad seemed to regard himself as the king of the country's stockholders. It was a far cry from the earnest Nader-like public interest mission pursued by the commission under Stanley Sporkin. Explicitly and implicitly Shad's priorities seemed to some of the senior staff to be an attack on the proud traditions of independence and moral leadership that the SEC had come to project under Sporkin's leadership. They feared above all that the era of high-profile enforcement cases against major corporations and investment houses was yielding to some sort of veiled Wall Street boosterism.

Shad only vaguely apprehended these resentments and he tried to ignore them. Once Pat was ensconced in New York, he settled into a routine. He would leave the SEC headquarters building on Friday afternoons and ride to National Airport across the Potomac in Virginia, where he would catch a plane to New York for the weekend. Reports filtered down to some of the staff that Shad sometimes dined on Saturday nights with old friends from Wall Street's elite corps of lawyers and investment bankers—whom he was now regulating. Those who opposed Shad's agenda saw this weekly commute as a disquieting metaphor: He had ushered in a new era of shuttle diplomacy aimed at bringing Wall Street and the SEC closer together.

3

A Giant of the Opera

To and from the racetrack, John Fedders slept. It was no easy feat for a man of his ungainly height to squeeze into the bus seat. He was six feet ten inches tall, much of it seemingly in his long, jointed legs. Standing up, wearing one of his well-pressed business suits, Fedders gave the fearsome impression of a neatly tailored human insect. In addition, he was often visibly tense, and his bald head was overlarge and egg-shaped. The tortoiseshell glasses he wore only emphasized the bulge of his eyes. But when he was sitting down and scrunched up, asleep on a bus rumbling through the Maryland countryside, it was possible to see another, less threatening image of Fedders: the awkward and solitary child trapped in an uncomfortable frame. As a young adolescent, Fedders had ridden back and forth over rural Kentucky roads to school, crammed into the back of a bus, studying and sleeping. His parents had pushed him to skip grades, so he was younger and taller than his classmates, isolated and excluded, and he had learned in the back of the school bus to block everything out, to sleep, study, or read despite all the noise and chatter, and despite his acute physical discomfort. He had learned, Fedders told those few who gained his trust, an almost meditative skill of concentration and a nearly obsessive determination. Those qualities—admirable to some, intimidating to others—would define Fedders's tenure as enforcement chief at the Securities and Exchange Commission and would reshape the culture on the fourth floor left behind by Stanley Sporkin.

It was John Shad who had arranged the day at the races. That fall of 1981 he invited the senior staff who constituted his new management team at the SEC—general counsel Ed Greene, market regulation division director Doug Scarff, and enforcement chief Fedders—to gamble on the horses at the harness track in Charles Town, West Virginia, sixty miles or so northwest of Washington. They met at one of the many elitist clubs Shad belonged to, the Chevy Chase Country Club, an establishment bastion hidden behind ivied walls on Connecticut Avenue. From there the bus took them north to Frederick and west to Harpers Ferry, where the Potomac and Shenandoah rivers join, and finally across the water to shabby Charles Town.

At the track, Shad volunteered to be the house, to play the bank.

No need to traipse back and forth to the betting windows, he said. Just give your money to me—I'll pay off whatever odds are posted on the tote board.

Fedders and the others said that would be all right.

So the crowd cheered the trotters to the wire and the chairman of the SEC changed money like a teller, doling out cash to the winners and taking profits from the losers. Shad thought he was doing his guests a favor, saving them from the walk to the windows and the long, smoky lines. It wasn't as if he was trying to bilk his staff. Money rarely seemed to be the point in Shad's wagering—he had plenty of money. It was the thrill, the competition, the numbers. It seemed to many of the SEC staff that Shad and Fedders both were gunning to establish some new culture of competitive edges at the commission, some attitude toward gaming and winning imported from Wall Street and the cutthroat world of corporate lawyering.

That trend was most visible in the enforcement division, the commission's most distinguished section, where Fedders had been brought in from outside to shake things up. The significance Shad attached to his selection of Fedders reflected the singular importance of the enforcement division itself, an autonomous and secretive domain within the SEC that had secured a worldwide reputation and had come to define the public character of the commission. The commission was organized into a number of major divisions, some larger than others, all nominally equal in bureaucratic importance. There was a corporation finance division, which reviewed the stock and bond issues of public companies in the United States. There was an investment management division, which tried to keep track of people who made a living dispensing financial advice. There was the market regulation division, which monitored the technical operation of the country's financial markets. And there was enforcement, whose power overshadowed the other divisions' entirely.

Fedders and Shad had much in common professionally, and their budding collaboration appeared to define where the SEC was headed in the early Reagan years. Shad had been determined to look outside the commission for an enforcement chief, to get away from the entrenched attitudes in the bureaucracy he had inherited. As the search began, Irwin Schneiderman, a New York securities lawyer and old friend of Shad's from Wall Street, agreed to advise Shad. Schneiderman was the first to talk with Fedders.

Hiring a new enforcement chief wasn't like searching for a new corporate vice president—you couldn't advertise in the newspapers or retain an executive-search firm. The game was subtle. Political and ideological credentials were critical. Republican fund-raisers and party stalwarts forwarded names or sent along résumés under cover letters of endorsement. Friends called upon friends. Rumors traveled freely in the circles of political conservatives who considered themselves the beneficiaries of Reagan's triumph at the polls.

Fedders had surfaced in a typical way. A partner at the large and prestigious Washington law firm of Arnold & Potter, he had been active in raising money for the Reagan campaign from fellow conservative lawyers. When the election was won, he let it be known that he was interested in a job in government. His chances of attracting at least some offer were good, since unlike many of the Republican activists who flocked to Washington on Reagan's coattails, Fedders had distinguished himself in his profession. Though relatively young, he had earned a reputation as one of the best corporate lawyers in the capital. After reviewing his résumé, Schneiderman flew to Washington and talked with Fedders over a bowl of soup in a restaurant near Arnold & Porter's plush downtown offices. Schneiderman was impressed. Fedders was articulate, smart, and forceful in his views about how the SEC should change its approach to law enforcement. Schneiderman suggested that Shad set up a meeting.

They were both busy and the only time they could find was a Saturday morning. Shad suggested a doughnut shop near his Georgetown hotel and Fedders drove in from his home in the Maryland suburbs. Once they started talking they found they couldn't stop, and they wandered through the cobblestone streets for hours. They talked about Stanley Sporkin, the history of the enforcement division, and about their own careers and ambitions. Shad was immediately taken by Fedders's self-confidence, his apparent leadership qualities. And Fedders made it clear that he shared Shad's ideological approach. He wanted to stop the enforcement division from harassing corporations over infractions such as overseas bribery or political payoffs—these were crimes beyond the jurisdiction of the SEC, Fedders said. He wanted to make the commission's prosecutions more orderly, more systematic, less dependent on the whims of a single chief such as Sporkin. And he wanted to create new priorities for division investigators, focusing their attention more on outright fraud in the financial markets and less on moral goose-chasing aimed at big corporations. All this accorded perfectly with Shad's ideas. And Fedders was articulate, deeply knowledgeable, able to muster specific cases and facts to make his points. Shad didn't know securities law in such detail. He needed someone on his team who did.

Can you afford to give up your private law practice? Shad asked finally. He had this way of getting to the bottom line. It was blunt, but effective.

Fedders said he could. It would be a big pay cut—more than 50 percent—but he could supplement his new government salary with real estate and other outside income. Moreover, he and Shad both knew that a stint as SEC enforcement chief was itself a kind of economic investment, since it would raise dramatically Fedders's value as a corporate lawyer when he eventually returned to private practice.

Shad engineered the hiring with the finesse of an experienced Wall Street investment banker. He provided Ted Levine, Sporkin's protégé, with a long and fair hearing. Shad was impressed by Levine's intelligence, and he made it clear that his inclination to hire from outside the commission was not a reflection on Levine's ability. He wanted Levine to stay—under Fedders. And to be sure that he did not ruffle feathers among his politically appointed colleagues on the commission—by law, two of them were Democrats—Shad sent Fedders to meet with every commissioner before any appointment was announced. Only when his colleagues expressed their approval did Shad go public with his choice.

Shad persuaded Sporkin to appear at the press conference where Fedders's appointment was announced, even though Sporkin had been working for weeks at his new job at the CIA. The appearance was meant to symbolize to commission staff and the public a smooth handoff of the SEC's most important staff job. Fedders said all the right words. He talked of Sporkin as a "legendary public servant." He pledged to avoid conflicts of interest involving clients of his old law firm and to pursue white-collar crooks with vigor and enthusiasm.

Away from the public spotlight, Fedders moved swiftly and decisively to implement changes in the enforcement division. There were superficial matters, reflecting his obsession with orderliness and detail. He insisted, for example, that all enforcement division attorneys fasten their ties and put on their suitcoats for meetings with outsiders. He banned enforcement employees from putting posters on their office walls. General Patton was one of his heroes, Fedders let it be known. Fedders viewed these edicts as part of a general campaign to make the enforcement division's investigative work more systematic and professional. During the 1970s, reflecting the looseness of Sporkin's leadership, the SEC sometimes let cases linger unresolved for years, never telling the targets of a probe whether they had been exonerated or not. Fedders said there had to be strict time limits on investigations and that potential defendants should be informed of a case's outcome within a reasonable period. Some of the staff welcomed these changes; others saw them as the arbitrary campaign of a tightly wound neurotic.

The enforcement staff received their first clear picture of Fedders's prosecutorial priorities during a three-day conference late in September 1981, to which all of the SEC's regional administrators were invited. The SEC had a centralized headquarters staff in Washington, where the division directors and the five appointed commissioners worked. But thousands of its employees were scattered about the country in the commissions' regional offices. There were offices in New York, Los Angeles, Atlanta, Dallas, Denver, and even a "Washington Regional Office" across the Potomac in Virginia, with responsibility for detecting fraud and inspecting investment firms in the immediate Washington, D.C., area. Some of the regional offices were crucially important. The New York office, for example, had primary responsibility for inspecting brokerage firms on Wall Street, where there were thousands of investment firms, large and small. Each SEC regional office was headed by a semiautonomous regional administrator. Policy was made in Washington, but new policies such as those being devised by Fedders and Shad would only be effective if they were adopted in the regional offices.

On September 19, the day before the conference began, Fedders drafted a "confidential discussion memorandum" to all the regional administrators. The enforcement program "should remain active and effective—not splashy," Fedders wrote. Staff attorneys should "avoid peripheral parties and exotic theories— they slow us down. . . . We cannot be all things to all men."

As for "what should the enforcement program look like; what should be emphasized," Fedders provided a list of priorities enumerated from the letter *A* to the letter *U*. Fedders later said that the list was in no particular order, but to the regional administrators it communicated an unmistakable shift of priorities. The hallmark of the 1970s—what the SEC had become famous for—was corporate bribery cases, particularly ones that ran afoul of the Foreign Corrupt Practices Act. But Fedders relegated such cases to near the bottom of his list, in between such irrelevancies as "the delinquent reports program" and a "program for processing applications for relief from disqualification."

At the top of the list Fedders distributed was "trading on the basis of non-public information," a crime popularly known as insider trading, a term to which Fedders mildly objected because it didn't distinguish between permissible stock trading by top corporate executives known as insiders and the use of confidential, inside information about corporate takeovers to make illegal stock trading profits.

Insider trading was a hot topic with Fedders that September. In part, he was responding to Shad. *Fortune* magazine, one of Shad's favorite publications, had published in August a long and persuasive cover story called "The Unwinnable War Against Insider Trading." The magazine argued that theft of confidential information on Wall Street was becoming almost endemic and that there was virtually nothing the SEC could do about it—the crime was too hard to detect and prove. The article riled Shad. Though he didn't know the extent of illegal trading, he disagreed with both its premises: that there was a major wave of dishonest dealing on Wall Street and that the SEC couldn't stop insider trading. Shad supported Fedders's efforts to make prosecution of such cases a priority.

A few months later, when what came to be known as the SEC's war on insider trading spilled into the newspapers, some former SEC lawyers described the new campaign as an effort to ease up on big business. Rather than pressuring large corporations and Wall Street firms, Shad and Fedders were proposing to spend their time chasing individual thieves. In truth, unlike some other area's of the SEC's franchise, prosecuting insider trading was a part of the commission's work about which John Shad felt no ambivalence. He was an avid Reagan man and a committed deregulator, but in his abhorrence of insider trading Shad dissented from the radical conservative precepts of some economists. Some disciples of the Chicago School of economic theory argued vocally in 1981 that insider trading should be made legal because the stock market would work better if there were no restrictions on the flow of information, however it was obtained. Though he valued efficiency in the stock market, that argument never registered with Shad—or with Fedders. What was wrong was wrong, they both said. And insider trading was wrong.

Fedders had put insider trading on the top of his list in part because he was looking for a chance to make his mark quickly in the way his predecessors at enforcement had done: by cracking a big fraud case in dramatic fashion. What Fedders needed was for some exceptionally greedy transgressor on Wall Street to provide him an opportunity.

As it happened, just weeks after Fedders handed out his confidential list to SEC regional administrators, Wall Street obliged.

"Maybe this is all a fluke," Gary Sampson had told himself on Friday, when word spread on the boisterous floor of the Pacific Stock Exchange that trading in Santa Fe International stock would be suspended until the following week. "Maybe this will all blow over." He tried to put it out of his mind over the weekend. But by Monday, October 5, 1981, he was beginning to feel the grip of panic.

There was talk of a possible takeover announcement, but Sampson, Steven Mitchell, and the other traders in the options pit could scarcely believe it. They were all self-employed market makers at the dingy Pacific Stock Exchange in San Francisco, one of the lesser financial markets overseen by the Securities and Exchange Commission in Washington. They spent their days in clusters of ten or fifteen, screaming madly at one another and waving hand signals like crazed sign-language interpreters. If you were young and gutsy and had a head for numbers, it was a pretty good business. Sampson had been at it four years. He had made a little, lost a little, accumulated some savings.

He did not imagine that it was possible to lose $2 million in a single day.

As market makers on the Pacific exchange floor, Gary Sampson and his brethren enjoyed monopoly privileges: They had exclusive rights to handle the purchase and sale of certain stock options. They also had an obligation to help maintain what the regulators in Washington called a "fair and orderly market." That meant, at any given moment on any given day, if the public wanted to buy stock options, Sampson and the others were required to sell. If the public wanted to sell, they had to buy.

Santa Fe International's stock options traded at the post where Sampson worked. The company was an industrial and natural resources behemoth headquartered in southern California. Not much appeared to be happening at Santa Fe that fall of 1981. Its stock price had been stuck between $21 and $23 per share for months, and it didn't move up or down very often. The stock options Sampson bought and sold were tied directly to Santa Fe's stock price. Unlike a share of stock, though, an option didn't last forever—every "call option" gave its owner the right to buy one hundred shares of stock at an agreed upon price, until the option expired in a particular month and year. Often when an option expired it turned worthless, like a losing lottery ticket after a drawing. Options were popular because they were dirt cheap. By spending a relatively small amount of cash, an investor could load up on Santa Fe options. By owning the options, he could control a big block of Santa Fe stock for a limited period of time. If the stock price advanced during that period, the value of the options would soar.

Strange things had begun to happen in Gary Sampson's trading pit during the last days of September. Orders poured in for Santa Fe stock options that were due to expire in just a few weeks. On Thursday, October 1, the number of Santa Fe options sold tripled over the previous day, to 3,993 from 1,153. Chaos reigned. The traders in the Santa Fe pit couldn't figure out why anyone would want to spend so much money on options that would be valuable for only a short time. They also couldn't learn who was buying the options. But they didn't dwell on it too much. It was hard to figure out the public—investors did a lot of stupid things. And the traders in the pit, all of them in their late twenties and early thirties, worked more from instinct than from sophisticated analysis. If somebody wanted to buy, they were willing to sell. Sampson sold hundreds of contracts worth tens of thousands of dollars each. He wasn't too worried. He could only get burned if Santa Fe's stock rose suddenly and dramatically in price before the options expired, something that had never happened before.

On Tuesday it happened. The clacking wire services that carried the news of the outside world to the Pacific exchange floor told the tale: Kuwait Petroleum Corporation, an arm of the Persian Gulf government of Kuwait, had agreed to buy all of Santa Fe's stock in a corporate takeover for $51 a share—double the current market price. Sampson was shocked. Giant takeovers were relatively rare events in those days and the truth was that he had never thought it was possible. He calculated the damage in a matter of minutes. All of his personal trading capital—$108,000— had been wiped out. He figured he owed about $2 million to the San Francisco firm that provided him with financing. Steven Mitchell made the same calculation and said that he was out about $1.75 million. Among the group the losses exceeded $6 million. It was odd how they reacted, Sampson thought—each according to his personality, some morosely, some with humor. Sampson was pissed off. Whoever bought the stock options he had sold knew there was a takeover announcement coming—that was illegal. The buyers must have had inside information.

"Shit," Sampson told his friends in the pit. "I'm going to try to get my money back."

He said he was going to call a lawyer. He said he was going to call the Securities and Exchange Commission.

Sampson's complaint helped spur the SEC into action. But even before his detailed explanation of unusual trading reached the enforcement division in Washington, the Santa Fe matter had galvanized Fedders's interest. Market surveillance officials at the Pacific exchange had begun to report unusual activity in the Santa Fe options pit. After the takeover announcement by Kuwait Petroleum, it was obvious to Fedders that someone, or some group of people, had made millions of dollars illegally by purchasing Santa Fe options from Sampson and the rest while knowing that a merger was about to be announced. Working with the Pacific exchange, Fedders quickly obtained trading records to see who had placed the mass of orders during the last week of September and the first days of October.

And immediately Fedders hit a brick wall.

The vast bulk of the Santa Fe options suspiciously purchased before the takeover had been ordered through trading accounts at Credit Suisse, one of the largest banks in Switzerland. Swiss banking laws prevented the SEC from finding out who owned the accounts.

The shroud of Swiss banking secrecy had recently become an enormous frustration at the enforcement division. In March 1981, just before Shad was confirmed in his new position, the SEC's New York office had filed a major enforcement action in a situation similar to the one involving Santa Fe. Someone using secret Swiss bank accounts had earned millions by purchasing large numbers of stock options in St. Joe Minerals Corporation, shortly before a publicly announced takeover of the company. Robert Blackburn, an SEC attorney in New York, had been fighting in court for months to find out who was behind the Swiss accounts, but to no avail. Now Fedders assembled a team of lawyers in the Washington enforcement office to try to find out the same thing in the Santa Fe matter.

Quickly, they came up with a novel idea. At a closed SEC meeting in October chaired by Shad, Fedders proposed filing a lawsuit against "Certain Unknown Persons" who had bought massive amounts of Santa Fe stock options from Gary Sampson and the other traders in San Francisco, and also against giant Credit Suisse, where the unknown persons had their secret accounts. The idea of filing suit against someone unknown was an unusual and creative legal approach, but neither Shad nor the other commissioners blanched at Fedders's proposal. They approved the lawsuit. On October 25, Shad flew to New York and met with editors and reporters at the *New York Times*, declaring over lunch that the SEC was about to "come down with hobnail boots" on illegal insider trading. The next day, the unknown-persons suit was filed in New York federal court and Judge William Conner issued a temporary order freezing millions of dollars held in the suspected Credit Suisse accounts.

In the meantime Blackburn of the SEC's New York office, working with Fedders in Washington, had put the final touches on an aggressive strategy in the parallel St. Joe case. Frustrated by his inability to obtain the names of the account holders at Banca Della Svizzera that he suspected of reaping illegal profits on St. Joe stock options, Blackburn had submitted a brief to the judge in his case, a feisty older jurist named Milton Pollack, arguing that the only way to break through the Swiss banking laws was, in effect, to hold a gun to the bank's head.

A traditional and compelling defense of Swiss bank secrecy law was that the rules had been established to stop Hitler's Reich from seizing assets of Jews and others fleeing Nazi Germany. The neutrality of Swiss law cut two ways, the Swiss argued. It might protect crooks who traded on inside information about U.S. corporate takeovers, but it also was a safeguard against tyranny.

Blackburn had found a way to turn an aspect of this historical defense on its head, and to use it against the Swiss bank he was suing. He had learned that in Switzerland it was a serious crime for anyone to disclose the name of a Swiss-bank-account holder. That was why the banks refused to turn over the names in American courts—they would be breaking Swiss law. But there was an exception in Swiss tradition: If someone was under imminent duress, they could reveal account holders' names with impunity. Blackburn told his judge that the exception dated from the days following World War II when, behind the newly erected Iron Curtain, guns were literally held to the heads of Swiss bank employees by Russian occupiers who were trying to stop the flight of capital out of Eastern Europe. Lawyers for the Swiss banks said they didn't think the issue or the history was as clear as Blackburn and the SEC made it seem. In any event, Blackburn tried to hand Judge Pollack a gun to use against the Swiss banks: He proposed the judge levy massive fines against Banca Della Svizzera, fines so large that it would jeopardize the bank's financial standing. Then, under imminent duress imposed by the American court, the bank would be free to turn over the names of its account holders to the SEC.

Judge Pollack had his own ideas about the theories that might justify levying such massive and unprecedented fines on a Swiss bank, but he also was evidently impressed by the SEC's arguments. On November 6, he delivered a decision that within hours of its issuance would rock the tight-knit Swiss banking fraternity in Zurich and Bern.

"There is something wrong with having somebody standing out there invading the market over here, doing something illegal and saying, 'You can't get me because I'm anonymous,'" Pollack announced from his courtroom bench to an awestruck Blackburn. "The game has proceeded long enough and the SEC should not be any longer put off."

Fedders had won—it was a total victory. Pollack's decision not only devastated modest-sized Banca Della Svizzera, it immediately threatened Credit Suisse, the bank sued by the SEC in the Santa Fe case. Within days, lawyers for the Swiss banks and political officers from the Swiss embassy were peppering Fedders's office with phone calls, urging compromise. There was even talk of a new, landmark treaty between Switzerland and the U.S. For the SEC's new Reagan Republican leaders, viewed with suspicion by their staff, it was a public victory to savor. And within weeks, Fedders was launched on a transoceanic diplomatic odyssey that would carry both him and Shad to international renown, cementing the SEC's new image while sending a strong and largely unexpected message to Wall Street.

Fedders and a diplomatic delegation from the Reagan administration flew to Switzerland to open negotiations aimed at solving the bank-secrecy crisis. SEC enforcement division staff had prepared fat, black briefing books for Fedders about the intricacies of Swiss banking politics, including sensitive portraits of the leading personalities in Bern and Zurich. Secrecy was a billion dollar business for the Swiss banks. They were not about to yield their franchise to a bureaucrat from Washington.

Fedders devoured the briefing books. Already he had proved to his skeptical staff that he was willing to work harder than any of them. When he touched down in Switzerland, he was well-prepared. At first there were the usual cocktail parties and stiff meetings dominated by protocol. A diplomatic note had been prepared beforehand with the help of the U.S. State Department. At the Swiss Justice Ministry, Fedders attended a preorchestrated meeting where the diplomats read from scripts and articulated their preconceived ideas. Fedders performed skillfully; he was commanding and concise. And there was progress amid the protocol. The governments agreed that they should develop a new treaty arrangement to permit the SEC to obtain the names of alleged wrongdoers from Swiss banks—after following certain legal procedures supervised by the Swiss government.

But the success of the trip hinged on whether Fedders could yet persuade the major Swiss banks to participate in the diplomacy. One of Fedders's aides advised him that the bankers were deeply suspicious and that, if the leading executives in Zurich did not consider a treaty to be in their interest, no treaty would be signed. That was a fact of Swiss political life, the aide said.

A few days after they arrived in Switzerland, Fedders and some of his delegation flew to Zurich for a luncheon sponsored by the Swiss-American Chamber of Commerce. Fedders was told that he would have to deliver a winning speech to a vast audience of Swiss bankers. If he impressed them, there was a chance they might yet obtain the names of the account holders at Credit Suisse who had earned millions of dollars at the expense of Gary Sampson and the options traders in San Francisco. If Fedders failed, the enforcement division would be back virtually where it started.

The suspicion, even hostility, among the Swiss bankers was palpable to some of the U.S. lawyers and diplomats who took their seats in the ballroom of the ornate Doldergrand Hotel that afternoon. The Swiss banking executives saw Fedders as the imperial American bogeyman, a caricature familiar even in sedate Switzerland. As far as the bankers were concerned, it was Fedders who had pointed the gun at Banca Della Svizzera's head and who had pointed one as well at venerable Credit Suisse. The chief executive of Credit Suisse, Rainer Gut, was to introduce Fedders to the audience. The room was tense and hot. Television lights flooded the dais. Fedders sat in the guest of honor's chair.

Fedders had done a fair amount of speaking while in private legal practice and he enjoyed it; he was drawn to the attention and applause. He had prepared a bland, safe speech about the growing internationalism of the securities markets and the importance of intergovernmental cooperation. But he had been told in the last few days that it was essential that he open his talk with some light remarks complimenting the Swiss and their system of banking and government. Fedders had been mulling this challenge over and had come up with an idea, which he shared with no one. The idea was inspired by a story in a local Zurich newspaper, which described an annual Swiss opera singing competition for young vocalists from around the world. Fedders had never heard of the competition before, but he asked Jim Fall, a Treasury attaché at the U.S. embassy in Bern, to find out the name of the local opera house in Zurich and the names of Switzerland's three best operas. Fall, puzzled, made the inquiries.

Rainer Gut of Credit Suisse presented Fedders with a big silver plate during the introduction, and all Fedders could think about was how he was going to have to give this thing back to the U.S. government because of the federal laws proscribing public servants from accepting foreign gifts. Then the applause died and Fedders was standing at the podium, the center of attention. In a deadly earnest tone, he began to tell an elaborate, and under the circumstances, hilarious story from his youth.

"It has been a great, great opportunity to come back here to Switzerland," Fedders told the bankers. "I was here once before, years ago. I came over to Switzerland at the age of eighteen for the first time as an aspiring opera star for the renowned youth singing competition here in Zurich. My sole ambition in those days was to be an opera star. Actually, on that trip, I met Rainer Gut for the first time, when I was only eighteen . . ."

Here Fedders paused and looked over at Gut, who appeared puzzled.

"Mr. Gut was in the audience when I performed," Fedders continued, saying that Gut had actually been in the first row, one of the judges.

He turned to the Credit Suisse chief executive. "You gave me a great ovation at the end of my performance, and the audience called, 'Encore! Encore!' And I sang the song again and there was more applause. 'Encore!' And I sang the song again.

"And the fourth time I sang the song, I leaned down to Rainer Gut and I said, 'How many times do I have to sing it?'

"And he said, 'Until you get it right.' "

The bankers laughed and applauded loudly—the self-effacing conclusion struck the right note, especially since it deferred to the powerful Gut. Afterward, the U.S. diplomats and lawyers praised Fedders heartily. Even after the story was retold as fact in the Zurich newspapers the next day, hardly anyone—and certainly not Fedders—made a point to note that the anecdote was a complete fabrication, made up from whole cloth.

The story served Fedders's purpose and the remainder of his speech was well received. The Swiss trip ended triumphantly: The government and the bankers agreed that a new treaty arrangement was necessary. Six months later a Memo of Understanding was signed in Washington, establishing new procedures for the SEC to obtain the names of alleged inside traders who used Swiss bank accounts to protect their identities. The insiders who bought Santa Fe stock options from Gary Sampson and his colleagues in Santa Fe were identified as a host of Kuwaitis, American executives, lawyers, accountants, and even a Washington, D.C., lobbyist. Much of the money lost in the Pacific exchange's options pit was eventually recovered. The SEC's Blackburn, too, identified a stockbroker named Giuseppe Tome as the alleged inside trader who had tried to hide behind an account at Banca Della Svizzera, and in that case the SEC won another important victory, recovering several million dollars. Most important of all, the SEC enforcement division had broken partially through fifty years of Swiss banking secrecy, one of the biggest obstacles to successful insider trading prosecution. A new phase in international law enforcement had been inaugurated during Fedders's first months on the job.

Fedders returned to Washington feeling triumphant. It was a sensation he savored, but it would not last for long.

4

Closed Meeting

Jack Shad sat at the head of the table in his high-backed swivel chair, and saw that he was outnumbered by the SEC staff—as usual. There were at least seven of them across the polished table ready to participate in the day's debate, all of them lawyers, none with extensive experience in business or on Wall Street. These were the people Shad had been warned against by some of his brokerage colleagues and some senior SEC officials before he came to Washington—bureaucrats who had never traded a share of stock in their lives, but who nevertheless exercised wide control over the nation's business.

The gaggle of staff in the eighth-floor meeting room at SEC headquarters that day was led by the lean and towering Fedders, the only one of them who had been recruited to the SEC by Shad. Several of the others seemed increasingly frustrated by Shad's policies. They had come to the commissioners' meeting that Tuesday morning, December 22, 1981, three days before Christmas, prepared to do battle for a cause in which they fervently believed.

To the enforcement staff led by Associate Director David Doherty, the SEC's three-year investigation of questionable financial dealings by the New York–based, multinational bank holding company Citicorp was more than an important case in its own right, involving legal violations the staff considered serious. It was also an important symbol of how the SEC intended to police Wall

59

Street and the corporate world during the Reagan years. Would Shad's SEC have the courage to punish any corporate violator, no matter how large or politically influential? Would the commission send a message to Wall Street that the inauguration of Ronald Reagan did not signal a relaxation of white-collar prosecutions? Would the SEC's fearsome reputation during the 1970s, when its investigations shook the boardrooms of Fortune 500 companies, continue to provide deterrence to wrongdoing in this new political era of business boosterism?

Shad, too, saw the Citicorp case in broad and even symbolic terms, but the questions he wanted to ask were different. Could the SEC's bureaucratic enforcement staff be persuaded that it did not have the power to impose its morality on corporations and brokerages, regardless of the law? Could the enforcement staff understand that the costs and benefits of its prosecutions—for the economy, for the federal government's budget—had to be balanced? Could it accept that most businessmen and Wall Street financiers were not crooks?

"It's a big one," Shad said of the Citicorp case as the meeting began. About that, if nothing else, everyone in the room agreed.

For months the case had been festering inside the SEC. Debate over the investigation had gradually intensified, settling finally into a bitter stalemate. The controversy was unknown to the public; the case, like most SEC investigations was a tightly guarded secret. The facts uncovered by the enforcement staff would be revealed only if the politically appointed commissioners voted to file charges. While the commission's overseers focused that fall on public battles over the size of the SEC's budget and its campaign to break down Swiss-bank secrecy laws, the fight over Citicorp had been carried on privately inside the commission's downtown headquarters.

John Fedders, Shad's new enforcement chief, thought that the passions stirred within the commission by the Citicorp case had at least as much to do with personalities, politics, and institutional change as with the actual facts of the investigation. When Fedders arrived at the SEC, he saw almost immediately that the case was fraught with difficulties. There were about eight hundred open enforcement investigations in the division when Fedders got there, and the Citicorp case was one of the biggest—for three years, the investigation had been draining manpower and resources. The staff was only now considering whether it was time to file fraud charges against Citicorp and its subsidiary Citibank, one of the largest multinational banks in the world.

At issue were questionable dealings by the bank in the exploding and largely unregulated foreign currency markets, where banks and other traders speculated—sometimes wildly—on which of the world's major currencies were going up in price and which were going down. The transactions under investigation by the commission had produced about $46 million in profits for Citicorp, a large amount in absolute terms, but a relatively small percentage of the bank company's massive revenue. Currency trading was not an area where the SEC had any natural jurisdiction—it was outside the scope of the federal securities laws the agency enforced. Moreover, there were other federal regulators in Washington—the Comptroller of the Currency, the Federal Deposit Insurance Corporation, and the Internal Revenue Service—that oversaw aspects of Citicorp's foreign exchange dealing. Still, the SEC's aggressive enforcement staff had been drawn to the case because it involved alleged illegal schemes and tax evasion that nobody else in the capital had detected or prevented. At the closed meeting in 1978, when he sought and received authority from the SEC to issue government subpoenas for Citicorp's records, Stanley Sporkin had argued that the investigation was necessary in part to sustain the public perception that the commission was afraid of no one, not even a giant bank. "One of the great benefits we have from our program is that we [have] got all kinds of confidence out there," he had said. He believed that Citicorp had made misleading disclosures to its shareholders about the legal and financial risks involved in the way it traded money around the globe. He wanted the bank to make a full disclosure of its questionable conduct in the SEC's public-filing room, something all the world would see.

That summer and fall of 1981, some of the enforcement lawyers who talked with Fedders about the case said they wanted to widen the probe's scope and keep pushing for new information. In his corner office on the fourth floor, in between his work on insider trading and his efforts to reorganize the enforcement staff, Fedders received a series of briefings from Thomas von Stein and Robert Ryan, two lawyers who had been chasing Citicorp since 1978. Fedders heard them out, but he was unimpressed—he thought von Stein and Ryan had failed to prove that Citicorp had done anything illegal, and he told them so. Fedders wanted to shut the case down.

In the end he hadn't done it, though. So far, Doherty had managed only to convince Fedders that if he killed the Citicorp case peremptorily, without allowing the commissioners to vote, he would badly alienate his staff. Fedders had compromised because he was having enough trouble winning the hearts and minds of the enforcement division lawyers who had worked so many years at the commission before his arrival. The Citicorp dispute had come just as he was beginning to gain ground. For one thing, he was starting to recruit his own people to the division from private practice—young, well-dressed, well-trained lawyers from private practice, "the preppies," as they were sometimes called derisively by the more motley veterans. Also, the successful campaign against insider trading was stirring some enthusiasm in the division. But the Citicorp case presented Fedders—and Shad, too—with a potentially dangerous pitfall. Fedders decided to allow Doherty and the others to present their own memo to the four commissioners, recommending charges against Citicorp. At the top of the memo, Fedders included his own recommendation that no charges be brought against the bank. It would be up to Shad and the other commissioners to choose between the conflicting recommendations of Fedders and Doherty. That was why the commissioners and staff had gathered in the closed meeting room three days before Christmas, in an atmosphere of considerable tension.

"I perceive," David Doherty declared as the discussion got under way, "that I may have a slight uphill battle on this one."

A bevy of memos describing the competing positions had already been drafted and circulated to the four commissioners who would consider the case. One SEC commissioner, Barbara Thomas, had removed herself from voting on the matter because business dealings she'd had with Citicorp before she was appointed to the SEC created the appearance of a conflict of interest.

"I'd like to compliment you, John Fedders, for the decision that you made to bring this to the commission," Shad said from his perch at the center of the table, reminding his fellow commissioners that a less magnanimous enforcement director might have killed the matter on his own. To Doherty, Shad added, "I'd like to compliment you for the courage and the conviction to go against the viewpoint of the other divisions and the integrity of your viewpoint."

Shad, too, was campaigning to win hearts and minds at the commission, and, like Fedders, he was beginning to succeed. His deregulatory campaign was in full swing. The deal he struck with Philip Johnson, the chairman of the Commodity Futures Trading Commission, to free new stock-index-futures products from their regulatory quagmire had progressed well. Other efforts to make the commission's regulations simpler and more efficient were under way. Shad had thrown the weight of his office behind plans to simplify the process by which corporations filed annual reports and other statements at the SEC—Shad thought the changes he was pushing would save the country billions of dollars by helping companies raise money quickly in the stock and bond markets, without unnecessary delays caused by the commission. The most controversial change Shad was backing that winter was known as rule 415, the "shelf registration" rule, which would allow companies to avoid repetitious disclosures of the financial aspects of their business operations each time they tried to raise money in the stock and bond markets. Critics warned that the proposed rule would allow big companies to hide problems from stockholders and investors. Shad disagreed, and his enthusiasm for the change had impressed some of the SEC staff wary of his Wall Street background—the big Wall Street investment houses, such as the one where Shad had spent his career, opposed the rule change because it would cut into one of their lucrative businesses.

But Shad hadn't bowed to any pressure from Wall Street, at least so far.

There was another way that Shad was ingratiating himself with the SEC bureaucracy—it was evident in the way he complimented Doherty for his "courage and conviction," even though Shad evidently disagreed with him about the Citicorp case. From the beginning the staff had wondered how Shad's obviously ambivalent attitude toward the SEC—on the one hand he distrusted the bureaucracy, but on the other he respected its mission and aspired to leadership—would be expressed at closed meetings, where the commission's serious business was conducted. (SEC meetings to which the public was invited were called open meetings; the public was barred from closed meetings.) What they had learned in the preceding five months was that while Shad held strong opinions about how the SEC should change its ways, he also wanted to work within the system, and he craved collegiality and respect. Before Shad's arrival, some closed SEC meetings erupted into emotional name-calling sessions. Shad put a stop to that immediately, setting a more formal tone by addressing division directors by their "Director" title and insisting on a professional decorum. Shad didn't go in for Machiavellian politicking or intrigue. He said what he meant and he was used to getting what he wanted. On Wall Street they said Shad was the sort of investment banker who didn't mind leading with his chin.

A few of the senior commission staff understood something Shad didn't, though, something they thought he would learn soon enough. To someone like the new SEC chairman, who was uninitiated in the ways of Washington, it was hard to explain in so many words, but it had to do with the ends of power and the means of its exercise. You could put it this way: In the nation's capital, if a man led with his chin, there was usually someone around ready to throw a sucker punch.

"I would like to take a few minutes and lay out where we are and what our position is and, hopefully, in the process, simplify what is a pretty complex situation," Doherty began when everyone was settled at the commission table.

The spools of a tape recorder turned silently nearby. The law required it—no one from outside the SEC attended closed meetings, but if there ever was a question about what went on, Congress could ask for the tapes. They were stored securely at commission headquarters and eventually shipped to a storage facility in suburban Maryland. It was only in the 1970s that the practice of taping meetings had begun, in the aftermath, ironically, of the Watergate scandal.

Doherty summarized the facts of the Citicorp case.

The whole thing had begun, as many SEC proceedings did, with a complaint from someone who thought the commission could help him. A junior official at Citicorp named David Edwards, distressed by what he thought were improper dealings by the bank, hired a lawyer and arranged to meet with the SEC's enforcement staff in Washington. He brought with him documents that appeared to show a deliberate scheme by the bank's currency-trading department to evade tax and currency-exchange laws in a number of countries, mostly in Europe. The bank bought and sold millions of U.S. dollars, British sterling, French and Swiss francs, German deutsche marks, and Italian lira every day. To avoid paying taxes and to escape restrictions on currency speculation, the bank allegedly arranged bogus deals with subsidiaries in island tax havens like the Bahamas. The bogus deals were called parking transactions because the bank allegedly "parked" its money in the Bahamas for short periods of time to evade the law.

"Our view is that Citicorp had a policy of parking that was known by management, and management was at least aware of the questionable legality of the practice," Doherty told Shad and the other commissioners that December morning. "Indeed, Citicorp itself, in various memos, described the practice as transparent, rinky-dink, and artificial. So I think it was perceived within Citicorp as, at many levels, a highly questionable practice."

Edwards, the Citicorp whistleblower who got the SEC investigation started, was fired by the bank a week after he squealed to the commission, Doherty continued. Meanwhile, Citicorp retained a prestigious Manhattan law firm, Sherman & Sterling, to conduct an internal investigation of the bank's currency trading practices. The law firm produced a carefully worded report that purported to describe the bank's practices and denied any wrongdoing. Sensitive to the precept that any questionable conduct by a corporation should be disclosed publicly in the SEC's filing room, Citicorp filed the Sherman & Sterling report at the commission. But Doherty and the other enforcement lawyers felt the report was intended to deceive the public. "We believe this report is misleading," Doherty said. "It basically indicated [the parking] was a sporadic, isolated kind of conduct. The impression it left is that Mr. Edwards was wrong in his allegations as opposed to being right."

For more than half an hour, Doherty went on without interruption. He talked passionately about how important it was that the SEC not change its policy of forcing big corporations like Citicorp to disclose fully their improper conduct to the public.

In addition to Fedders, other senior commission staff opposed Doherty. Among the memos that had been submitted to Shad and the other commissioners prior to that day's meetings was one from Jack Shinkle, the SEC's associate general counsel. Shinkle's office, called the counseling group, was supposed to express an opinion about every recommendation that went to the full commission from the enforcement division. (The group was formed under former chairman Harold Williams, who had used it as a check on enforcement chief Stanley Sporkin's power.) The counseling group sometimes submitted legal briefs to the commissioners, opposing the enforcement division's recommendations. In this matter, Shinkle argued that under certain provisions of the federal securities laws, the commission could only force a corporation to make *corrective* disclosures in the SEC's public-filing room—the agency had no power to force a company to disclose something it had never mentioned in previous statements to investors. In other words, if a corporation said in its publicly filed annual report that it did business legally and honestly, and the SEC found out that it actually was crooked, then the commission could force the offender to correct its earlier public statement and admit its improper conduct. But if, on the other hand, a corporation never asserted publicly that it was honest in the first place, the SEC had no authority to force the company to admit that it was crooked.

It was a strange logic, and Doherty was evidently outraged by it. Warming to his argument, he told the commissioners a story about how a few years back the enforcement division had found out that a publicly owned company in the scrap-metal business was deliberately short-weighting its shipments to customers. When a customer bought a hundred tons of metal, Doherty said, the company loaded only seventy-five tons into its trucks, and made up the difference with bricks and stones. To avoid discovery when the trucks were unloaded, it paid bribes to the customer's receiving agent. "My reading of the general counsel's office theory . . . is that you could not charge a violation . . . under those circumstances because there's no affirmative representation in the annual report that management was honest, that books and records were honest, that they were conducting their business in an honest manner. . . . I would urge the commission not to take such a restrictive point of view."

In Doherty's long speech he kept drifting away from the details and toward broader, more emotional themes. They kept letting him talk, never asking questions, never challenging him, as if they were politely indulging him before delivering the hard truth that the view of the SEC's role that Doherty was articulating no longer would prevail.

"We can't prove this case," Fedders declared when his deputy was done. "We have no ability to establish today that the conduct engaged in by Citicorp was illegal. We have circumstantial evidence; we have evidence that tends to indicate that there may have been improper conduct. But we could not walk into an administrative proceeding or to a court today and establish this case, that there was illegal conduct."

Later, Fedders considered this to be one of his finest hours at the SEC. He had been on the job only months, he faced resentments and suspicions and management challenges, yet he had stuck to the facts and he had given Doherty and the others beneath him in the enforcement division a chance to make their case before the commissioners. Fedders prided himself on his "intellectual honesty," by which he meant rigorous attention to the facts and to the letter of the law. Attorneys like Doherty, in Fedders's view, were intellectually dishonest because they stretched the federal securities statutes and the SEC's powers to suit their needs. Shad shared this basic view about enforcement. In the Citicorp case, Shad thought not only that the enforcement staff had failed to prove any illegality, but also that it had delayed far too long in bringing its proposed fraud charges to the commission table.

"May I ask, why wasn't it brought before now?" Shad inquired. "Why this extraordinary delay?"

"Let me answer that," said Robert Ryan, the enforcement staffer who reported to Doherty and who had devoted nearly three years of his life to the Citicorp investigation. Ryan could see that the meeting was going against him and he sounded frustrated. "Number one, the first delay was the commission. The commission told us to wait until Sherman and Sterling filed their report."

"Well, but that was in seventy-eight," Shad said.

"That was the first delay, sir. The second delay was Sherman and Sterling and Citicorp in delaying getting documents to us and arranging witnesses. Third, the complexity of the case; and fourth, quite frankly, disagreement among the staff as to the scope of the case."

"Well, but how much of—let me characterize it baldly. How much of the delay was due to stalling or dilatory tactics by Citicorp?" Shad pressed. "Where did that end up?"

"I can't break it down and talk to that."

"It certainly hasn't been going on for three years."

Shad planned to vote against filing any fraud charges against Citicorp. The question was whether Doherty and Ryan could win at least two votes from the remaining three commissioners, thus forcing a 2 to 2 deadlock. In that event, there were certain procedures by which a tie might be broken, but the procedures were little used and it wasn't at all clear what would happen. Throughout its history the commission had not been an adversarial body; the majority of its votes were unanimous and usually followed the recommendations of staff. If there was a tie, certainly there would be a new round of discussions and arguments, and perhaps one of the commissioners would change his or her mind. But from whom could Doherty win two votes?

Under federal law, two of the commission's seats were reserved for Democrats and two for Republicans. The president appointed the chairman, and so a majority of commissioners at any given time belonged to the president's political party. But when John Shad arrived at the SEC, party affiliation was not a significant factor with the commissioners; it was the ideology of Stanley Sporkin, not the ideology of Republicans and Democrats, that divided the members of the SEC. When the SEC staff in the room that day looked at the three commissioners who flanked Shad, they could sort them most easily in terms of their attitudes toward the enforcement program. Phil Loomis, a Republican, had spent time on the commission staff and respected Sporkin and his enforcement division, but lately Loomis had grown increasingly resistant to the enforcement division's expansive policies. John Evans, a Republican appointee of Nixon, was Sporkin's great defender on the eighth floor, the one commissioner who had consistently opposed the changes being pushed by Shad, Fedders, and the others. The swing vote belonged to Bevis Longstreth, a recently appointed Democrat whose views were largely unknown. Longstreth was a Manhattan attorney who specialized in bankruptcy law during his long career.

"I agree that what Citicorp did here was questionable," Loomis began, when it came time for the commissioners to air their views. "Perhaps, probably, it did involve, technically, an evasion of the rules with respect to the amount of the currency they held overnight. But, on the other hand, there are the arguments that Mr. Fedders makes, which I think are quite forceful. . . . It's not really a securities case; it's a foreign currency case, and a banking case, and in view of the fact that there are difficulties of proof and other factors, I quite agree with Mr. Fedders, in the exercise of discretion, not to bring this."

That made it two votes to none against Doherty and the staff.

"Commissioner Evans?" Shad said.

"I find this a very difficult case," he responded.

Evans began to talk about the facts, the amount of money involved, the foreign tax and currency laws in question. But as he went on, as had happened to Doherty, Evans glided into sweeping, emotional themes—a defense of a vigorous, activist SEC, one whose enforcement division provided deterrence against crime in the boardrooms and executive suites of the country's largest financial institutions. Evans thought that Fedders had a point about the Citicorp case—the amount of money involved was relatively small compared to the bank's revenue, and the case was certainly old. But there was another issue that Evans thought was more important. Fedders seemed to be saying that if you're big enough, and if you keep your illegal conduct on a well-managed scale, then the commission will never be able to prove a specific case. Evans thought this was a dangerous development. If you stopped holding Wall Street and executives at the country's largest corporations responsible for the little things that went wrong in their organizations, then soon enough the top people would start to look the other way when bigger problems arose.

"I think it's appropriate that people understand that the commission expects them to adequately disclose transactions of this type," he said. "And just because it's the largest bank in the United States or the largest bank dealing in foreign currency transactions in the world doesn't mean that this is not . . . in my opinion, doesn't mean that this is not material.

"I think it means that the commission should be willing to take on a responsibility of adequate disclosure even in a case where you have the largest institution in the world. If we don't, who will?"

With that flourish, Evans said that he thought the SEC should file charges against Citicorp.

Eyes in the room shifted to Bevis Longstreth, the former bankruptcy lawyer who now held the decisive vote.

Longstreth had much in common with Shad. He commuted between Washington and New York, spending the week at a rented basement apartment in Georgetown and the weekends at his spacious Manhattan flat. Longstreth differed with Shad on some economic and ideological issues, but they were fast becoming friends, brought together in Georgetown by the tragedy of Pat Shad's stroke and by a streak of giddy playfulness they shared. Shad kiddingly referred to Longstreth's basement apartment as a "den of iniquity" because of all the attractive coeds and professional women who walked the neighborhood streets. Some nights after work, Shad and Longstreth would eat sushi together at a Japanese restaurant on Wisconsin Avenue. Occasionally, they wandered over to the Little Tavern hamburger stand on Wisconsin and poured quarters into a Pac-Man video-game machine at the back of the restaurant. Shad had grown enthusiastic about Pac-Man—he liked the game's geometric and mathematical aspects, especially the fact that he could keep track of his score, measuring his improvement in numbers. He drew Longstreth into a running competition in which they wagered on the outcome of Pac-Man games, with Shad often spotting Longstreth the number of points by which he had beaten him in the previous game. Sometimes Shad's prowess at the game would drive Longstreth into debt until he could win a match and bring the account back to zero on a double-or-nothing bet.

"I share the agonies around the table," Longstreth said that morning, "because it is a tough case, an awfully tough case. I guess my bottom line is that, in the exercise of prosecutorial discretion, I guess I wouldn't bring the case."

"Would not?" Shad asked.

"I think it's very hard for the SEC to prove that [Citicorp was] wrong, at least in a case as fuzzy as this."

The vote was finished—Shad and Fedders had prevailed at the commission table, 3 to 1, with Shad joining the majority. There would be no charges against Citicorp.

The enforcement lawyers were deeply disappointed. They had given three years of their lives to this case; lived it, sweated it. During the investigation, they hadn't thought there was much chance that it would come to nothing; the only question was how big a case it would be when the charges were finally filed. Tom von Stein, the staff lawyer who had worked hardest on the investigation and who sat silently through most of the meeting that day, couldn't let it drop. The commissioners, except for Evans, had all sounded so reasonable, so devoid of commitment, as if proposed fraud charges against one of the world's biggest banks were somehow a routine matter.

"The evidence is there," von Stein broke in dramatically. "There are hundreds of documents which describe the practice."

"The evidence is arguably there," Shad answered him. "In your view it's there, and in the opinion of the other two divisions, it's questionable." Shad was talking about the memos submitted by the SEC's Office of the General Counsel and the Division of Corporation Finance, which regulated filings at the commission by publicly owned corporations, including Citicorp. Both memos supported the view of Shad and Fedders that the Citicorp case should be dropped.

"I'm the only person in this room who has read all the documents, and I'm telling you," von Stein said ardently.

Fedders cut in. "I've reviewed the case and I stand by what I said."

"You said that with a little more work you could probably show that they were illegal," challenged Evans, joining von Stein.

"A hell of a lot more work. . . . We don't have any evidence to prove illegality," said Fedders. ". . . We could not go in court tomorrow and establish this case."

"On that basis, I concur with the other two commissioners," Shad said, putting an end to it.

"Thank you very much," he added. And with that, the meeting was dismissed.

That wintry week the hallways and offices of the North Capitol Street headquarters emptied as Shad, Longstreth, and the others headed off to spend the Christmas holidays with their families. Shad wasn't one to gloat, but the flush of victory in such a difficult and deeply felt debate could hardly fail to make an impression on such a competitive man. He was winning now. The old was on the way out, the new was on the way in; it was that season of the year. Within months Doherty would be gone from the SEC, joining his old mentor Sporkin at the CIA. Some of the other holdovers would be leaving soon, too. There was every reason for Shad to believe that the new year would bring with it new momentum, an acceleration of his deregulatory program and consolidation of his influence inside the SEC.

There was every reason for optimism.

5

The Hunted

From an anteroom off a cavernous marble hallway, Jack Shad and his two counselors from the Securities and Exchange Commission crossed into a vast inner office. One of them lugged a box filled with confidential documents. They were supplicants on a political pilgrimage—the box was a kind of offering. On a winter's day early in 1982, Shad and his staff lawyers had been summoned to the second floor of the Rayburn House office building by Congressman John D. Dingell, Democrat of Michigan, the chairman of the House Energy and Commerce Committee, whose responsibilities included oversight of Wall Street and the SEC.

Trophies rimmed the walls—Dingell was a hunter, and he had mounted the heads of caribou, wild boar, and rare white deer. The first time he saw the place, Shad was struck by the political metaphor of the congressman's interior decoration, and a frightful, impish idea jumped into his head. He imagined his own head stuffed and mounted on a wooden plaque, hoisted right up there between the animals. He said something along those lines and Dingell laughed. At least he had a sense of humor. Once Shad found himself seated next to Big John, as the six-foot three-inch, two-hundred-twenty-pound congressman was known on Capitol Hill, and Dingell started talking about what it was like to hunt in the Michigan woods in winter. Dingell said he wore a white hunting suit as camouflage and stalked his prey through thick foliage

73

draped in blinding white snow. As he listened Shad visualized Dingell tromping through the woods, all but invisible, with a big bull's-eye around him formed by a flock of dead crows. It was hard to say what Shad's vision meant, but if there was a dreamlike intensity to the way he thought about Dingell, it was because the congressman loomed large in Shad's life.

Dingell was always lamenting what he saw as the culture of greed on Wall Street, and he demanded that the SEC protect ordinary investors from crooked stockbrokers and the economy from sophisticated financial corruption. When he talked about Wall Street and the SEC, Dingell sounded like a prairie populist, a righteous defender of the little people against the clutches of corporate excess. The irony was that there were few congressmen of either party in Washington more beholden to big business than Dingell. His father had been a congressman before him, and Dingell knew intimately the importance of protecting hometown constituents—as it happened, Dingell's suburban Detroit district was home to the headquarters of the Ford Motor Company, one of the world's largest automobile manufacturers. Thanks largely to Dingell's support as chairman of the powerful Energy and Commerce Committee, Ford and its brethren automakers had successfully fought off a litany of consumer-backed reforms of the industry. Laws to require airbags in cars, to toughen auto-safety standards, and to reduce air pollution by limiting carbon dioxide emissions in auto exhaust, all were blocked by Dingell. Unfortunately for Shad, any ideological inconsistency between Dingell's genuflection to Detroit and his populist support for the SEC mattered little in the capital. What mattered was that Dingell chaired a powerful committee, and that he was virtually unbeatable at reelection.

For Shad, an unhappy phase in his tenure as chairman of the SEC began that day early in 1982, when he and two top commission aides arrived in Dingell's office with their box of documents. Dingell had contacted Shad to say that he was about to launch a congressional investigation into Shad's personal finances. Staff members on Dingell's oversight and investigations subcommittee thought they smelled something improper in the stock transactions through which Shad began to sell his more than $10 million fortune in E. F. Hutton shares before leaving Wall Street for the commission. Shad didn't know why Dingell's staff was suspicious. He had heard that lawyers at the oversight subcommittee simply couldn't believe that he would willingly pay the $2.5 million in capital gains taxes due the U.S. Treasury upon sale of the stock— the congressional lawyers were going to see if he had secretly "parked" his Hutton shares, hiding them temporarily and planning to get them back later. On the other hand, there might be another, more obvious explanation for the probe: partisan politics. Ronald Reagan's conservative revolution was sweeping the capital, but Dingell had launched a one-man counterattack.

Shad handed over his box, which contained a pile of confidential, personal financial records documenting his holdings and stock trades. Shad also gave Dingell a copy of a letter that had been drafted by the commission's ethics counsel. The ethic's counsel's job was to make sure that SEC staff and commissioners didn't violate any of the Byzantine laws proscribing conflicts of interest by government officials, and also to discipline staff who leaked secret commission information to the public. The letter said that Shad had complied with both the letter and the spirit of the relevant laws. He was selling his Hutton stock; he had established a blind trust for his fortune, managed by his old friend Barton Biggs at the Wall Street investment firm Morgan Stanley & Company; and he had avoided participating in SEC decisions when there might be a question of financial conflict of interest.

Shad said he wanted this wrapped up as promptly as possible. When it was over, if Dingell hadn't found anything improper, he also wanted a letter of exoneration.

Dingell said that Shad would be treated fairly.

There was another thing: Shad said emphatically that he didn't want any of this to be leaked to the press, a tactic that he surmised was commonplace among congressional committees, particularly those run by Dingell. The very fact of an ongoing investigation, if it were publicized, would unfairly imply wrongdoing and tarnish his reputation, Shad said.

There won't be any leaks, Dingell responded.

Perhaps Dingell meant what he said. It was hard to know some-times how much of what happened in Dingell's name was person-ally approved by him, and how much represented the independent work of his large staff. Dingell usually accepted responsibility for what they did, and certainly he basked happily in the publicity they generated. There were more than a hundred people on the con-gressman's payroll, at least a dozen of them full-time investigators whose work often found its way into the pages of the country's larg-est daily newspapers. At the libel trial between Mobil and the *Wash-ington Post* that involved the SEC's probe of the oil company, one of Dingell's investigators testified that he routinely leaked infor-mation to reporters as part of his effort to win notice for Dingell's committee. Reporters, at least those who didn't feel too ashamed of themselves, competed ferociously for Dingell's leaks—the staff in-vestigators' work was often thorough and genuinely newsworthy. But the targets of Dingell's probes—Republican government offi-cials, defense contractors, and businessmen—often felt they were victims of politically motivated, calculated campaigns of character assassination.

John Shad felt that way on March 18, not long after the meeting with Dingell, when he awoke to find a headline splashed across the pages of the *New York Times*'s business section: MORGAN STAN-LEY'S LINK TO SEC CHIEF STUDIED. The story, by the investigative reporter Jeff Gerth, cited "congressional sources" as saying that Shad had been asked to turn over documents to Dingell's over-sight subcommittee, and that the committee was probing possible improprieties in the SEC chairman's stock dealings. Gerth re-ported that Dingell was investigating whether Shad's financial ties to Morgan Stanley might influence his consideration of the pro-posed SEC rule known as 415, which would affect the Wall Street firm's business if adopted. By simplifying procedures for public companies to file financial disclosure documents at the SEC when they sold new securities to investors, 415 could cut into Morgan Stanley's and other Wall Street firms underwriting and financial-advisory fees. Shad backed 415 wholeheartedly, so it was hard to see where he might be influenced by Morgan Stanley. Shad was convinced, too, that key facts about his financial dealings with

Morgan Stanley—facts that would have demonstrated he had no conflict of interest—were deliberately left out of the story. The story questioned whether Shad improperly had joined the other four SEC commissioners in voting to implement the new rule on a one-year trial basis only—partly because of howls of protest from the Wall Street firms. The story questioned whether Shad might have accepted the one-year compromise because of his relationship with Morgan Stanley, and there were questions, too, about the adequacy of Shad's financial disclosures.

Furious, Shad tromped over to Capitol Hill and met again with Dingell, beneath the stuffed animal heads on the second floor of the Rayburn building.

You leaked this story to Gerth, Shad charged.

Dingell denied that he had done any such thing. Pressed by Shad, a member of Dingell's staff acknowledged that he talked sometimes with Gerth, but he, too, denied that he was the initial source of the reporter's story. There was nothing else Shad could do. After another talk about fairness and confidentiality, he retreated to his office at SEC headquarters.

The press was driving Shad to distraction that winter. Apart from Big John Dingell, if there was anyone in the capital whom Shad had come to view as his personal nemesis, it was *New York Times* reporter Jeff Gerth. It had started during his first weeks on the job, back in the summer of 1981, when Gerth had come to visit Shad at the SEC for an interview. Shad talked about the changes he hoped to implement at the commission—he said that he wanted, among other things, to make it easier for companies filing financial statements and annual reports at the SEC to write in language ordinary investors could comprehend. Too often, Shad told Gerth, it was the lawyers who wrote a company's annual reports, and lawyers were such a cautious, even paranoid, lot that they overstated a company's negative aspects while drowning the reader in qualified legal jargon. This was something Shad felt strongly about because developing corporate reports for investors had been one of his responsibilities in the corporate finance department at E. F. Hutton. After the interview, Gerth published a story that implied, Shad felt, that the new SEC chairman only wanted "happy news" in corporate reports, as if he were some bimbo television news director bent on relieving his audience from the gloom of truth. Shad was livid—Gerth had "bagged" him, he told anyone who would listen. Ever since, he had been fuming about Gerth's reporting about the SEC.

Then, in February of 1982, Shad felt he got bagged by Gerth again, this time with even more devastating effect. On the front page of the *Times* appeared a long story describing how the SEC had decided, after a long investigation, not to file securities fraud charges against Citicorp over the banking company's questionable dealings in the foreign currency markets. The story rocked the SEC—rarely did newspaper stories describe decisions made at closed commission meetings. From his reading of Gerth's story, Shad thought the leak had come at least in part from Dingell's oversight committee, which could have learned of the probe from a disgruntled attorney in the SEC's enforcement division. Dingell threatened to hold public hearings to investigate why the SEC had not acted. Such hearings would help the Democrats in Congress discredit the deregulatory approach championed by Shad.

Now, on top of all this, there was Gerth's story in March, which used the "news" of Dingell's investigation of Shad's finances to raise questions about the SEC chairman's personal stock dealings and the adequacy of his disclosures under government ethics laws. The questions and accusations about him were rising to a crescendo; one story justified another, and then another. In an attempt to respond, Shad paid $70,000 to Joseph Califano, the former Health, Education, and Welfare secretary, for public relations and legal advice. Perhaps Califano worked hard for such a steep fee, but in the immediate aftermath of the *Times* stories none of it seemed to do much good.

Competition between the newspapers only intensified the drive for information about Shad's dealings, and new stories appeared. The *Times* found that since his appointment as SEC chairman, Shad had donated $1,000 to Senator Alfonse D'Amato, a Republican from New York, who sat on the Senate committee responsible for SEC oversight. It was a measure of Shad's naïveté about the ways of Washington that he couldn't understand why this was news; he had always given money to Republican senators from New York, he said. In what Shad viewed as a "me too" effort by the competition to catch up, the *Wall Street Journal* also ran a front-page story calling Shad a "flabby cop" and reporting that lawyers and commission staff feared the SEC's glory days were finished.

When the newspapers failed to provide what Shad considered adequate space for his defense, he sent a letter to the editor. He also demanded an audience with Gerth's superiors. Some of Shad's colleagues in the Reagan administration—the ones who had served in the previous Republican administrations of Nixon and Ford—might have told him to relax, to keep things in perspective, that this was how politics was played in the capital. The best approach was to go easy, be careful about how your words and deeds might appear in public, and keep an eye out for compromise.

But that wasn't Shad's way. Though the SEC never responded to press inquiries or stories about its confidential investigations, except to say that it would neither confirm nor deny the existence of a probe, Shad decided to make an exception in the Citicorp case. It was painful for him to watch from the sidelines as he and the agency got battered in the press. The SEC issued a public statement on March 5, 1982, explaining its decision not to press charges or take any other action against Citicorp.

"Certain members of the enforcement staff believed that Citicorp violated the commission's disclosure rules," the SEC statement said. "However, the Director of the Division of Enforcement, the Office of the General Counsel and the Division of Corporation Finance were of a contrary opinion."

The SEC listed reasons justifying its decision—the allegations weren't proven, and even if they had been, the case was outside the commission's jurisdiction. Then the SEC lashed out at the newspaper stories that prompted this extraordinary public statement in the first place.

"The illegal disclosure to the press of confidential commission proceedings is also a serious cause of concern," the SEC said. "It violated the rights and interests of private parties, inhibits the commission's ability to obtain essential cooperation of the private sector in its investigations and undermines the candid debate of critical issues by members of the commission and the staff necessary to well-considered decisions. It is for these reasons that the commission normally does not comment on actions not brought.

"In view of the distorted impressions created by statements in the press, the commission would welcome the opportunity to provide a full account of its handling of the Citicorp matter before an appropriate Congressional committee."

On Wall Street, when Shad had a problem, he had dealt with it head on, without shrinking or shirking. That was how he was going to handle things in Washington, too. He thought that he and the SEC were being unfairly lumped in with all the sleazy scandals and conflict of interest probes that made Washington seem morally bankrupt to those who earned their livings outside the Beltway.

Shad was outraged. He wasn't going to play by the capital's rules—he was going to fight.

Jack Shad had been warned.

Not long after he arrived in Washington, Dingell had joined him for lunch at the Monocle, the Capitol Hill watering hole where Shad cut his stock futures deal with Philip Johnson. Dingell wanted to explain how things were going to work. He wanted Shad to understand that while all of Washington might be excited about the Reagan triumph, and the chance to streamline the bureaucracies and establish new priorities of deregulation, he, Dingell, wasn't going to let that happen at the commission. The Senate was in the hands of Republicans, so the Senate committee overseeing the SEC was unlikely to be aggressive. Dingell intended to take up the slack in the Democratically controlled House of Representatives. There was too much history at the SEC, he said. He wasn't going to allow all of what had been accomplished to be undone.

I'm tough, Dingell said, but you'll know where I'm coming from. I won't sandbag you, but I'll stick to my guns.

It was at that lunch that the rules of the hunt seem to have been explained. But what was Shad supposed to do—run off into the woods and hide?

He respected Dingell's "machismo" and blunt resolve; Shad used to say that if he ever had to fight in a trench war, "Rambo" Dingell was the sort of guy he'd like to have at his side. But it irked Shad that Dingell could be so affable in private—at meetings in the congressman's office or over lunch at the Monocle—and then so brutal and partisan in public. Shad's legislative director at the SEC, Ethel Geisinger, a young Republican who had worked as an aide to the Senate banking committee before joining the commission, tried to explain that Washington not only tolerated such hypocrisy, the capital thrived on it. Everybody had a job to do, a role to play in front of the television cameras. But that didn't preclude public enemies from developing private friendships. No matter how hard she tried, though, Geisinger couldn't persuade Shad to accept such duplicity as the ordinary course of business.

That winter of 1982, when he was having so many public difficulties, Shad kept asking Geisinger to arrange lunches with the congressmen and senators who were giving him the hardest time, whether over the budget, deregulation, or his personal finances. They would meet in a private dining room on the Hill, or downtown at the Metropolitan Club, *mano a mano*, with no staff allowed. Afterward, Shad would walk beaming into Geisinger's office, declaring the session a great success.

"I think I have an understanding with him now," Shad would say.

And then, the next day or the next week, when the SEC chairman was summoned back to Capitol Hill for another public hearing—bam, the same congressman or senator would tear into him with great ferocity, accusing Shad of all variety of transgressions. In the car afterward, on the way back to SEC headquarters, Shad sometimes railed emotionally against those who had attacked him at the hearing. He would say that he couldn't understand how they could treat him like that, after all that had been said in private. For their part, the congressmen felt so much strain at the lunches with Shad that after a while Geisinger had trouble getting anybody to accept the chairman's invitations.

There were times when Dingell, especially, was just as intimidating behind closed doors as he was in public. During the first round of budget battles late in 1981, Shad publicly supported the Reagan administration's plan to reduce the SEC's personnel by 6 percent. With its budget of about $80 million and its approximately 2,000 employees, the SEC was a small agency by federal government standards. The commission also was ostensibly an independent law-enforcement agency, but as a loyal Reagan team player Shad felt obliged to defend the president's budget with enthusiasm. He charged up to the Hill with an eighteen-page memo drafted by the SEC's executive director's office, which handled the commission's budget, administrative, and personnel matters. The memo explained how the commission could do its job with fewer resources—by increasing productivity, the SEC could maintain its programs while implementing the 6 percent personnel reduction.

But the Democrats would have none of it. Congressman Tim Wirth, chairman of a key Dingell subcommittee, publicly ridiculed Shad's notion, which he said amounted to an assertion that the SEC could do more with less. Wirth and Dingell summoned the SEC chairman to a private meeting in the basement of the Rayburn building, where Dingell made it clear in no uncertain terms that Shad was not going to get away with reducing the commission's budget. Wirth recalled that Shad was "almost shaking" when Dingell's lecture was finished.

And in public, Shad's lack of political finesse undermined his cause even further. Several of his fellow commissioners, including Democrats Barbara Thomas and Bevis Longstreth, disagreed with Shad's position on the budget—Thomas warned that proposed budget cuts would "cripple the commission." At a key hearing on Capitol Hill, Shad allowed the dissenting commissioners to voice their opinions after he delivered his official testimony, cementing the impression that the SEC was divided within itself over Reagan's proposals. Shad's political advisers had warned him to avoid such an appearance, but the chairman seemed not to understand the impression split testimony would make on congressmen and the media.

Hearings on the Hill terrified Shad, which was unfortunate,

since there were a lot of them. He grew preoccupied with his preparations—he thought of the hearings as final exams, and he was determined to cram. Nobody in the hearing room was going to know more about the topic at hand than Shad. Perhaps he thought such encyclopedic knowledge would make up for the discomfort he obviously felt when speaking in public, but in truth it only seemed to make him more tense. When a hearing approached, Shad kept his staff at SEC headquarters late into the night, rehearsing questions and answers, pouring over briefing books, struggling to write and rewrite his opening statement. Shad thought the rehearsals were critically important. Once, during a particularly touchy legislative fight concerning the SEC, Ethel Geisinger recommended that Shad place personal phone calls to a number of key congressmen in an effort to influence their votes. Shad was so uncomfortable that he insisted she rehearse the calls, with Geisinger playing the congressmen and Shad playing himself. Still, though he worked hard, his performance didn't improve.

Shad took the worst shellackings when his drive to implement broad changes at the SEC ran afoul of Dingell. One of Shad's projects during his time at the commission was an attempt to establish a new, electronic filing system that would cut down on the massive amount of paper processed by the SEC. The $10 million electronic system was known as EDGAR—Electronic Data Gathering and Retrieval—and Shad launched into it with typical insistence and enthusiasm. It made perfect sense to Shad that, in the computer age, public companies should stop delivering reams of paper to the SEC, and start filing their financial statements electronically. But he made a characteristic mistake—he forgot to consult with Dingell and make the congressman's staff appear to be an integral part of the project's planning. When EDGAR reached the pilot stage, Dingell's staff attacked. They commissioned studies to show that the SEC was rushing too fast, that Shad was wasting taxpayer dollars by choosing the wrong technologies. On relatively short notice, Shad and his staff were summoned to Dingell's hearing room in the Rayburn building for a public discussion of the project.

That morning, Shad sat at the back of the hearing room as

Dingell and the other Democrats on his committee tore into the SEC staff lawyers responsible for EDGAR, accusing them of incompetence and poor judgment. Shad fumed—he detested these media events, where the Democrats mugged for the cameras and embarrassed his commission. And the hearing that day struck him as especially unfair. None of the Republicans on Dingell's committee were present; it was strictly a partisan attack. By the time it was Shad's turn to sit before the microphones, lights in his eyes and a cigarette at hand, he was steaming.

"I came with a prepared opening statement," Shad told Dingell. "But having heard the testimony this morning I would like to make some preliminary observations. . . . Mr. Chairman, I know how strongly you feel about treating people fairly—in fact, bending over backward. But these hearings have not been fair to the people that have been subject to this cross-examination, particularly members of the staff that have just been on the stand. First of all, these hearings are not bipartisan. There are no Republicans present. But neither are the hearings objective."

Dingell was outraged—he would not stand for Shad's impertinence. "It is not for you to complain about whether these are bipartisan. These hearings are being held in full conformity to the rules of the House, and I will interpret those for your benefit as opposed to your interpreting them for mine."

"Well, I appreciate that. You are much better qualified than I am."

"We will proceed more comfortably once you recognize that."

It was the same point Dingell had made back at the Monocle, during Shad's first weeks in Washington. The SEC chairman would be much better off if he would just play by Dingell's rules. But Shad wasn't listening. He carried on as if Dingell hadn't said anything.

"As I understand it, there is an issue about the composition of the committee—"

"Mr. Shad, that is not any of your business. That is a matter for the decision by the members of this committee and not for the SEC."

"Well, all right."

"You have a broad writ at that institution, but it does not go to the composition of this committee, and you are so informed."

"Thank you." But Shad would not stop. He didn't seem to understand that he was hurting himself.

"Nor do I think these hearings have been objective," he went on. "I do not think these have been objective or unbiased."

"I am curious about how hearing from your staff shows a lack of objectivity," Dingell inquired sarcastically.

"The case," Shad answered; "if you want to call it the case for the prosecution—"

"There is no prosecution here, this is a committee which is inquiring into your conduct of the public business."

"Somebody is laughing in the background on that comment," Shad said with a touch of bitterness.

The quip was a rare score for the SEC chairman, but overall, the hearings went badly for him. It was Dingell who controlled the podium, the witness list, and the agenda—Shad was merely a player in the congressman's drama. There were those of Shad's rank in government who, in similar circumstances, managed to relax and speak their lines. Shad never could, and when he did speak at hearings, he mumbled as though he had a mouth full of marbles. Most of the SEC staff found their chairman's political naïveté charming, if occasionally frustrating. It was part of what made him accessible, vulnerable.

Surely Dingell, too, understood that Shad was overmatched, but it was hard to tell whether the congressman ever felt much sympathy for his prey. As 1982 wore on, and the questions and controversy about Shad's personal finances and his drive to change the SEC's philosophy and rules mounted, Dingell and his allies in Congress pushed harder and harder.

One way they pushed was by gathering information. Staff lawyers who worked for Dingell and for the Senate banking committee talked regularly with attorneys in the SEC's enforcement division. Dramatic change was under way in the division because of Fedders, and resentment was building.

As was true for frustrated citizens across the country, there remained a course of last resort—angry SEC staffers could always talk to their congressmen.

*   *   *

By the late summer of 1982, the Citicorp matter had escalated into a public fiasco for Shad, Fedders, and others at the commission. After the Gerth stories about the 3 to 1 commission vote to kill the case, and after his congressional staff had poured over the relevant documents, Dingell had decided to tear into the matter. Fedders told his friends and allies at the SEC headquarters on North Capitol Street that Dingell's staff, which included among its number a former enforcement staff lawyer who had clashed with Fedders, was out to destroy his public career and embarrass the Reagan administration at a crucial early juncture.

There was reason to be concerned. In August, Bevis Longstreth, the Democrat whose vote in Citicorp's favor had been decisive at the closed meeting, was excoriated at a Senate hearing because the New York law firm where Longstreth used to work had represented Citicorp, creating the appearance of a conflict of interest. Although he had said he would not vote on matters that presented conflict of interest problems, Longstreth had not disqualified himself from hearing the case. Longstreth protested that he personally had represented Citicorp only on rare occasions in the 1960s and mid-1970s, and that he had represented many clients whose interests were opposed to Citicorp's. But Democrats on the Senate banking committee criticized him sharply. Of course, even if Longstreth had withdrawn from the case the vote would still have been 2 to 1 in Citicorp's favor. Still, Longstreth was embarrassed by the hearing and he vowed privately not to let it happen again.

Fedders, in the meantime, decided to counterattack. He realized that the only way a target of one of Dingell's "investigative" hearings could defend himself effectively was to work within the committee, behind the scenes. Unlike Shad, Fedders wasn't afraid to soil himself in the gamesmanship of realpolitik. When he heard that Dingell planned to call Sporkin, Doherty, and von Stein to testify, but would not allow rebuttal testimony from Fedders, the enforcement chief got in touch with some of the Republicans on Dingell's committee. Minority members of the Energy and Commerce Committee often were stymied by Dingell's intimidating rule; there was virtually nothing they could accomplish at the committee without Dingell's approval. Fedders said that he needed help—here was a chance for the Republicans to make a splash at one of Dingell's hearings. Working with Bob Whittaker, an obscure junior Republican from Eureka, Kansas, Fedders drafted a series of tough questions—drawing on his inside knowledge of the Citicorp case—that could be used to embarrass the former SEC lawyers who were scheduled to testify, including David Doherty, Stanley Sporkin, and Thomas von Stein, all of whom believed strongly that charges should have been filed in the case.

Shortly after the proceedings began in Dingell's brightly lit hearing room on September 13, 1982, Whittaker jumped in, interrupting Dingell with procedural points and pressing for a chance to conduct his own examination. Dingell put him off for a while and allowed Doherty and von Stein to describe damaging details about the way Citicorp conducted its foreign-currency-trading business. Finally, it was the minority side's turn. Reciting in rapid-fire fashion the questions prepared with Fedders's help, Whittaker, an optometrist by profession, sounded like a student reciting in proud tones a poem that he had recently memorized.

"Mr. Doherty, is it correct that the commission's Citicorp investigation took three and a half years to complete? . . . Mr. Doherty, in the course of the commission's investigation, did Mr. von Stein prepare a lengthy report of his findings and conclusions? . . . Mr. Doherty, did you disagree with portions of Mr. von Stein's report? . . . Mr. Doherty, was Mr. Fedders invited to testify here today? . . . Mr. Doherty, was it the commission's responsibility to exercise the final judgment as to whether an enforcement action should be brought against Citicorp? . . . Mr. Doherty, do you have any reason to believe that the commission undertook and fulfilled its obligation in bad faith or with a lack of integrity?"

The more Whittaker went on, the more obvious it became that he, like Dingell, had had help from inside the SEC. How else to explain that an eye doctor with less than four years' experience in Congress could begin to quote, as Whittaker did, a host of obscure legal cases describing the standards by which SEC enforcement actions were filed? "Mr. Doherty, are you familiar with the 1976 decision of the U.S. Supreme Court in the case of *TSC Industries, Inc.* versus *Northway, Inc.*?" he asked. And a few minutes later: "I would assume then, you are familiar with the July 11, 1979, decision in the U.S. District Court for the Southern District of New York in the case of *Amalgamated Clothing and Textile Workers* versus *J. P. Stevens and Co.*?"

Fedders considered Whittaker's performance a rare and inspirational victory over Dingell's unrelenting partisanship, and perhaps he was right. But the newspapers paid little attention to the Republican's questions; their stories concentrated on Dingell's charges that Citicorp had conducted itself improperly and that the SEC had failed to sanction the company. It might be fun to win from time to time, but the truth was that the sparring with Dingell too often seemed a demoralizing distraction from the commission's business. So much time, so much worry went into the fight.

And while Washington's regulatory factions pummeled one another that fall of 1982, struggling for advantage in a contest of partisan politics, Wall Street was moving on to another game altogether. It might not have been obvious to John Dingell, or even to Fedders or Shad. But while they scrapped with one another in capital corridors and hearing rooms, the Manhattan financial district they were supposed to be regulating was whirling into a new orbit, beyond their control.

6

Trick or Treat

Jack Hewitt had to know. That was the way he always approached investigations for the SEC. The only way to do the job was to find out as much as he could about people before he sat down to question them. He had to know personal details, not just where somebody worked and lived, but whom he spent time with on weekends, where he went on vacation, how he spent his money. Motivations, values, obsessions—it wasn't easy trying to get inside somebody's head, especially somebody he had never met before. But that was how Hewitt prepared.

On the day before Halloween, 1982, Hewitt sat at a conference table seventeen floors above palm-tree-lined Wilshire Boulevard, a congested business thoroughfare that sliced thirty miles through the L.A. basin, from downtown to the sea. It was early on a Saturday morning, a languid hour in hazy southern California, but Hewitt was alert and intense. He was trying to assess the man across the table—in this case, a trim, reticent, dark-eyed bond salesman, age thirty-six, wearing an obvious toupee.

Before he flew to Los Angeles, Hewitt had formed certain preconceptions about Michael Milken, a target of the SEC enforcement investigation he was pursuing. Hewitt thought Milken and the investment firm he worked for, Drexel Burnham Lambert, might have profited illegally by manipulating the stock and bond markets.

The case hadn't started that way. A tip that unusually heavy trading, late in 1981, by Carl Lindner, the aggressive chairman of Cincinnati-based American Financial Corporation, might reflect improper dealings, had been passed through the SEC enforcement division and landed finally on staff attorney Hewitt's desk. Although one of Hewitt's superiors, the number two man in the enforcement division, Ted Levine, was especially eager to see a case developed against Lindner, the matter wasn't a priority for Levine's boss, Fedders. The tip was interesting, but it was like dozens of others. Hewitt was told to follow up. With relatively little direction or support from his superiors, Hewitt ultimately had taken the case in a different direction, focusing on Milken and Drexel, rather than Lindner. Drexel at the time was a mid-sized but aggressive, rapidly growing Wall Street investment house. Milken ran its office in Beverly Hills. It appeared to Hewitt that Milken and some of his clients—insurance companies, savings banks, and the like—had traded securities suspiciously in connection with a corporate takeover, improperly arranged bogus stock and bond trades, manipulated stock and bond prices, and otherwise run roughshod over the federal securities laws. As he prepared for the interrogation Hewitt found that Michael Milken's raw power to set prices when he traded and sold certain bonds reminded him of the greedy financiers who rigged markets prior to the Great Crash in 1929. Before he ever met him, Hewitt thought Milken was a dangerous man.

To get started, Hewitt punched Milken's name into a computer at the SEC's North Capitol Street headquarters in Washington. The screen indicated that lawyers in the commission's New York office had questioned Milken in 1980 about his trading activities, so Hewitt dug out the deposition transcript and read it. He could hardly believe Milken's description of his work in Beverly Hills— Milken was like a component in some high-speed telephonic machine. During one of his typical days on the Beverly Hills trading floor, Milken had said, he held roughly two hundred telephone conversations, at times talking with one party while "I'm at the same time carrying on ten other conversations. I would say that I listen to no more than twenty-five percent of the conversations I have with anyone during the trading day. . . . I would come in and out, buy and sell securities during any conversation."

Milken's self-image as a whirlwind money-making machine intrigued Hewitt, and he had decided that when he got to Los Angeles, he would ask some questions about the salesman's daily routine. In this case and others, Hewitt was drawn to moral and social questions raised by the uses of vast sums of money by traders such as Milken. He was no philosopher, but in 1968 he had spent thirteen bloody months as a platoon commander in the jungle and fields outside Da Nang during the Tet Offensive, and he had learned a few things about how humans make moral choices. After he came to the SEC, the experience of Vietnam became one filter through which Hewitt evaluated the people he met "in the field," as law enforcement officials referred to the workaday world.

What would Jack Hewitt have thought of Michael Milken if they had met in 1968, in the days of rage, rather than across a government conference room in 1982? Hewitt was only two years Milken's senior, but a chasm of class, culture, and experience separated them. Jack Hewitt had been the kind of soldier that Hollywood lionized in its versions of the Vietnam War. He had blue eyes and brown hair, and was a middle-class Catholic from Pittsburgh, Pennsylvania, the son of a supervisor at a railroad-equipment manufacturer. A broad-shouldered offensive lineman, he went to college on a football scholarship, played on two undefeated teams, and then enlisted in the Marines because it seemed the right thing to do. After officer candidate school, they tossed him into the jungle. First Hewitt and his platoon chased the Vietcong in circles through the bush, then came the offensive led by the North Vietnamese Army, and suddenly it was an overwhelming, brutal war. Hewitt won a silver star for gallantry in action during the Tet Offensive, when his platoon of about sixty men defended Da Nang against an enemy force believed to be at least ten times larger. But when he came home—before they made the movies and built the Vietnam Memorial and had all the parades to set things straight—there were people who thought of him as a murderer. Hewitt got along all right, however; he didn't become absorbed or obsessed by the rejection he met, but he understood why some veterans couldn't take it.

And suppose he had met Michael Milken then? Milken wasn't one of the hippies, one of the radicals fighting against the war Hewitt believed in. That would have been something Hewitt could grapple with. Instead, it was as if Milken lived in some parallel universe that never intersected with Hewitt's world. Upper-middle class, Jewish, and driven to achieve, Milken was the son of a prosperous southern California accountant who took him along to visit clients and enlisted his help preparing their tax returns. In high school, forty pounds lighter than Hewitt, Milken was the head cheerleader, the prom king, and an honors graduate who excelled in math and got a D in woodshop. While Hewitt was in the jungle, Milken was at the University of California at Berkeley, but amid all the campus craziness—the Black Panthers, the communes, the Summer of Love, the protests against the war—Milken concentrated on his studies and his fraternity, as if the rest of it didn't matter one bit. He led an almost monastic life: no drugs, no beer, no tobacco, no escapades. After college he married Lori Anne Hackel, his childhood sweetheart, and headed straight for Philadelphia to get his master's degree in business administration at the University of Pennsylvania's Wharton School. From there he joined the Drexel investment firm and, by the fall of 1982, when Hewitt's SEC investigation brought him to the conference room high above Wilshire Boulevard, Milken had returned to his old neighborhood, bought the old Clark Gable estate in Encino for around $700,000, and had become one of Drexel's most important and successful executives. At thirty-six, Milken earned millions, more money in a year than Hewitt could realistically hope to earn in a lifetime at the SEC, with its more rigid government salary scale.

That morning, Hewitt asked Milken what, exactly, he did for a living.

"Trying to make money for the firm in the purchase and sale of securities," Milken answered vaguely.

By "securities" Milken meant stocks and bonds. He was laconic to the point of condescension, as if Hewitt's questions were an utter waste of his time. How could Hewitt or the SEC really hurt an executive like Milken? The commission's subpoena power could force him to testify, as he was doing this Saturday. But its fraud investigations often dragged on for years, and even then it was usually possible for someone with Milken's resources to reach a harmless, civil settlement—no big fines, no jail time. If Hewitt's investigation uncovered serious securities fraud, the SEC might refer the matter to the Justice Department for criminal prosecution, and the commission could itself bar Milken from the brokerage business. But such severe sanctions were rare. Milken's indifference to Hewitt seemed to be reinforced by the high-priced lawyer beside him, Thomas Curnin, from a prestigious New York firm. Curnin was the sort of litigator who liked to make deposition testimony as unpleasant as possible for the lawyer on the other side—especially a less-experienced government lawyer. He repeatedly ridiculed Hewitt and his inquiries.

Hewitt asked Milken to give him a rundown of a typical day in his Beverly Hills office. It was a simple, softball question, a way to get a sense of Milken's personality before moving on to the substantive questions about fraud and manipulation.

But Milken was argumentative. "There's no such thing as a typical day," he replied. "I don't know what a typical day is. Let me describe what generally happens. I could do that?"

"Yes, if you could. . . ."

"I come in, in the morning between four-thirty and five o'clock. I generally read the *Wall Street Journal*. I generally write notes for the people in the department, put them on an administrative person's chair. By five-fifteen, she's put them on everyone's chair in the department, so if they're not in they can't sit down without picking up their note."

Hewitt didn't interrupt. It was obvious now that he had struck a chord. Milken apparently didn't mind bragging about how hard he worked.

"I then direct administrative people to make phone calls for me and get people on the phone, and that generally runs till around two o'clock in the afternoon," he continued. "Sometime around ten forty-five to eleven-fifteen [A.M.] they put some food on my desk, which I eat in anywhere from one to five minutes. Sometimes in the afternoon, it's possible corporations would come in for meetings [about raising money with Milken's help]. . . . Sometime between four o'clock and six o'clock, a position sheet is put out as to what the [stock and bond ownership] position is for the department, which I start to review. And if I'm not too tried, I then start writing out notes for the people in the department, asking them why they bought or sold a security—if I have an opinion, or I don't think that's a good idea, or that it might be a good idea. When I'm exhausted I go home and I get ready for the next day."

". . . Do you have any role or participation in the trading at the department?" Hewitt asked.

"I have good hearing, and over the years it developed that I can hear most conversations in the department," Milken said. ". . . I might overhear someone doing a trade that I don't think's a good idea and might scream at them before they've completed that trade or try to provide direction."

There was a part of Hewitt that admired Milken's dedication to work, but there was a part of him, too, that considered Milken a threat. Hewitt didn't know that Saturday morning where the tip about Milken's alleged stock and bond manipulation would lead, how serious the matter was, or whether he would eventually muster enough evidence to impress Fedders, who was several layers above Hewitt in the enforcement division's hierarchy. Still, because it involved allegedly deliberate manipulation of the stock and bond markets by powerful financial interests, this was exactly the sort of investigation Hewitt thought the SEC should be concentrating on.

Hewitt had been attracted to the commission in the late 1970s by Stanley Sporkin, whose charisma reminded him of the late football coach Vince Lombardi. He had enrolled in a nighttime masters program at Georgetown University Law School in Washington and had agreed to write a long research paper on market manipulation. Day after day Hewitt sat in the SEC library, reading transcripts of the Pecora hearings, the landmark congressional hearings held in the 1930s, in the aftermath of the stock market

crash and in the depths of the Great Depression. The hearings
exposed the rampant corruption prevalent on Wall Street during
the 1920s, particularly a series of brazen, secret stock and bond
manipulation schemes carried out by some of the financial community's most respected denizens. The soaring stock market of
the 1920s, it turned out, had been driven by speculation and a
web of complex, conspiratorial frauds—that was why it had
crashed so disastrously in October 1929, the hearings showed.
Hewitt was certain that Wall Street in the 1980s was more honest
and better regulated than Wall Street in the 1920s. But as he
studied Michael Milken's life and career, especially the way in
which Milken was rapidly building a dominant role for himself in
the fastest-growing segment of the bond market, Hewitt con-
stantly was reminded of the Pecora hearings. Certain parallels
between Milken and Wall Street figures from earlier in the century took shape in his mind.

Since the 1970s, Milken had devoted himself to an obscure
corner of the bond market shunned by Wall Street's respectable
firms, and he was beginning to build in Beverly Hills an innovative, enormously profitable franchise, selling bonds for small,
growing companies that most of Wall Street considered too risky
to finance. Soon the national press would be comparing Milken to
the legendary financier J. P. Morgan, who dominated Wall Street
and the economy during the 1920s—and the comparisons would
be made with uneasy ambivalence, as if the sheer scale of Milken's
influence augered repetition of earlier disasters. (Milken's friends
and colleagues said such doubts reflected typical small-
mindedness in the face of innovation; every genius was labeled a
heretic in his own time, they said.) Hewitt's concerns were reinforced by the evidence he had accumulated about Milken's potentially shady dealings. Hewitt was convinced that the economic
strength of the United States was wholly dependent on effective
enforcement of the securities laws. To Hewitt, there was more
involved in all of this than just keeping a few brokers or traders
honest; the SEC was saving the economic and political system
from the sort of turmoil that prevailed after the 1929 crash.

That Saturday, Hewitt found Milken an elusive quarry. He was

distracted by Milken's attorney, Curnin, who interrupted continually. Depositions constituted the bulk of an SEC lawyer's field
work. There was no judge to resolve disputes, so an experienced
defense litigator like Curnin could test the patience and skills of a
commission lawyer like Hewitt with virtual impunity.

Hewitt tried to press for explanations of some specific stock and
bond trades that had aroused his suspicions. Some of the trades
involved shares of Reliance Group, a giant New York–based insurance company headed by corporate raider Saul Steinberg, with
whom Milken had a close relationship. Steinberg had announced
a takeover bid for Reliance—meaning he would buy back all of its
shares in the public stock market and turn it into a private corporation no longer subject to the same degree of SEC regulation.
Hewitt thought there was a web of potential conflicts of interest
and suspicious trading before and after the deal was announced.
Steinberg was Milken's client, and it looked as though Milken had
acquired a big block of Reliance stock on Steinberg's behalf. But
Milken was also trading Reliance stock for his own account and
for Drexel. Milken could potentially have been trading illegally on
inside information about Steinberg's takeover plans for Reliance.
Then, too, there was a series of trades involving another intimate
of Milken's, Fred Carr, an insurance executive. It appeared unusual to Hewitt that one Carr subsidiary had sold Reliance stock to
another Carr subsidiary, brokered in the middle by Milken.
Hewitt also had questions about the prices of these trades. He
wondered about the sales calls allegedly made by Milken's brother,
Lowell, a lawyer who was supposed to be concentrating on compliance with SEC rules and administrative matters, not selling
bonds. It was all exceedingly complex, and it was hard for Hewitt
to read the Drexel trading records and gain any clear understanding of what scheme, if any, had motivated the web of trades Milken
had engineered. Milken didn't operate like an ordinary stockbroker who took orders from customers, recommended attractive
investments, and sold new issues of stocks and bonds. Instead, in
his flurry of two hundred phone calls every day, Milken did it all
at once—he was a middleman one minute, a principal the next; he
was a broker; a buyer; a seller; an adviser; a deal maker. Hewitt

thought the complexity of Milken's Beverly Hills operation might hide a variety of secret, illegal schemes: tax evasion, insider trading, and evasion of a host of technical SEC regulations. What the schemes might have in common, Hewitt suspected, was the tight control over the trading of Reliance's stocks and bonds that Milken exercised from his command post in Beverly Hills at the center of the Drexel trading floor.

Milken said he had no idea what Hewitt was talking about.

"Do you know what a wash trade is?" Hewitt asked, referring to bogus trades of stocks or bonds, designed to evade taxed or generate risk-free profits.

"As it relates to tax purposes?" Milken asked.

"No, as it relates to the securities laws."

". . . I recall that term more in relation to tax transactions."

"All right. Do you have any understanding at all as it relates to the securities laws?"

"I'm not familiar with that specific term as it relates to the securities laws."

"How about a match sale?"

"I'm not familiar with that specific term. . . . I don't use that in my terminology."

"What about a prearranged trade?"

"I've heard that term before."

Now Hewitt was finally getting somewhere. Perhaps Milken was going to admit to setting up prearranged trades that violated securities laws even as they generated profits and served his clients. But when Hewitt asked him to explain, Milken instead went on to tell some vague story about placing orders on the floors of the New York financial exchanges and finding out later that the orders hadn't been accepted because of "prearranged" trades by floor brokers. Whenever Hewitt pressed for specifics, Milken dodged. Milken's claims of ignorance stretched Hewitt's credulity. When Hewitt asked him about stock trading in accounts established for Milken's children, Milken said he didn't know who made investment decisions for the accounts. Hewitt also asked about the trading activities of Belvedere Securities, a Chicago brokerage in which Milken was the majority owner—it had been established to generate tax benefits by trading government bonds. Hewitt thought it was unusual that Drexel would let Milken have his own, separate brokerage firm that traded bonds in apparent competition with Drexel. Milken said he hardly knew anything about it.

"I knew I had an investment in something called Belvedere," he said. "I didn't know what the last name was or what it was. . . . I believe my brother, Lowell Milken, came to me and suggested I make an investment in this entity."

Finally, with an air of desperation, Hewitt pulled out a list of Wall Street firms whose trades had shown up in the records he had examined back at SEC headquarters in Washington. He asked Milken if he had any business relationship with each of the firms.

"Do you deal with the Bear Stearns firm on a regular basis in your trading?"

"No."

". . . Any association with the Queen City Securities Corporation of Cincinnati in the trading in your department?"

"No."

"How about the L. F. Rothschild firm?"

"No."

"How about the firm titled Seemela, S-e-e-m-e-l-a, brokerage firm?"

Milken paused. That was the firm run by Ivan F. Boesky, one of Wall Street's most powerful and aggressive independent stock traders who specialized in shares of companies involved in corporate takeovers. Like Milken, Boesky was fast becoming a figure of national importance, and his trading in connection with takeover bids was rapidly changing the way Wall Street and the economy functioned. Hewitt didn't know all that much about Boesky, and he didn't notice that Milken had failed to answer his question about whether he had any relationship with Boesky's brokerage firm. Without stopping, Hewitt plowed on with his list of Wall Street firms, provoking a new chorus of noes from Milken, followed by a sarcastic, contemptuous question:

"Are these potential customers," Milken asked, "that we should be taking their names down?"

The interrogation wound slowly to a close. Hewitt knew that he

faced months of work ahead, much of it mind-numbing recon-
struction of the stock and bond trades about which he had questioned Milken, before he would be ready to present a memo to
Fedders about the case. Milken remained something of an enigma
to Hewitt. What stayed with Hewitt, after that weekend in Los
Angeles, was that he had looked Milken in the eye, asked him
simply what he did for a living, and yet Milken had given no
answer, or at least none that was satisfactory to a man from Pittsburgh, where people knew what they did and what they made—
sheets of steel for cars and girders for buildings and ball bearings
for tanks. There had been something about Milken's manner during the deposition, something about his arrogance and evasions
that struck Hewitt as fiendish.

They ended at nine-thirty Sunday night, in the darkness of
Halloween night. During his questioning, Hewitt never returned
to the point where Milken had unaccountably paused when asked
about his relationship with stock speculator Ivan Boeksy. Later,
looking back on it all, it was clearly a missed opportunity.

That fall of 1982, when Hewitt flew west to interrogate Michael
Milken, the first signs of an epochal change on Wall Street—a new
kind of cowboy capitalism—were beginning to appear. Hewitt was
unsettled by what he saw of Milken's business, and by his demeanor during the interrogation, but he couldn't be sure that the
parallels with the 1920s that kept jumping to mind were valid.
Besides, reaching such grand conclusions wasn't generally part of
an SEC investigator's job.

But they were certainly part of John Shad's responsibilities, and
for his part, in his chairman's suite at the Securities and Exchange
Commission's headquarters in Washington, and on weekends with
his friends and family in Manhattan, Shad saw no reason to be
worried.

The truth was that Shad did not grasp what was happening now
on Wall Street. He had been away from the Street for less than
two years. He might just as well have been away for twenty.

It was the SEC's primary charter to supervise and regulate Wall
Street, and certainly there was no one at the commission who

knew Wall Street more intimately than Shad. The trouble was that the Wall Street Shad knew—the place where he had worked for thirty years—was disappearing. There were those who said afterward that Shad's Wall Street died in August of 1982, when the most bizarre and controversial corporate takeover fight in U.S. history was launched, and simultaneously, the greatest surge in stock prices since World War II began.

As an investment banker. Shad had made his fortune as a specialist in corporate finance, the business of advising companies on the best ways to raise money to pay for their future growth. Should a company borrow funds for a short term or a long while? Was it better to issue new stock or new bonds? Should it build a factory this year or wait until next year? Did bad news about an unprofitable subsidiary have to be disclosed to public investors through the SEC or could it be concealed? These were the kinds of questions with which Shad grappled. In many ways it was a comfortable, slow-moving world, with business conducted under the same general guidelines and principles set down in the 1930s, when SEC rules governing corporate finance were first established. Personal relationships and trust were paramount. A handshake was all that was required to complete a deal and the ties between Wall Street firms and the companies they advised were informally binding. If a corporation's top officials forged a relationship with investment bankers at a particular Wall Street firm, the relationship usually became a hallowed tradition that lasted decades.

Besides corporate finance work, Shad also served as an adviser to companies on mergers and acquisitions. Many of these deals were an outgrowth of the financial advisory work he was already doing. Shad thought takeovers could be beneficial for all parties involved, provided they were prudently financed and made sound business sense. He also had a reputation among his Wall Street and corporate colleagues for opposing mergers he thought were overpriced—he put the long-run interest of his corporate client above the large fees he might earn as an adviser on any given deal. In general, the takeover work Shad had done involved a friendly agreement between a party who wanted to sell and another who wanted to buy. Shad's standards of conduct were evidently so high, and his financial analysis was so thorough, that during a highly litigious period, he was never the subject of any lawsuits arising out of investment banking transactions in which he had played a major role.

It was the relationships, not just the individual deals, that mattered—the clubs, the friends, the corporate clients, the class-mates from school. Shad arranged deals of significant magnitude for former Harvard Business School classmates who had risen to senior positions in major corporations. But Shad was not bound by tradition. He also did deals with small companies whose growth he shepherded. His role was clear; as an investment banker he was an agent, a provider of financial services to a client—the cor-poration was the principal, and its people made the decisions. There was a sense of paternal duty attached to the profession: Shad became a mentor for the young men he hired out of Har-vard, personally responsible for their progress. Investment bank-ing was like some medieval craft guild, with carefully planned apprentice and master stages. Some complained that the system favored the well-born and the well-connected, and discouraged free competition based on merit, but Shad's own personal history—his rise from the dirt farms of Utah to the duplex on Park Avenue—showed that in some cases, at least, a man could forge his own success on Wall Street. (A woman would have more trouble. Finance in those days was exclusively a boys' club.) The centrality of personal relationships and the primacy of the client were evident in Wall Street's lexicon. In the prime of Shad's years there, a stockbroker often was referred to as a customers man.

In 1975, not long after Shad assisted his firm, E. F. Hutton, in selling shares in itself to the public, the brokerage business un-derwent dramatic change. Sales commissions, which had been fixed at set levels for generations, were deregulated at the urging of the SEC. A new era of aggressive competition erupted between established Wall Street firms and start-up, cut-rate discount bro-kerage houses that emphasized price, not quality. The flowering of competition made it cheaper for individual investors to buy and sell stocks, and it put the squeeze on some of the comfortable Wall Street investment firms. In the late 1970s, attitudes about clients, customers, and the nature of investment banking began to shift. The imperatives of profit loomed larger at the big firms than they had before.

Those changes paled, however, beside the forces unleashed in August 1982.

It started with William Agee, the ambitious chairman of a Michigan-based company called Bendix Corporation. The problem was that Agee was getting bored. Running a giant auto parts and aerospace company near Detroit apparently dulled his senses, which were otherwise stimulated by his Ivy League–educated young wife, Mary Cunningham, who had been Agee's assistant at Bendix until their personal relationship became a notorious corporate affair. (Cunningham took a job at another company.) Egged on by his Wall Street advisers at venerable Salomon Brothers, Agee had Bendix secretly accumulate an almost 5 percent stake in Martin Marietta Corporation, the giant Bethesda, Maryland–based defense contractor that was several times the size of Agee's company. On August 25, Agee declared war on Martin Marietta, announcing a $1.5 billion, $43-per-share hostile takeover bid for Martin Marietta's publicly traded stock.

A retired Navy admiral named Thomas Pownall was the proud, deeply conservative chairman of Martin Marietta. Adhering to the precepts of his Annapolis training, he decided to fire back at Agee. At Pownall's side was a young, brown-haired, strikingly handsome, Harvard-educated Wall Street investment banker who would do much in the coming years to alter the way his profession operated.

Martin A. Siegel's story was reminiscent in some ways of Shad's—he had been raised without riches or privilege, his father had struggled in business, but Siegel had exhibited enough talent to zip through Harvard Business School. There the similarities ended, however. Siegel had the charm and élan of a smooth investment banker that Shad lacked. He commuted to Wall Street by helicopter from his seaside Connecticut estate; he relished press attention; and he seemed to find his wardrobe in the pages of *Gentlemen's Quarterly*. Everyone called him Marty, and though he was a talented strategist when it came to developing a takeover defense, his most obvious skill was as a salesman. He could work a corporate boardroom like a bible-toting preacher at a southern revival meeting. In part he preyed on the fears of staid, comfortable corporate chief executives like Martin Marietta's Pownall, when they were threatened by the possibility of a corporate takeover. Pownall might be an admiral, but Marty Siegel was known on Wall Street as the Secretary of Defense.

After Agee's hostile takeover bid was announced, Siegel huddled with Pownall for a week and then disclosed his stunning plan: in response to Bendix's takeover offer for Martin Marietta, Martin Marietta would issue a hostile takeover offer for Bendix. It became known as Marty Siegel's Pac-Man defense, named after the popular video game in which glowing goblins try to eat each other. The astonishing spectacle of two corporate behemoths trying to devour simultaneously one another's assets attracted front-page headlines across the country. The fire spread. Agee, annoyed and in the curious position of both bidder and target, turned to a new team of Wall Street advisers, Bruce Wasserstein and Joe Perella of First Boston Corporation. Agee understood that to fight someone of Siegel's youth and audacity, he needed investment bankers who were similarly unconstrained by Wall Street traditions—and in the dynamic duo of Wasserstein and Perella, Agee chose the right pair. Wasserstein, a former public interest lawyer who had once worked for Ralph Nader's Raiders but had decided to devote his life to the acquisition of capital, thought the ancient Wall Street order of trust and friendship should be torn down, to be replaced by a new system of free and aggressive competition. Wasserstein started fighting Siegel furiously and publicly. The game was now about winning, not preservation of past relationships.

There were offers and counteroffers, press releases, and pompom girls leading pep rallies at Bendix headquarters in Michigan. More companies and Wall Street firms piled on—United Technologies Corporation, advised by the ostensibly conservative Wall Street house Lazard Frères, launched a rival billion-dollar takeover bid for Martin Marietta. Allied Corporation, advised by Lehman Brothers, considered a rescuing bid for Bendix. By September, four major corporations, five Wall Street investment firms, and a host of New York lawyers were jetting around the Eastern seaboard at a dizzying pace, for a purpose that increasingly escaped conservative business leaders and congressmen in Washington. In the end that September, Bendix bought about 70 percent of Martin Marietta, Martin Marietta bought about 50 percent of Bendix, Bendix agreed to sell all its shares to Allied, Allied bought the Martin Marietta shares owned by Bendix, and the fight was over.

There were few outside of Wall Street who understood what had happened. The newspapers figured out this much: Allied would end up owning all of Bendix; Agee would lose his job; Martin Marietta would remain independent; Pownall would keep his job; and, in the process, the Wall Street advisers would become exceedingly rich.

The fees billed by the investment bankers were staggering, typically calculated as a financial advisory fee plus a percentage of the money involved in the deal. For one month's work, Lehman Brothers earned about $6 million for advising Allied; Wasserstein's First Boston Corporation made $8 million; Salomon Brothers $3 million; Lazard Frères and Siegel's Kidder, Peabody & Company $1 million each. And there was a magic about this money—it came without risk. Wall Street firms had been long accustomed to putting their own capital at risk in stock and bond trading, making millions of dollars one quarter and losing millions the next if the markets took an unexpected turn. But in the Martin Marietta–Bendix fight, there was no capital invested, nothing at risk, only millions of dollars in quick advisory fees.

It became obvious that summer that whatever their consequences for the nation, hostile takeovers were certainly good for Wall Street, which had seen its profit margins erode in the retail brokerage and traditional corporate finance businesses because of deregulation during the 1970s. The generation of investment bankers and traders that rose to influence on the Street in the early 1980s, when Shad came to the SEC in Washington—the generation led by Siegel, Wasserstein, Milken, and the rest—wanted to ensure that the takeover game continued. In the after-

math of the Martin Marietta–Bendix spectacle, there were some
calls for reform in Washington and a bit of publicly voiced self-
criticism on Wall Street. But behind closed doors at the nation's
leading investment houses, there spread a strong hunger for the
next deal.

In the lobby of a Manhattan hotel late in 1982, Martin Siegel
nervously awaited a courier dispatched by Ivan F. Boesky, the
independent stock trader whose audacity and wealth were beginning to attract attention on Wall Street. When the man arrived,
Siegel uttered a password, and the courier turned over a briefcase
containing $125,000 in cash.

It was, in the annals of Wall Street, as blatant a crime as had
ever been concocted by respectable men of finance. It was also
carried out well beyond the reach of the Securities and Exchange
Commission.

During the chaotic, controversial public fight between Bendix,
Martin Marietta, and the others, John Shad had sounded no public warnings about the potential dangers of hostile corporate takeovers. It wasn't just that he considered mergers and acquisitions to
be essentially good for the country, it was that he was occupied
that summer and fall with other concerns. The Dingell investigations into Shad's personal finances continued. And in September,
when Agee's cowboy antics reached their zenith, Dingell convened
days of embarrassing public hearings, not to discuss Wall Street's
bizarre new takeover tactics, but to rehash the Citicorp case.

There was much that John Dingell and Jack Shad did not know
that fall. They did not appreciate how the operations and priorities of the biggest Wall Street investment firms were changing.
And certainly, they did not know that Marty Siegel and Ivan
Boesky were crooks.

In August 1982, in the midst of the battle between Agee and
Bendix, Siegel and Boesky met at the Harvard Club in midtown
Manhattan. Boesky hadn't gone to Harvard, but he apparently
wished he had, because he spent nearly every afternoon at the
club, conducting meetings and playing squash. Siegel, too, was
vastly insecure—and he was, to his way of thinking at least, finan-

cially strapped. Siegel found the cost of maintaining a home on the Connecticut shore, an apartment in Manhattan, and a lifestyle appropriate to both places too much to handle on his six-figure Kidder salary and bonus. But Siegel had something to sell: inside information about the takeovers he worked on, such as Martin Marietta's fight with Bendix. At the Harvard Club, Siegel agreed to leak secrets about upcoming takeover events to Boesky in return for a percentage of any stock-trading profits Boesky earned. Siegel wanted the money in cash. It helped to make ends meet; he would eventually use some of the money to pay an off-the-books salary to his child's nanny.

It was hard sometimes for Siegel to see what was wrong with his arrangement. By leaking information to Boesky about Martin Marietta's planned bid for Bendix, he was able to stimulate massive trading in Bendix stock, driving its stock price up and giving his client's offer greater credibility. That sort of trading greased the skids of the deal, making Siegel's defense strategy more effective, and if it produced stock-trading profits for Boesky as well, who was the loser? Presumably, whoever sold his stock to Boesky without the benefit of Siegel's inside information did so voluntarily. And there were some conservative economists who thought the trading by Boesky only increased market efficiency, rapidly driving the Bendix stock price closer to the level it would eventually reach anyway when the offer for the company became public.

As chairman of the SEC, Shad had already considered such arguments and dismissed them. Insider trading was unfair and hurt the integrity of the market, he believed. Shad had vowed publicly to crack down on insider trading, even as he encouraged the very corporate takeovers that provided Siegel and Boesky with their opportunities.

Almost inadvertently, the commission's policies that summer and fall of 1982 began to revolve more and more around corporate takeovers, though the thrust of the policies sometimes seemed at odds. In the enforcement division, Fedders was attacking Swiss-bank secrecy that blocked inquiries into takeover-related trading. Jack Hewitt had embarked on an investigation of Michael Milken's trading in takeovers and other deals, one of many insider trading probes under way. With one hand Shad pushed Fedders to press his ambitious law-enforcement campaign, while with the other hand he paddled in a different direction. He began to implement a new, hands-off policy at the commission toward corporate takeovers, even hostile battles like the one between Bendix and Martin Marietta.

That fall Shad took a major step in promoting a free market approach to takeovers by hiring Texas A&M economics professor Charles Cox to be the agency's first "chief economist." Shad's view was that the commission had too many attorneys who applied convoluted legal thinking to issues that begged for a simpler, more economic, approach, including the quantification of the costs and benefits of regulation. By creating the new office of the chief economist, Shad sought to reduce the SEC's reliance on legal reasoning and increase its emphasis on economic analysis.

Shad's hiring of a free market economist sent a clear signal to Wall Street that new priorities were being set in place at the SEC. The hiring also sent a distinct message of a different sort through the commission's bureaucracy. When Cox arrived at the SEC to take up his post, Shad told his top aides that he wanted the new chief economist to report directly to him. To accommodate Cox in an office near Shad, a decision was made to move Phil Savage, the SEC's equal-employment-opportunity officer, to the basement. The impression created by Savage's move to the basement—that Shad and his top staff cared most about free market economics and least about equal opportunity—wasn't lost on some blacks and women at the commission. Savage, a former civil rights worker, complained that Shad wouldn't even meet with him. Some senior SEC staff vigorously defended Shad against charges of racism or sexism, noting for example that he appointed women to several key staff positions and relied on them heavily for advice. But it was also true that during Shad's watch, with Savage relegated to the basement, several serious harassment and discrimination cases arose that deeply embarrassed the SEC after Shad was gone.

Cox was oblivious to the controversy inside the SEC about his office. He was enlivened by the mission Shad had laid out for him—to analyze, quantify, and document the chairman's free market views on the most important regulatory issues of the day. Corporate takeovers were an ideal issue for Cox to tackle first. With controversy over the Martin Marietta affair raging and calls for reform mounting, Shad wanted to quickly quantify the costs and benefits of takeovers. He wanted a clear economic analysis—based, of course, on Shad's own free market assumptions about economics—of the impact of any proposed changes in the rules that governed the merger game. Shad's gut told him that takeovers were good and that tampering with the regulatory system to control them would create more problems than it would solve. Now he had an economist who could crunch the numbers to support his views.

That would be no intellectual compromise for Cox, who had received his doctorate in economics from the University of Chicago. Cox was one of the university's true believers—the graduate students and economists who flocked to Washington to change the way government worked. To them, the political changes inaugurated by Ronald Reagan offered a chance to implement a radically conservative version of the Marxist concept of praxis—the melding of revolutionary theory and practice. Cox subscribed fervently to the view that free, unfettered markets offered a more efficient and effective means to solve society's problems than government did.

He and Shad hit it off from the start. In their first conversation before Cox was hired at the SEC, they talked about how economic analysis could play a role in decision making at the commission. They agreed that the SEC staff was generally too reluctant to quantify the economic impact of regulatory decisions. The more they could quantify, Shad and Cox agreed, the better their decisions would be. Of course, since it was typically much easier to quantify the cost of a proposed rule or regulation than it was to quantify its benefits—which might include abstract ideas such as the quality of life or the safety and soundness of the financial system—there were some at the SEC who saw the new emphasis on numbers as a disguised effort to reduce the commission's regulatory role.

With Cox in place as chief economist, Shad had implemented an important institutional mechanism that he hoped would transform the SEC. Shad was at last firmly pushing the commission bureaucracy in a new direction. Fedders had won international renown for the agency's campaign against insider trading; the biggest overhaul in history of the SEC rules governing how corporations raised money from investors was well under way; Cox was ready to draft papers declaring that takeover fights like the one that rocked the country in August merely represented the invisible, albeit indelicate, hand of capitalism at work; and Shad even succeeded in pushing his first bill through Congress. On October 13, President Reagan signed amendments to the securities laws that resolved the turf battle between the Securities and Exchange Commission and the Commodity Futures Trading Commission, thereby permitting new stock futures to come into existence. This was the deal struck by Shad and CFTC Chairman Philip Johnson, over lunch at the Monocle restaurant on Capitol Hill. In Shad's view, the bill was tantamount to an emancipation proclamation for shareholders, who were free now to trade a panoply of new financial instruments without undue regulatory interference.

Finally, too, the withering battle with Dingell began to ease. About two weeks after Jack Hewitt returned from Los Angeles to report on his interrogation of Michael Milken, Shad received a letter from Dingell's office. "It is the staff's conclusion that there was no wrongdoing in the method of disposition of the Hutton securities or in the transfer of the proceeds thereof to your trust," Dingell wrote. "While the transactions were complex, they appeared to satisfy all existing statutory and regulatory requirements." It was exactly the letter of exoneration Shad had requested when the investigation into his finances began—or as close to a letter of exoneration as John Dingell knew how to write.

Before Shad moved from Wall Street to Washington, Nicholas F. Brady, an executive at the Dillon, Read investment house and a former senator from New Jersey, warned him about capital politics. You come to Washington with a fine reputation and you want to be sure you leave with it, Brady had said. And when

Dingell had come after him, it was Brady who suggested that Shad hire Joseph Califano to fend him off. It irritated Shad enormously that he had to pay Califano $70,000 in fees and that his personal integrity had been questioned publicly. Yet, that November, Shad adopted a moderate tone in the public statement he released to the press along with the Dingell letter. "It has taken seven months and $70,000 in personal legal fees, but I am glad to get it over with," Shad said.

He had survived his initiation into Washington's partisan rituals. He had established his authority over the SEC's staff, partly through compromise. He had put in place new mechanisms through which to translate some of his free market views into federal policies. What remained was for John Shad to put broadly into practice the ideas about economics and government he shared with Ronald Reagan and the conservatives who had come to Washington to change the relationship between government and business.

Shad sincerely believed that such a program—he refused to call it deregulation, partly because that was a word the Democrats used to bludgeon the Reagan administration—would lead the United States toward growth, prosperity, and strength. He believed adamantly that such a readjustment of priorities in favor of unfettered markets would work, because he shared his president's sunny optimism about American business and American businessmen. The dark suspicions about venality and greed in corporate boardrooms that seemed to underlie the SEC's enforcement program before his arrival seemed to Shad an overreaction, an essential misreading of Wall Street's moral turpitude. He was prepared to stake his tenure as SEC chairman on his conviction that most everybody in American high finance—and, for that matter, at the commission—was honest.

7

The Chicago School

In mid-February 1983, a heavy snow blanketed the capital, clogging roads and paralyzing traffic. SEC enforcement chief John Fedders was trapped at his spacious home in Potomac, amid rolling hills and horse farms and white rail fences, unable to navigate by car the narrow roads that led into the city. Snow in Washington was rare and much resented by the local populace, but in the wealthy Maryland suburbs along the river, it transformed pedestrian suburban tracts into winter landscapes of bright, manorial splendor.

At Fedders's house the mood was not bucolic. His marriage was deteriorating quickly, and for weeks he had offered little but silence to his wife, Charlotte. When the snow fell, it seemed to Charlotte that her husband became immediately angry and frustrated. Like a drill sergeant, he ordered the five boys to shovel the driveway clear. When they finished, Fedders climbed above the garage to clean the drain and inadvertently loosened a small avalanche of snow from the roof onto the drive. Though the boys were now inside, resting, he insisted that they return with their shovels. Charlotte began to scream, and she threw a wooden toy at him. Fedders smacked her so hard that he broke her glasses and blackened her eye.

A few weeks earlier, confounded by his silence, Charlotte had written the SEC's enforcement chief a note: "Do you realize the responsibility you have to find out what your problems are to help your children now and in the future? Do you realize you are more likely to succeed further (i.e., cabinet position, etc.) if your problem is taken care of now by counseling and/or medication than if your neighbors and friends and coworkers begin talking to investigative agents about your bizarre treatment of your family? . . . I know you are a good and decent man when you are healthy."

Now she decided to act. She dropped the boys with a friend, had her bruise photographed, and drove to the Rockville police station. They said all they could do was arrest him if she swore out a warrant. She said she didn't want him to go to jail, and went home. A few days later, Fedders left for Florida on SEC business. He didn't tell her where, or when he would return.

The telephone rang one afternoon while she was home alone with the boys. It was John Shad. Charlotte had met him a few times, once at a commission Christmas party she and Fedders hosted in Potomac. As Charlotte recalled:

"Do you know when he's coming home?" Shad asked.

"I don't know and I really don't care. He has just given me a black eye."

"I'm sorry, but he has been under a lot of pressure lately," Shad said.

Perhaps Shad was thinking of Dingell's investigations. The congressman's probes of Shad had ended, but Fedders was the target of several continuing, politically motivated investigations. They would eventually come to nothing, but they put pressure on Fedders and kept his name in the newspaper.

"No," Charlotte replied. "It's been happening since the beginning of the marriage."

"I'm really sorry," Shad said. She was convinced he meant it. Shad said later that Charlotte hadn't mentioned a black eye.

When Shad saw Fedders the next week, he told him, "Get away and relax. Spend time with Charlotte and the kids."

"Yes, yes, but—" was Fedders's reply.

"I mean it, John," Shad said.

That was a suggestion Charlotte Fedders might have found frightening, but Shad thought that many marital problems were caused by stress faced by the husband at work, and that the problems could be eased if the stress was reduced and the husband spent more time at home. In his days on Wall Street, Shad had seen that sort of thing often enough. He did not discipline Fedders, nor demand that he seek professional help, nor did he investigate Charlotte Fedders's condition—whether she and her children were in imminent danger, whether they needed assistance. Shad felt that he didn't know the facts about the Fedderses' marriage, and in any event, he was reluctant to get involved with what he viewed as a personal family matter, even one that involved the top law enforcement official at the SEC.

Charlotte Fedders wasn't sure why she had told Shad; never before had she talked to one of her husband's colleagues about the violence. Later, when Fedders came home from Florida and she asked him to move out of the house, she told him that Shad knew that he was "a wife beater."

After that moment, Charlotte said later, her husband never spoke to her again until he moved in July to his own apartment on Massachusetts Avenue in Washington. To Fedders, Charlotte thought, talking to Shad about the beatings was her ultimate betrayal. In any event, as a cry for help, it was useless.

At one level, Shad seemed not to comprehend the magnitude of the secret he was harboring. This was a trait with which Shad's senior staff at the commission had grown familiar. Shad often justified his free market policies at the SEC in strong moral terms. He described his own life decisions in the same language of right and wrong. And yet at times his own views of ethics and morality seemed sharply at odds with those of his colleagues or the public.

A stunning example of this gap in ethical perceptions had been a closed SEC meeting two weeks before Shad's call to Charlotte Fedders. At the meeting, the commission was to consider a controversial investigation into allegedly improper accounting practices at Aetna Life & Casualty Company, the insurance giant. Senior SEC staff wanted to file public charges, but the insurer had lobbied vigorously in its own defense, arguing through written briefs that the practices questioned by the SEC were generally accepted in its industry. As the climactic decision by the SEC approached, Aetna retained Joe Flom, the Wall Street takeover lawyer Shad had invited onto an SEC takeover advisory panel, to press its case at the commission. At stake was $203 million in profits that Aetna would have to wipe off its books if the SEC decided against it. Flom flew to Washington with Aetna's chief executive in an effort to make a personal presentation to Shad and the other commissioners. To the amazement of the SEC staff, Shad invited Flom into a closed commission meeting and allowed him to make an oral argument on Aetna's behalf. No outsider had been permitted into a closed commission meeting for more than a decade. That Flom was Shad's old friend from Wall Street compounded the transgression in the eyes of some senior commission staff, who were convinced Aetna had hired Flom because of his personal relationship with Shad. One commissioner vocally objected to Flom's appearance at the closed meeting, and the vote went against Aetna. Afterward, what appalled many of the SEC staff involved was Shad's obliviousness to the implications of his actions. He didn't understand that he had violated sacred SEC tradition and offended some who took that tradition seriously. Nor did he understand that such favoritism to an old friend from Wall Street looked bad politically, inside the commission and out. What would John Dingell do if he found out about Flom's appearance?

But there were no embarrassing hearings on the matter, because Dingell never found out. Secrecy, of course, was one of the commission's most cherished traits. It was a credit to the commission's culture of secrecy, and to the personal affection Shad was beginning to earn from the staff, that the partisan investigators on John Dingell's staff never learned what happened in the Aetna case. Though it had merit in some instances and was a sign of the intense loyalty felt by the SEC staff to the agency, the uses of secrecy at the commission also highlighted some of the worst tendencies of bureaucracies and bureaucrats in Washington. Most importantly, secrecy protected the symbiotic relationship between the agency and the corporations and Wall Street firms it regulated. Secrecy had its legitimate functions—protecting the right to privacy of innocent people under investigation and enhancing the commission's ability to conduct many of its sensitive probes. And both sides felt they benefited from the fact that neither the public nor the Congress knew what was happening. SEC officials felt they benefited from secrecy in part because no one could second-guess their votes or examine the evidence on which they based their decisions. The corporate and individual defendants in commission cases avoided the costs and embarrassment of publicity and full disclosure. On another level, though, the agency's obsession with secrecy was replete with hypocrisy. The SEC pushed corporations and Wall Street firms to disclose all material information to investors, but it disclosed relatively little of the agency's own most crucial dealings, making it difficult for the public to evaluate enforcement settlements and other issues. There was a way, too, in which the culture of secrecy percolated into the personal and professional attitudes of SEC officials. They became endowed with prestige and power. It was exciting to work on a secret case, one that could be resolved only in the revered privacy of a closed SEC meeting.

Some of the commission staff lawyers had decided that either Shad didn't care about how Flom's appearance at a closed meeting looked or else he didn't understand, and truthfully, they weren't sure which it was. As the truth of Shad's knowledge about the dark secret of Fedders's marriage eventually spread, these staffers felt the same puzzlement. Despite Shad's expressions of sympathy to Charlotte Fedders on the telephone, he took no action. The irony was that among officials of his rank in the Reagan administration, there were few who grappled more regularly with ethical questions or who described their work in moral terms more articulately than Shad. The commission's charter demanded it— the agency's job in part was to develop and enforce rules about fair dealing and ethical conduct on Wall Street. Shad's argument for the crackdown on insider trading led by Fedders was as much moral as economic. Insider trading was just wrong—it was unfair—he kept saying, and it must not be allowed to undermine the integrity of the stock market. Away from the SEC, so often had Shad repeated to his friends his Mormon grandmother's precept that a person should spend one third of his life learning, one third earning, and one third serving, that it had become a kind of cliché among them when the topic of Shad's character arose. How many Wall Street millionaires had prefaced their careers by fasting in an attempt to induce a religious revelation? Yet the conflicts within Shad were obvious to those who knew him well, or who saw him operate inside the commission. His competitiveness, his love of wagering, his chain-smoking, his dedication to family and work, the way he drove cars and boats too fast—at times the only thread binding his impulses seemed to be his absolute intensity.

On a boat in the Pacific in the 1940s, Shad had declared himself an agnostic, but at the commission he was sometimes seen as a true believer, not about God but about free market economics. The first impulse of commissioners and staff who tried to assess Shad's ideology was to lump him in with the "Chicago School" conservative theorists so prevalent among the Reagan appointees. That was easy to do, since Shad was attracted to economic theorizing generally and to the work of the Chicago professors specifically—his recruitment of Charles Cox to head the commission's new office of the chief economist emphasized the point. By early 1983, though, it was becoming clear that Shad's approach was not so coldly utilitarian as that of the hard-line Chicago intellectuals, who tended to think that every aspect of human life could be measured and assessed in terms of the free market. The Chicago economists' laissez-faire attitude about markets had a libertarian corollary in their approach to social issues. Just as the government should keep away from the nation's financial exchanges, it should stay out of the country's bedrooms, too.

Though Shad believed in free markets more fervently than almost anything else, his vision of the ideal society included—in fact, demanded—a prominent place for human trust and benevolence. The Chicago economists who had never tried to make a living on Wall Street thought free markets worked because, abstractly, they provided the best system in which individuals could make choices about their self-interest. The amalgamation of self-interested choices would protect and promote the collective interest. Shad thought that was correct as far as it went, but that the theory didn't take account of the environment of personal trust that was essential for the markets to work fairly.

To the public, whether before Congress or in interviews with the press, Shad repeated over and over a handful of cherished aphorisms, each time as if they were new revelations. The one he repeated most often was "America has today by far the best securities markets the world has ever known—the broadest, the most active and efficient, and the fairest. Last year, securities transactions in America amounted to about $40 trillion, about nine times the gross national product. By the highest conjecture, securities frauds amount to a fraction of one percent of such transactions, most of which are executed over the telephone in reliance on the other party's word."

Over and over again, Shad implied a key reason the markets worked so well was that most human beings were trustworthy enough to honor their word. Shad also argued that fraud was not systemic on Wall Street, so there was no need to become hysterical about the relatively small incidence of insider trading his SEC was uncovering. Perhaps on the Wall Street where Shad had worked before heading to Washington—in the world of men's clubs and Ivy League degrees and quiet wealth—honor and trust were exalted, even enforced. If such a culture had ever existed broadly in the financial world, as opposed to what went on in the exclusive suites and clubs where Shad worked and socialized, it was fast eroding in that January of 1983, under the ancient pressures of speculation and greed.

The Securities and Exchange Commission had been created precisely because the country had learned, in the devastating financial panics of the 1850s, the 1870s, the 1890s, and the 1920s, that when there were large sums of money to be made, the people who controlled the financial markets could not be trusted to police themselves. Shad seemed to accept the necessity of the commission's role, but not all of its assumptions about human nature. Shad often said that if new laws or regulations were passed, 99 percent of the people would follow them and the 1 percent of the people they were aimed at would find new ways to break the law. He didn't believe new laws and regulations would raise the general standards of conduct. Above all, he embraced freedom of choice for investors. Yet in his genuine enthusiasm for innovation and efficiency, he seemed unable to see that lax discipline, in the face of vast temptation, could bring out the worst in people, threatening rather than strengthening, the markets to which he was so devoted.

There were people Shad respected who warned, late in 1982 and early in 1983, that ominous change was occurring on Wall Street. The takeover free-for-all between Bendix and Martin Marietta was one signal. Trading in stock index futures, the new financial instruments whose birth had been ensured by the regulatory deal cut by Shad and Philip Johnson in the summer of 1981, was perhaps an even more obvious sign, since debate in Washington over whether to allow stock futures had been conducted in the same ideological and even moral vocabulary so often used by the commission chairman. "In my judgment, a very high percentage—probably at least 95 percent and more likely much higher—of the activity generated by these [stock index futures] will be strictly gambling in nature," the investor Warren Buffett had written to Congress at the height of the debate in 1982. Shad admired Buffett; during his first months at the commission, he had invited the Omaha investor to brief commission staff about certain insurance issues, partly to acquaint the bureaucrats with the wisdom of an accomplished capitalist. In his warning to Congress about stock futures, Buffett had concluded, "In the long run, gambling-dominated activities . . . are not going to be good for the capital markets."

Gambling—that was a loaded word in the Mormon community where Shad was born, a word of sin. Shad was adamant that the constant wagering he engaged in, since it didn't involve casinos or large sums of money and was driven by competitiveness and a pure quest for excitement and fun through risk taking, wasn't really gambling, at least not in the sense that a Mormon might think of it. During the critical congressional debate over whether the SEC should accede to the creation of stock futures, Shad took a similar position—he didn't think that trading stock futures would lead to widespread gambling, at least not in the sense that

Buffett meant. Some increased speculation would be good for the financial markets, he thought. But in Shad's view the private choices of investors, whether speculative or prudent, were best left alone by the government. To enact the laws that authorized stock futures, Congress had to use the prerogatives of the federal government to preempt certain state antigambling statutes that otherwise would have prohibited such speculative trading. Still, Shad had no basic moral or economic objection to stock futures. And he did not think stock futures would alter fundamentally the way the stock market worked.

About that, at least, it turned out that Shad was wrong.

Early in 1983, in a pit on the floor of an obscure commodities exchange in Kansas City, Missouri, the first stock index futures contracts changed hands amid great fanfare and ceremony, all of it mustered in the hope that a new era was at hand. It was, but unfortunately for those gathered in the pit, little of the massive wealth generated by trading in stock index futures during the 1980s would find its way to Kansas City.

The futures industry had been headquartered for decades in Chicago, and there stock futures trading would flourish. That was appropriate in a way, since it was the conservative economists at the University of Chicago, the ones Jack Shad had so admired, who had helped to invent stock futures in the first place. On Wall Street, too, futures trading would soon generate tens of millions of dollars in fees and commissions annually as new products proliferated and grew in popularity. Some on Wall Street came to believe that futures trading contributed to the great bull market already under way that winter. Since the previous August, when the economy's recovery from recession finally seemed assured, the Dow Jones Industrial Average had raced from the mid-700s past 1,100, an increase of about 50 percent in only half a year.

Later, in 1987, when the market crashed and the politicians in Washington fretted over what to do about it, there was a great deal of public talk about whether stock futures were good or bad for the country. The trouble was that few in Congress or at the White House understood what stock futures were or how they had changed the financial markets. Bemused economists in Chicago said that that was typical of Washington, that federal regulators and legislators were often years behind in comprehending innovation in the industries they supervised. In the case of stock futures, the problem was compounded by the conflicting ideological assumptions that different factions carried to the debate. It was a peculiar facet of the futures business that ever since its birth, a century earlier, people had been trying to outlaw the industry on what boiled down to moral grounds.

The conflicting American impulses of religious rectitude and boyish abandon visible in a man like John Shad were evident, too, in the tangled history of stock futures. The futures markets were born on the hardscrabble midwestern plains of the nineteenth century in a spontaneous attempt to quell the effects of what were then commonly called acts of God—violent storms, howling tornadoes, and devastating droughts. The seasons and the weather formed a repeating, treacherous economic cycle for farmers, who depended on rain at the right time and in the right amount to eke out sustenance for their families, many of them recent migrants from the more comfortable East. In the spring, a farmer went deeply into debt to buy seed, fertilizer, and other supplies for planting. If the weather cooperated, he profited. At harvest-time late in the summer, he hauled his crop to market, sold it at the prevailing price, paid off his debts, and stashed away the profits. Next spring, he began again. But if the weather failed, he was ruined. If it rained too much and there was a bumper crop, plummeting prices caused by the oversupply prevented him from earning enough to pay off his debt. If it rained too little and his crop failed, he might not have enough to sell to pay back his spring borrowings. Every year, then, the farmer, often an austere and deeply religious man devoted to the land, involuntarily gambled on the weather.

In Chicago and Kansas City and other Midwestern cities, a free-market answer to the farmer's predicament sprang up. Fly-by-night speculators and profiteers came west and offered to make deals with the farmers. In the spring, at planting time, a farmer might contract with a speculator to "presell" the crop he would harvest later. The farmer would get the speculator's cash, receiving the prevailing market price for wheat or whatever crop was to be planted, and he would agree to deliver the goods at harvesttime. The speculator was betting that crop prices would rise so that he could make a killing. The deal between the farmer and the speculator involved what economists came to call risk transfer. The risk of bad weather was shifted from someone who couldn't afford to bear it, the farmer and his family, to someone perfectly willing to gamble, the speculator.

As time went on, the speculators started to swap crop contracts. The modern futures market in Chicago actually began in loose, raucous crowds of speculators who gathered in the mud near the railroad depots where the crops came in. A rough system of market pricing developed, and slowly the speculators began to build institutions for themselves, places some of the farmers' organizations denounced as casinos. There was always tension between the farmers and their unruly financial partners in the cities—mainly because the farmers rightly suspected the speculators of manipulating crop prices in their unsupervised marketplaces. For a hundred years, price manipulation and crop-cornering schemes were virtually commonplace in the agricultural futures pits where trading took place. Scandal and corruption on Wall Street prompted the SEC's creation during the 1930s, but the futures markets received no such vigorous oversight, though they continued to prosper and grow in importance. Despite futures scandals, one reason there was little push for federal regulation was the low involvement of small investors in the futures markets and the success of futures traders—who opposed federal regulation—in political fund-raising. Until 1974, when a particularly outrageous series of scandals led to the formation of the Commodity Futures Trading Commission, the Chicago futures exchanges were supervised by a small, ineffective office in the federal Agriculture Department.

It was a diminutive, wiry, palpably energetic speculator named Leo Melamed who changed everything. The only child of Polish immigrants, Melamed had started out as a clerk at the Chicago Mercantile Exchange, then a lesser institution known in part for its trading in egg futures. He went broke in the pits three times before he rose to power at the exchange, winning a seat on its executive board and building a coalition that eventually transformed the Merc into one of the world's most important financial institutions. Melamed was an erstwhile science fiction writer; he eventually published a thriller in which characters named Rafflo, Nan Nan, and Slib Fru jetted between planets dubbed Qalm, Quut, and Usma, indulging themselves with morsels of Zamotian fruit. His writing was original, but back on planet Earth, Melamed demonstrated a remarkable talent for taking other people's ideas and turning them into money.

Free market economist Milton Friedman provided him with the breakthrough that ended the cycle of boom-and-bust that had defined Melamed's career. In 1967, Friedman became convinced—correctly, as it turned out—that the international monetary system was about to undergo revolutionary changes as the prices of foreign currencies became subject increasingly to free market forces. Friedman wanted to gamble on his analysis, and he asked a Chicago bank to let him make a down payment of $30,000, borrow $270,000, and then sell short $300,000 worth of British pounds, meaning that Friedman would profit if the price of British pounds declined. The bank refused. For one thing, Friedman was asking the bank to lend him 90 percent of the purchase price—in the stock market, ever since the crash of 1929, individual investors had been required by the federal government to put up 50 percent of the purchase price in cash, in an effort to quell dangerous speculation. As it happened, about three weeks after the bank's rejection, the price of pounds plummeted so steeply that had Friedman been allowed to borrow the money to place his bet, he would have more than doubled his original investment. Friedman vented his frustration with the Chicago futures-market officials he knew, urging them to take advantage of the upcoming volatility in the currency markets by establishing new futures products based on the world's major currencies. Leo Melamed was among the few who listened to him.

In theory—and theory was the Chicago School's specialty—Friedman's proposal traced back to the economic idea that underlay the alliance between speculators and farmers a century earlier: risk transfer. What was the difference between a farmer worried about changes in the weather and a giant, multinational bank concerned about fluctuations in the value of the dollar in Japan, where the bank might have huge loans outstanding? The price of the dollar relative to other currencies was just as unpredictable as the weather. Melamed, sensing that he had stumbled onto a potential bonanza, began to work with Chicago School economists and officials of the Chicago Mercantile Exchange, which had long been dwarfed by its rival, the Chicago Board of Trade. Melamed and his competitors came up with futures not just for foreign currencies, but for Treasury bonds, Treasury bills, corporate bonds, mortgage-backed securities, and, finally, stocks. A pension fund, for example, could hedge against a drop in the overall stock market by "preselling" some of its stocks through the use of stock index futures.

They found it was theoretically possible to transfer any economic risk imaginable.

By 1983, when stock futures began trading, it was hard sometimes to recall the original impulse—the eagerness of speculators and drifters heading west to make fast money gambling on the weather—that gave birth to the futures markets in the mud down by the railroad tracks. The approval and supervision of so many new financial products by regulators in Washington during the Carter administration and in the early Reagan years had produced a blizzard of well-reasoned papers and briefs written by lawyers and economists, all designed to justify financial futures on theoretical grounds. The once-humble idea of risk transfer was extended and expanded and contorted into charts and graphs until it began to resemble some philosopher's ontology of the universe. When he flew into Washington to testify before Congress or the CFTC, Milton Friedman liked to talk about theories of capitalism. He didn't digress into why he personally had wanted to wager $300,000, several times the annual salary of a college professor, on the future price of British sterling, or what exactly he planned to do with all that money if his bet paid off.

Yet the terms of Friedman's proposed bet on the price of the pound told exactly why financial futures were booming in Chicago, and why they might eventually effect the way the stock markets on Wall Street worked. The key was *leverage*.

That winter of 1983, most financial regulators in Washington, including Shad, weren't sure that stock index futures would ever become popular. Large institutions that owned a lot of stocks— university endowments, pension funds, and mutual funds— tended to view the Chicago futures exchanges as seedy hotbeds of speculators. Why would these big traders abandon the venerable New York Stock Exchange? The answer, it turned out, was that they could buy more with less, just as Milton Friedman had proposed to control $300,000 worth of sterling with only $30,000 in cash.

Stock index futures were contracts containing promises about the future. As with stock options, every contract had a date on it: an exact day, month, and year sometime in the future guaranteeing the delivery of the financial value of stocks for a price negotiated in the present. The "index" part of the contract referred to the basket of stocks to be delivered. The Standard & Poor's 500, made up of stocks of five hundred big U.S. corporations, would eventually become the most popular basket. The S&P 500 futures contract promoted by Leo Melamed succeeded because it took less cash to buy the stock future in Chicago than it did to buy the corresponding five hundred stocks in New York. Instead of the 50 percent down payment required of individual investors in the stock market, a speculator in the futures markets was required to put up only about 10 or 15 percent in cash. Stock futures traders got more bang for the buck than anyone in the stock market, just as a home buyer with $20,000 on hand can buy a bigger house if the required down payment is 15 percent rather than 50 percent.

During the stock market crash of 1929, highly leveraged speculation by individual investors not only contributed to the steepness of the market's fall, but also wreaked financial devastation on thousands of the middle class who seemed to think, as they borrowed and borrowed to buy stocks, that the market could only go up. A deep skepticism about the uses of debt never left the generation that witnessed the crash and lived through the Great Depression. John Shad was one of them—even as he maneuvered with Phil Johnson at the CFTC to unleash trading in stock futures, he expressed concern to Federal Reserve Board Chairman Paul Volcker about the relatively low down payments required of stock futures investors. Volcker was worried as well, but there was a part of him that just didn't want to get involved with the futures markets. The Federal Reserve already had to regulate the size of the nation's money supply, assure the safety and soundness of the banking credit system, and oversee the use of borrowed money in the stock market. Volcker was afraid that if the Fed was seen as a kind of universal financial safety net, prepared to protect people against even the most outrageous speculative losses in the futures markets, then it would only encourage more and more speculation. Volcker's thinking was that if a tightrope walker knows he has a net underneath him, he is encouraged to take all sorts of foolish chances on the wire.

So, despite the misgivings, a new market for stock futures was born. Shad heralded the freedom of choice for investors, believing that restrictions on innovation would do more harm than good. Like so many other complex issues, it was for Shad a simple equation of costs and benefits.

Inauguration of stock futures trading sealed off Jack Shad and the SEC from regulation of one of the fastest-growing sectors of the country's financial markets, since the original deal between Shad and CFTC Chairman Johnson precluded the SEC from supervising stock futures trading. That meant the markets in Chicago were regulated by Johnson's CFTC, while the stock markets in New York—increasingly influenced by the stock futures trading—continued under the supervision of the SEC. Those who had opposed this act of regulatory segregation warned that the SEC should protect investors from abuses arising from the trading of any financial product, including stock futures, that directly affected the stock market.

But Shad had promoted the agreement not only because it suited his deal-making and deregulatory instincts, but also because it helped to fulfill a specific, almost utopian vision he harbored about how the country's financial markets should ideally work. Shad saw as potentially beneficial the same speculation that prompted an investor like Warren Buffett to issue a warning about the ill effects of gambling on the health of the public markets. He believed that some speculation enhanced the stock market's efficiency. One of Shad's favorite words was *liquidity*, which he used to conjure up the image of money flowing through the stock market and the economy like water through a fertile delta. Shad thought of faltering economies as dry gulches where the flow of money had been cut off; the solution was to open a spigot and let cash pour again, until it lapped into every parched corner and brought barren land to life. Stock futures and the speculators who might trade them helped promote liquidity by making it easier for companies to find money to pay for growth.

There were times when Shad's views about liquidity sounded almost like a religious revelation. "The millennium to which mankind can aspire is that great day when capital will be permitted to flow, with safeguards against fraud and with the ease of water, into every nook and cranny of economic opportunity, first within nations, second throughout the Free World, and ultimately throughout the earth," he declared.

It wasn't just stock futures that Shad wanted to free in the hope that increased trading would help to "liquify" the economy, it was old-fashioned stocks as well—the securities traded at the New York Stock Exchange, the American Stock Exchange, in the National Market System, and at other venues directly under the regulatory control of the SEC. The commission's division of market regulation was responsible for day-to-day supervision of the stock markets. When he first came to Washington, market reg, as it was called, was the directorate Shad viewed with the most reservation—its very name, with the emphasis on regulation, provoked a visceral dislike in him. Shad's intuition had been reinforced by Doug Scarff, the director in charge in 1981, a nervous, chain-smoking lawyer whose inexperience with the actual business of trading stocks seemed to irritate the chairman. Shad was always asking why, questioning the assumptions and the fundamental purpose of the division's work, and his approach had the predictable effect of putting market reg's staff lawyers on the defensive. He said the same words over and over—*liquidity* and *efficiency, liquidity* and *efficiency*—but Shad's broad vision of an economy enriched by the unfettered flow of money, and of a government that regulated only when absolutely necessary, did not square with many of the commission staff lawyers who spent their days forcing the big Wall Street firms to comply with the division's minute rules.

When it came to resources, Shad favored enforcement over market reg. Shad and the market reg staff had different ideas about how the commission should enforce morality in the stock market, and what sort of morality it should endorse. During the 1970s, the market reg division had shared the enforcement division's enthusiasm for regulatory expansion and moral righteousness. Shad tried to change some of the market regulation staff's assumptions about the division's role in the markets. During 1982, for example, a group of lawyers in the division conducted a big investigation of allegedly abusive trading practices in the stockoption pits of the Philadelphia Stock Exchange and the Chicago Board Options Exchange. The lawyers found, after months of study, that traders in the pits were fixing options trades to generate bogus tax losses for investors, and that the exchanges weren't doing anything about it. So prevalent was the bogus-tax-loss trading that daily volume figures about the numbers of options traded in the Philadelphia and Chicago pits, which were disclosed to the public so investors could evaluate the general level of interest in specific options, had become distorted and false. The trading was wrong, the market reg staff felt, and they wanted to find a way to stop it.

That same winter of 1983, when stock futures began trading, the market regulation division sent a confidential memo to the commission recommending that the SEC crack down on the tax trading schemes at the options exchanges. The memo conceded that tax violations were not part of the commission's jurisdiction, but said the distorted volume figures posted at the exchange were a securities-law violation. But Shad opposed the recommendation—he said he would not permit the commission to wander outside its jurisdiction. If the Internal Revenue Service was concerned about bogus trading in options, then let the IRS attempt to stop it, he said. The market reg memo went nowhere.

Even some inside the SEC who generally shared Shad's political ideology could be frustrated by the chairman's view that the stock market was essentially an honest place, that its principal purpose was to promote capital liquidity for the nation, and that the government ought to let the stock exchanges regulate themselves.

Shad sided with those aligned with the New York Stock Exchange who wanted to block the construction of a sophisticated computer surveillance system that would allow the commission to track the names of buyers and sellers in every transaction on the exchange floor—information that had always been closely guarded by the Wall Street investment firms. The surveillance system, whose purpose seemed obvious and essential to some in the commission's enforcement division, had been proposed during the 1970s. The technology for it was already available. As its development progressed, the Wall Street firms who were members of the NYSE became alarmed by the possibility that the government would soon be able to monitor buyers and sellers on the exchange floor—it would be like Orwell's Big Brother, they said. When Shad arrived at the commission, many of his colleagues on the Street wanted the development of any such government surveillance system stopped. He initiated a market regulation division review of the proposal and decided finally to end the program, assuring those staff lawyers who disagreed with him that he would support alternative private-sector programs through which the SEC could collect names and other data about players in the stock market. Shad thought the alternatives he backed were cost-effective; others inside the commission thought the New York Stock Exchange had taken the SEC's teeth away.

Yet it was an irony of Shad's relationship with many of the senior staff responsible for the commission's regulation of the stock markets that, despite their sometimes heated internal battles, the staff seemed increasingly to forgive and respect him. John Wheeler, secretary of the SEC for two years under Shad, felt as much as any of the senior staff, and perhaps more so, that the decision to kill the system of computer surveillance of the stock market could turn out to be a grave and even irresponsible mistake. He thought the raw power of the stock exchange's member firms had succeeded against the commission, and that Shad's position had been influenced in part by the hysterical, self-interested fears of Wall Street executives who dreaded the prospect of accountability to the SEC. But any anger Wheeler harbored against Shad was less political or ideological than filial, the disappointment of a son in the weaknesses of his father. That was how Wheeler thought of Shad—as a father figure to him and to other senior commission lawyers, especially Fedders. And Shad was no saintly, benevolent patriarch. He liked to bet; he liked to smoke; i.e., he "sinned." That was part of what attracted Wheeler and the others to him.

Wheeler was highly visible away from the commission as the leader of a controversial effort to build a memorial to veterans of the Vietnam War. Opponents of Wheeler's plans continually attacked his credibility and his motives. When he started his crusade, Wheeler asked Shad for permission, knowing that he was going to attract heat and controversy to the commission, and Shad had said it was all right. Then Wheeler's opponents dug up his private military records, which showed that he had been reprimanded for stealing a jeep in a combat zone. Worried about how Shad would react to the disclosure, Wheeler hurried to the chairman's expansive office suite and asked for an audience. That was no problem—Shad's doors were almost always open to the senior staff, who moved in and out in a series of ad hoc, informal meetings. Wheeler decided to go right up to Shad and blurt out his preemptive confession.

"Boss, in Vietnam I was reprimanded for using a jeep that I got from a motor pool without permission. It was a hot jeep, and my God, I feel so guilty," Wheeler blubbered.

Shad looked at him and laughed. "Don't ask me about the jeep I used in China," he answered jokingly. That was it. When the news about Wheeler came, Shad didn't bat an eye.

All around Shad that year—in the personal problems of his top officials, in the debates over how financial futures and corporate takeovers and junk bonds were changing the markets and the economy, and in the secret enforcement cases being developed against Michael Milken and other powerful financiers suspected of corruption—notions of morality and ethics were becoming increasingly central. And yet, within the commission, nobody, least of all Shad, was able to confront the quandaries head on. It was Shad's conviction that the SEC had to stop thinking of itself as the Securities and "Ethics" Commission, the Wall Street–thought police, the way he believed it had before his arrival. So the questions unasked and the contradictions unresolved just simmered and bubbled, gathering heat as the months passed. When at last it boiled over, there was nothing John Shad could do.

8

High Yield, High Risk

In August 1983, not long after Jared Kopel settled into his new and larger office in the commission's recently built, concrete headquarters on Fifth Street, one of his bosses, associate enforcement division director Ted Levine, stopped by to see him.

Bearded, broad-shouldered, forceful, and excitable, Levine intimidated some of the staff lawyers who worked for him, but Kopel was one of his protégés, and the pair had an exceptionally smooth relationship. Levine recently helped to promote Kopel to branch chief, a mid-level position that brought with it prestige within the enforcement division, a little extra pay, and the chance to supervise the investigative work of a handful of attorneys.

Levine handed Kopel a confidential memo. We have to decide what to do about HO-1395, he said.

The memo had been drafted by Jack Hewitt, the staff lawyer and decorated Vietnam combat veteran who had been pursuing for more than a year his theory that Michael Milken and the investment firm Drexel Burnham Lambert fraudulently manipulated the stock and bond markets in connection with a corporate takeover and other transactions. Hewitt was one of the attorneys in the enforcement branch Kopel had just taken over, and HO-1395 was one of the cases Kopel had inherited.

There may be some questions about this investigation, Levine told Kopel. Read the memo and we'll talk.

131

So Kopel read. He knew that contrasting personalities within the enforcement division had already affected the course of the case, which was officially captioned "Trading in the Securities of Certain Issuers." (The case was most commonly referred to by its file number, HO-1395. *HO* stood for Home Office or the SEC headquarters in Washington; 1395 was the sequentially assigned number of the case.) As in any large institution, the enforcement division had its cliques and petty personal rivalries, and inevitably decisions were influenced by who was up, who was down, who was in, or out of, favor. In this case the problems were especially complex. For many months Jack Hewitt had been pouring himself into the Milken investigation, but he hadn't really had much guidance from his supervisors. Hewitt hadn't gotten along very well with his former branch chief, Dwayne Cheek, whom Kopel had replaced. Hewitt, who as an ex-military man respected the importance of chain of command, didn't think this was his fault— Cheek didn't seem to get along with some of the other attorneys in the branch, either. Hewitt was older than many of his peers at the commission, he lost his temper from time to time, and there were those who thought Cheek was outright intimidated by him. The peace was kept mainly through isolation, leaving Hewitt largely on his own as he chased Milken and Drexel.

Perhaps that was why Kopel had trouble comprehending Hewitt's memo as he read it that summer—perhaps the presentation would have been sharper if a senior attorney had been working at Hewitt's side. As it was, Kopel found much of the memo's contents hazy and imprecise. In particular, Kopel was mystified by Hewitt's sweeping allegations that Milken was at the center of some far-flung market-manipulation scheme designed to produce special favors for Drexel clients.

It wasn't that Kopel didn't think such a scheme was conceivable. He understood the complexities of high finance. He had been educated firsthand during the 1970s when, as a reporter, at the *New York Post*, he had covered New York City's fiscal crisis. His job then had been to examine large quantities of complex financial information and zero in on the most important elements.

That's what Kopel and his superiors said was missing from

Hewitt's memo about Milken and Drexel. They called Hewitt to roundtable meetings in their offices, where they reviewed the investigative testimony he had taken from Milken and others and grilled Hewitt about the conclusions in his memo.

Kopel, Levine, and the others kept saying the same things to him. What, exactly, is this scheme that Milken has supposedly concocted? Yes, there are trades and deals here that look suspicious. But what's the motive? What's going on here?

Hewitt tried to explain. But they felt that he wasn't clear enough about the alleged manipulation scheme. It was extremely complicated—the most sophisticated frauds always were, Hewitt thought.

The weeks passed and Hewitt drafted his final memo on the case, taking care to make his allegations clear. Thick, printed transcripts from his interrogations of Milken and others were stacked around him. Hewitt didn't think of himself as an exceptionally talented writer—one of the things Kopel criticized was his writing ability—nor did he see himself as a legal scholar. But as he scratched the words that laid out his theory of Milken's manipulation of the markets, he was satisfied that his superiors would grasp the essential details and accept his thesis.

To a degree, he was at their mercy. Kopel, Levine, and possibly even Fedders, all would have to accept his recommendation to file charges against Milken and Drexel before any presentation was made to John Shad and the other SEC commissioners. Hewitt knew that if things got that far, and he brought his case to the table, the commissioners would evaluate his proposed lawsuit by an exacting standard: Could the SEC win in court, where it would have to persuade a judge or jury by a preponderance of the evidence that fraud had occurred? Rarely did SEC lawsuits actually go to trial, but the commission had to assume in each case that a trial would result. Though he didn't know for certain, Hewitt thought Milken would go to trial, fighting rather than settling any charges brought against him by the commission. Most SEC defendants opted for the easy way out, settling their cases without admitting or denying the allegations and agreeing not to commit similar wrongful acts in the future. In some cases a defendant might agree to make certain changes in his business operations. From the SEC's point of view, the advantage in settlement was that the agency wouldn't have to devote people and money to a lengthy court battle, where there were no guarantees of success. In a settlement, wrongdoing would be disclosed publicly, albeit in closely negotiated, carefully limited documents. The commission relied on publicity from settlements to deter wrongdoing on Wall Street. While suffering a certain amount of negative publicity on the day a settlement was announced, a defendant also benefited by avoiding the expense, uncertainty, and long-running public exposure of a trial. There was a convenient symbiosis between prosecution and defense that had grown up around SEC settlements, which made Hewitt's belief that Milken would fight in court all the more exceptional. Still, as he rewrote his memo, Hewitt was confident the commission would prevail if it took his case to court.

Hewitt had come to believe that Milken and Drexel were at the center of a massive fraud. At the beginning, Hewitt's investigation had focused on suspicious stock trading late in 1981 by Cincinnati-based American Financial Corporation and its chairman, Carl Lindner. Hewitt didn't know whether anyone at American Financial had knowledge of any scheme involving Milken. But, over the months, Hewitt had come to believe that clients of Milken's were mere appendages, customers for whom favors may have been done and who may have obliged when called upon by Milken, who was the master of a scheme.

Proving it was another thing. Market manipulation could be a difficult crime to establish in a court of law, Hewitt knew. If someone such as Milken were a big trader of stocks and bonds, and through his massive trading affected, or at times even dictated, prices, that might be a natural and lawful extension of his market prowess rather than illegal manipulation. Defendants in SEC manipulation cases generally didn't admit to criminal intent—they always had a rationale that ostensibly explained their trading and market activity. Such cases usually rested on circumstantial evidence—trading records, telephone records, and financial statements—rather than on direct testimony by a participant who admitted to fraud. Lacking any inside witnesses, often the commission lawyers had to guess at motive and intent, and the success of their cases depended in part on how plausible their guesses were. In this case Hewitt thought he could articulate a complex but undeniable motive.

It wasn't anything as simple as money. Usually in SEC cases that's all there was to it—greed. Hewitt had known one stockbroker involved in a securities trading scam who rushed out when it was completed and bought a white Rolls-Royce and a yacht. The defendant's conspicuous consumption weakened his case. With Milken, it was clear that he wanted to accumulate large amounts of wealth, Hewitt thought, but there had been no apparent change in life-style, no conspicuous consumption. The money might be a scorecard of sorts to chart Milken's progress, but Hewitt saw something else, something perhaps more intoxicating than dollars and cents to a man who was working sixteen to eighteen hours each day, building a new bond market that would alter fundamentally the course of American finance—power.

Controlling access to billions of dollars in capital and, in the process, creating whole new companies and even industries; being strong enough to dictate prices on your own terms; having clients and customers who do what you tell them and become extensions of your own ambition; deciding whether and when a huge corporate takeover would occur—these were the facets of Michael Milken's financial power that Hewitt both admired and resented. As he saw it, Milken had directed trading in certain stocks late in 1981 to manipulate their prices upward, partly so that he, under the terms of a special employment agreement with Drexel, would receive a bigger paycheck. And there was more, Hewitt thought. Through a complex scheme that involved the trading of shares of the Reliance insurance company headed by Saul Steinberg, Milken had rigged a corporate takeover by helping Steinberg buy his company's shares in a series of trades that involved secret accumulations of stock by certain Drexel clients and by other accounts Milken controlled, Hewitt concluded. He called it a "warehousing" scheme, since he believed Milken and his clients held the Reliance shares temporarily and had no real economic risk—they made secret arrangements to sell the shares later, if necessary, without suffering any financial loss. If Hewitt were right, these phony purchases violated securities laws. So sophisticated, in Hewitt's view, was the scheme that Milken could direct trades to assist one of his clients one day and then involve that client in trades helping Drexel or yet another client the next day. It wasn't a simple quid pro quo, where there were direct cash payoffs or bribes. It was more of the "You scratch my back, I'll scratch yours" variety, complex and insidious and effective, with Milken sitting at the helm deciding who would scratch whom and when.

The rapidly growing Drexel firm "appears to have a major supervision problem," Hewitt wrote in his revised memo. Moreover, secret buying and selling by Milken and his cadre violated certain SEC rules requiring disclosure of the purchase of securities, he charged. At the least, Hewitt figured, even if his superiors did not accept his market-manipulation theory, they would be willing to pursue a case pressuring Drexel to beef up its internal management supervision and fraud-detection procedures, which were handled by most Wall Street firms in a "compliance department." Wall Street firms like Drexel stood at the bottom of a totem pole of federal securities regulation, with the SEC on top and so-called self-regulatory organizations, like the New York Stock Exchange, in between. One of the actions the SEC could bring against a brokerage house such as Drexel was a "failure to supervise" proceeding, with potentially serious sanctions, though under the former brokerage executive Shad, the commission's approach to such cases was changing.

Late in October, Hewitt finished his thirty-three-page, single-spaced memo, and handed it back to Kopel and Levine. It had taken about two years' work to finish it—and this, Hewitt hoped, was just the beginning of a new phase.

What are we going to do with this? Levine asked Kopel when they had both read Hewitt's new memo. They both saw major problems with the case, not the least being that they did not believe Hewitt could prove his sweeping allegations of fraud in a court of law.

Kopel kept tinkering with the memo and talking with Levine.

He said he wanted to find a smaller piece of Hewitt's broad case to pursue. Kopel had only taken over the branch a few months earlier; Hewitt was one of his lawyers, and it was a general imperative of bureaucratic turf that it was better to hold on to what you had, not to let anything go, lest your authority be undermined. Kopel didn't want his first act as a branch chief to be one that took something away from him.

But Levine wasn't so sure. Back when the investigation began, Levine had favored a case focusing on Cincinnati's Carl Lindner. Hewitt had gone off on his own and he had come back, after questioning numerous witnesses and spending thousands of dollars on travel, with an enforcement memo focused on Milken and Drexel that wasn't strong enough to lead to immediate action against anyone, Levine said. Perhaps Lindner had committed some technical violations in his securities trading, but the enforcement staff would be embarrassed if it brought a narrow case like that to the commission after so much work. Enforcement would look like it was stretching, trying to bring *any* case to justify its work, and it would lose credibility with Shad and the other commissioners.

Moreover, in reviewing the transcripts of testimony that Hewitt had taken, Kopel, Levine, and others in the division saw major holes, and concluded that many of the subjects would have to be questioned again if the investigation were going to be pursued any further. Though he seemed to ask many of the right questions initially, Hewitt failed to ask the follow-up questions that Kopel perceived to be crucial—as in the time he had asked Milken about his relationship with stock speculator Ivan Boesky, but didn't press when he got no answer.

Hewitt was a competent lawyer, a solid litigator, but the truth was that the average SEC staff lawyer, even in its vaunted enforcement division, was no match for the three-hundred-dollar-an-hour litigator from the big Wall Street firm who typically defended the target of a commission investigation. That sort of mismatch often created problems in SEC investigations, and this one was no exception. Though he was assisted by a financial analyst from the SEC, Hewitt suffered because he was operating on his own without the direct involvement of a seasoned SEC enforcement lawyer. It wasn't necessarily a matter of talent; the most successful lawyers generally had decades of experience, whereas many of the enforcement division's staff attorney's were in the early stages of their careers. In his drive to recruit exceptional young lawyers to the SEC, enforcement chief Fedders was hiring a flock of associates from the most prestigious firms in Washington and New York. But when these former associates, many of them in their twenties and thirties, went into the field to conduct investigations, they were matched against the most senior partners of their old firms. Milken's lawyer, Thomas Curnin, for example, had been through deposition proceedings countless times before, and he knew how to control the flow of the interrogation. When Hewitt attempted to review complex trading records from Milken's Beverly Hills office, Curnin successfully held him at bay.

Hewitt's problems reflected a larger difficulty at the commission: There was simply no way for the SEC to match the legal and financial resources of the individuals and companies it was charged to police and investigate. This was true for many federal regulatory agencies, but at the commission the problem was especially acute. SEC investigations were often complicated and protracted, requiring a commitment of legal manpower that sometimes stretched over years. Moreover, the facts and issues involved in SEC cases were almost uniformly complex, requiring mastery of the law, finance, accounting, and the ability to interpret regulatory codes creatively in defense of one's position. Targets of SEC investigations, particularly those at large Wall Street firms or corporations, could afford to meet this challenge—they had the money both to sustain a defense for years and to hire the best legal minds in New York and Washington. The Manhattan and D.C. bars had developed a subindustry of legal specialists in SEC cases, experienced and frequently brilliant attorneys at large firms whose own work was backed by research and support from dozens of young associates who were from the country's best law schools. Because of its strong reputation, interesting work, and the kind of legal experience it offered, the SEC—especially in its enforcement division—was able to attract some bright young attorneys from the best schools. But these lawyers often worked without adequate secretarial or paralegal support, with little supervision from seasoned attorneys, and then, after they gained experience, they often left the commission for lucrative private practice, where they defended financiers and corporations against SEC probes. Division directors at the SEC often were excellent lawyers, capable of matching the skills of blue-chip private-sector partners, but below the directors, the ranks were uneven and frequently mediocre. Young lawyers might be talented but were inexperienced. Older SEC staff frequently hadn't displayed the abilities that would permit them to leave the commission for a lucrative job at a private firm. During the 1980s, the financial gap between attorneys at the SEC and their private-sector adversaries grew, aggravating the problem. A young attorney several years out of school could expect to earn more than $100,000 annually at one of Manhattan's best corporate law firms, while at the SEC, he or should would have to accept less than half of that.

The problems with the Milken investigation that fall were by no means all Hewitt's fault or the result of his being outmatched legally. There were other complications, including the fact that Milken operated out of Beverly Hills. A California court had ruled that autumn that the SEC was required to provide all the witnesses in its private investigations with extensive information about their status—whether or not they were potential targets of fraud charges, for example—as well as detailed information about the testimony of other witnesses. Though the ruling was later overturned in the Supreme Court, that fall it was creating major obstacles for anyone at the commission who contemplated pursuing an enforcement case with a California connection.

As associate director, one notch below Fedders, responsibility for the Milken probe lay with Levine, and the choices were clear. They could send HO-1395 up to the commissioners and recommend charges; they could send Hewitt and perhaps other attorneys back into the field to do more investigative work; or they could drop the matter altogether.

As they talked Levine and Kopel agreed first off about one thing: There was no sense passing Hewitt's memo upstairs to the commissioners. With enforcement chief Fedders shying away from long-shot litigation and Shad opposing any enforcement case that smacked of marginality, they would only be inviting trouble.

Enough time and money has been spent without conclusive results, Levine finally told Kopel. Let's bring this thing to a close.

The word was passed to Hewitt—a decision had been made to kill the case, although rather than shutting the file entirely, Hewitt's memo would be sent to the SEC's Los Angeles Regional Office, which was pursuing certain Drexel inquiries on its own. Some of Hewitt's superiors rationalized their decision by saying that since Hewitt's work had been sent to Los Angeles, it hadn't really been quashed. But they were willing to admit, too, that the chances anything would come of the L.A. Regional Office's work were slim. Perhaps it was only hubris, but many senior enforcement attorneys at SEC headquarters in Washington regarded the regional offices, with the exception of the New York regional branch, as poor stepchildren of the commission, unable to retain qualified lawyers or mount sophisticated prosecutions.

Hewitt was bitterly disappointed—not only did the investigation represent two years of his working life, he thought he had uncovered a major fraud in a powerful quarter of the financial markets. He understood that his proof wasn't perfect, but after all, much of the information that would be needed to establish the fraud incontrovertibly had been inaccessible because the subjects of the investigation, especially Milken, were so uncooperative. Shouldn't that reveal something to his superiors? Didn't it matter, even if they didn't accept his arguments about market manipulation, that the Drexel firm had a major supervision problem?

Hewitt understood that it was hard for Levine, Kopel, and the others to accept his theory that a single individual could dominate sectors of the financial markets the way Hewitt thought Milken was doing. But didn't it look suspicious that one man and his brother directed trading in scores of personal accounts, while at the same time trading on behalf of Drexel and clients?

While Hewitt didn't know it—one of the questions he had failed to ask Milken was an omission that hurt his ability to sell the case to his superiors—Drexel Burnham paid Michael Milken $45 million in salary and bonus in 1983, which came out to more than $123,000 per day if Milken worked 365 days that year. If Hewitt had known that one small fact, he might well have piqued the interest of Levine and Kopel enough to salvage his case. In Los Angeles the year before, Hewitt had asked Milken what, exactly, he did for a living, and it seemed to Hewitt that Milken evaded him elaborately. No wonder. How could a bond salesman justify to a government lawyer what he had done to deserve annual compensation greater than the revenues of all but the largest corporations in the country?

Perhaps the real question was whether the Securities and Exchange Commission, with its limited resources and limited talents, had the vision to pursue a complex enforcement case of that magnitude in 1983, especially one that did not fit neatly into the campaign against insider trading sponsored by John Fedders and Jack Shad.

The fact was that Jack Shad had come to admire Michael Milken. For one thing, there was an important friendship that linked their careers. And unlike Jack Hewitt, Shad thought he understood why Milken's innovations in the financial markets helped to explain Drexel's enormous profits.

On Wall Street, Shad had helped companies raise money through the traditional method of selling stocks and bonds to the public, subject to the SEC's regulations. The traditions and protocols of the business were well established, and in many cases, it wasn't that difficult a job. If a company already had shares of stock that were traded on the New York Stock Exchange or another major market, it was easy enough to convince investors to buy new shares, since the existence of a public-trading market gave them confidence that the stock could be readily convertible into cash at any time, simply by picking up the phone and placing a sell order with a broker. In Shad's vision, that sort of liquidity—the routine conversion of stock to cash—helped capital to wash through the economy to the dry patches where it was needed to create jobs. If a company had no stock already trading in the market, the sale of a new issue of shares was more difficult, but such "initial public offerings" were commonplace and usually easy to complete if the company was well-known and the price was right.

What was true of the stock market was also true of the bond market: During the decades Shad worked on Wall Street, the country's largest corporations had no difficulty selling bonds to the public. While stock represented an ownership interest in a company, and share prices fluctuated with the company's future earnings and growth prospects, bonds were more stable investments—they were borrowings that a company agreed to pay back at some future date. A bond investor typically held on to the securities and received periodic interest payments. The more risky the company, the higher the interest rate investors demanded on the bonds. Unlike stocks, publicly traded bonds were sold on the basis of a well-developed rating system. For years, at Hutton, Shad had used the services provided by the Moody's and Standard & Poor's rating services when evaluating bonds. These services rated bonds on the basis of the perceived risk of a default, with AAA (triple A) being the highest, or safest rating. Any bond blessed with a superior rating was called investment grade, and the rating was a key factor in determining a bond's interest rate. The existence of a liquid public-trading market for top bonds, in which the bonds could easily be converted to cash on demand, was at the heart of the system by which giant corporations borrowed money from investors.

If a young, growing company—a company too small or too new or too risky to receive an investment grade rating—wanted to borrow money from investors by selling bonds, it normally couldn't. There was no public bond market similar to the "initial public offering" market for stocks. Small companies, then, were forced to try their luck with the banks, which often would not provide them with as much cash as the companies wanted. The only other alternative was the so-called private-placement market, a kind of ad hoc market for risky debt, which was expensive and heavily regulated. The result was that some companies simply couldn't raise the capital they needed to grow—and when that happened, one of the things they often did was complain to their Wall Street investment banker. Shad heard such complaints from his stable of smaller clients at Hutton, a second-tier firm that had to compete ferociously for corporate-finance business. In the 1970s, Shad tried to help some companies to sell newly issued, riskier bonds to the public, but while he managed to complete a few deals, he found the whole enterprise exceedingly difficult. There just weren't enough investors willing to take chances on high-risk bonds. The attraction of the bonds Shad tried to market was their high interest rates—considerably higher than the interest paid by investment grade bonds. The problem was that no ready market existed if an investor wished to convert them to cash on the spur of the moment. The liquidity that Shad had seen as the raison d'être for stock index futures was lacking for these bonds; the market was dry.

Michael Milken had changed all that by the time Jack Hewitt wrapped up his fraud investigation in the summer of 1983. He had changed the world of finance irrevocably by creating a liquid, multibillion-dollar market for newly issued bonds that were shunned by the Wall Street bond-rating services. The bonds Milken traded became known as junk bonds, a term Drexel and Milken would unsuccessfully strive to replace with the friendlier "high-opportunity bonds" and later "high-yield bonds." While creating his market, Milken earned millions of dollars for Drexel by trading junk bonds and selling new junk issues for princely fees. One of his strategies was to sell more bonds to investors than a company actually needed to finance its economic growth. Then Milken would encourage the company, now a loyal and grateful client, to use its excess proceeds to buy a piece of his next junk bond offering. Thus many of Milken's clients became both issuers of, and investors in, junk bonds. The web of financial relationships that grew up around Milken, and his power at the center of things, had prompted Hewitt's suspicions that there was foul play at work. But Shad looked at the same picture and saw something else: liquidity, capital flowing freely to the very same kinds of companies Shad had tried but failed to assist during his years on Wall Street. In Shad's eyes, it was as if Milken had developed a new product, like the videocassette recorder, and profited first by being the inventor and then through salesmanship—Milken was the sort of innovator-implementer that a free market capitalist system was designed to motivate and reward. Drexel deserved to be profitable and Milken deserved to be rich, Shad thought.

Certainly, Milken felt no guilt about his immense wealth. The more he came to prominence and influence, the more he talked about his work as some grand mission of public service. He had long been fascinated by the market for riskier bonds, and had even bought and sold them as an undergraduate on the tumultuous Berkeley campus during the 1960s. Milken convinced some of his father's accounting clients to give him some money to manage on their behalf—the deal was that Milken would agree to absorb 100 percent of the losses if they would give him 50 percent of the gains. The terms of his arrangement gave Milken a strong incentive to be careful, but it pushed him to find an edge. At Berkeley he read a historical study that argued that investors who bought a diverse mix of riskier bonds with high interest rates tended to do better than those who bought the corporate bonds blessed by the Wall Street rating services. It was true that junk bonds had a slightly higher rate of default, but their exorbitant interest yields appeared to more than make up for the increased risk. Milken preached that the bond-rating system so revered for decades, with its reassuring lettered codes and strict gradations, was an economic anachronism. Investors clung to the rating system because it provided them with a false sense of security, reinforced by the institutional power of the biggest firms on the Street. But the emperor, Milken saw, was wearing no clothes. There was more money to be made by ignoring the bond ratings than by adhering to them.

It was Fred Joseph, whom Jack Shad hired out of the Harvard Business School and trained as one of his first recruits at E. F. Hutton, who helped to make Michael Milken into something more than just a wealthy bond trader. In the mid-1970s, Joseph joined Drexel in New York as an investment banker in charge of its corporate-finance department. Just as Shad had done years before at Hutton, Joseph directed Drexel's attempts to develop new business toward small and medium-sized companies, cognizant that he had little chance to snare giant, blue-chip corporate clients away from Wall Street's old-line investment firms like Salomon

Brothers, Morgan Stanley, and Goldman Sachs. Early on, Joseph stopped by the bond-trading floor to meet Milken, whom he had heard was making a lot of money for the firm, buying and selling junk bonds. Milken told Joseph the market was potentially enormous, and that if he had additional supply, he was confident he could sell more and more junk bonds.

Joseph and Milken became a tandem. Joseph identified the companies that needed capital, and Milken sold the junk bonds. Soon Milken became involved in all facets of the business, advising companies, trading, selling. He succeeded where others had failed, by guaranteeing investors that if they wanted to get rid of their "junk"—if they wanted to turn their bonds into liquid cash—Milken and Drexel would stand ready to buy them back. The fees for selling new junk bond issues were 3 or 4 percent, meaning Drexel made about $4 million for every $100 million in new bonds Milken sold. By tradition, Wall Street firms invited other houses to participate with them when they sold new issues, but over time, Milken did that less and less, believing that since he was the one who had developed the market, and the buyers, there was no need to play by the old rules. In every way, Milken bucked Wall Street tradition. And since only about 1,000 corporations in the country actually qualified for investment-grade ratings, the potential for issuing new junk bonds was huge. Meanwhile, insurance companies, savings and loans, wealthy individuals, specially designed junk bond mutual funds catering to individual investors—and even pension funds—flocked to Milken to buy the high-yielding bonds.

By 1983, the junk bond market had nearly doubled from about $20 billion in 1977 to $40 billion, largely because of Milken and Joseph. Shad watched them with respect and admiration from the commission's headquarters in Washington. In the age of Reagan, in a period of economic recovery and celebration of the country's self-imagined entrepreneurial culture, Milken symbolized all of what Shad believed was good and right in the financial markets. His troops in Beverly Hills were making liquid capital available to companies like MCI Communications, the long-distance upstart that raised $1 billion through Drexel in 1983 to fund its challenge to the establishment bulwark of the telephone business, AT&T. Officials at the Wall Street firms whose business was threatened by Milken's rise warned that he was adding billions of dollars in debt to the balance sheets of scores of companies, leaving them and the economy vulnerable to catastrophe during the next economic downturn. But that summer of 1983, there was no recession in sight, and when Jack Shad looked ahead, he seemed to see an auspicious horizon.

Late that year, Milken and Joseph hatched another golden plan. Drexel was making mountains of money in the junk bond market, more than any other Wall Street firm. But ever since the wild takeover fight between Bendix and Martin Marietta, Drexel's rivals on the Street had been reaping millions of dollars in fees by advising companies on corporate takeovers. Drexel was on the sidelines—it didn't have the big corporate clients involved in such deals. At a series of meetings in the Beverly Wilshire Hotel and next door in Milken's offices at the posh corner of Rodeo Drive and Wilshire Boulevard, the firm's top executives laid plans to transform the junk bond into a takeover warhead. During the prior year Drexel had sold some junk bonds to help finance friendly leveraged buyouts—corporate takeovers in which the management of a public company and other investors bought all the company's outstanding stock with borrowed money. Former Treasury Secretary William Simon had provided Milken and Joseph with a model. In 1982, Simon had purchased the Gibson Greeting Card Company from RCA Corporation with mostly borrowed money, and in 1983, he sold stock in Gibson to the public, making an apparent $70 million profit virtually overnight. In Beverly Hills, Milken, Joseph, and other Drexel executives decided to explore a similar plan: they would finance multibillion-dollar hostile corporate takeovers—raids by renegades on the bastions of the corporate establishment—by selling, or promising to sell, junk bonds.

It was an idea that would alter radically the corporate-takeover game and the nation's economy during the 1980s. And it would pose, too, the greatest challenge of all to John Shad's tenure as chairman of the Securities and Exchange Commission.

* * *

Through the double doors at 11 Wall Street they came, past the security checkpoint, into the attended elevator, through the hushed, carpeted hallways on the sixth floor, and finally into a majestic boardroom beneath high stained-glass ceilings. Shad had called them here, and when the meeting began, he sat in an emerald-colored chair before a colossal walnut table.

It was an informal tradition at the New York Stock Exchange that you had to be dead fifty years before they hung your portrait in the boardroom, which perhaps explains the sternness of the visages gazing down on the members of Shad's takeover advisory committee that morning in 1983. The portraits were of the stock exchange's founders and caretakers during the nineteenth and early twentieth centuries, men in frock coats and top hats, with pink skin and elaborate gray whiskers. Artifacts of the exchange's self-conscious history adorned the room. In one corner stood a gargantuan, solid-marble-and-sterling-silver urn, a gift of the Russian czar Nicholas II upon the successful sale of a bond issue to finance construction of the Siberian railway—a junk bond deal if ever there was one.

To some of the commission staff 250 miles away in Washington, the meeting that day symbolized the growing ties cultivated by Shad between Wall Street and the SEC. The tender-offer advisory committee had been formed under considerable political pressure from Capitol Hill, and amid disagreements within the commission, to recommend how the SEC should respond to the boom in wild corporate-takeover fights. The meeting had been convened in New York solely for the convenience of its members, who happened to include a number of Jack Shad's old friends from Wall Street. Joe Flom, who had attended the Aetna meeting, was there. Martin Lipton, the takeover lawyer whom Shad consulted before accepting the SEC chairmanship, was invited. There was Irwin Schneiderman, the attorney and friend who advised Shad about his hiring of John Fedders; and Bruce Wasserstein, the investment banker who had played a central role in the fight between Bendix and Martin Marietta.

Months earlier, when Shad announced the appointment of seventeen Wall Street takeover experts to a blue-ribbon SEC advisory committee on mergers, there had been those on the Hill and inside the commission bureaucracy who voiced resentment about Shad's decision to look outside the agency to Wall Street for advice. But to Shad it made perfect sense. Staff lawyers at the commission who had never traded a share of stock in their lives certainly didn't know what it was like to be in the middle of a hostile corporate-takeover fight, he thought. How could the staff possibly know what should be done? Shad had wanted to appoint professional experts to the committee, though after hearing of the views of key congressmen, he agreed to add an elder statesman, the sort of person who always showed up on Washington policy-making committees.

Arthur Goldberg, the liberal former Supreme Court justice, was a late addition. The committee had met previously, but the session at the New York Stock Exchange was Goldberg's first. When they asked him to make some introductory remarks early on, he said what few of them wanted to hear.

"The principal interest of the committee should be that of the public," he announced baldly. He added that takeovers had an increasingly bad reputation because of perceived manipulative and abusive practices and that the committee had to help the SEC "reassure the public that regulatory agencies are acting to prevent gross abuses."

"Thank you for your comments," said Dean LeBaron, the committee chairman, when Goldberg was through. LeBaron was the head of Batterymarch Financial Management, a Boston-based money-management firm that relied on computers and quantitative analysis to manage billions of dollars in pension-fund money and other assets, much of which was invested in stocks. Reflecting his bias toward the rights of stockholders, Shad had picked LeBaron as committee chairman. LeBaron directed the committee's attention to the day's detailed agenda, which included discussion of a host of proposals designed to modify complex laws and SEC rules governing takeovers. Throughout the hours of discussion that followed, the public wasn't mentioned again.

There were undeniable limits on what a group of financiers and takeover lawyers gathered in the august boardroom of the New York Stock Exchange was going to recommend about curbing corporate takeovers. The takeover game was making most of them wealthy beyond their wildest imaginings. There was much talk, as the discussion wound on, about protecting shareholders, which was the sector of the public whose interests Shad thought the commission should defend. But the bottom line was that experts like these were destined to find a way to keep the takeover game going by balancing the interests of bidders and targets, to permit an unlimited number of takeover fights.

Gregg Jarrell, the Chicago School economist and academic who was a member of the advisory committee, watched his colleagues that day and thought he saw another purpose in their work—while preserving a level playing field that would encourage takeovers, Shad's friends from Wall Street wanted to create just enough regulatory delays during the battles to enhance the market for legal and financial advice. In the committee's work Jarrell thought he saw Wall Street using Washington to create a demand for its services. To do it, it seemed to Jarrell, they were willing to adopt the language and protocols of public servants, and to push for complex regulations, even though at heart their economic views were as radically conservative as any economist's at the University of Chicago. "When they got together in this committee setting [with the] audience and the big chairs, they wanted to sound like concerned policymakers," Jarrell said afterward. "What you had were a bunch of diehard capitalists apologizing for making $4 million the previous month. . . . It was a strange thing to watch." Underlying the committee's position was the Williams Act, the 1968 law which called for a balance between bidders and targets in takeovers.

When it was over, the SEC advisory committee approved an enormous document of commentary and advice that was remarkable for what it did not do. Shad's experts declared that they had no opinion on whether takeovers were good or bad for America.

"On the strength of the evidence presented, the committee does not believe there is sufficient basis for determining that takeovers are, per se, either beneficial or detrimental to the economy or to the securities markets in general, or to issuers or their shareholders, specifically. . . . The purpose of the [Securities and Exchange Commission's] regulatory scheme should be neither to promote nor to deter takeovers; such transactions and related activities are a valid method of capital allocation, so long as they are conducted in accordance with the laws deemed necessary to protect the interests of shareholders and the integrity and efficiency of the capital markets," the committee's final report said. Later, when the hefty document was transmitted to Congress, the committee went further: "Takeovers . . . should be allowed to take place. For this reason, the committee does not believe the government should act to encourage or to discourage or to evaluate the merits of takeovers."

Thus was born an essentially amoral school of economic ideology about takeovers, articulated by some of the most influential financiers on Wall Street, and protected by the political and financial power of the Street's institutions. Its central doctrine was the notion that it was not possible to know what was right or wrong, whether takeovers were good or bad.

Still, the committee recommended dozens of detailed regulations aimed at balancing offensive and defensive interests in a takeover fight. That approach outraged Chicago School economists like Jarrell, who wanted to push Shad toward policies in which the commission would retreat from regulation, not adopt new rules. And partly from his conversations with key commission staff close to Shad, Jarrell understood the buzz words favored by the SEC chairman. In a strong dissent, Jarrell and a Chicago School colleague played explicitly to Shad's campaign within the commission to focus less on legal reasoning and more on economics and cost-benefit analysis. "The most striking thing about the advisory committee's report is that the committee offers no explanation of tender offers, no treatment of costs and benefits, indeed, not even a definition of 'abuse,' which is the cornerstone of the recommendations for 'reform.' How can we identify, let alone rectify, 'abuses' without some idea about why [takeovers] exist, what costs and benefits are associated with them, and what effect our 'reforms' would have on the number of offers. . . . The best of all worlds is the termination of federal regulations."

As senior SEC staff read this dissent that fall many of them recognized that Jarrell's arguments would appeal naturally to Shad. The question was whether or not the SEC chairman—and his commission—would go along.

9

Naked Options

T. Boone Pickens, Jr., looked out at the sea of Texas rich and Republican faithful gathered before him. The scene was redolent with diamonds and designer dresses, wildcatters and wine.

"I hear Ringling Brothers is thinking of buying Cities Service," Pickens said into the microphone, referring to the staid, giant oil company against which he had launched a hostile takeover bid a few weeks earlier. "They want to get the clowns that are running that company."

President Ronald Reagan chuckled at the dais; a ripple of laughter fanned across the cavernous Albert Thomas Convention Center in downtown Houston. It was a June evening in the midst of the president's triumphant first term. Reagan had flown to Texas to spur on the conservative political movement then sweeping what formerly had been Democratic bastions in the South. The Reagan ethos—entrepreneurialism, Chicago School economic and social theory, a misty optimism about the American people—was taking hold nowhere more than in Texas, battered though the state's economy was by a sharp fall in oil prices. For his part, Boone Pickens, who was the evening's master of ceremonies, considered himself a standard-bearer of the Reagan way. The hostile takeovers he pioneered would shake up the musty, entrenched corporate establishment centered on the East Coast, he said, creating wealth and opportunity and growth for the nation. Reagan, by his laughter, seemed "in sync" if not in agreement.

Superlatives swirled from the podium. The political fund-raising dinner that evening would add a record $3.5 million to the reelection coffers of Texas Governor Bill Clements, it had been announced. This was a triumph shared by Pickens, who was rapidly becoming the best-known corporate raider in the country, as well as one of the most successful money men in the Republican Party. Moreover, if his $5 billion chase for reluctant Cities Service Company succeeded, Pickens would have pulled off the third-largest corporate takeover in history. Cities Service, the country's nineteenth largest oil company, was roughly six times the size of Pickens's Mesa Petroleum; an oil man for three decades, Pickens liked to think big.

Yet the truth was that despite his glibness and the glamour all around him, Pickens felt uneasy. Mesa Petroleum was under attack that night because of the battle he had initiated with Cities Service. As a tactical defense against Pickens's $50-per-share take-over offer, Cities Service had launched a retaliatory $21-per-share takeover bid for Mesa—a version of the controversial "Pac-Man" defense that stirred Shad to form the SEC's takeover advisory committee. (The committee of Wall Street specialists recommended to Shad that Pac-Man defenses be permitted by the SEC.) There was a chance that Pickens's company could be swallowed whole before Mesa's takeover offer for Cities Service succeeded. Pickens was anxious to fly, in his private jet, to New York, where his team of advisers—led by the ubiquitous takeover attorney Joe Flom—was plotting to save Mesa and defeat "the clowns" at Cities Service.

That same June day, from a sawmill in the small Midwestern town of Neopit, Wisconsin, a thirty-five-year-old accountant named Wayne Knauf telephoned his stockbroker at Smith Barney, the giant Wall Street brokerage house that had branch offices all across the country.

"What looks good for the next series?" Knauf asked his broker. Knauf had a copy of the *Wall Street Journal*. He had scanned the tables in the back of the newspaper that listed the prices of stock options.

"Can't find anything good," said his broker, R. Dennis Herrmann, known to his customers as Denny.

"I can't find anything good," Knauf agreed.

"Well, you know, gees, this Cities Service is at an eighth and that's three days," Herrmann said. "You put on forty of those at an eighth, that's five hundred bucks for three days."

The Smith Barney broker was talking about the riskiest type of stock options trading: naked option writing. They called it naked because if you did it, you were exposed theoretically for everything you had, down to the shirt on your back. Herrmann was pointing out to Knauf that the options were priced in such a way that he could earn $500 in just three days if he "wrote," or sold, 40 options on Cities Service stock. (Each option would obligate Knauf to sell 100 shares of Cities Service stock at current prices, though it seemed unlikely that anyone would demand such a sale of 4,000 shares—40 options contracts times 100 shares per contract—unless the price moved sharply. For each option contract he sold at the prevailing price of one-eighth, Knauf expected to receive about twelve cents. The $500 he hoped to make was the product of multiplying twelve cents per share times 4,000 shares.) Knauf's trade was a gamble on Boone Pickens's takeover fight with Cities Service, similar in many ways to a bet on a horse race. Afterward, it wasn't clear whether Knauf understood it that way or not.

"Five hundred for three days—that doesn't sound too bad," Knauf answered.

He had made that sort of decision countless times in the last several years, and it came easily now. A whole group wrote naked options up at the Rhinelander, Wisconsin, office of Smith Barney, which was located above the drug store and just down from the coffee shop along the town's main thoroughfare. There was Larry Graf, the unemployed heir to a modest Milwaukee soda pop fortune, Larry's unemployed girlfriend Judith Bergquist, "Doctor Tom" the dentist, and David Kuenzli, an expressive, theatrical man who was unemployed, divorced, and living with his mother.

Helping to bind this odd lot together were Denny Herrmann, the broker, and Wayne Knauf, the accountant, whose offices were across the hall from one another and who rendered professional services to the entire group. Over the years, Knauf had referred about twenty of his accounting clients to Herrmann, and Herrmann had referred a similar number of his brokerage customers to Knauf.

Rhinelander—which had a population of about 8,000—and surrounding towns like Neopit were isolated in northern Wisconsin's lake wilderness, nearly two hours' drive from Green Bay and twice that from Milwaukee. There were a few prosperous lake resorts nearby, but mainly the area's economy depended on the fortunes of a local paper company, which was in sharp decline. The nascent Reagan years had been rough for many in Rhinelander; unemployment was up, hopes were dampened. But the downtrodden did not include Denny Herrmann, Wayne Knauf, or the dozen or so others who had discovered the wonders of naked options. Larry Graf, the unemployed soda pop heir, earned $66,500 in 1980 and $81,000 in 1981 writing naked options. Herrmann didn't write naked options for his own account, but he brought in handsome brokerage fees for assisting and encouraging the others. Herrmann earned about $120,000 in each of 1981 and 1982, a fortune by the standards of a small town like Rhinelander. And as Herrmann prospered, so did Smith Barney, which took in hundreds of thousands of dollars in commission revenue from the Rhinelander group.

Smith Barney advertised on television that it made money "the old-fashioned way," by earning it. But the group that gathered most mornings above the drugstore had discovered that writing naked options did not require perspicacity, patience, or experience. It was a way to try to get rich quick. Herrmann's success was evident most days in the odd scene around his desk at Smith Barney. There, his customers clustered in twos and threes, punching up options prices on the office computer and chatting about the market or the Green Bay Packers or the latest gossip from the coffee shop. Larry Graf had a learning disability and gave the appearance of a mild mental retardation, and yet he was perhaps the most active trader of them all.* Knauf would come over most mornings, carrying his *Wall Street Journal* and scribbling the results of his carefully planned "system" for naked options writing. Knauf directed some trading for his accounting clients, as did Denny Herrmann on behalf of Larry Graf. The group had grown with dizzying speed. "Doctor Tom" Butler's decision to join was typical. As Knauf recalled later, "I had some dental work done, and I told Doctor Tom what I had been doing in my own particular account, basically writing naked options and just been doing super . . . And [Doctor Tom] said, 'Maybe I'll do that.' I don't know if he really understood anything."

He understood this much: Stock options were dirt cheap. As with the new stock futures whose trading in Chicago Jack Shad had helped to unleash, an investor in stock options could get a big bang for his buck. (Like stock futures, stock options required only a small down payment; one of the only important differences between a stock option and a stock future was that most options were linked to stocks of individual companies, such as IBM or AT&T or Exxon, while futures were linked to broad measures of the stock market such as the S&P 500 average. Also, because of Shad's deal at the Monocle, options were regulated by the SEC, while futures were regulated by the Commodity Futures Trading Commission.) Some stock options cost less than twenty-five cents a share. Without putting up much cash, a buyer or seller of options could speculate in a big way on the future price of individual stocks.

* In a subsequent court proceeding, Graf was questioned about his education, and he acknowledged that he had sought special assistance for his learning disability. This exchange occurred during the examination:
Q. You do know how to read?
A. Very slowly.
Q. Do you ever read books?
A. No.
Q. Do you ever read magazines?
A. Not really.
Q. Do you ever read the newspaper?
A. Occasionally.
Q. What newspaper do you read occasionally?
A. Occasionally I look at the *Wall Street Journal*.

For example, on the day Boone Pickens appeared on the dais in Houston with President Reagan—the same day Wayne Knauf called Denny Herrmann from a sawmill in Neopit, Wisconsin— the price of oil giant Cities Service stock closed at $36.50 a share on the New York Stock Exchange. But the options Wayne Knauf "wrote," or sold, by telephone—called Cities-Service-45 options— were priced at only about twelve cents per share. They were cheap partly because the options were due to expire in three days, at which point they could become totally worthless. The other reason had to do with the number "45" in the option's title. A Cities Service–45 option provided the owner with the right to buy a hundred shares of Cities Service stock at $45 per share anytime before its expiration date, in this case three days away. Since Cities Service was trading at just $36.50, that meant its price had to rise by more than $10 in a very short time or the options would expire worthless. The options cost just twelve cents that June day because people in the options market figured that the likelihood of Cities Service stock rising from $36.50 to more than $45 per share in just three days was remote.

Wayne Knauf and the others in Rhinelander figured the same thing, and that's why they were willing to sell Cities Service options. The twelve cents per share Knauf would receive as the seller seemed, on the surface, virtually a sure thing. He and the others had been doing this for years. If they sold cheap options just before they were set to expire, the chance of a sudden explosion in the stock's underlying price was very small. That might have been true for the group's trades in the past, but selling naked options on a stock that was a takeover target was incredibly risky due to the possibility that a takeover bid could send the stock price shooting up at any moment. While Knauf was only at risk if the price of Cities Service stock skyrocketed above $45 within three days, if that happened Knauf's exposure was theoretically unlimited. If the stock rose to $95 per share, for example, he would be liable for the $50 difference between the $45 option price and the $95 market price—in his case, $50 per share times 4,000 shares, or $200,000. If the stock price went higher, so would Knauf's liability.

Such a catastrophe had never befallen Knauf, Graf, Kuenzli, or the others who met in the Rhinelander office of Smith Barney. Never, that is, until Boone Pickens came along.

Two days after his appearance with President Reagan in Houston, Boone Pickens sat with a band of his advisers in the dimly lit recesses of the famous 21 Club in midtown Manhattan. Empty bottles of wine cluttered the table. The restaurant was popular with the pretentious Wall Street investment bankers and corporate executives whom Pickens claimed to deplore, yet it was one of the Texas raider's favorite New York watering holes. In contrast to the bonhomie Pickens usually displayed to the restaurant's maitre d' and black-tied waiters, the mood at his table that evening was subdued. The battle for Cities Service was over, and all the alcohol was meant to soothe what for Pickens had been a disappointing, though far from unprofitable, outcome.

A white knight had arrived that afternoon at 1:00 P.M. to rescue Cities Service from Pickens's clutches. From its Tulsa, Oklahoma, headquarters, Cities Service had announced that following two days of intense and secret negotiations, it had agreed to a friendly merger with Gulf Oil Corporation for $63 a share. In trading at the New York Stock Exchange, the price of Cities Service stock skyrocketed above $60. Pickens had been defeated, but he wouldn't go back to Texas empty-handed. Partnerships he controlled owned about four million Cities Service shares, bought for an average of about $45 per share. Even after his expenses, Pickens would pocket a sizable profit from his failed takeover bid.

Still, in the burgeoning culture of takeovers on Wall Street, winning sometimes mattered as much as money, and the competitive Pickens hadn't gotten what he said he wanted. As they drank that night Pickens and his advisers comforted themselves by noting that while they hadn't won control of Cities Service, they had at least altered the company's destiny by forcing it into Gulf Oil's arms. And they had come out of nowhere, using very little of their own cash to do it.

"We put a $5 billion deal in play with no money," said Robert Stillwell, one of Pickens's lawyers.

Surely they could be proud of that.

That same Thursday afternoon, a Western Union telegram from Smith Barney was delivered deep in the peninsula wilderness to soda pop heir Larry Graf's home in Ironwood, Michigan, about forty miles from Rhinelander.

DUE TO THE PROPOSED TENDER OFFER BY GULF OIL TO PURCHASE SHARES OF CITIES SERVICE AT $63 PER SHARE. . . . IT IS NECESSARY THAT YOU REMIT A CHECK IN THE AMOUNT OF $1,233,500.00 BY 12 P.M. NEW YORK TIME . . . OR WE WILL BE COMPELLED TO LIQUIDATE SUFFICIENT SECURITIES FOR YOUR ACCOUNT.

David Kuenzli burst into the Smith Barney office above the Rhinelander drugstore.

Something is very wrong here, Kuenzli angrily said.

That much was obvious to the rest of the group. They had lost more than a million dollars among them in just two days, far more than their combined net worth. All of their trading accounts had been liquidated by Smith Barney to cover the losses, and still, they were hundreds of thousands of dollars in debt.

This smells like a conspiracy, Kuenzli continued. The timing of Gulf Oil's takeover bid for Cities Service looks suspicious. Was it merely a coincidence that the merger was announced two days before the June options they sold were due to expire?

Kuenzli thought not. There had been considerable trading in Cities Service stock and options on Wednesday, the day before Gulf's announcement. Kuenzli thought he detected insider trading. And his theory went further. Somebody, maybe Gulf, maybe Cities Service, maybe some big stock traders on Wall Street, deliberately timed the merger announcement to wreak havoc on the options markets and allow some crooked traders to escape with huge profits—profits made at the Rhinelander group's expense. The logic of his theory was difficult to accept, but the argument was strongly felt.

Who could stop this conspiracy? Kuenzli demanded of Denny Herrmann, the Smith Barney broker who had helped to get them into this mess. But he didn't wait for an answer—he already knew. He went to a typewriter and began to peck out a letter.

He typed the address: The Securities and Exchange Commission, Washington, D.C.

"We are writing . . . in the direst hope that you will be able to intercede to straighten out this terrible affair," Kuenzli began. He recounted the publicly reported news events of the last several days, ascribing to them a variety of sinister meanings. "The final manipulation was to keep you out of this affair, and it was done via the adjustment of the entire timing to conclude coincident with the expiration of the June options, and hence via that the simple fact that the whole affair would be completed on a Friday afternoon. You would be supposed to, at best, belatedly realize that there was not time to act on the same day, and by Monday the natural psychological buffer of the weekend would place this event beyond reclamation. . . . The lives of trusting, decent men are being ruined by this. Please, if you can, would you straighten this matter out."

There is no time to waste, Kuenzli declared when he was finished.

He urged Denny Herrmann to join him in signing the letter. Herrmann was reluctant, but he was in a difficult spot. Others besides Kuenzli in the naked-option-writing group were angry, but they were focusing their anger not on an imagined Wall Street conspiracy, but on Herrmann and Smith Barney for failing to anticipate and stop the fiasco. Kuenzli's theories, however bizarre they might seem to Herrmann, were in some ways preferable to having the blame focused on him. In any event, Herrmann signed the letter.

The SEC had to act immediately, Kuenzli continued, once Herrmann had agreed to sign. The mails were not fast enough. Kuenzli announced that he was going to fly to Washington that weekend and deliver his letter by hand at the commission's headquarters. While he was in the capital, he would see his congressman as well. Herrmann was a little incredulous at this proposal—he wasn't sure where it would lead—but he couldn't talk Kuenzli out of it.

On Monday, David Kuenzli arrived at the new SEC building on Fifth Street in northwest Washington, just down from the city's imposing courthouse on Indiana Avenue. The lobby was cool and spacious and formal, with a buffed stone floor and walls of poured concrete. Walk-in complainers at the SEC were not unheard of, and they ordinarily received courteous but perfunctory treatment. Kuenzli made an impression. One SEC official recalled that after demanding an audience with a commission attorney, Kuenzli trembled and began to cry. In any event, he was granted a personal audience with an enforcement division lawyer upstairs. He told the lawyer all about his conspiracy theory. And he described, too, the group of investors who had been gathering for several years in the Rhinelander office of Smith Barney to write naked stock options.

Few inside the SEC thought of it this way, but the story David Kuenzli outlined that day was in some respects a disaster of the commission's own creation. Stock options, like stock futures, had for years been a source of controversy and debate inside the SEC. But in contrast to the debate over futures, in which policy makers tended to focus on sweeping economic issues like liquidity and speculation, the disagreements over stock options centered in large part on whether they were good or bad for ordinary investors like the group in Rhinelander, Wisconsin. And in the end, the SEC had decided that the benefits of options for individual investors outweighed their risks.

The "individual investor" had always been a kind of abstract icon inside the SEC, akin in the pantheon of political mythology to the "mom and pop" small businessperson, or the "man on the street" in every congressional district. On Capitol Hill and in speeches across the country, SEC officials routinely paid lip service to protecting the individual investor from fraud and from unfair trading practices on Wall Street. The commission's public concern about individual investors dated back to the 1920s, when millions of naïve and newly rich middle-class investors had poured their money into stocks, only to be burned by the outlandish manipulations of Wall Street insiders and by the 1929 crash. When the SEC was founded, it was seen not only as an institution that would root out crooks from the corner of Broad and Wall streets, in lower Manhattan, but also as one that would ensure that ordinary, middle-class investors would never again face such abuse. It was the middle class's hard-earned money, after all, that fueled the country's economic growth, and thus it was essential that the "individual investors" have faith in the integrity of the financial markets. The federal paternalism inherent in the SEC's charter irked some conservatives, but during the great rush of the New Deal, when the commission was created, there was a broad consensus in Washington that extensive regulation was necessary to restore fairness to the markets and to protect the quality of life for the middle class and, to a lesser degree, the working class as well.

By the time Jack Shad arrived in Washington in 1981, the commission's public devotion to protecting individual investors had congealed into a cliché, a piece of conventional wisdom so soft and malleable that it was used to justify sharply divergent positions on economic issues. Partly the problem was that the economic world of the 1920s no longer existed. The country's middle class still invested as individuals in stocks and bonds, but their role in the financial markets was overshadowed by the huge institutional investors that had come to prominence during the 1960s. The money controlled by these big institutions—pension funds, university endowments, insurance companies, and bank trust departments—dwarfed the money controlled by individuals. Institutional money usually belonged in one form or another to the middle and working classes, as was the case with pension funds and stock mutual funds, but it was no longer managed by individuals. Instead it was controlled by big money managers on Wall Street who had the expertise and economic clout to profit from stock and bond trading. Thus it could be argued that protecting individual investors now required defending the interests of the large institutions that managed their money. Inside the SEC, though, the image persisted of the individual investor as a hard-working, middle-class homeowner who lived somewhere on the great plains of the Midwest with 2.4 children and a garage for his car. The image wasn't entirely false: millions of such investors did exist. David Kuenzli and the group of naked options writers in Rhinelander, Wisconsin, were evidence of that.

But what was the commission supposed to do about David Kuenzli and his friends? Risky options trading of the kind carried on in Rhinelander was sanctioned by the SEC, with certain restrictions concerning the "suitability" of individual investors to participate. Because of their leverage—the bang-for-the-buck they offered—stock options had become popular during the 1970s. Regulation was lax, however, and a widespread scandal in the options markets led the SEC to impose a moratorium on some options trading during Jimmy Carter's presidency. After a lengthy study, and over the objection of those who thought options were too speculative, the SEC decided finally that the "liquidity and efficiency" options promoted were fundamentally good for the nation's financial markets, and that public trading and the introduction of new stock options should be allowed. But to prevent repetition of scandal and to protect individual investors from risks they didn't understand, the commission adopted strict standards whereby Wall Street brokerage firms were required to supervise closely the riskiest trading strategies of their customers. In its 1978 options study, the SEC said that customers should be made aware "on an on-going basis of the risks of any and all options transactions undertaken. . . . A brokerage firm should not be permitted to recommend any options transaction to a customer unless the firm reasonably believes the customer is capable of both evaluating the risks and bearing the financial burden of those risks."

With ambiguous, legalistic phrases such as "reasonably believes," the SEC left plenty of room for debate about what exactly a stockbroker was supposed to do when his customers, inspired by illness or misjudgment or merely the speculative fever of the times, wished to take enormous risks by writing naked options. By authorizing the growth of public options markets, the SEC had tacitly blessed the sort of trading carried out by the Rhinelander group. Yet the commission insisted that brokerage firms be sure that their customers knew what they were doing, even though the firms' reason for being was to make money by encouraging, rather than discouraging, trading. It was in some ways like asking a casino to judge whether one old man at a slot machine, as opposed to another, was fully apprised of the risks of gambling and could afford to lose a bucketful of quarters. Without strict government supervision, could a Wall Street brokerage really be expected to fulfill such a paternalistic responsibility?

The story David Kuenzli told that day at SEC headquarters was a case in point. Had Kuenzli known what he was doing when he sold naked Cities Service stock options? What about Larry Graf, the unemployed soda-pop heir with a learning disability? Whoever was responsible for the idea, selling naked options on the stock of a company involved in a public takeover fight was foolish almost beyond comprehension. The basic risk in writing naked options was that some unexpected event would cause the stock of the company in question to rise dramatically and suddenly in price. The event most likely to have such an effect was a takeover. While writing naked options, it was impossible to completely eliminate the risk of an unexpected takeover announcement that might send the price of a target company's stock soaring. Yet the risk could be reduced substantially by avoiding companies that were being stalked publicly by Boone Pickens, or whose managements were being referred to as "clowns" to the amusement of the president of the United States. When the Rhinelander group wrote options on Cities Service stock, the company was already in receipt of a $50-per-share takeover offer and was fighting for its life against Pickens. It wasn't clear to investigators from the commission who in the Rhinelander group had been aware that Cities Service was in the midst of a takeover fight. Details of the battle were chronicled almost daily in the *Wall Street Journal*, which several of the group professed to read. It was plausible, although hard to believe, that none of them understood what might happen.

Denny Herrmann sat bundled in his overcoat. The lawyers were all around him. They had been crawling all over him for months now, or so it felt to Herrmann. He had never been through anything like it in his life. And now, the week before Christmas, 1983, the SEC attorneys had summoned him to an interrogation in this ugly federal building in downtown Milwaukee, where the heat didn't work, where the walls seemed gray and forbidding. The deposition was supposed to last for days, and Herrmann wasn't sure that he could make it.

"All these accounts had a strategy in common," he wanted them to understand. "They felt they'd really found the golden goose. . . . I felt I had warned these people time and time again."

During a preliminary interrogation in August, SEC attorney Susan Pecaro had asked him how he knew when it was all right for a particular customer to write naked options. Herrmann replied: "Well, to answer that question without trying to make this sound silly, it would be like how does a father know the first time his daughter can stay out to midnight?"

This was Herrmann's defense: His clients were old enough and mature enough to gamble with their life's savings.

Now Susan Pecaro bore in at him from across the conference table. Herrmann understood that she was not impressed. Young and relentless, Pecaro was the enforcement division attorney who had been running the SEC's confidential investigation of Herrmann and Smith Barney, captioned in the commission's files as HO-1480, "Trading in the Securities of Cities Service Co." The probe had begun the day David Kuenzli presented himself in the lobby of the SEC's Washington headquarters. Pecaro had interviewed most of the members of Denny Herrmann's options trading group, subpoenaed records, and interrogated his superiors at Smith Barney headquarters in New York. Herrmann felt pressure from all sides. Wisconsin state-securities regulators had initiated proceedings against him, saying that Herrmann had failed to supervise properly the naked options writing of the Rhinelander group, that he had doctored options-trading application forms, and that he had failed to follow Smith Barney's internal rules. And Smith Barney wasn't happy with Herrmann, either. After initially expressing support at a breakfast meeting in Rhinelander just after the Cities Service takeover was announced, Smith Barney executives had begun to keep their distance from him, it seemed to Herrmann. For one thing, they were furious about his decision to sign Kuenzli's protest letter to the SEC. It had only prompted the commission to initiate an investigation of Smith Barney.

Pecaro and her superiors in the enforcement division thought it was clear that Herrmann and Smith Barney had violated the securities laws. The SEC rules about options trading admittedly were vague, especially the standard that required a brokerage firm to refrain from recommending options trades "unless the

firm reasonably believes that the customer is capable of both evaluating the risks and bearing the financial burden of those risks."
Such a rule could only be enforced on a case-by-case basis, with
the discretion of a prosecutor. But in the months since Kuenzli's
flight to Washington, Pecaro and her colleagues had ferreted out
evidence that Smith Barney and its employees had grossly ig-
nored the SEC rules. Documents subpoenaed from Smith Barney
showed, for example, that the brokerage's executives in New York
had been warned repeatedly about the impending calamity in
Rhinelander, yet had failed to respond.

Denny Herrmann's boss, Robert Heck, who was the Rhine-
lander-branch supervisor, was required each month to report to
Smith Barney's lawyers at its Wall Street headquarters on the state
of his office. Pecaro discovered that in the six months leading up
to the Cities Service takeover announcement, Heck had reported
clearly and repeatedly that the naked-options-writing group assembled under the eye of Denny Herrmann was headed for serious trouble.

"Compliance Department has been advised repeatedly re: the
tremendous option activity in various clients accounts," Heck had
written six months before the Cities Service calamity. "New York
should also continue to assist in monitoring option activity," he
wrote again three months later. He wrote the same thing in his
next report. The following month, in a final act of prophecy,
Heck warned: "Continue to be concerned about large naked positions re: option activity."

The Smith Barney lawyer responsible for the firm's compliance
with the SEC rules never saw Heck's reports, Pecaro learned. The
clerk at Smith Barney's Wall Street headquarters who received the
monthly reports filed them away in a drawer; they were never
circulated to either the compliance or general counsel's offices, as
the brokerage's procedures required. Pecaro and some of her
colleagues in the enforcement division regarded this as an egregious failure—and clear evidence that Smith Barney, as well as
Herrmann and Heck, should be publicly charged with securities-
law violations. They were preparing, that December of 1983, to
mount a securities-fraud case against all of them.

Denny Herrmann told Susan Pecaro that day in the frigid Milwaukee conference room that she was wrong. Herrmann was a savvy, articulate, sometimes defiant, man, and for a while during the interrogation he was able to project an air of confidence. He was a gambler who spent Thursday nights playing poker at Rhinelander's country club, a weekly game where the loser might drop two or three hundred dollars. He had grown up in Des Moines, Iowa, and spent most of his life in Wisconsin, so he had become accustomed to the leisurely pace of the rural Midwest, but Herrmann also fancied himself a tough man, a realist, especially about money.

He considered the SEC's investigation of him essentially unjustified. Sure, Herrmann conceded, he might have broken a few rules, but his customers all knew what they were doing—they talked together about their gambling in options nearly every day of the week. The way Herrmann figured it, there was nothing wrong with making a bet, whether on a poker hand or the stock market or the outcome of a corporate takeover, so long as you were prepared to pay up if you lost. Herrmann claimed he always paid his bets out at the country club and didn't grumble about it. In the time since Kuenzli had started the whole affair, some of those who had been writing naked options in the Rhinelander office had settled their accounts without much complaint. The accountant Wayne Knauf, for example, readily acknowledged that he knew the risks he was taking by selling Cities Service options, and though he didn't have enough money to pay the huge debt he owed Smith Barney, he had agreed to pay off his losses on an installment plan. The others—including Graf and Kuenzli—had merely been dealt a bad hand in the options market, and now they were trying to make a federal case out of it, Herrmann said.

Susan Pecaro showed him a document. It was the application Larry Graf had filled out at the Rhinelander office when he first began to trade stock options. As part of its compliance with SEC "customer suitability" rules, Smith Barney required an investor who wanted to trade options to disclose detailed information about his finances and sources of income. Graf was described on the form as "self-employed," with a net worth of $350,000 and an income of $75,000 annually—both numbers were exaggerations.

Other application forms from Herrmann's customers contained similar misstatements, and some of the forms had been filled out in Herrmann's handwriting.

Herrmann said he had tried to check the information provided by his customers, that he hadn't deliberately invented or exaggerated any information about them.

Pecaro opened a fat legal book and began to read aloud from sections of the U.S. criminal code concerning forgery.

Herrmann's head began to whirl. Every question seemed to challenge him. He had a lawyer with him from a big Milwaukee firm retained by Smith Barney, but Herrmann thought the attorney might be more interested in protecting the brokerage firm that paid his bills than in defending one of its stockbrokers.

At one point, while explaining the long history of his own trading in stock options, Herrmann said that he had mostly "sold options short" in the months before his customers lost their life savings in the Cities Service takeover. By selling short, Herrmann was betting that stock prices would go down. One of the SEC lawyers pounced on him.

"You mean, you were shorting options prior to the bull market?" the lawyer asked incredulously.

"That's ridiculous," he practically shouted in reply. "What—am I supposed to be able to predict a bull market?"

Afterward, Herrmann recalled the exchange vividly—he regarded it as one of his few triumphs during the days of interrogation. Increasingly, he felt the pressure mount on him. On the last day, at about three-thirty or four in the afternoon, he felt that he had reached his breaking point. He was agitated, exhausted. All of what Herrmann had built for himself in Rhinelander—the six-figure income, his second marriage and children, the Thursday poker game at the golf club—appeared to be in jeopardy. He seriously believed that he was about to have a breakdown. And it seemed to Herrmann, finally, that Susan Pecaro saw how he felt, and that she relented.

"I guess we've done enough," Pecaro told him, and she began to gather her papers.

That evening the SEC lawyers returned to Washington for the

holidays. It was nine months before Herrmann heard from them again. There was no answer, no resolution—everything was left hanging.

So Herrmann went about his business in Rhinelander, reporting to the office each day, advising his customers on stock and bond and option trades.

Back in the capital, Jack Shad would soon embark on a surprising mission that would put him at odds with the White House on the most pressing financial issue of the day.

10

The Leveraging
of America

John Shad called the commission meeting to order a few minutes late, just after he and commissioners Charles Cox and Jim Tread-way settled into their swivel chairs on the raised platform illuminated by the hot television lights. Before them the public citizenry was assembled, or at least its salaried representatives, in the form of lawyers and Wall Street consultants and journalists. They had come to the SEC's basement conference room, in the cool deep of its headquarters on Fifth Street, drawn by the rare chance to watch the commissioners wrestle openly with the most divisive and pressing economic issue of that spring of 1984, the unprecedented boom in corporate takeovers.

Shad seemed in a hurry, oblivious to the political opportunity presented by such a well-attended public forum.

"We'll be able to do it, I hope, in a rather abbreviated form," he mumbled in the direction of his microphone. He was referring to the commission's agenda, which included a final vote on what new rules the SEC planned to adopt or recommend to Congress to curb corporate mergers.

The room was tense, not least because the commission had opened its deliberations under the Sunshine Act, the ironically titled law that permitted the SEC to hold nearly all of its important debates in the sanctified privacy of the closed-meeting room six floors above. The meeting took place amid fiery political de-

171

bate about takeovers. That Tuesday morning, March 13, 1984, the newspapers were filled with startling reports that two prominent Democratic senators hoped to enact a six-month moratorium on mergers in the oil industry. The immediate causes of the senators' distress were the continuing takeover raids of T. Boone Pickens, Jr., and a recently announced $5.7-billion takeover bid for Superior Oil by Mobil Oil, a deal so big it would have been almost unimaginable months before. The White House was under pressure. Informed of the proposed congressional ban, spokesman Larry Speakes publicly waffled, saying that Reagan hadn't expressed any "concern or opposition" to takeovers, but he wasn't ready to express approval, either.

"I find there definitely is some sentiment for us to act," an emboldened Senator Howard Metzenbaum, a liberal Democrat from Ohio, had told reporters on Monday. "Reagan would be very hard put, in view of the political picture, to veto" any congressional ban on takeovers.

This was exactly what Shad had tried to avoid—a political frenzy about the takeover issue—and now he was right in the center of it, stationed before the cameras on a raised platform at the head of the commission's basement meeting room. That morning, voters across the South were flocking to the polls in a chaotic electoral event dubbed Super Tuesday, a host of simultaneous Democratic and Republican primaries in the 1984 presidential campaign. Reagan's position within his own party was secure, but Democrats felt the vigor of an electric battle between two senators, Gary Hart and Walter Mondale, with Hart claiming that his youth, charisma, and "new ideas" held the only hope for defeating Reagan in the fall. Shad's colleagues in the Republican party and at the White House were concerned—a private poll completed the day before showed Reagan ahead of Hart by only four points, while the president held a sixteen-point lead over Mondale. Hart's economic advisers, drawn principally from Harvard University, offered a sharp rebuttal to the laissez-faire approach to takeovers advocated by the right-wing Chicago School economists. On the campaign trail across the South, Hart and Mondale each attacked the Reagan economic program as fundamentally unfair, and the boom in big takeovers provided an easy target for their populist rhetoric.

Shad and his fellow commissioners found themselves uncomfortably in the center of this political storm. For the first time since the surge in wild and hostile corporate takeovers began in the summer of 1982, the SEC was poised to act. Shad's takeover advisory committee, dominated by his friends and former Wall Street colleagues, had submitted its muddled report the summer before, and only now, after months of private tinkering and review, was the commission prepared to accept or reject or alter its recommendations. In the interim, more and more mergers had been announced each month for greater and greater sums of money, each one greeted by the assessment that such an audacious takeover "would have been unthinkable" weeks earlier. Stock prices surged and gyrated daily on the floor of the New York Stock Exchange amid speculation about which previously untouched corporate giant was to be the next target. The good news for Shad and Reagan was that usually at the end of the week stock prices were higher, buoyed by the continuing economic recovery and teased upward by rumors of new and bigger deals.

Shad's takeover advisory committee hadn't suggested any fundamental program to slow mergers—the members of the committee profited enormously from the takeover boom. But in the months since their report was completed, the SEC staff had gone to work on it, and some of the lawyers and consultants who gathered in the commission basement that Tuesday weren't sure whether Shad and his colleagues had capitulated to the outcry for sweeping new regulations.

"Any commissioners . . . have any dissent or comments on the first eight recommendations of the advisory committee?" Shad asked from the platform. "Mr. Treadway or Mr. Cox?"

Members of the audience shuffled through their papers—what eight recommendations was Shad talking about? they asked each other. Many of them had nothing to follow, but Shad was not going to slow things down by providing special explanations. And the commission's senior staff, who had helped to organize the meeting, sat at a table near the front of the room, facing the commissioners but with their backs to the public.

"On the general proposal about [takeover bids] being a valid method of capital allocation, which regulation should neither promote nor deter, I agree completely with that," answered Charles Cox, the conservative economist who, with Shad's backing, recently had been elevated from chief economist to SEC commissioner, by President Reagan. "I think there's a substantial body of empirical evidence assembled by financial economists showing that combining firms . . . is in general economically beneficial. . . . It is not the place of regulation to determine which is a beneficial [takeover bid] and which is not."

"I would essentially concur in what Commissioner Cox has said," added Treadway.

Shad began to race through the list like an actor anxious to get off the stage. Number nine. . . . Number ten. . . . Numbers eleven through nineteen. . . . Any objection? None was voiced. Murmurs rose in the audience—few people were sure exactly what the commission was voting on, or whether it was voting at all. Piles of paper rested before the three Republicans on the platform, and some in the audience were able to follow the rapid decision-making by looking at old copies of the takeover advisory committee report, but there was no substantive debate about controversial issues, no back and forth. Virtually every vote was unanimous, seemingly scripted. It wasn't always clear whether the three commissioners were adopting a rule, making a recommendation to Congress, or suggesting a proposal to SEC staff for future consideration.

In part, the proposals had been designed by Shad and his senior staff to reduce political pressures on the commission through the adoption of a middle course—recommendation to Congress of laws that would eliminate the most egregious takeover abuses, without interfering fundamentally with the takeover process or disturbing the flow of profits to Wall Street. But when it was over that Tuesday, Shad's commission had managed to please few outside of its own staff. Partly it was a failure of presentation. So accustomed were the commissioners and senior staff to the casual intimacy of their private meetings that they had difficulty adjusting to the demands of public scrutiny. Skillful grandstanding and speech-making and contrived debate so common on Capitol Hill were rarely practiced at commission headquarters. The open meeting that day marked the first in a series of public-relations failures for the SEC in the area of takeovers and insider trading—failures that built one upon the other, sometimes putting Shad and the commission on the defensive even at moments of unqualified triumph. The commissioners and senior staff were like a breed of regulatory bat: In the pitch darkness of their own cave, they flew with precision and skill, but in open spaces they seemed to grow disoriented.

Shad's problems, however, were not wholly in the realm of public relations. Amid mounting calls for the SEC to do something, *anything*, about takeovers, he was being tugged and pulled from four sides—from his friends and former colleagues on Wall Street, from the conservative intellectuals in the Reagan administration, from Democrats in Congress, and from his own staff. In the months since his takeover advisory committee completed its work, Shad had become increasingly convinced that the public outcry surrounding certain abusive takeover practices demanded a measured response. He also was growing more concerned about the risk to the economy posed by heavy reliance on borrowed money to finance takeover bids. He was intrinsically uncomfortable with anything so drastic as a moratorium on mergers, such as the one proposed by Metzenbaum, but in private discussions that spring, he also rejected the arguments of Chicago School economists like Gregg Jarrell, who had written in his dissent to the advisory report that terminating federal regulations of takeovers was "the best of all possible worlds."

In part, Shad's views had been influenced by Linda Quinn, a top official in the SEC division of corporation finance whom he admired greatly and who had served as the staff link between the takeover committee and the commission. In the months leading up to the open SEC meeting in March, Quinn had been analyzing the committee's proposals and crafting compromise positions among the three Republican commissioners. She was closest to

Shad's. Quinn and other senior SEC staff wanted to see the commission take some action on takeovers to end perceived abuses and enhance the agency's regulatory clout. Quinn argued vocally with Jarrell, who saw her as the embodiment of the bureaucratic instinct to meddle. But Shad viewed Quinn in contrast to the legal-minded staff at the SEC who he thought had little appreciation for the financial markets. The chairman listened to Quinn that spring. She had worked for several years at the top-drawer Wall Street law firm of Sullivan & Cromwell, and Shad considered her brilliant.

In a series of meetings in Shad's office, Quinn proposed in March that the SEC adopt dozens of recommendations made by its takeover advisory committee, and that it reject others. As the SEC essentially was a bottom-up agency, no substantial takeover proposals came to a commission vote without staff recommendations, which only were made after considerable analysis at levels in the hierarchy far below the commission. Since the takeover panel recommendations had been limited in the first place, there were those to the left of Shad's views inside the SEC who thought that the votes taken at the open meeting—once it was deduced what the votes meant—were ineffectual. But even some Democrats in Congress were cheered by the unusual unity Shad mustered at the open meeting. Nearly all the recommendations made by the three commissioners were adopted unanimously. Proposed takeover laws were being introduced almost daily on the Hill, and the SEC's recommendations, however limited, added the weight of the Reagan administration to the momentum for reform. The SEC was ostensibly an independent agency, and it wasn't clear where the White House would come down on the issue, but the support of a loyal Reagan man like Shad added credibility to the Democrats' cause. Any final legislative package might be far more aggressive than what Shad's SEC proposed—the important thing now to the Democrats, in the midst of a hothouse election year, was to create the political impetus to move *all* the takeover bills through Congress.

And as a baseline for political debate, the proposals adopted by Shad and his fellow Republicans on the commission were, at the least, a far bolder regulatory program than anything previously proposed by members of the Reagan administration. Among the proposals was one that would force takeover bidders to disclose more rapidly their holdings of 5 percent or more of a public company, a change that would give target companies more time to mount defenses. Another SEC staff recommendation supported by Shad would restrict "golden parachutes"—lucrative severance agreements for executives who lose their jobs in a takeover—and "greenmail"—the payment of a premium to a corporate raider who agrees to sell his stock in the target company and drop his takeover bid. In the case of greenmail, Shad thought such payments should be permitted only with stockholder approval, and not simply at the whim of a corporate management wishing to rid itself of a suitor and preserve its power and perks.

Greenmail had become a lightning rod for controversy in the capital—that March, St. Regis Corporation, the giant paper manufacturer, had paid tens of millions of dollars to Anglo-French financier Sir James Goldsmith to encourage him to drop his takeover bid. The payment seemed a rank form of extortion, and as a political issue, it cut through the complex, delicate arguments about whether mergers were good or bad for the economy. Nobody was in favor of greenmail—yet Shad was ambivalent. His "middle course" recommendation that managements seek shareholder approval for the payments was consistent with Shad's view that stockholders were the SEC's most important regulatory constituent. But Shad knew, too, that corporate managements possessed wide powers to control shareholder votes, and that even if his proposal became law, it would have a marginal effect in many instances.

Amid all the public rhetoric about reining in the wild corporate takeovers that spring, the complexities of the commission's role—the personal and ideological connections linking Shad, some senior SEC staff, the practitioners of the takeover game on Wall Street, and the conservative intellectuals in the Reagan administration—escaped notice and comment. The commission's public and private dealings with T. Boone Pickens—who even more than Goldsmith had become in Washington the symbol of a new, and to many people a distressing, trend in finance and the economy—encompassed all of that.

One month after the commission meeting on takeovers, the SEC's enforcement division filed charges against the oil company Pickens headed—Amarillo, Texas–based Mesa Petroleum Company. The case involved Pickens's relationship with Drexel's Michael Milken. Several months before, in January 1984, Pickens asked for Milken's help in financing the first-ever junk-bond–backed multibillion-dollar hostile takeover bid, ushering in a new era of debt-driven merger mania. His target was Gulf Oil, one of the nation's leading refiners and marketers of crude and a familiar citadel of the country's corporate establishment.

The SEC possessed only a handful of legal and regulatory tools with which to examine and review corporate takeovers. One of the most important was a rule known as 13D, which required a bidder, once he accumulated 5 percent of his target company's stock, to disclose the size of his stock holdings and the nature of his intentions—whether, for example, the stock was purchased for investment purposes only, or whether he intended to seek control of the target. Typical of SEC regulations, the rule left wide latitude for interpretation as to what a bidder like Pickens actually had to say in his filings at the commission—the rule required him, among other things, to disclose his state of mind, which presumably was known only to Pickens. In the Gulf deal, Pickens had initially tried to win stockholder support through a proxy contest, and the 13D statements he filed at the SEC said that a proxy fight, in which shareholders cast ballots, was what Pickens intended. In a volatile atmosphere of lawsuits, mutual recrimination, and accusations, Gulf had defeated Pickens by persuading 53 percent of its shareholders to vote in favor of the incumbent management. Soon afterward, Pickens and his wife boarded their private jet in Houston and flew to Los Angeles, where Pickens had arranged an "audience" with Milken in Beverly Hills.

I want to explore the possibility of raising billions of dollars to finance a new takeover bid for Gulf, Pickens told Milken in a fourth-floor conference room off the Drexel junk bond trading floor in Beverly Hills.

"That's a lot of money," Milken answered succinctly.

I deal with a lot of money, but do you realize how much the $2 billion we are talking about is?

"Anything we have attempted we have performed," Milken answered.

This was exactly the deal Milken had been looking for—only weeks earlier he had met with Fred Joseph and other Drexel officials in Beverly Hills to discuss the use of junk bonds in hostile takeovers. Now Pickens was offering Drexel a foothold in the biggest, albeit the most politically controversial, takeover available. Milken said he would send his people down to Texas to get to work on the deal.

Pickens's meeting with Milken, and his decision to dip into Drexel's junk bond war chest, was a potentially decisive event in the battle for control of Gulf, its $20 billion in assets, and its 40,000 employees. After buying a nearly 9 percent stake in Gulf, Pickens declared that Gulf management needed to take steps to increase its stock price. But the company didn't budge until Pickens mounted a credible threat with Milken's help. Yet the meeting and Milken's financing work remained a secret—Pickens did not promptly amend the 13D statements in the commission's public-filing room to disclose that he had changed his tactics, that, in the aftermath of his defeat in the proxy contest, he now planned to launch a junk bond–financed hostile-takeover bid. Pickens did not make the change even after Milken took steps to raise $2.2 billion from his network of junk bond buyers. Not only did Gulf Oil, its executives, and employees know nothing of Pickens's alliance with Milken, neither did anyone at the Securities and Exchange Commission.

Inside the commission bureaucracy, daily review of developments in the fight for Gulf Oil was bifurcated between two divisions, enforcement and corporation finance. The latter had responsibility for reviewing all the paper filed at the SEC, while the former attempted to prosecute securities-law violations. Often they tried to work in tandem, since irregularities in public filings spotted by the lawyers in corporation finance provided tips for the enforcement staff. Even within corp fin, as the division was called inside the SEC, review of takeovers was split and segregated. In the most important section, the office of tender offers, SEC lawyers spent much of their time on the phone with Wall Street bankers and takeover attorneys embroiled in takeover fights, answering questions and providing informal advice about commission rules. But the office of tender offers competed for regulatory supremacy with other sections of corp fin—the office of chief counsel, the office of disclosure policy, and corp fin director John Huber's front office. Cooperation was difficult, not so much because of the occasional personality clashes, but because responsibility was split through the bureaucracy like light through a prism.

Some of the lawyers who dealt with day-to-day SEC regulation of takeover fights inside the corporation finance division were talented and dedicated—the increasing number and quickening pace of new deals, and the evolution of questionable tactics devised by Wall Street advisers forced staff like Joseph Connolly, who headed the office of tender offers, to work late into the night and through weekends and holidays. Yet even the best of them were aware of an uncomfortable truth: They were treading water, struggling each day just to return the phone calls that poured in from Wall Street takeover lawyers. There was barely time to review the mounds of new filings carted by the ream into the commission filing room downstairs. And there was certainly not enough people or time to conduct a systematic review of even the most controversial takeover fights to be sure that the participants were playing by the rules, or to consider new interpretations of existing regulations in order to curb abuses.

In a case like the battle for Gulf, where a corporate raider had failed to disclose a key change in his plans, one of the only ways lawyers inside the SEC could realistically hope to learn of the omission was if somebody ratted on Pickens. Indeed, belligerents in protracted takeover fights were discovering, that spring of 1984, that it was possible to use the SEC to gain an advantage against an opponent. If one side in a takeover battle discovered that the other side might be in violation of an SEC regulation, its lawyers inundated the corp fin and enforcement staffs in Washington with telephone calls and documentary evidence, urging them to bring an enforcement action that might alter the outcome of the takeover. Lawyers in corp fin looked carefully at the evidence that came in, but they were sometimes reluctant to act unless the purported violation was clear and egregious—they sensed correctly that the ordinary balance of power between regulator and regulated had been reversed, that the SEC was in danger of becoming a tactical pawn in a game controlled by lawyers and investment bankers on Wall Street. Pickens suspected that the SEC's investigation of him had been initiated because of allegations made by Gulf.

Then, too, even if the evidence of a violation was clear and compelling, it wasn't easy for the SEC to act fast enough to make any difference. By the time evidence was passed over to the enforcement division that spring, demonstrating that Pickens had failed to disclose properly his financing arrangements with Milken, and by the time the enforcement lawyers prepared their case, offered Pickens a chance to submit a defense, and at last secured approval for the action in a closed SEC meeting, the destiny of Gulf and its employees was decided. On March 5, 1984, to dodge the threat posed by Milken and Pickens, Gulf agreed to be acquired for a premium price of $80 per share by Chevron Corporation. At $13.3 billion, it was the biggest corporate merger ever. Milken and Drexel made millions of dollars in fees for arranging financing for Pickens's bid, including securing a loan of $300 million from raider Carl Lindner. Pickens and his investor group made a whopping $760 million profit, before taxes, on their Gulf stock. The SEC case charging Pickens with improperly keeping secrets about his plans during the battle—charges Pickens agreed to settle without admitting or denying wrongdoing—wasn't filed until April. If the case had been filed earlier, it probably wouldn't have changed the outcome of the takeover or deprived Pickens of his riches, but at the least, it would have provided the SEC with meaningful authority in the midst of the biggest merger deal on record. Pickens felt the SEC was unfair, because he was merely exploring a junk bond bid and had not yet made up his mind. The

SEC, for its part, was trying to force bidders to disclose key relationships earlier so that all stockholders had access to information that could affect stock prices.

As it was, the Gulf deal only fueled suspicions that the commission was being left behind by a new and powerful alliance linking Milken, the corporate raiders he was beginning to finance with junk bonds, and the arbitragers on Wall Street who profited by speculating, spreading rumors, and acquiring inside information on the outcome of takeover deals. The SEC investigated suspicious trading in Gulf stock which appeared linked to Milken's communications with potential junk bond buyers, but it brought no case. Merely by threatening Gulf, and without actually raising a dime of capital from Milken's junk bond investors, Pickens had been able to earn hundreds of millions of dollars in stock trading profits, and force Gulf into a merger that would throw thousands out of work and add billions of dollars of debt to Chevron's balance sheet. Moreover, the success of the Gulf deal made it easier for Milken to sell $500 million in junk bonds to help Pickens plan his next raid, and to stake other corporate raiders, such as Saul Steinberg, who launched a hostile raid on Walt Disney Company that spring. It was reported that in a single week Milken raised $1.3 billion for Metromedia, $1.2 billion for Occidental Petroleum, $325 million for Steinberg, and $100 million for a new client, a leveraged-buyout firm called Kohlberg Kravis Roberts & Company. Drexel doubled in size between 1979 and 1984, from 3,000 to 6,200 employees. Milken didn't go unrewarded; he earned $123.8 million in salary and bonus that year. Ivan Boesky, the arbitrager who in 1982 had begun to bribe investment banker Marty Siegel for inside information about takeovers, took home a reported $70 million in stock-trading profits from Pickens's raid on Gulf. To many of the commission staff in Washington, who lived on salaries of $25,000 or $30,000 annually and struggled with the banalities of checkbooks and mortgages, the scale of this instant wealth was numbing.

The SEC case against Pickens was minor and it seemed clear even to Shad that much of the illegal trading and dealing on Wall Street went unchecked. "In law enforcement," Shad said, "what you don't know is the extent of undetected fraud." Early in 1984, the SEC did bring an impressive insider trading case. But the case wasn't against a sophisticated stock market professional. Instead, the defendant was Paul Thayer, deputy secretary of defense, whom the SEC charged with violating the insider-trading laws by leaking information to a ring of friends and associates, including his mistress. (Before joining the administration, Thayer had access to inside information about takeover plans because he was chairman of the board of LTV Corporation, and a director of the Anheuser-Busch and Allied corporations.) The Thayer case generated a lot of favorable publicity for the SEC, but the fact remained that unlike the savvy traders on Wall Street who knew how to cover their tracks, Thayer was a relatively easy target. The rule-13D fraud charges filed publicly against Pickens in April provided a glimpse of only one aspect of the corporate raider's complex, multifaceted relationship with the SEC. That spring, Pickens traveled to Washington frequently to lobby against a merger moratorium on Capitol Hill and to appear before various congressional committees. In private meetings and public testimony, Pickens justified his raids in language that appealed intuitively to SEC Chairman John Shad—he used the vocabulary of the shareholder. Takeovers, even hostile takeovers, were good for the country because they helped shareholders reclaim control of large corporations from "entrenched" management coddled by big salaries and country club perks. Pickens proclaimed loudly that Gulf Oil wasted millions of dollars a year exploring for new oil and paying salaries to legions of expendable executives. Pickens understood that it was cheaper to buy control of an oil company in the stock market than it was to go out and drill for new oil—cheaper, that is, if the government would permit you, in the first place, to borrow billions of dollars to buy the stock. Gulf's stock price was undervalued and did not reflect fully the value of the company's known oil reserves. Pickens's rhetoric about shareholder rights, and the way his basic strategy seemed to rest on an insight about the free market system, appealed to Shad in many respects.

Pickens had another link to the SEC—through the conservative economist Gregg Jarrell. After Charles Cox was promoted, with Shad's assistance, from chief economist to commissioner, Cox recommended Jarrell to be the next SEC chief economist. Shad agreed. Even more than his predecessor, Jarrell was committed to the doctrine and empirical work of the University of Chicago, where he had received his doctorate in economics. Soon, with Shad's blessing, he was churning out studies at the SEC purporting to demonstrate that takeovers were good for shareholders and the country. Jarrell's studies attracted widespread attention in the capital and across the country.

Pickens noticed, and he telephoned Jarrell one day to tell him how much he admired the economist's work. Soon they became friends—Pickens liked to call Jarrell the "boy economist" because of his youthful face and puckish manner. When Pickens came to Washington, he would call Jarrell and invite him to play racquetball. At lunchtime, Jarrell would stand out on Fifth Street, gym bag at his side, waiting for the sleek limousine in which Pickens invariably traveled to pick him up. The slick concrete veranda before the entrance to SEC headquarters was a popular picnic ground for commission staff on sunny days in spring and summer, and Jarrell sometimes felt that he was the target of icy, disapproving stares from enforcement lawyers when he climbed into Pickens's limo. Jarrell didn't mind. He thought the whole scene was funny. He was committed deeply to the cause of free market deregulation, and he generally thought of his colleagues in the SEC bureaucracy as amiable but confused people who didn't understand what was good for the country. If the limousine coasting down Fifth Street and the racquetball games and the casual telephone calls from Pickens were a symbol of how much was changing at the SEC, Jarrell thought it was all for the better.

As he flew to New York that June, miles above the familiar corridor—fingers of the Chesapeake poking the Maryland shoreline, the gray brown grid of Philadelphia, down over the muddy industrial wasteland of northern New Jersey, banking finally into LaGuardia—Jack Shad must have understood that, for the first time, he was about to change the nature of the political debate in Washington over corporate takeovers.

In this SEC meeting room closed to the public, John Shad and his colleagues deliberated on secret investigations of Wall Street fraud, economic policy, and internal commission disputes. *The Washington Post*

In 1981, John S. R. Shad became the first SEC chairman to come from Wall Street since the agency was founded in the aftermath of the 1929 stock market crash. He waged a kind of guerrilla warfare to pull the SEC back from crusading about morality in corporate boardrooms and focus instead on enriching stockholders by making sure financial markets were fair and orderly. *The Washington Post*

Outgoing SEC enforcement director Stanley Sporkin, whose aggressive investigations earned the commission a formidable reputation on Wall Street, introduces his successor, John Fedders, at a 1981 press conference. The towering Fedders resigned in 1985 following revelations that he beat his wife several times during their marriage. *The Washington Post*

SEC San Francisco office director Bobby Lawyer traveled to Washington, D.C., to persuade the commission that it should bring securities fraud charges against Merrill Lynch after SEC Chairman John Shad tried to block the case. *AP/Wide World Photo*

Gary Lynch succeeded John Fedders as SEC enforcement director and led the commission's historic investigations of Ivan F. Boesky and Michael Milken. *The Washington Post*

Although John Shad was a bulldog in private negotiations, he mumbled and seemed way off balance when he testified before Congress. In his straightforward way, Shad led with his chin, and there often was a Democrat waiting to throw a sucker punch. *The Washington Post*

In February 1986, at the height of Ivan Boesky's career as a Wall Street stock speculator, SEC Chairman John Shad invited him to Washington to provide advice on takeover regulation at a public commission meeting. Seven months later, Boesky admitted he traded on inside information and became a cooperating witness in the largest SEC investigation of Wall Street fraud in history. *The Washington Post*

While on frequent furloughs from prison to testify against Wall Street colleagues, a bearded Boesky tried to find time to play squash. *The New York Post*

Called charismatic and brilliant by employees, greedy and devious by prosecutors, Michael Milken earned more than $1 billion during the 1980s by
building a market for junk bonds. Here he smiles at applauding supporters
while leaving a New York federal courthouse during legal battles that ended in 1990 with a ten-year prison sentence. Reuters

Soon after he came to Washington, John Shad declared the SEC was going to come down on insider trading with hobnail boots. Five years later, amid the success of the agency's campaign to clean up Wall Street, the SEC staff presented Chairman Shad with this pair of commemorative boots. *The Washington Post*

The speech he carried in his briefcase represented a major departure from the SEC's public posture about corporate take-overs. There could be no doubt about its impact. In the months since the SEC's open meeting in March, the political controversy about Milken and Pickens and junk bonds had only deepened. Reform legislation, some of it drastic, was moving quickly through the House and Senate. It still wasn't clear where the White House stood—amid the volatility of the continuing election campaign, some strategists in the administration were urging caution. Since Reagan wasn't inclined to push for drastic curbs on mergers, it was hard to see how his campaign could capitalize on the political controversy over takeovers. A potentially large number of blue-collar workers and others felt that their jobs and communities were threatened by the takeover boom, but there was no political constituency in favor of takeovers, other than wealthy corporate raiders, investment bankers, stock traders, and conservative intellectuals—a narrow spectrum of Reagan loyalists. Silence from the White House on the takeover issue heightened interest in the SEC's position, not only because of the agency's regulatory juris-diction, but also because Shad was a Reagan appointee who had toed the administration's line on other controversial issues, such as the budget.

The SEC was supposed to be an independent agency and the truth was that so far, Shad had developed little intimacy with the White House. Perhaps if Pat hadn't fallen victim to the stroke, if they had taken the house in Kalorama and worked their way onto the right social lists, it would have been different. But commuting every week between Park Avenue and Georgetown, Shad had little time for Washington society. On week nights, he buzzed in and out of cocktail parties, quickly returning to the SEC or to his hotel room to work and to eat alone. So divorced was Shad from doings on Pennsylvania Avenue that once, when he wanted to discuss financial regulation with Vice-President Bush, he had to dial directory assistance to get the White House phone number. When he reached Bush's office, Shad had trouble persuading the aide who answered the phone that he was actually the chairman of the SEC. Those who knew who Shad was generally considered him a loyal soldier, but Shad was not a member of Reagan's cabinet and was not required by law or custom to submit to the administration's views on political or economic issues.

Yet Shad felt acute pressures that spring to take a bold stand on takeovers. Ever since the takeover frenzy on Wall Street had begun, Shad had been worried about the debt being amassed on corporate balance sheets—that was the one aspect of the new merger game that didn't square with the way Shad approached corporate finance during his own career on Wall Street. Moreover, two of the social and professional friends he respected most, Wall Street takeover lawyer Marty Lipton and former SEC commissioner A. A. Sommer, continually urged him in private to stop the takeover wave before it undermined the nation's economic base. Sommer even gave Shad an antitakeover article he had written, titled "Hostile Tender Offers: Time for a Review of Fundamentals," as a key part of his effort to spur Shad to action. Executives from the powerful Washington lobby called the Business Roundtable, whose corporate members were directly threatened by takeovers, also urged Shad to speak out, to fill the political vacuum created by the White House.

Shad began to write a speech—a bold new assessment of the takeover boom. Before he left for New York to deliver it before a gathering of the New York Financial Writers Association, Shad circulated a draft to several of his senior staff.

"The Leveraging of America" was its title, and when he saw it, Gregg Jarrell was stunned and alarmed. "B.S.!" he scribbled in the margin, making so many marks on the page that he turned his copy red. "You've got no evidence." Commissioner Cox, Jarrell's soul mate from the Chicago School, told Shad outright that delivering the speech was a bad idea.

A lot of the things in that speech don't have any sound economic basis or support, Cox told Shad. They seem to be out of character with the stance you have taken on takeovers in the past.

Shad defended himself. He said he was going to deliver the speech.

"My purpose is not to sound a note of alarm," he said when his audience in the midtown-Manhattan ballroom of the Sheraton Centre Hotel had quieted, "but to ventilate some of the major issues." Few paid much attention to this disclaimer. Shad's speeches tended to repetition, and a phrase like "ventilate some of the major issues" sounded like a euphemism for "put everyone to sleep by telling them things they already know." The SEC staff made fun of Shad because he not only talked about the same topics over and over, but also used the identical words in speech after speech. He sounded like an old political sound truck, repeating a single message as it circled the streets.

But this night was different. "In today's corporate world, Darwin's 'survival of the fittest' has become: 'Acquire or be acquired,' " Shad intoned boldly. ". . . The more leveraged takeovers and buyouts today, the more bankruptcies tomorrow."

Shad acknowledged that shareholders reaped huge economic benefits from the premiums paid for stock in takeovers, but he warned that if the effect of mergers was to substitute debt for stock across the economy, not only shareholders but also the nation would be at risk. "The leveraging-up of American enterprises will magnify the adverse consequences of the next recession," he said. Shad's analysis ranged far beyond the normal purview of the SEC, to a discussion of global economic policies. He argued that highly leveraged takeovers—and there could be little mistake on that early-summer evening in 1984 that Shad was referring in large part to Drexel's roaring junk bond machine—hurt the ability of U.S. companies to compete abroad effectively because they had to devote too much cash to paying off debt.

Most startlingly of all, Shad attacked the central theory on which Pickens and Milken and the rest politically justified their debt-financed hostile takeover bids.

"The theory that contested takeovers discipline incompetent managements is of limited veracity," he said. "Corporations have momentum. Today's corporate performance and stock prices are in large measure a function of yesterday's decisions by prior managements—whether good or bad. . . . Outstanding executives are often engaged to turn around ailing enterprises. The market prices of such companies' shares often lag their improving prospects, and they become attractive takeover candidates because of the competence—not the incompetence—of the managements.

Also, contrary to a discipline, the increasing threat of being taken over is an inducement to curtail or defer research and development, plant rehabilitation and expansion, oil exploration and development, and other programs which entail current costs for long-term benefits. . . . Companies that do not replace aging facilities and declining resources become increasingly inefficient."

Shad hedged by adding that "it would be as wrong to overreact to these issues as it would be to ignore them," but that qualifier did little to alter the impact of his speech. As the first serious public doubts about the efficacy of the takeover boom voiced by a member of the Reagan administration, Shad's remarks made news worldwide. For anyone who had followed his career at the SEC, it was clear that he had journeyed far beyond the usual tired phrases about liquidity and efficiency and the United States having the best, the broadest, the fairest capital markets in the world. Instead, the chairman of the SEC had delivered a major economic-policy statement and come down clearly on the side of those who said that, in the long run, the leveraging of America through corporate takeovers was perilous to the nation's health. So proud was Shad of his address that when he returned to Washington, he asked an aide to mail copies to business leaders throughout the nation, including the chief executives of the Fortune 500—the largest corporations in the U.S.

That mailing list suggested that Shad understood the constituency for his manifesto: not most of his old colleagues in Wall Street investment banking but, rather, their clients, the chieftains of the corporate establishment. They were the ones who feared the power of Milken's junk bond warhead most of all, just as Boone Pickens had been saying all spring on Capitol Hill. As the import of Shad's speech filtered and circulated through the capital, it was hard for some to reconcile its ideas with the oft-stated views of the SEC chairman. In some ways, "The Leveraging of America" mirrored precisely the lobbying pamphlets of the Business Roundtable and the position papers of congressional Democrats. To them, the speech provided the clearest endorsement yet for the takeover reform legislation pending in the House and Senate.

Even those closest to Shad professionally were dumbfounded by his speech. They didn't understand where it had come from—it was like a shot from the blue. In nearly every other way, Shad had guided his tenure at the SEC by the lights of Chicago School theory. What could have prompted him to deviate now? Chicago School adherents like Jarrell speculated that Shad must have been influenced by the Wall Street friends he saw on weekends—lawyers and investment bankers who earned their livings defending large corporations against takeovers, and who were looking to help their cause by restricting the availability of debt for their opponents in the game. Friends of Shad on the Business Round-table side of the issue saw it differently: After much effort, they thought, some people Shad trusted, such as takeover attorney Martin Lipton, had finally knocked some sense into the SEC chairman. But the truth was that Shad's speech was an enigma. It was in many respects inconsistent with other policies he believed in, and it was unsupported by other speeches or private comments by Shad expressing serious doubts about takeovers.

Did Shad understand the political implications of his speech, coming in the midst of a volatile election year? What if legislation to curtail mergers, implicitly endorsed by Shad, somehow spooked Wall Street, leading to a sharp fall in stock prices and fears of a recession just as the election approached? The possibilities were myriad—and to more than a few senior Reagan administration officials, disturbing. Whether or not Shad appreciated the full political consequences of his speech, some key conservative officials in the administration and at the SEC were determined to make him understand. Within weeks after Shad delivered his remarks in New York, a private campaign was under way within the administration to alter drastically the SEC chairman's public approach to corporate takeovers.

11

Leaking

When Jack Shad started seeing stories in the newspapers about confidential SEC studies on takeovers, he suspected he knew the source of the leaks. The way to figure out where leaks came from in Washington, Shad had learned from his early experiences with Dingell, was to pinpoint who stood to gain. Sometimes that was difficult, because the bureaucratic competition or office politics from which a leak arose might be hidden entirely from public view. But in the case of the stories about corporate takeovers that began to appear after Shad's "Leveraging of America" speech in June 1984, the calculation was relatively simple. The point of the stories was that the SEC had begun to discover, through careful and empirical study, that hostile corporate takeovers—even those involving such controversial practices as greenmail and golden parachutes—actually were beneficial, not potentially harmful, to the economy. Confidential studies undertaken by Jarrell's office of the chief economist were quoted from in the newspaper stories, and it was clear that somebody familiar with Jarrell's work was talking regularly to reporters in violation of SEC policy. Shad thought the source likely was Jarrell himself.

As the SEC's chief economist, Jarrell was working feverishly to develop studies "proving" that the fears Shad had expressed in his landmark "Leveraging of America" speech were unfounded. Shad had departed from his previous public statements and sounded warnings about the potentially disastrous long-term consequences of debt-driven corporate takeovers. Since then, during meetings in Shad's office, in the commission's hallways, and at every available opportunity, Jarrell had pushed the SEC chairman to rethink the views he expressed in New York—views Jarrell had characterized as "B.S." when he marked up an early draft of Shad's speech with a red pen. It wasn't clear how deep Shad's skepticism about takeovers ran, since the merger boom in 1984 was providing clear benefits to stockholders, the group Shad saw as the commission's most important constituency. Indeed, takeovers had been a driving force behind the great bull market in stocks that in little more than two years had taken the Dow Jones Industrial Average from the high 700s to more than 1,200, an increase of more than 425 points and more than $400 million in stock market value. Still, that studies from the SEC chief economist's office supporting Jarrell's position on the takeover issue suddenly appeared prominently in the press did not, under the circumstances, seem a deep mystery.

And then Jarrell was exposed. Not long after Shad's June speech, Jarrell leaked to a reporter from *Barron's* an advance copy of a confidential SEC study he had drafted demonstrating that greenmail, the antitakeover tactic of buying off corporate raiders by paying them premiums for the stock they owned, was actually good for shareholders. The reporter had promised Jarrell anonymity, but on a Friday night, as *Barron's* went to press, she called him with what Jarrell later characterized as "a big sob story about how her editor made her identify me." Jarrell had leaked the reporter a rough and aggressively worded draft of his study, which she used to prepare her story. Then he spent all weekend polishing a new version that toned down his conclusions and included lots of "wiggle words," as Jarrell referred to moderate, qualified language.

After he saw the *Barron's* article, Shad tore into Jarrell at SEC headquarters on Monday morning. "We don't do these sorts of things here," the chairman said in an intimidating baritone.

"It's much easier to beg for forgiveness than ask for permission," Jarrell answered.

"That works once," Shad said, and turned on his heel.

But Jarrell, determined to play a role in preventing any possible SEC action that might restrict corporate takeovers, couldn't help himself. The leaks continued, one after another, and often they were poorly disguised. "I had to deny, deny, deny that I had leaked my studies," Jarrell admitted later, but even after Shad caught him again, he kept on. Shad treated his chief economist the way an indulgent, curmudgeonly uncle might treat a wayward but promising nephew; he was always willing to give him one more chance.

Shad's indulgence seemed in defiance of logic to Jarrell's rivals among the senior SEC staff. They didn't share the chairman's concern that it would be difficult to hire a new chief economist if Jarrell were fired, and it seemed to them that Jarrell got away with things that no one else at the commission could hope to try— including, for example, his friendship with corporate raider Boone Pickens. Jarrell even attacked his colleagues publicly, a common-enough practice in Washington, but virtually unheard of at the SEC. Once Jarrell gave an on-the-record interview to the *Wall Street Journal*, attacking the decisions of Clarence Sampson, who headed the SEC's office of the chief accountant, in a matter involving changes in oil-industry accounting. When the story was published, there was an outcry in Washington—Shad felt pressure from several quarters of the capital, including from the Secretary of the Interior.

"Why did you have to leak it?" Shad asked Jarrell when he angrily called him to his office.

"Well, at least I didn't pose as an unofficial source and try to hide behind some shield of anonymity," Jarrell answered, disregarding the fact that anonymity was his usual tactic when he leaked to reporters.

"Yeah, well, that's just stupid," Shad said.

That afternoon Jarrell drove off to Delaware, where he had grown up in the small capital city of Dover, and where his parents still lived. What he didn't know was that the *Journal* reporter to whom he had given the original interview denouncing Sampson had decided to write two stories. The next day another story appeared, and Jarrell was again quoted prominently, still criticizing his colleagues at the SEC. He was in the front yard of his parents' house when his sister appeared on the doorstep.

"Gregg, you have a phone call—do you know a guy named Chad?"

"I might have your office cleared out," Shad said when Jarrell got on the phone. "What am I going to do to get you to understand?"

"Sir, there is an explanation."

"Well, I am just giddy with anticipation."

When Jarrell told him that the reporter had made two stories out of one interview, Shad seem unimpressed. The chairman was fuming when he hung up—but he said nothing more about cleaning out Jarrell's office.

Jarrell had figured from the beginning, when he first accepted the position of chief economist at the SEC, that there was a good chance he would be fired for breaking the rules. That didn't bother him. In some ways, getting fired was the easy way out.

If Shad had decided to let him go, the SEC chairman would have confirmed for Jarrell the wisdom of Milton Friedman and George J. Stigler, the Nobel Prize recipients who were the intellectual and spiritual leaders of the University of Chicago's graduate-school program in economics, where Jarrell studied during the 1970s and early 1980s. Jarrell's career prospects at the SEC had been the topic of several discussions at the famous (among conservative intellectuals) Thursday lunch group, where Friedman and Stigler led a savage roundtable exchange with their graduate students about the political, social, and economic policy implications of Chicago School free market theory. There was a great deal of self-consciousness among the group, a sense that the Thursday lunches were a forum for developing the vanguard to the next great political revolution in the United States: the triumph of free market theory. Yet when the Chicago School's political champion, Ronald Reagan, swept to power in 1980, the éminences grises of the Thursday lunch group reacted with ambivalence rather than elation. Heated discussions ensued about whether it was politically correct for a free market intellectual,

who believed that government should play the smallest role possible in society and the economy, to actually join the government
and attempt to promote change. Jarrell's dilemma about whether
to accept the SEC chief-economist job offered by Shad in 1984
became a model for the application of this theoretical dispute.
Stigler—who had been approached indirectly, soon after Reagan's
1980 victory, about taking an SEC post and had spurned the
idea—cautioned Jarrell that Washington was an "efficient political
market," which in Chicago School jargon meant that the entrenched bureaucracy was too big and too powerful for one person to make any difference.

Jarrell thought otherwise. "How can we possibly know the answers and marshal all this evidence and then concede that we can't
convince anyone who's in power to make different decisions?" he
asked.

He possessed an undeniable, even insidious, charm. Slim and
sandy-haired, with an unblemished, boyish visage, Jarrell gave the
appearance of a clever, pleasant elf—he was the Chicago School's
Peter Pan. He was brilliant and incisive in conversation, but also
mocking and funny and virtually unself-censored in word and
thought, like a frolicking child. In college, during the 1960s, he
had been a committed hippie, and even after his deep conversion
to a free market outlook, there remained in him the impulses of
a merry prankster, someone who distrusted the establishment and
liked to tweak its nose at every opportunity.

Jarrell respected Friedman and Stigler, his mentors at the University of Chicago, but he thought their cynical attitude toward
government reflected their ages as much as anything else. They
had seen it all, or so they believed, and they thought nothing in
Washington could be changed fundamentally. A younger economist such as Jarrell had the enthusiasm and arrogance and enough
outrage about the status quo to believe he could make a difference. Jarrell convinced them finally that he would go only for a
few years, that he would approach the SEC job like a guerrilla
fighter infiltrating the enemy command, and that he would escape
Washington at the first sign that he actually enjoyed the place.

He listened politely to what Friedman and Stigler said, but all along, in the back of his mind, he thought, "I'm going to get in there and I'm going to do what I do. I'm going to rely heavily on the empirical work and stay away from the rhetoric and try to show them that the economist from Chicago doesn't have to be a lunatic—and trick them. I'm going to try to be as big a backslapper as these people are—in Washington, you slap them on the back and then you go into chambers and call them thieving maniacs. There are rules and I'm going to learn them and compete very, very hard and see if we can't get some kicks out of it." At worst, Jarrell thought, if he went too far, he would be fired by Jack Shad over some matter of principle, and that didn't seem so bad at all. He could return to Chicago like some celebrated prisoner of war released to his family.

Though his views were to the far right of the political spectrum, Jarrell in many ways resembled a clandestine Marxist revolutionary when he arrived at the SEC in 1984. Like the Marxists, Jarrell subscribed to a sweeping, often dogmatic, doctrine of economics that he used to explain a panoply of social and political phenomena. Change was urgent. The growth of the federal bureaucracies during the 1960s and 1970s, the interference in the economy by agencies like the SEC and the Justice Department, and their attempts to prescribe standards of regulatory morality, provoked a visceral reaction in Jarrell. He felt enormous intellectual disdain—almost disgust—for what the regulators had done in fields like antitrust. Failing or marginal companies used antitrust cases brought by Washington bureaucrats to protect themselves from free market competition, Jarrell believed.

He applied a similar analysis to the SEC. Investment bankers and lawyers on Wall Street lobbied for complex takeover regulations at the commission to increase demand for their interpretive and advisory services. Old-line traders on the floor of the New York Stock Exchange used SEC rules to stem the introduction of new and competitive technologies at the country's financial exchanges. Lawyers and bureaucrats in the market regulation and enforcement divisions vied for power by pushing trivial rules that, far from ensuring the fairness of the financial markets, only distorted and inhibited their efficiency. The SEC bureaucracy didn't protect the public, Jarrell believed, but was instead an instrument for interest groups—economic classes, in Marxist vocabulary—to improve a given group's position at the expense of its rivals.

That was the way Jarrell saw the unfolding debate in 1984 over computerized program trading of stocks and stock futures. There were those at the commission who wanted to slow Wall Street down, to put controls on the "quant jocks," those academics-turned-Wall-Street-traders whose computers and mathematical models linking stock and stock-futures trading increased the speed and volatility of market activity. Jarrell was convinced that new trading regulations would merely benefit the old guard, the gray-haired Wall Street traders who were not keeping up.

Shad, who ran his own life at high speed and found the pace exhilarating, generally agreed with Jarrell that it was best to let technology and the markets race ahead. In Shad's view, computerized trading made the markets more efficient and increased trading volume, which meant stock prices reflected all available information more rapidly than before. Liquidity and efficiency, liquidity and efficiency—that's what Shad wanted for the markets, and he thought the computers and stock index futures would help.

The rise of computerized trading by big institutional investors and major Wall Street firms whipsawed prices back and forth in 1984, prompting the first major cries for regulatory reform since stock index futures had been created. But Shad believed that the gyrations and volatility, while highly visible, obscured many important but less obvious benefits, such as the ability of institutional investors to move large blocks of stock in a short time. The real question was whether the stock index futures and computerized trading techniques Shad endorsed would reduce risk in the markets through various risk-transfer techniques, or whether the theory of risk transfer would be used as a rationalization, a shield hoisted by powerful market players to disguise massive speculation.

The debate inside the SEC over computerized trading paralleled the battle for Shad's heart and mind on the issue of takeover regulation. On one side were the free market theorists, led by Jarrell, who told Shad that the changes were healthy, and that to oppose the introduction of new computer-trading strategies would be a form of regulatory Luddism—irrational fear of technology. On the other side were the senior staff of the market regulation division. Cognizant of Shad's suspicions about market regulation of any sort, the staff proposed no drastic restrictions, and indeed backed some proposals that made certain forms of computerized trading easier. But they were not so sanguine about it as Jarrell.

The truth was, the SEC staff didn't really understand what was going on as the markets in New York and Chicago became linked on the computer screens of high-powered traders. When traders began profiting in 1984 by doing complex transactions linking the stock market in New York and the stock-futures market in Chicago, Jarrell was delighted. It helped to prove his conviction that regulators in Washington were always years behind the universities and quant jocks in their approach. The principal issue at the SEC, and during congressional debate when the Chicago stock futures had been created in 1981, was whether the new financial futures would generate excessive speculation. No one had even considered whether computers and mathematicians and Wall Street rocket scientists would find ways to link the markets. Jarrell urged Shad and the other SEC commissioners to move cautiously on the issue. There was plenty of emotion generated by the issue, he said, but no quantitative proof that computer-driven trading was bad.

Jarrell had acquaintances and intellectual allies all through the administration—young, committed, heavily ideological economists and lawyers who had taken key posts at various federal agencies. Their youth, the generational experience they had shared during the 1960s, and their self-awareness as leaders of a potentially powerful political and intellectual force, distinguished them from the old-guard conservative Republicans who held the most important senior cabinet posts in the Reagan administration. And yet the Chicago School "cabal," as Jarrell liked to call it, was well positioned to influence economic policy. Charles Cox was now an SEC commissioner. Douglas Ginsburg, later denied a seat on the Supreme Court after admitting he once smoked marijuana, was the antitrust chief at the Justice Department. Tom Campbell had begun to shake up antitrust enforcement at the Federal Trade Commission. Christopher DeMuth headed the economic policy section of the powerful Office of Management and Budget (OMB), which worked closely with the White House. Joseph Grundfest, an attorney who had become an advocate for some aspects of Chicago School economics, was in charge of takeover issues at the White House Council of Economic Advisers.

They were called by some the "movement" conservatives, a self-conscious appellation derived from the antiwar movement of the 1960s. Jarrell and his brethren not only fought against the bureaucrats and the Democrats but also fought at times against the entrenched establishment of their own Republican administration—against men like Jack Shad and Treasury Secretary Donald Regan and Chief of Staff James Baker, who had strong emotional and material links to the Wall Street and Washington establishments.

In fact, *conservative* seemed an inadequate word to describe both Shad and Jarrell. Shad often seemed a traditional conservative, in the sense that he wanted to conserve, or preserve, institutional agendas that he thought were good for the country—those of Harvard and Wall Street, for example. Jarrell, on the other hand, was the sort of "conservative" who didn't want to conserve much of anything. He wanted to foster radical change. Shad's outlook had been shaped by experiences such as the patriotic fervor of World War II and the economic dislocations of the Great Depression. In contrast, Jarrell had grown up amid cynicism about Vietnam and the runaway inflation of the 1970s that devalued savings and encouraged consumers to accumulate debt. They seemed bound more by a shared spirit for adventure than by similarities of experience. Jarrell admired Shad because the SEC chairman was still full of life and curiosity late in his middle age. When Michael Jackson came to Washington, Shad bought a ticket from a scalper and went out to Robert F. Kennedy Memorial Stadium by himself to see what the fuss was about. Another time he hurt his ankle while parachuting with Senator Jake Garn, Republican chairman of the banking committee that oversaw the SEC.

The idea that Shad jumped out of an airplane for thrills impressed Jarrell. But the issue that galled him more than any other at the SEC, and the one that most provoked his adolescent and rebellious tendencies, was the commission's regulation of corporate takeovers. He couldn't stop thinking about Shad's speech warning of the dangers of takeovers. Jarrell, like nearly everyone else from the Chicago School, believed that takeovers were fundamentally good for the economy and the country because they brought free market discipline to the entrenched corporate managements of the target companies and also increased shareholder wealth. Among the University of Chicago ideologues generally, Justice Department antitrust policy was the issue that stirred the greatest emotion, but SEC takeover regulation was a close second, and it was one of Jarrell's fields of specialization. As one of only two academics on Shad's takeover advisory committee, Jarrell had struggled against the Wall Street bankers and lawyers to produce a manifesto for laissez-faire theory.

Jarrell was disappointed when, at the SEC open meeting in March of 1984, Shad and the other SEC commissioners responded to the advisory report by recommending new laws to Congress. But he was horrified three months later when Shad traveled to New York to deliver his "Leveraging of America" speech. Jarrell feared Shad's speech would add momentum to the push for sweeping takeover restrictions in Congress.

Shad's speech set off alarm bells across the Reagan administration, and within weeks there was talk that Shad had met with Treasury Secretary Regan to clarify his position on takeovers. For months prior to the speech, the White House had done nothing about the swelling debate over takeovers in Washington. The election campaign was in full swing and an air of caution had settled over administration policy-making. Shad's speech, which was received as a major economic policy pronouncement by the Reagan administration even though it was never cleared by the White House, helped to shake the administration from its lethargy. A task force was formed hastily at the White House—Shad wasn't invited to join—to develop an official administration position on takeover policy and legislation. And privately, unofficially, relentlessly, Gregg Jarrell began a campaign inside the SEC to influence Jack Shad about takeovers and pull the commission back from any attempt to restrict or regulate them. "I tried to move him wherever the administration wanted to go," Jarrell said later. "The administration's view was that Shad was off the reservation." In conversations with Ginsburg, DeMuth, and others, Jarrell assured his allies that he would do everything he could to prevent Shad and the SEC from pushing tough new laws or regulations restricting junk bonds or corporate takeovers.

Jarrell's private campaign was multifaceted. Leaks of his economic studies to the press attracted attention for Jarrell's free market theories supporting takeovers and helped to undermine the public impact of Shad's caveats about debt and junk bonds in his "Leveraging of America" speech. Working within the SEC, Jarrell began to arrange lines of informal communication between Shad and key economic policy makers in the administration. Jarrell thought he was only helping Shad by putting him in closer touch with the White House, which held the keys to Shad's political future. In June, shortly after Shad's speech, Chris DeMuth at the Office of Management and Budget had sent a memo to the cabinet recommending that the administration study takeovers and speak out against unnecessary curbs—action was necessary, DeMuth's memo noted, not only because the Democrats were pushing drastic legislation in Congress, but also because John Shad and the SEC supported new rules and laws with which the administration might be uncomfortable. Jarrell wanted Shad to understand how key policy makers and economists in the administration reacted to his speech. He invited Doug Ginsburg to a brown-bag lunch in Shad's office with the chairman and some of his senior staff. One of the topics discussed over lunch was the danger of attempting to regulate greenmail, and Ginsburg was articulate, forceful, and persuasive. Later, Shad invited Ginsburg to testify at a public SEC meeting called to reevaluate the commission's position on pending takeover reform bills in Congress. Jarrell considered the budding intellectual alliance between Shad and Ginsburg one of his greatest achievements in government, though others at the commission thought Jarrell's role in this and other matters was not as important as Jarrell tended to view it.

Jarrell wanted to do more than lobby Shad and issue studies in favor of takeovers, so he developed relationships with key senior SEC staff who had responsibilities for takeover regulation. Among them was Joe Connolly, who headed the Office of Tender Offers in the corporation finance division. Connolly had come to the SEC straight out of law school in Washington, and had worked his way up through the bureaucracy to a position just beneath division director John Huber. Connolly's father had been a staff attorney at the SEC during the 1940s, before embarking on a career as a securities lawyer in Manhattan—Connolly, then, was a second-generation SEC bureaucrat. Because he talked daily with the Wall Street lawyers involved in takeover fights, Connolly and his small staff wielded considerable authority over the commission's day-to-day approach to takeover regulation. His office also proposed technical changes to the SEC's takeover regulations, changes that sometimes had a significant influence on the merger game.

Jarrell watched Connolly carefully, and he kept his eye on the commission's calendar of closed meetings. Whenever a takeover rule change came up for an SEC vote, Jarrell would rush down to Connolly's office and try to obtain from him in advance the staff memos and other documents that would eventually be submitted to the commissioners. If he succeeded, Jarrell would promptly draft a rebuttal paper promoting his free-market viewpoint, and at times he would meet with his intellectual ally, Commissioner Cox, to discuss his position on the issue. Connolly opposed Jarrell on takeover issues occasionally, but Jarrell considered him compliant. "Joe was a guy who knew where his bread was buttered," Jarrell said. For their part, Connolly and other senior staff who supervised takeover regulation within the corporation finance division viewed Jarrell as the single most influential SEC official on takeover issues, and as someone who exercised increasing influence over Jack Shad's positions.

It wasn't just Jarrell's personal energy and influence that intimidated senior SEC staff who were otherwise inclined to take a bolder approach to takeover regulation, in 1984 and 1985, as more and more mergers and greater amounts of debt swept through the nation's economy. When the staff tried to check abusive takeover tactics through direct, hands-on regulation and law enforcement—as opposed to the changes in rules and laws backed by Shad at the open meeting in March 1984—they were handed a series of devastating defeats in court.

In one case initiated by Connolly's office and backed enthusiastically by John Fedders and other attorneys in the enforcement division, the SEC sued the Los Angeles–based retailer Carter Hawley Hale for allegedly violating SEC rules governing the purchase of large blocks of its own stock during a takeover fight. To defend itself against a hostile takeover bid from The Limited, an Ohio-based competitor, Carter Hawley Hale purchased stock in the open market equal to more than half of its own shares, thus defeating Limited's attempt to buy a majority of Carter Hawley Hale's stock. Connolly, Fedders, and Gary Lynch, who had replaced Ted Levine as the number-two attorney in the enforcement division, agreed that Carter Hawley's aggressive tactic was a shortcut that violated SEC rules—the company shouldn't have scooped up its shares on the floor of the New York Stock Exchange, but should have conducted a formal tender offer to all of its shareholders that would have enabled Limited to continue to press its takeover bid.

The lawsuit attracted widespread attention because it marked one of the few times the SEC had intervened in the midst of an ongoing takeover fight. Since the commission chose to take the side of the raider, The Limited, the suit fueled congressional criticism that the SEC under Shad favored bidders over targets in takeover fights. Connolly and Fedders rejected that criticism, although Fedders conceded that on a personal level he tended to have more sympathy for raiders than for their corporate targets. Like Jarrell, Fedders thought takeovers were good for the economy and the country. During the Carter Hawley Hale case, the excitement of a contested lawsuit and the potentially decisive role the SEC played in the takeover created an atmosphere of camaraderie inside the commission. Old rivalries were set aside. Jarrell testified for the enforcement division that Carter Hawley Hale should be subject to the SEC's takeover rules. Enforcement attorneys worked late into the night for days in succession to draft their legal briefs, and Lynch led a team to Los Angeles, where the suit was heard in federal court.

But the excitement lasted briefly. The commission had asked the court in its suit to order Carter Hawley Hale to drop its antitakeover defense by ending the purchase of its shares in the open market. But federal judge A. Wallace Tashima ruled against the commission, saying the SEC had misinterpreted some of its own highly technical rules governing the conduct of takeovers.

The defeat was thorough, devastating, and in the tightly knit world of takeover law and investment banking, deeply embarrassing for the SEC attorneys. At first they blamed Tashima, muttering that since he lived and worked in Los Angeles, he was a hometown judge biased in favor of Carter Hawley Hale and its executives and employees. Later, however, the federal appeals court in California affirmed Tashima's ruling in all of its important aspects. Stung again, the SEC staff retreated. They grew increasingly reluctant to intervene directly during takeover fights for fear that they would be embarrassed again.

In effect, the SEC took Tashima's advice—instead of attempting to control the boom in takeovers and junk bonds through direct regulation or law enforcement, Shad and his colleagues focused increasingly on the economic policy debate about takeovers raging in Congress and within the administration. That was the forum Jarrell preferred. There he could influence Shad's positions; Shad relied on Jarrell for data and information and he sometimes asked Jarrell to draft the testimony he delivered before Congress.

Slowly Jarrell built connections between the ostensibly independent SEC and the key economic policymakers in the Reagan administration. He sent raw statistical data and advance copies of the studies about takeovers his staff produced to economists working in the Office of Management and Budget, and those economists in turn used Jarrell's work to bolster the Chicago School's position within the new administration task force on takeover policy.

Jarrell believed strongly that in the battle for Shad's heart and mind on the takeover issue, he and his Chicago School allies were competing against some of Shad's closest friends on Wall Street, people like takeover attorney Martin Lipton. An outspoken skeptic about hostile takeovers and junk bonds, Lipton clashed openly with Jarrell as a member of Shad's takeover advisory committee and later at SEC roundtable meetings in Washington, where experts were assembled to discuss takeover reform. As Jarrell explained it to his allies at Justice and OMB, the problem was that Shad flew each weekend to Manhattan, where he relaxed and dined with "these old cronies from Wall Street who were slamming Drexel and putting down junk bonds." Lipton was one of the people Jarrell had in mind. To counteract the effect on Shad's thinking of Lipton and other old Wall Street friends who were unnerved by the growth in takeovers—the value of corporate mergers more than doubled in 1984 to $126 billion, up from $52.6 billion in 1983, and there was about $90 billion in new corporate debt—Jarrell knew that Shad would have to be persuaded by his generational and political peers in the Reagan administration, men such as Regan and Federal Reserve Chairman Paul Volcker, with whom Shad consulted regularly about economic issues.

For Jarrell and the cabal, the biggest breakthrough came on September 25, 1984, three months after Shad's stunning speech about leverage, when with the approval of the administration's takeover task force, Treasury Secretary Regan sent a letter to John Dingell, setting forth, for the first time, an official Reagan administration stance on pending takeover legislation.

"Although some abuses have undoubtedly occurred, it is not sensible to enact legislation without more complete consideration of the consequences," Regan wrote. "We urge Congress to refrain from adopting legislation governing this area until there has been a full public debate. . . . Corporate takeover attempts perform several beneficial functions in our economy. First, they provide a means—sometimes the only feasible means—of policing management conduct in widely held public corporations. Second, they help identify undervalued assets and permit shareholders to re-

alize the true value of their investments. Third, successful takeovers help realize efficiencies by reallocating capital and corporate
assets into more highly valued uses; enabling merger partners to
generate joint operating efficiencies; and providing companies
with access to financial, management, and other resources not
otherwise available."

The stylized language—the references to "realizing efficiencies"
and "reallocating capital . . . into more highly valued uses" and
"joint operating efficiencies"—was drawn straight from the doc-
toral theses of the Chicago School economists. Takeovers were a
beneficial symptom of the invisible hand of capitalism at work,
Regan's letter declared. Jarrell and his cabal were ecstatic. Just six
weeks before a presidential election that already was shaping up
as a massive triumph for Reagan, the administration had taken a
public stand against the concerns about takeovers articulated by
Jack Shad the previous June. Under the circumstances, a land-
slide win for President Reagan would implicitly endorse the positions in Don Regan's letter. Moreover, Jack Shad never again
publicly repeated the warnings sounded in his "Leveraging of
America" speech—in the end, his speech was seen by friends and
opponents alike as a puzzling aberration, a brief moment of doubt,
or truth, expelled almost as quickly as it was voiced. Of course,
few but those at senior levels of the SEC understood the effort
Jarrell and his allies among the movement conservatives made in
the attempt to change Shad's position. Nor did they understand
what a dramatic difference it made that Shad, having been re-
buked for his words, forever abandoned his tough talk about the
dangers of takeovers. Without the support of either the chairman
of the SEC or the president of the United States, the takeover
reform bills moving through Congress in the fall of 1984 died.

And in the conduct of mergers and acquisitions, at least, the lid
on Wall Street came off.

12

Dr Pepper

Ivan Boesky sat in the back of a long, black limousine on a week-day morning in 1984 as his chauffeur negotiated the congested avenues of the capital, heading toward the corner of Fifth and D streets. He chattered on his car phone, speaking in short and sometimes cryptic bursts, as if this were just another trading day in the business of risk arbitrage, the arcane game of Wall Street stock speculation at which Boesky excelled. As his limo approached the SEC's headquarters, Boesky called his office in Manhattan, checking in with his secretary for messages one last time. He was late. It was nearly 11:00 A.M., almost an hour past the scheduled start of Boesky's interrogation by lawyers from the commission's enforcement division.

While Boesky cruised in his limo, his lawyers and aides had been milling around the SEC's cavernous lobby, wondering what had happened. They kept checking their watches—10:15, 10:30, 10:45—and still, no Boesky.

It's not a good idea to keep the SEC lawyers waiting, one of them had remarked anxiously.

Finally, they saw the stretch limo. Boesky hopped out and strode into the lobby. He wore a dark three-piece suit with an antique gold watch chain draped across the vest. With his silver hair, sunken eyes, and long, beaked nose, he seemed a caricature of the Victorian man of finance. In truth, it was an image Boesky cultivated assiduously.

"Gentlemen," he pronounced grandly as he entered the Securities and Exchange Commission, "I'm sorry I'm late. My plane was late."

There was no hesitation in his voice, no blinking or sideward glances, but several of the group suspected Boesky was lying. Some of them had taken commercial flights that morning from New York to Washington and had arrived without delay. Boesky had flown in his private jet, telling one of his advisers that he had some other business to attend to in Washington before the SEC deposition. Nevertheless, no one in the entourage challenged Boesky's account. After all, Boesky was a multimillionaire, he paid their six-figure salaries and exhorbitant fees, and he had risen to become one of the most powerful traders on Wall Street during the 1980s. There was nothing to be gained by confronting him.

Led by Boesky and Henry King, a prestigious trial attorney from the Wall Street firm Davis, Polk and Wardwell, who had agreed to represent Boesky before the SEC, the group passed a security guard's station and entered a restricted area within the commission building.

"Hi, Mr. Boesky," a young man piped up, stopping them in their tracks.

Boesky appeared puzzled; he looked at the fellow as if his face seemed vaguely familiar. The young man identified himself as the son of one of Boesky's friends.

I'm just finishing up with law school and doing an internship here at the SEC, he told Boesky proudly.

Boesky smiled indulgently. This was a chance to talk about himself, the sort of invitation Boesky rarely refused. His voice acquired the peculiar tone of the successful man who tells embroidered stories about his past.

When I graduated from law school, Boesky said, I wanted to intern at the SEC just like you. But I had a *clerkship* with a federal judge that I had to take.

Boesky made it clear to all within earshot what a far more prestigious honor he thought his clerkship had been. He neglected to mention, however, that the judge he clerked for in his hometown of Detroit—The Honorable Theodore Levin—

happened to be his wife's uncle. He also didn't mention that it wasn't a particularly prestigious clerkship.

Boesky and his attorneys left the young man in the hallway and proceeded to the end of a corridor on the fourth floor. A group of SEC enforcement-division lawyers was waiting for them in a small conference room. Boesky's appearance at the commission that day was voluntary, in the technical sense that the enforcement lawyers had not issued him a subpoena compelling him to testify. But there was no question that Boesky was a key subject of an insider trading investigation by the SEC.

The commission's interest had been piqued by suspicious trading in the stock of Dr Pepper, the soft-drink company, which recently had been involved in a complex takeover deal. Records obtained by the commission's staff lawyers showed that Boesky had made millions of dollars by trading in Dr Pepper stock before a takeover of the company was announced. At the same time, Boesky was an investor in the Wall Street firm that bought Dr Pepper. The circumstantial evidence raised an obvious question: Had Boesky acquired his Dr Pepper shares before the takeover because of illegal, inside information about what was about to occur?

It was the sort of question the SEC enforcement staff had asked again and again about Ivan Boesky, yet they never seemed able to prove a case against him. Commission lawyers had questioned Boesky about suspicious stock trading on numerous occasions, dating back to 1974. There was no program in the division to target Boesky, but his name kept popping up in records of stock trading before and after announced corporate takeover bids. Of course, it was Boesky's business to trade in the stocks of companies involved in takeovers, so it was only natural that his name would arise in records subpoenaed by the SEC, but the suspicious timing of his purchases and the huge sums of money he put into takeover stocks raised questions about where he got his information. For several years, Fedders had been frustrated by his division's inability to prove an insider trading case against Boesky or any other big-time Wall Street arbitrageur, and his frustration was shared by senior enforcement lawyers such as Associate Director Gary

Lynch. Some of the staff thought the Dr Pepper case offered the chance for a breakthrough.

Boesky, his lawyers and aides, and the SEC staff attorneys settled in chairs around a small table in the enclosed conference room. Boesky pulled a cigar out of his suitcoat pocket. Before he could light it, one of the SEC lawyers told him to put it away.

I have a right to smoke my cigar, Boesky said.

We'd appreciate it if you didn't, the lawyer answered. This is a small conference room and some of us are allergic to smoke.

I have a right to smoke if I want to, Boesky declared imperiously.

Please, as a courtesy, we ask you not to smoke.

I ask, as a courtesy, that you allow me to smoke.

Counsel, Boesky continued, turning to Henry King, I ask that you demand my right to smoke.

King appeared to be embarrassed.

My client would like to smoke, King said, repeating the obvious.

And so Ivan Boesky lit his cigar and began to fill the room with blue gray smoke, even before the first question was asked of him.

Ivan Boesky was an unusual man, and for the SEC, he presented an unusual challenge.

By that morning in 1984, when he appeared at the commission to testify in the confidential Dr Pepper investigation, Boesky was already famous on Wall Street, a symbol of a new era of takeovers and speculation and extravagant, sudden wealth. Indeed, he seemed to embody the forces that were changing the financial world's cultural mores and business practices: energy, speed, greed, and deal-making. When Jack Shad came to Washington in 1981, on the heels of Ronald Reagan's electoral triumph, Boesky was a little-known stock trader struggling in an arcane profession. By 1984, he had thrust himself to center stage on Wall Street, accumulated a personal fortune approaching $50 million, and helped to transform the corporate takeover game. Since at least August 1982, when he met the dashing, younger merger specialist Martin Siegel at the Harvard Club in Manhattan, and arranged to bribe Siegel for inside information about upcoming takeover events, Boesky had been systematically and audaciously violating the federal securities laws enforced by the SEC.

Siegel wasn't the most important financier who had a special relationship with Boesky. There was an alliance, too, between Boesky and Michael Milken. They had started doing business in a big way in the fall of 1983, when Milken sold $100 million of junk bonds for a hotel company Boesky controlled. A few months later, Milken, his brother, and some of the traders on the Drexel Beverly Hills junk bond trading floor bought a stake in one of Boesky's arbitrage firms. The investment gave Milken a direct financial interest in Boesky's trading of takeover stocks at the same time Milken was helping to finance the very takeover bids on whose outcome Boesky wagered.

So obvious was Milken's conflict of interest, and so great was the potential for leaks of illegal inside information from Milken to Boesky, that the freewheeling Drexel firm was probably the only major brokerage on the Street that knowingly would have permitted its employees to make such an investment. The Milkens' investment, and the $175 million in junk bonds Drexel sold for Boesky during 1984, provided Boesky the cash he coveted to play the risk arbitrage game.

Through these deals, Boesky and Milken became private partners, and by 1984, they had fallen into the habit of providing each other with favors when the need arose. If Milken needed Boesky to help rig the market so that a Drexel-financed takeover would succeed, all he had to do was ask, as he did in 1984 when Boesky helped Milken rig the outcome of a hostile takeover bid by amassing shares in the electrical giant Fischbach Corporation. If Boesky, for tax reasons, or to comply with SEC capital rules, needed temporarily to shift some of his stock and then buy it back later, he called Milken. In either case, the person doing the favor was protected against financial loss by the other—a promise was made that any losses would be made up in the future. A secret, off-the-books, illegal trading arrangement evolved to keep track of the favors and to tally who owed how much to whom. Boesky and Milken each enlisted a trusted accountant and stock trader to help carry out the arrangement and maintain its secret records; the paper trail they created to ensure that no one cheated would later come back to hurt them both.

Following orders from his superiors, Jack Hewitt had dropped his pursuit of Milken before learning anything about his ties to Boesky. And nobody in authority at the SEC knew of or even suspected the scale and extent of Boesky's illegal dealings. Many SEC lawyers and officials saw Boesky the same way most people in the financial world did—as an aggressive, hugely successful, personally idiosyncratic stock market tycoon.

There was a reason for that. Despite his far-flung criminal activities, Boesky worked hard, desperately hard, to cultivate an honest public image. To the press and in increasingly frequent public speeches, he described himself as a kind of Renaissance financier, an intellectual and philanthropist at heart who managed to profit through hard work and exceptional mental faculty. Boesky's risk arbitrage business essentially involved betting millions of dollars each day on the outcome of corporate takeovers. The truth was that Boesky rigged his bets by bribing Wall Street professionals to obtain inside information about takeover deals. In public, though, he claimed that his success was a result of exceptional acuity and skill. He authored a book titled *Merger Mania,* so that, as he wrote, investors large and small could employ technical analysis to profit at arbitrage and "be inspired to believe that confidence in one's self and determination can allow one to become whatever one may dream."

Naturally, Boesky was uncomfortable with the accusation that he was a cheater—a charge lodged with increasing frequency by his competitors during the mid-1980s. Yet, partly because the SEC was unable to mount any credible charges against him, Boesky was able to convince most people that he was successful because he was smarter and worked harder than anyone else. There were stories, which Boesky did nothing to discourage, that he employed people at private airports to track the movement of corporate and personal jets to determine the whereabouts of executives involved in takeover deals. (Such research, since it didn't involve special, inside tips about takeovers from people involved in the deals, would have been legal in most cases.) There were stories, too, about Boesky's almost inhuman dedication to work. It was said that he rose from bed before dawn at his sprawling country estate north of Manhattan, boarded a limousine to arrive at his office before the market opened, then manned a 160-line telephone bank that wired him to brokers and bankers across Wall Street. He cradled a phone against each of his ears for hours at a time and digested documents until late in the evening. He said that he slept just two or three hours each night. "Whoever has the most when he dies wins" was the slogan emblazoned on one of his T-shirts. On Wall Street, traders liked to tell the story of how Boesky, once walking along a beach in France with his wife, had asked her: What good is the moon, if you can't buy it or sell it?

It seemed crucially important to Boesky that he be known and respected for accomplishments outside of finance. He made heavy donations to various philanthropic and educational institutions, ranging from Harvard University to the United Jewish Appeal. Boesky never went to Harvard—he had attended Wayne State University in Detroit and graduated from the Detroit College of Law—but he spent many afternoons at the richly appointed Harvard Club in midtown Manhattan, presiding over business meetings and slipping off occasionally for a game of squash. And though he rose to become chairman of the United Jewish Appeal's fund-raising arm in New York, he had never set foot in Israel. There were times when Boesky did or said something that belied his social and cultural aspirations, exposing the raw nerves that seemed to twitch inside him. Once during a speech in Washington, pausing to accept a cup of coffee, he said, "This is my plasma. I was thinking, vampires live on blood. Well, I live on coffee. This is vampire's plasma." But usually he emphasized his supposed worldliness.

"I don't want you to think that I am just a greedy guy," he once told a college audience, flashing a creepy smile that more nearly resembled a nervous twitch. "I'm not *just* a greedy guy."

Despite what he implied in his speeches, Boesky was not entirely a self-made man—his wife, Seema, was independently and fabulously rich. When Boesky moved from Michigan to Wall Street in 1966, he was backed in part by Seema's father, Ben

Silberstein, who owned the Beverly Hills Hotel and other real estate properties. There were those who speculated that Boesky's obvious insecurities about his status and accomplishments traced in part to his relationship with Silberstein, who gave indications that Boesky, the son of Russian Jewish immigrants in the Detroit restaurant business, was unworthy of his daughter at the time of their marriage.

Silberstein helped him early on, but the rest was Boesky's doing. He sometimes found it difficult to work for other people, which helped to explain why he changed jobs so frequently after moving to New York. Even in the small and specialized field of risk arbitrage, Boesky was an outsider on Wall Street. Throughout the 1960s and 1970s, arbitrage had been the province of aggressive, well-known stock traders at major, prestigious Wall Street firms, people such as Gus Levy at Goldman, Sachs & Company and Salim B. Lewis at Bear, Stearns & Company. During the 1970s, Boesky traded stocks at several relatively small Wall Street firms, and then finally struck out on his own. His timing was fortuitous. In the early 1980s, spurred in part by the influence of Chicago School economists and the SEC's deregulatory policies, the corporate takeover market burgeoned. The boom created new opportunities to profit by speculating on the outcome of merger deals.

Boesky's edge was his willingness to make larger bets on the outcome of corporate takeover deals than virtually any of his competitors. He felt that arbitrage had too long been dominated by a handful of big Wall Street firms, and he set out to practice the craft in a manner bigger and bolder than any independent player who had come before. Although he sometimes had inside information, arbitrage was still a risky business, especially the way Boesky went about it. He invested millions of dollars in the stocks of companies he thought would become targets of corporate takeovers, and he borrowed heavily. If Boesky's information about a particular deal was uncertain, he was exposed to potentially enormous losses. If a deal fell apart, he could lose millions of dollars in just a few minutes when the price of a takeover target's stock tumbled. On the other hand, by borrowing heavily and taking such huge positions, Boesky could make Himalayan profits when a deal went his way. In his speeches and interviews, Boesky liked to argue that takeover arbitrage was less risky than picking individual stocks for investment, since the shares he bought and sold were primarily affected by the dynamics of a specific deal, and typically were immune to the sharp swings in investor sentiment that sometimes pounded the rest of the stock market without warning.

Research—legal and illegal—was at the heart of Boesky's business. Young analysts and investment advisers and lawyers who worked in his offices high in a Fifth Avenue skyscraper pored over public statements about corporate finances and management. Boesky worked the phones, nudging and badgering investment bankers, lawyers, and corporate executives for information about pending and upcoming takeovers. While it was illegal in most instances to acquire and then trade on inside information, such as the precise price of a secret takeover bid to be announced publicly at a future date, there was much information that fell into a legal gray area. To his colleagues and competitors on Wall Street, it often seemed that Boesky didn't care what was gray and what was black and white—he wanted to learn everything he could about takeover deals.

Arbitrage was for many years a quiet, obscure business. Boesky's competitors, large and small, abhorred his self-promotion. They dubbed him "Piggy" because of the massive amounts of stock he bought in certain takeover deals, squeezing out his competitors, and because of the aggressive borrowing techniques he used to accumulate ever larger positions. Federal Reserve rules instituted in the 1930s in response to the stock market crash generally restricted investors to borrowing only 50 percent of the purchase price of stocks, but Boesky employed legally questionable techniques to evade that limit and borrow more than 80 percent in certain situations. He also raised millions of dollars from wealthy individuals outside of Wall Street to fund his arbitrage operation, bucking unwritten rules on the Street by purchasing big newspaper ads soliciting investments in his firm.

Because he rapidly bought and sold huge blocks of stock in

companies involved in takeover fights, trading in and out of his shares within hours or days or weeks, Boesky became a powerful player in the hostile takeover game. He was a speculator, the ultimate short-term investor. His primary motive was to facilitate the completion of deals—he wanted to sell his stock to the highest bidder in the shortest possible time, and like the corporate raiders and their junk bond backers at Drexel, Boesky made his biggest profits when a company was sold or restructured. Corporations feared and shunned him. The last thing a stable company wanted was to have a large block of its stock fall into the hands of Ivan Boesky, an arbitrager who would push hard to see a takeover succeed.

The SEC's enforcement division questioned Boesky repeatedly as his influence in the stock market grew, but the commission adopted no rules or regulations designed to curb his aggressive, speculative trading techniques. In large part, that was because Jack Shad regarded Ivan Boesky as a legitimate and indeed admirable stock trader who poured buckets and buckets of the economic "liquidity" into the financial markets, cash that would "wash like water through the economy" and help to make it fertile.

Ever since his days on Wall Street, Shad had believed that risk arbitragers like Boesky provided crucial amounts of capital to make stock market trading efficient, especially during complex corporate-takeover battles. Boesky had millions of dollars of cash, much of it borrowed, to pour into the market, and by doing so, he made it easier for other investors to buy and sell stocks as they wished, Shad believed. Shad's view of arbitrage reflected the same Chicago School theories that had shaped his approach to the earlier debate over stock futures: some speculation, some gambling, was good for the financial markets and for the country.

Ignorant of Boesky's illegal dealings, Shad also thought Boesky's aggressive trading in the stocks of takeover targets helped small investors by providing them a way to achieve profits without significant risk. In a typical takeover, once a bid was announced, the target company's stock skyrocketed quickly to a level near the announced price of the merger. Since Boesky was so active buying up shares of the target's stock during this period, a small investor could sell out his holdings, reap a premium profit, and not worry about whether the takeover deal was completed or rebuffed. The transaction between Boesky and a small investor in that situation reflected the theory of risk transfer that underlay the futures markets in Chicago: The small investor, who was unwilling to speculate on the outcome of a takeover, transferred his risk to Boesky, who was more than willing to gamble on the deal. Without Boesky and other arbs gobbling up shares of the target's stock, the small investor would not be able to sell at a price close to the takeover offer. It seemed more appropriate to Shad for a market professional like Boesky to assume the risk that the takeover deal would fall through, profiting on his short-term holdings if the deal was consummated and losing money if things fell apart. Shad thought such arbitrage trading, if practiced legally, enhanced not only the efficiency but the essential fairness of the stock market.

Some of Shad's more conservative friends from Wall Street, those such as takeover attorney Martin Lipton, who had praised his bold "Leveraging of America" speech, argued to Shad privately that he was missing the point. Arbs such as Boesky, they said, were merely short-term speculators who teamed up with raiders and Wall Street deal makers like Milken to make fast profits by putting companies "into play" in the merger market, forcing them to be sold. There were even some who took their criticism of Shad's policies public. "In its opposition to any restriction on takeovers, the SEC, founded to protect the investor against the financial wolves, has now become the protector of the wolves," wrote management consultant Peter F. Drucker, in a prominent newspaper column in 1984, when Boesky's influence in the stock market was rising rapidly.

But Shad held firm. Shad pretty much saw Boesky the way Boesky wanted to be seen: as an intellectual, a stock-trading craftsman who built his business on research and strict adherence to complex, technical, mathematical formulas. As a general matter, Wall Street was an honest place, Shad thought, and he saw no reason to distrust Boesky, though he had some reservations because of the constant rumors that Boesky profited by cheating.

Fedders and others among Shad's enforcement staff became concerned during the mid-1980s about Boesky's increasing forays into what was called premerger arbitrage, the practice of buying large blocks of stocks in potential takeover targets before any merger bid was announced. Some among the enforcement staff saw Boesky's consistent pattern of successfully predicting takeover targets as circumstantial evidence of insider trading. But Shad defended the practice. Much of this sort of trading, he argued, mirroring Boesky's claims, was based on detailed research into corporations and observation of market-trading patterns. And some of it, Shad said, was based on straightforward financial analysis that helped to predict which companies were likely to become takeover targets.

Fedders's enforcement staff, despite their devotion to prosecutions of insider trading, had not been able to present evidence to Shad that Boesky engaged in illegal conduct. Boesky had been a subject of enforcement inquiries since before Shad arrived at the SEC. An early commission investigation, in 1974, was typical of those that followed. SEC staff noticed that Boesky, then an employee of the Wall Street firm Edwards & Hanly, had aggressively purchased shares of the movie company Twentieth Century Fox and then sold them at a profit to an investor named David Merrick, before it was known that Merrick was considering a takeover bid. The SEC asked Boesky to testify about where he had gotten his information, but during the interrogation, which occurred two months after Boesky's suspicious trading, the arbitrager claimed that he could not remember much of anything about the deal. "I specifically don't recall any of my discussions with anyone, but I probably had some discussions," Boesky testified. "If you asked me fifty-eight days ago what my conversations were, I probably would have had a more specific response." He even denied knowing who it was he had sold his stock to at a profit. He only found out it was Merrick, he said, "when I read about it in the newspaper."

The investigation went nowhere, for the same reason that most SEC insider trading probes of active Wall Street traders like Boesky went nowhere. Boesky was trading in the stock market all day long, buying and selling shares, talking to lawyers, chatting with investment bankers, trading gossip with other arbitragers. When asked during an investigation how he learned a particularly profitable piece of information about a takeover, Boesky could claim that he read it in a newspaper, that he did not recall, that he overheard two men talking in an elevator, or that he pieced it together from random conversations with numerous market professionals—all perfectly innocent explanations. In most insider trading cases filed by the SEC, the defendant was someone who rarely traded stocks and got caught because he made an exceptional purchase based on inside information, a purchase that was difficult to explain if the buyer didn't have an inside tip. Boesky, though, always had a reason to be trading the stocks of takeover targets. After all, that was his business.

Driven by Shad's edict to crack down on insider trading, Congress passed a new law in 1984 that substantially increased the financial penalties for insider trading. Instead of a slap on the wrist that involved only giving up illegal profits, inside traders could be forced to pay treble damages. While the SEC filed as many as two dozen insider cases each year during the early 1980s, none were against the powerful market professionals who operated at the heart of Wall Street. Without a cooperating witness, a stool pigeon who could contradict the memory lapses and vague claims of witnesses like Boesky, many of Fedders's top enforcement staff felt there was nothing they could do. All they typically had was sketchy circumstantial evidence, certainly not enough to take to court.

Many of the enforcement lawyers who questioned and investigated Boesky did not doubt his word or consider him dishonest. On the contrary, though Boesky could be arrogant and difficult, he also was regarded by some enforcement lawyers as a highly knowledgeable and exceptionally valuable source of information about how the stock market really worked. Boesky testified in more than ten confidential SEC investigations during the 1970s and 1980s, but usually he appeared voluntarily and provided what was believed to be useful data about events and patterns of trading in specific takeovers. During the late 1970s, the SEC questioned Boesky about trading in takeovers involving United Technologies and British Oxygen Corporation, and in the early

1980s, he was questioned as part of an investigation into a take-over battle involving the Wall Street firm Paine Webber. But Boesky was not the sole target of these SEC investigations, and the commission never filed insider-trading charges against him.

In its two principal areas of responsibility—making regulatory policy and enforcing the securities laws—John Shad's SEC had done little by 1984 to hinder Ivan Boesky's extraordinary rise on Wall Street. The Dr Pepper case, the investigation that brought Boesky to SEC headquarters in his limousine on a weekday morning in 1984, was supposed to be different.

Not only had Boesky profited enormously by trading in Dr Pepper stock in advance of a public takeover announcement, not only did he have a web of personal and financial connections to people involved in the takeover, but Fedders's staff had developed credible evidence that Boesky had tried to obtain inside information about the Dr Pepper deal before he traded in the company's stock.

The enforcement attorneys had pieced together a colorful, detailed chronology of Boesky's involvement with the Dr Pepper takeover even before Boesky arrived at SEC headquarters and began to blow cigar smoke at the staff. The chronology was based on records subpoenaed by the commission and testimony provided by some of the executives and Wall Street bankers who had participated in the deal.

The story, as the SEC staff understood it, began in 1978, when Ted Forstmann, a former Yale hockey goalie with a knack for sales, visited Boesky in his lower-Manhattan office and asked if he wanted to become a limited partner in a new investment firm called Forstmann Little & Company. The firm, Forstmann said, would specialize in leveraged buyouts, deals in which public companies were acquired using mostly borrowed money. The goal was to identify stocks of public companies that were undervalued, seek control of those companies through friendly takeovers, and then try to make money.

The profits would come in several ways, Forstmann explained. Generally, an investor like Boesky could expect to make a hefty financial return of five to ten times his money within three to five years. In some cases, the profits would come when Forstmann Little sold the companies it acquired. In other cases, after improving operations and giving the managements of the acquired companies ownership incentives to run their businesses more efficiently, Forstmann Little would profit by selling shares in the companies back to the public. Though the deals were risky, Forstmann was cautious—he was fearful of doing a bad deal and wanted to proceed carefully.

Boesky agreed to become a partner. Not only could he make a lot of money, he figured, but working with Forstmann would widen his network of contacts and keep him attuned to the flow of information about takeovers on Wall Street.

Boesky and Forstmann had never met before Forstmann solicited the arbitrager's investment, but in the next few years they developed a closer personal relationship, especially as Forstmann Little grew and prospered, becoming one of the most successful leveraged-buyout firms in the country. Forstmann Little's first acquisition—the $420 million purchase of a North Carolina furniture company in 1980—had led to a public sale of stock that reaped ten times the initial investment for Forstmann's partners. Boesky decided that he wanted to know Forstmann better, so he invited him to appear as a guest lecturer at a finance course Boesky taught at Columbia University.

Boesky pressed to get even closer. In the fall of 1983, he invited Forstmann and corporate raider Boone Pickens, along with some Wall Street executives, to a Sunday dinner at Boesky's Westchester County estate. (Boesky told Pickens to dress casually, so he wore an open-neck shirt and blazer. Boesky, clad in a double-breasted navy blue suit, offered to lend Pickens a tie. "I don't borrow ties or shotguns," Pickens replied.) Before dinner, Boesky asked Forstmann to take a walk with him through the sculpture gardens he maintained behind his mansion.

"Are you guys busy these days?" Boesky asked Forstmann as they strolled past Renaissance busts and ancient Greek torsos.

"Yes."

"What are you working on?"

"Dr Pepper," Forstmann answered.

"What do you think it is worth?"

"I don't know, I have no idea," Forstmann said.

In the weeks that followed, Boesky pelted Forstmann with telephone calls, asking him how things were going. For Boesky to buy Dr Pepper stock on the basis of confidential information about an upcoming Forstmann Little takeover bid would violate insider-trading laws. But Forstmann, who thought of Boesky as a partner and investor in his firm, rather than as a professional speculator who might buy Dr Pepper shares, often answered Boesky's questions.

On November 17, 1983, Forstmann and his partners submitted a $22 a share, $623 million cash offer to take control of Dr Pepper. The company's directors approved the Forstmann offer and a final agreement was signed on December 3. Boesky earned millions of dollars in stock trading profits by selling the Dr Pepper shares he had accumulated before the takeover was announced.

It was the walk in the sculpture garden that most intrigued the SEC enforcement staff. It seemed clear to the commission lawyers that Boesky had acquired inside information about Forstmann Little's interest in Dr Pepper. The question was whether the SEC could prove in court that Boesky had used that information to purchase Dr Pepper shares.* One problem was that the *Wall Street Journal* had published a story before the walk in the sculpture garden saying Dr Pepper was for sale. Fedders's staff knew that Boesky might claim he had bought the stock on the basis of rumor or newspaper reports or the phases of the moon. "I swear I didn't know Forstmann Little was going to make a [$22 a share] bid," Boesky told a colleague in New York before he flew to Washington for his interrogation at the SEC. To this colleague it sounded more as if Boesky were rehearsing for a play.

---

* After the SEC investigation of Boesky's Dr Pepper trading, Forstmann Little & Company asked Boesky to sign an agreement promising that he would not be an active trader of the stocks of companies that Forstmann Little was pursuing. Boesky initially resisted signing such an agreement, but later did. However, it is believed that he did not live up to all of the agreement's terms, and continued trading in certain situations where Forstmann Little had an interest in making an acquisition.

Boesky parroted that denial in the fourth-floor conference room clouded with cigar smoke that day in 1984. The commission lawyers pressed him about his Dr Pepper trading. Why had he bought the stock? How had he learned of an impending takeover at the company? What did he make of Ted Forstmann's responses in the sculpture garden?

Boesky refused to yield. He told the SEC lawyers that he hadn't traded a single share of Dr Pepper stock on the basis of inside information. About the details of the enforcement staff's chronology, Boesky was somewhat vague. Witnesses in SEC insider trading investigations often were.

Ivan Boesky understood this much: Without an inside witness against him, without a Marty Siegel or Michael Milken, there was no way the Securities and Exchange Commission could touch him.

When the deposition was over that afternoon, Boesky and his entourage rode the elevator back down to the commission lobby. Boesky climbed into his black stretch limousine and rolled away— he planned to fly back to Wall Street on his private plane. To his lawyers and colleagues, he appeared confident about how things had gone. None of them knew about Boesky's secret, criminal alliances. None of them knew, either, whether Boesky had told the truth upstairs on the fourth floor.

For their part, the senior attorneys in the enforcement division, led by Fedders, felt frustrated. They felt it was important for the division to mount an insider trading prosecution against a major market professional. The Dr Pepper case had seemed promising, but after Boesky's deposition, the investigation was stymied—the circumstantial evidence was so limiting, and if charges were filed, the trial would come down to Boesky's word against the commission's. That wasn't enough for Fedders to make a positive recommendation to Shad and the other commissioners. Besides, Fedders's staff had only its suspicions, no real proof that Boesky had traded Dr Pepper stock specifically because of his sculpture garden talk with Forstmann. In effect, Boesky had employed successfully the same defense he offered during the early SEC investigation of his trading back in 1974—"I read it in the newspaper." In ten years, nothing much had changed.

13

Confrontation

Be reasonable," Fedders told him over the telephone, but the words only seemed to make Bobby Lawyer angrier.

There is no question but that Merrill Lynch and Company deserves to be publicly charged with fraud, Lawyer kept saying, his voice rising each time he had to argue the point again.

Yet he couldn't get through, and he was frustrated. Lawyer was in San Francisco, where he headed the commission's Bay Area branch office, while Fedders was on the fourth floor of SEC headquarters in Washington. Lawyer could only defend himself and the work of his office by telephone, a limited means of communication for an attorney used to prancing and arguing in a courtroom. It was late in 1984—more than two years after Lawyer's office had initiated a major confidential investigation into alleged securities fraud by a Merrill Lynch broker in San Francisco, and into the failure of the largest Wall Street brokerage firm to detect and stop the broker's wrongdoing. Now Fedders was telling Lawyer that one of the San Francisco office's main recommendations, that Merrill Lynch be named in the case as a defendant, was meeting stiff opposition in Washington.

All Lawyer had was the telephone, so he kept using it. He peppered the commission's headquarters with calls—to Fedders, to the general counsel's office, to the staffs of individual commissioners, to the commissioners themselves. He argued, prodded, questioned, and generally made himself a nuisance. Lawyer and some of his colleagues in San Francisco had decided that even if their stridency somehow hurt their careers by angering their superiors at headquarters, they would push as hard as they could. Within weeks they had set the stage for a tumultuous confrontation over commission policy with SEC Chairman John Shad.

It came just as Shad was consolidating an uneasy truce with the SEC bureaucracy. The senior staff who on most days of the week drifted in and out of loosely structured meetings in the chairman's expansive office suite in Washington were loyal to Shad. Fedders had a tight grip on the policies of the enforcement division, and he consulted regularly with the chairman. Linda Quinn, who had managed the takeover advisory committee and then become Shad's chief of staff, was indefatigably efficient, able to match the chairman's relentless pace. Dan Goelzer, Shad's first chief of staff, had moved over to become general counsel, a job he had always coveted, and his personal rapport with Shad along with his unique skills as a politician within the bureaucracy gave the chairman a new control over the commission's legal policies. Rick Ketchum in the market regulation division seemed more amenable to Shad's deregulatory approach than his predecessor had been.

There were new and friendlier faces among Shad's four commission colleagues as well. When free market economist Charles Cox came on board as a commissioner, he replaced John Evans, the Republican and former SEC staff member who had so often opposed the chairman on enforcement matters. Shad's rival on budget issues, Barbara Thomas, also was gone. The two Democratic commission seats were occupied by newcomers, former congressional staffer Charles Marinaccio and Los Angeles attorney Aulana Peters. Neither of them shared Shad's ideology but they had no history at the commission, either; no emotional ties to the staff or its agenda. One of the Democrats had replaced Bevis Longstreth, the Manhattan attorney whose friendship with Shad had helped to bridge the political differences between them.

Longstreth's 1984 farewell party in commission headquarters had focused attention on the friction in Shad's relationships with the other commissioners and especially with the staff. At the party, Longstreth had a piano hauled into the room and he serenaded Shad and the gathered staff with an original solo—"Ruler of the SEC"—to the tune of "When I was a lad" from Gilbert and Sullivan's *H.M.S. Pinafore*.

> When Shad was a lad he served a term
> As office boy to the Hutton firm.
> He crunched the numbers and made deals galore
> And fed himself abundantly on free market lore.
> He praised the free market so zealously
> That Reagan made him ruler of the SEC.
>
> He signed on Fedders as enforcement mate
> And pledged him sternly to deregulate. . . .
>
> In laying plans John failed to note
> That Congress allotted him just one vote. . . .
> Yes, the Congress had decreed for the SEC
> A five-headed beast to act collegially.
>
> How we would vote was hard to tell:
> Each wanted power, had no vote to sell.
> 'Gainst inside trading there was broad concensus
> But on the budget Shad stood against us.
> In budgetary matters we agreed to disagree
> With the Reaganomic ruler of the SEC.
>
> Our Chairman said I'm for competition,
> But on 415 to the Street I'll listen. . . .
> Yes, shelving the rule might be the key
> To industry affection for the SEC.
>
> Commissioners come and Commissioners go,
> Hemming in their Chairman, be he John or Joe.
> And Congressmen, feigning oversight,
> Holler to the press and pretend to fight.
> Yet to each comes this discovery:
> It's the staff who rule the roost at the SEC.

"Bevis," Shad declared amid resounding laughter, "leave us." They could laugh with and at each other in SEC headquarters, bound by mutual dependence, familiarity, and genuine affection. Yet in some respects the import of Longstreth's lyrical insights was greatest for those staff who never heard his song. Out in the SEC's far-flung bureaucracy, among a number of the staff who did not meet with Shad daily, whose careers were not lifted by his patronage, resentments festered. This was especially true in the fifteen SEC regional and branch offices scattered around the country, where hundreds of attorneys, accountants, and investigators worked on enforcement cases and inspections that often seemed tedious and unappreciated by headquarters. Nearly all the headline-grabbing insider trading cases were managed by an elite group that worked closely with Fedders and Shad in Washington.

To some senior attorneys in the regional offices, Shad was only a distant caricature perceived as a knee-jerk, budget-cutting former Wall Street tycoon hostile to the commission he now ran. Shad helped his cause little when, in a speech to a conclave of stock traders in Boca Raton, Florida, he joked that he recently had been told that the definition of a "damn shame" was a busload of government officials going over a cliff—with five empty seats. The remark was reported in the press and Shad apologized, but the incident only reinforced suspicions in the regional offices. All the regional managers struggled because of the budgetary restraint supported by Shad. Secretaries, computers, even desks and chairs, were sometimes hard to come by in the mid-1980s, and it seemed to some that the headquarters staff in Washington didn't much care. It angered and appalled Ira Lee Sorkin, chief of the commission's busy New York office, that while Shad commuted every weekend between Washington and his Park Avenue apartment, in four years the chairman stopped by the New York Regional Office only once or twice—so unknown was Shad that an employee there once mistook him for an intruder and asked to know who he was and what he was doing.

Bobby Lawyer in San Francisco shared Sorkin's indignation about Shad. Litigators possessed of raucous demeanors and politically liberal outlooks, Lawyer and Sorkin talked occasionally by telephone, as did other disgruntled regional office attorneys.

When the Merrill Lynch case erupted into an emotional confrontation with Shad's office, Lawyer's crusade became a vessel for some pent-up frustrations among certain commission staff in Washington and at the regional offices.

Around the time of Bobby Lawyer's crusade, for instance, frustration was also building in the regional office closest to SEC headquarters—the Washington Regional Office (WRO) in suburban Virginia. Though it was just a short distance from the commission's imposing headquarters in Washington, where the flags and the bustle and the sense of urgency in every hallway contributed to the SEC's culture of self-importance, the forty-employee WRO seemed a world apart. Shad apparently never visited the place.

In theory, the WRO was supposed to function like the major regional offices in Los Angeles, New York, and Chicago, all of which had troubles of their own partly because of Shad's neglect. But the WRO's difficulties were even worse. On paper, its mission was to enforce federal securities laws along the Eastern Seaboard in a five-state region that included Pennsylvania, Delaware, Virginia, West Virginia, Maryland, and the District of Columbia. But the truth was that, when a prestigious or politically charged case came along—the sort of case that might catapult the WRO to prominence and attract talented lawyers—senior lawyers at SEC headquarters took over.

The big problem at the WRO wasn't turf, though—it was sex, drinking, and discrimination, or so said staff attorney Catherine Broderick.

Before Broderick filed a formal grievance in 1984, it was hard to know whether the antics she encountered so routinely in the WRO were known to Shad and the senior staff at nearby SEC headquarters. Broderick's grievance was the opening shot in the SEC's Equal Employment Opportunity (EEO) process, in which disgruntled employees had the right to file documents laying out their complaints. The EEO process was lengthy and rarely satisfying, and it was something Shad and many of the other senior level appointees paid little attention to during the Reagan years. In part, that was because those who held political authority at big agencies like the SEC knew they likely would be in government a relatively short time and felt no identity of interest with the huge class of permanent government employees beneath them. And in part it was because early in the EEO process there was no way to weed routine and illegitimate complaints from those allegations that were serious and meritorious. Moreover, many of the ideological conservatives who held the government's most important posts during the 1980s were utterly indifferent to the issue of employment discrimination.

At the SEC, John Shad said he saw the issue of employment discrimination the way he saw most everything else: through the filter of free market theory. After he came to Washington, Shad said on numerous occasions that he had learned many years before, in a case at the Harvard Business School, that discrimination was bad for the bottom line. He boasted publicly that he was promoting more women to senior positions at the SEC than ever before. His daughter, Leslie, was in law school, and Shad clearly wanted to see her treated with respect whether she worked in private practice or government. Though senior SEC officials praised Shad's handling of EEO issues, there were those inside the commission and out who doubted Shad's commitment to civil rights and the eradication of racial and sexual discrimination. For Catherine Broderick and some other mid-level employees at the SEC, the gap between Shad's public rhetoric and daily reality seemed immense. To them, Shad's priorities had seemed clear since the day that the EEO director's office had been moved to the basement of SEC headquarters to make room for the new Office of the Chief Economist that Shad created.

Broderick found working in the WRO humiliating and embarrassing. Far from a bastion of the public service ideal, the Washington Regional Office seemed at times like an oily swingers' pad from some camp Hollywood movie of the 1960s. As time went on, Broderick discovered that she wasn't the only one in the WRO who had uncomfortable experiences with some supervisors who made crude remarks, solicited sexual favors from subordinates, and granted favorable evaluations and other awards in exchange for sexual favors. Broderick declared on her grievance form that supervisors in the office maintained a "hostile and oppressive working environment" and discriminated against her by giving her unfair performance evaluations because she refused to take part in office parties and other social activities.

Broderick sent a memo to Shad, outlining some of her complaints, and then waited to see what would happen. EEO Director Phil Savage—the civil rights veteran whose office had been shifted to the basement in favor of Shad's chief economist—was immediately intrigued and amazed by Broderick's allegations of womanizing and boozing during work hours. He began to look into her claims. Typical of the pace of workplace discrimination cases, it would take years before the matter bubbled to the surface and became public, putting John Shad and the SEC's self-conscious traditions of excellence on trial. In the meantime, the matter would remain, like so many other things on the sixth floor of commission headquarters, a closely guarded SEC secret.

To those who knew him and believed in him, including the mostly young and liberal staff in the SEC's San Francisco office, there was nobody at the SEC better qualified to lead a righteous crusade than Bobby Lawyer. He was a balding, energetic, perceptive black man with unruly tufts of hair on the sides of his head, protuberant teeth, and an ego bigger than Mississippi, where he was born. Lawyer had grown up in the racially divided Old South, the middle of seven children. His father was an interstate truck driver and his mother worked odd jobs until the last of her children finished school—all seven went to college, though neither of Lawyer's parents had gone themselves. As a child in Vicksburg, Lawyer had to walk past three of the white elementary schools to get to the segregated school for black kids. There were all-white swimming pools, all-white restaurants, all-white bathrooms, all-white seats on the bus. Later, it was Lawyer's habit to shrug off the obstacles he had faced without bitterness. "What can I say?" was one of his signature phrases around the SEC office in San Francisco. On the topic of Vicksburg, the question posed to himself was followed by: "I was a kid. It was segregated. . . . You knew it didn't seem right. You knew that for sure."

There was no explanation for his peculiar surname, other than the guess that it reflected the occupation of some long-ago slave-owner. Still, Lawyer came to Harlem as a teenager in the late 1950s suspecting that he might become an attorney even if it meant, as it did, that he would have to attend high school and college during the day while working through the night. He lived on 145th Street and took the "A" train down to the garment district, where he pushed hand trucks and delivered dresses to the finest Manhattan department stores, like Saks Fifth Avenue. He started out majoring in chemistry but switched to prelaw, drawn by the romantic image of the trial lawyers he saw on television and at the movies. He told others he wanted to be the kind of trial attorney who could dominate a crowded courtroom and triumph with dramatic cross-examination. After enrolling at Columbia University Law School in 1965, he became active in the civil rights movement, and once he finished, he spent two years working with a group of criminal attorneys in an experimental antipoverty law office in East Harlem. From there he was recruited to be an assistant U.S. attorney—a federal prosecutor—in the prestigious Southern District of New York, the Manhattan office that brought big, complex criminal cases against the city's political bosses, the Mafia, and errant titans on Wall Street. One of Lawyer's office-mates was a young, ambitious prosecutor named Rudolph W. Giuliani, who as Manhattan U.S. Attorney during the 1980s would lead, in tandem with the SEC, the most ambitious prosecutions of Wall Street corruption ever.

Stanley Sporkin brought Lawyer to the commission in 1975. After two years as a trial lawyer in Washington, he headed for the West Coast. He was named chief of the San Francisco office, with a staff of forty, less than two years before Jack Shad came to the SEC.

Three thousand miles from Washington, Lawyer had the freedom and autonomy to choose the investigations he wanted to pursue aggressively. He had no particular interest in the insider trading prosecutions urged by Fedders and Shad; his preference was for cases where there were more tangible victims, real people or companies who had been defrauded and whose losses could be

restored or at least avenged. In that respect, at least, the Merrill
Lynch investigation was the kind of cause Bobby Lawyer liked
most of all. Before it was over, the matter that generated so much
controversy inside the SEC that fall of 1984 would bring Lawyer
face-to-face with Shad in a dramatic confrontation at the commission table. Lawyer didn't mind that, either.

> He is now [saying]—just get rid of [the customer]—he no longer
> is of any value to Merrill Lynch—he has no more money! Uncon-
> scionable behavior for a Merrill Lynch broker. The customer feels
> as though he has been taken for a ride—and I'm having difficulty
> in defending our position. Please review the above and advise what
> action you want me to take.
> —Memo from Merrill Lynch manager Louis Trujillo to super-
> visor Robert Fisher, July 22, 1981.

On a busy summer weekday, John J. Bruns, an investigator on
Bobby Lawyer's staff, strode unannounced into the Merrill Lynch
branch office in San Francisco, situated in a financial district store-
front amid the towering skyscrapers and Lego-like shopping con-
courses engulfing the eastern tip of the city peninsula.

Coincidentally, as Bruns walked through the door, halfway
across the country the Smith Barney naked-options-writing group
was being visited by financial catastrophe in Rhinelander, Wisconsin. But Bruns knew nothing about that case, at least not at the beginning. Soon it became clear to the SEC staff that both the Smith
Barney and Merrill Lynch matters revolved around the same question of when to punish an investment house for the misconduct of
a stockbroker. But all Bruns knew then was that a disgruntled customer of Merrill Lynch had written to the commission complaining
of the allegedly fraudulent sales techniques of a stockbroker
named Victor Matl, and of the failure of Matl's supervisors to make
amends.

Bruns identified himself and said he was there to conduct a
surprise inspection of the Merrill Lynch office on behalf of the
Securities and Exchange Commission. He asked to speak to the
branch office manager, Robert Fisher, or whomever else might be
in charge. He said he wanted to see Merrill Lynch's customer
complaint file.

The office managers scrambled to accommodate him, and soon Bruns was flipping through a file of complaints that dated back to the 1970s. The file raised serious questions about stockbroker Victor Matl's conduct and also about Merrill Lynch's decision to keep him on as a salesman in the face of so many fraud allegations by his customers. About thirty-five complaints had been lodged against Matl since 1978—many more than against any other of the approximately seventy-five account executives in the office. At one point recently, Matl had been generating a complaint every week. And the accusations against him were far from trivial. They ran the gamut from forgery to unauthorized trading in brokerage accounts to clearly improper sales techniques.

When he finished reading, Bruns trundled back across Market Street to the SEC's dreary offices in the low-rent Tenderloin district. He told his superiors what he had found. Within days, Bobby Lawyer authorized a full-scale inquiry into Matl's conduct and Merrill Lynch's supervision.

Commission attorneys and investigators fanned out across the Bay area, interviewing customers whose names appeared in the complaint file. The SEC staff was led by Cary Lapidus, a young SEC lawyer who had come to the San Francisco office from headquarters in Washington in part because he wanted to work for Bobby Lawyer. The stories Lapidus and the others heard appalled them.

Max L. Christensen, an Episcopal priest in San Francisco nearing his retirement, said he had opened a money market account with Merrill Lynch by depositing $42,000, nearly all of his worldly wealth, through the mail. Victor Matl soon telephoned, saying that he had been assigned as Christensen's stockbroker. Christensen said he didn't want to do anything with his money except let it earn interest for a few months. Matl said he understood, but then suggested that the priest use his money as collateral for loans that would allow him to play the stock market in a big way. Christensen demurred. A month later he received an account statement showing that without authorization, Matl had borrowed about $30,000 from the priest's account and had sunk it all into a risky oil stock. When Christensen called to protest, Matl assured him everything was safe. There was a way Matl had of making even the most preposterous ideas seem safe and desirable. There was plenty of hard sell in his approach, but his aggression was tempered by kindly, mollifying assurances. Matl had a thick Czech accent, and he spewed financial jargon as if it were a secret code only he understood. He cajoled, pressured, cajoled, pressured. Christensen explained to the SEC investigators that he had trusted Matl.

"I've been forty years in the ministry and I've seen all kinds," he said. "He had a style that fooled me."

The oil stock plummeted in price, forcing Christensen to sell at a loss to pay off his borrowings. Matl pushed him to invest in another little-known oil company and to begin trading risky stock options. He sent application forms to Christensen so that extensive options trading could be authorized—unsure what the forms were, Christensen and his wife signed them without filling in any of the financial information required. The SEC investigators requested the records from Merrill Lynch and found that Matl had filled in the blanks himself, without permission. Instead of writing in the Christensens' actual net worth of about $50,000, Matl entered a figure of $500,000. The form was approved by an office supervisor, and Matl began trading options aggressively in the priest's account. Christensen had heart trouble, and his health deteriorated along with his finances. He was hospitalized for surgery, and even while Christensen was flat on his back, Matl continued to trade the account without permission, earning commissions for himself while steadily losing the original $42,000 balance. One year after mailing in his deposit, Christensen had only $7,000 left. "That was my inheritance and my savings," the priest said. "It was a disaster in terms of what we thought of as future security. . . . I didn't contemplate jumping off a bridge, although I was quite close."

There were other stories. Albert Iaccarino and his wife, Rose Scalise, both doctors, said that when Matl took over their accounts, he sold off more than $100,000 worth of conservative utility stocks and replaced them with more speculative investments—without telling them or seeking their permission. Robert Reeves, a junior high school principal, said he told Matl that his investment goal was to help his children buy homes. Matl then pushed Reeves into speculative stocks and he lost $10,000 in three months. Jan Haraszthy, a retired wine merchant, deposited $15,000 into an account assigned to Matl, who quickly recommended that Haraszthy invest in a tax-exempt municipal trust. Haraszthy declined but Matl ordered the trade anyway.*

As they built their case, conducting interviews, organizing documents, and taking formal testimony from Merrill Lynch officials, it became increasingly clear to Lawyer, Lapidus, and the other SEC staff that they had a solid foundation for fraud charges against Matl. What intrigued them as much as the breadth and depth of Matl's violations of securities law, however, was the possible culpability of Merrill Lynch and some of its supervisory officials. What they had in mind was a special type of disciplinary action the SEC could bring naming a brokerage—a 15c4 administrative proceeding commonly called a "failure to supervise" case. Though legally it was not as serious as many other types of SEC charges, a failure-to-supervise action hurt a firm's reputation and was designed for situations where there had been a systemic breakdown in monitoring the conduct of employees.

For the San Francisco staff, the issue seemed measurable in dollars and cents. Victor Matl's boss, Merrill Lynch branch manager Robert Fisher, supervised a booming office in San Francisco, one that generated about $20 million in revenue each year. That was hardly a decisive amount for a worldwide giant the size of Merrill Lynch, the largest brokerage firm in the United States, but it wasn't small change, either. Fisher's own compensation depended to an extent on the profitability of his office. That profitability, in turn, depended on the commissions generated by his brokers, known as account executives. From top to bottom, the retail brokerage business depended on commissions. And that gave Fisher an incentive to ignore the complaints about Victor Matl.

* SEC records do not reflect Matl's response to these specific complaints, but Matl said on several occasions that he was authorized to make the trades that customers were complaining about.

The account executives in Merrill Lynch's San Francisco branch handled more than 25,000 accounts, but as with most sales forces, there were only a handful of exceptional salesmen. These big sellers—producers, as they were called in the brokerage business—generated a disproportionate amount of the office's revenue and profits. Matl was one. He was consistently among the top five producers in San Francisco, and by some measures, he was the biggest producer of all. Between 1977 and 1983, Matl generated about $1.8 million in sales commissions, of which he personally kept about $600,000. A producer like Matl had special leverage over his employer. Not only would Merrill Lynch lose a considerable stream of revenue if he left, but he was the sort of broker who, because of his personal charisma, might take customers with him if he joined a competitor. In that event, Merrill Lynch would lose both commissions and deposits.

Inevitably, there was tension within a firm like Merrill Lynch—Lawyer, Lapidus, and others at the SEC called it a conflict of interest—over the need to generate commissions and the need to treat customers fairly. On one hand, it was in Merrill Lynch's own interest to enforce the rules governing the behavior of stockbrokers. Unhappy customers were no bargain; at the least, they would take their business elsewhere, and at worst, they might sue the firm over rule violations. On the other hand, aggressive salesmanship was essential to making profits. The qualities that made Victor Matl a big producer—the way, as one customer told the SEC investigators, he "brainwashed" and "tranquilized" his clients—also made it likely that people would complain about him. That didn't mean Matl had committed fraud. The question was whether a profit-driven firm like Merrill Lynch, which Shad believed had the industry's best internal compliance system, truly was capable of detecting and responding swiftly to fraud when it occurred.

It appeared to Lawyer and his staff as their investigation unfolded that for three years Merrill Lynch had done virtually nothing to restrain Victor Matl. From time to time, Matl's immediate supervisor, Louis Trujillo, confronted the broker with customer complaints about his more egregious conduct. But Trujillo's admonishings, and his occasional memos to Fisher about problems with Matl, provoked no action from above. Those customers who hired lawyers and pressed a case against the brokerage were either offered a cash settlement—always less than the amount of the customer's losses—or were shunted into a Wall Street arbitration system for settling customer disputes that was stacked against them. Before investigator Bruns walked unannounced into the Merrill Lynch branch, the brokerage had paid $75,000 to six of Matl's customers to settle legal claims.

Bruns's appearance and the document requests generated by Lawyer's office suddenly changed Merrill Lynch's attitude toward Matl. Senior lawyers from the brokerage's Wall Street headquarters were dispatched to San Francisco. When the lawyers read the customer files, they threatened to fire Matl, but the broker begged to keep his job. "Please save me and give me a fresh start," he wrote to Fisher just days after the surprise inspection. "I don't want to be fired." Merrill Lynch's top in-house attorney, senior vice president and general counsel Stephen Hammerman, interviewed Matl for three hours and decided not to fire him. He and other Merrill Lynch executives were impressed by Matl's sincerity and his considerable selling skills. Matl was told to tone down his aggressive tactics and attend a short training course in New York at his own expense. Meanwhile, the SEC investigation of Matl and Merrill Lynch proceeded in secret, with neither Merrill Lynch nor the SEC informing Matl's old or new customers either of the probe or of the complaints.

Merrill Lynch's lawyers claimed afterward that the threat to fire Matl made him into a "changed man." To the staff in Bobby Lawyer's office, that claim seemed absurd. In any event, if Matl did change his ways, it wasn't for long—in the midst of the continuing SEC investigation, new complaints came into the Merrill Lynch office about trades Matl allegedly had made without approval from his customers. After another brief round of handwringing inside Merrill Lynch, Matl was summoned to Robert Fisher's office and fired. He later attended law school in San Francisco and applied for a summer job at the SEC. He was turned down.

*   *   *

John Fedders faced a sensitive dilemma when the long, confidential memo authored by Lawyer and Lapidus recommending fraud charges against Merrill Lynch and its employees arrived at SEC headquarters in the summer of 1984.

Fedders's power as enforcement chief, and the trappings of his position in government that were so important to him, derived in large part from his continuing good relations with Jack Shad. On the other hand, ever since *Citicorp,* Fedders had been working assiduously to build morale and loyalty among his staff, and to a considerable degree he had succeeded. At the table in closed meetings, Fedders was supposed to be the staff's champion. After reading Lawyer's memo, Fedders had two reactions. First, he thought it needed to be rewritten—the arguments weren't clear enough. Second, Fedders understood that the case Lawyer proposed against Merrill Lynch was likely to lead to conflict with Shad. And there was another memo circulating through enforcement that summer that was likely to exacerbate the conflict: Susan Pecaro and her supervisors in the enforcement division had decided to recommend fraud charges against Denny Herrmann and Smith Barney for failing to crack down on the naked-options trading in its Rhinelander office.

At issue was a basic question about who was responsible for detecting and preventing fraud on Wall Street. The debate within the commission dated to the days of Stanley Sporkin and before, but recently it had acquired new life and urgency at SEC headquarters.

Of all the changes Shad had attempted to implement, there were few that stirred emotions more than his effort to alter the standards by which the commission held big Wall Street firms accountable for wrongdoing by their employees. By recommending that charges be filed against Merrill Lynch because of Victor Matl's conduct, Bobby Lawyer brought the conflict to a head.

Shad was pulling the SEC back from close scrutiny of Wall Street investment firms' operations, particularly in the area of stockbroker sales practices. It was axiomatic of Shad's attitudes about Wall Street that he thought top executives at the major brokerages were almost uniformly honest and responsible. He believed, too, that the brokerages and the stock exchanges to which they belonged were well equipped to police themselves and that the SEC's resources were too limited to meddle in individual stockbroker disputes.

Federal regulation of stockbrokers and others at Wall Street firms was structured like a pyramid, with the SEC at the top, followed by the stock exchanges and the brokerage houses themselves. The SEC could bring civil charges against anyone or any firm if there was sufficient evidence of securities fraud. The SEC also routinely monitored some operations of registered brokerage firms through filings the firms made to the commission and occasional SEC inspections. As a practical matter, though, it was impossible for the SEC to closely examine all of a firm's operations; during the period of Shad's tenure at the SEC, the number of stockbrokers alone nearly doubled from slightly more than 200,000 to more than 400,000, while total SEC employment remained flat at about 2,000.

Beneath the commission were the other layers of regulation and responsibility. Merrill Lynch, for example, was a member of the New York Stock Exchange, a so-called self-regulatory organization, or SRO. The exchange could discipline Merrill if the firm violated its rules for dealing with customers—rules that were approved by the SEC. Then, too, Merrill Lynch had certain obligations as an exchange member and a brokerage registered with the SEC to oversee the conduct of its employees.

Increasingly, during Jack Shad's tenure at the SEC, the burden of regulation in the sales-practice area was shifted from the commission down to the lower levels of the pyramid. The role of the self-regulatory organizations was emphasized more and more. Shad argued this made the regulatory system more efficient and effective, but no less vigilant. Transferring some responsibility to the stock exchanges would free up SEC resources for other programs, Shad said. The SEC would do its part by monitoring how well the stock exchanges handled their new duties. But a number of the SEC staff contended in internal debates that Shad's approach only exacerbated the conflict within Wall Street firms between their drive for profits and their obligations to the law. Filing big cases and "jawboning," or talking tough, about charging firms helped encourage compliance with the law. Conversely, shifting enforcement responsibility to Wall Street and resisting proposals to file charges against big brokerage firms for wrongdoing by employees in branch offices could lead to a breakdown of discipline at the largest investment firms, these SEC staff lawyers felt. It was an issue that was already taking on added significance within the commission because of the questions raised by Jack Hewitt's probe of fraud allegations against Michael Milken and other employees in the Beverly Hills office of Drexel Burnham Lambert—a branch office that wielded growing influence across the economy because of the giant junk-bond-financed takeover bids and other transactions it spawned.

Ever mindful of shareholders, Shad sometimes argued that it was the stockholders of the defendant firm, rather than the executives charged, who got hurt most when a brokerage firm was charged, especially if the individual culprits already had been fired. In the absence of bad faith on the part of the company or high-level executive corruption, Shad opposed charges not only against large Wall Street firms but also against major industrial corporations. However, when it came to Wall Street he showed his deepest sentiments, arguing that it was unfair to charge a Wall Street house for bad deeds by an individual broker, because other firms would use the negative publicity to steal clients and because it was simply too costly to demand such perfection. It's the brokerage house customers who ultimately will foot the bill for higher compliance costs, Shad argued. An irony of his position was that consumer-activist Ralph Nader, with whom Shad saw eye-to-eye on very few issues, had pushed during the 1970s for the SEC and other law enforcement agencies to charge individual executives with wrongdoing, rather than the firms and corporations where they worked. Nader thought that approach would give executives in positions of responsibility an incentive to avoid public humiliation by acting ethically and disciplining their institutions. If Shad had cast his own approach in Nader's language, he might have found the SEC staff more receptive.

But some among the commission staff thought Shad's views were affected by his personal identification with potential defendants. Shad must have understood that during his days on Wall Street, had the SEC held senior firm executives responsible for wrongdoing by lower-level employees, he might have been named as a defendant in an enforcement case even though he personally had violated no laws. That assessment wasn't just academic. Around the time that the Merrill Lynch and Smith Barney matters came before the commission early in 1985, Shad's alma mater, E. F. Hutton, pleaded guilty to 2,000 counts of wire fraud in connection with a firm-wide check-kiting scheme to earn additional interest income through illegal overdrafting of bank accounts. As soon as the matter came to the SEC's attention, Shad recused himself; the SEC proceeded to examine the chairman's old firm without his input, due to the conflict of interest his participation would have posed. The Hutton money-management scheme, carried out in branch offices with the support of some members of senior management, began in 1980 while Shad was still at the firm, though there were never any allegations that he knew about the highly profitable, unethical scam. Ironically, while Shad's approach to enforcement involved charging individuals rather than firms, both the SEC and the Justice Department charged the Hutton firm, but no individuals, leading to criticism that the regulators had failed—no scalp, no deterrent, the argument went.

Bobby Lawyer wanted to charge both the Merrill Lynch brokerage and its employees, and in pressing his argument, he tried to utilize his geographical distance from Washington and secure regional office fiefdom to his advantage.

Lawyer's memo about the Merrill Lynch case circulated to Shad's office, the office of the general counsel, and to other division directors. Meantime, Cary Lapidus wrote to Merrill Lynch's lawyers in Manhattan informing them that the staff had decided to recommend fraud charges against the brokerage. Merrill Lynch was invited to make a so-called Wells submission, named for an attorney who originated the idea—the submission was a defense brief in which arguments against prospective charges were sent in writing to the commission. Lapidus told Merrill Lynch that if the firm wanted to submit a Wells, it had two weeks to do so. A confidential, twenty-page letter from the Wall Street firm arrived at SEC headquarters in mid-August. The document contended that neither Fisher, Louis Trujillo, nor Merrill Lynch itself should be charged with fraud, because the brokerage and its officials had acted responsibly in trying to control Matl.

Merrill Lynch's executives in Manhattan were deeply concerned about the prospect of SEC charges. A big retail brokerage depended on the trust of its customers; publicly filed fraud charges might undermine that trust severely. To press its defense inside the commission, the firm retained two lawyers with personal connections to the SEC: Robert Romano, a former enforcement division trial lawyer who had worked on Fedders's early campaign against insider trading and Swiss-bank secrecy, and Irv Pollack, a former SEC commissioner and enforcement division chief who had been a staunch ally of Stanley Sporkin. Pollack now earned a lucrative living as a legal consultant to those who had trouble with the commission.

Just after Labor Day, Romano called Bobby Lawyer's office in San Francisco.

I just want you to know that we're going to do everything we can to defend ourselves at the commission, Romano said. I've put a call in to John Fedders and asked for a meeting in Washington and it looks like they'll grant it. I'm letting your office know because I don't want you to think we tried to go around you dishonestly.

Lawyer said he appreciated the call. Of course, it was clear to the staff in San Francisco that Romano was trying to go around them— all of them knew that Merrill Lynch was likely to receive a more sympathetic hearing from the Republican appointees in Washington than from the former civil rights activists in San Francisco.

On the appointed day, Romano and Pollack arrived at Fifth and D streets and were cleared upstairs. In a conference room they were greeted by a virtual army of enforcement division staff and other SEC lawyers, led by the towering Fedders.

Merrill Lynch did everything that could be expected to curtail Matl's conduct, Romano argued. When we determined that there were problems with his dealings with customers, we fired him—what more can a brokerage do?

But Fedders and the others inundated Romano and Pollack with questions about Merrill Lynch's internal compliance procedures, and about why it appeared that the firm had done little until an SEC investigator walked into the San Francisco branch and demanded to see the office files. When the meeting concluded, Romano and Pollack were handed a list of about twenty written "interrogatories," or investigative questions, to be answered in writing and submitted later to the staff.

A messenger lugged the answers into the SEC lobby on October 19, 1984—the brief weighed as much as a small phone book. There was a forty-page memo and about twenty-five exhibits attached. To show that Merrill Lynch had monitored Matl closely, the brief quoted from the memos Trujillo had written to his superiors detailing his concerns about Matl's behavior. A copy of the fat document was sent out to Lawyer in San Francisco. Taking account of the Wall Street firm's defense, his original memo was revised. But it contained the same recommendation: Merrill Lynch should be charged publicly by the commission for failing to supervise Victor Matl.

The closed meeting room was packed when Lawyer and Lapidus arrived from San Francisco. Word of their impending confrontation with John Shad had circulated through headquarters, and an unusually large crowd of staff had come to the sixth floor to see who would prevail.

Fedders, Lawyer, and Lapidus took their seats across from the five commissioners. Shad was in the center, flanked by James Treadway and Charles Marinaccio on one side, Charles Cox and Aulana Peters on the other.

Whispered rumors about the case had risen to a crescendo in recent weeks. Shad denied it, but it was said that the chairman, through a subordinate, had ordered Lawyer's case off the commission's closely guarded calendar of closed meetings because he was opposed to naming Merrill Lynch as a defendant.

Moreover, the counseling group under General Counsel Dan Goelzer—the cluster of attorneys organized in Harold Williams's day to contain the power of Stanley Sporkin and which now reviewed all enforcement recommendations—had drafted a memo opposing charges against the Wall Street firm. It was said that lawyers in the counseling group had originally agreed with Bobby Lawyer's proposal that Merrill Lynch be named, but had been told to take the opposite side by the chairman's office. Again, Shad said it wasn't so, but there was little doubt where he stood on the issue. A few weeks earlier, Susan Pecaro's case against Smith Barney had finally wound its way to a commission vote. At that meeting, all five commissioners had supported filing charges against Denny Herrmann and his boss in Rhinelander, Robert Heck. But Shad had argued vigorously against naming the Smith Barney firm as a defendant in the case, and it was only after a heated discussion that the staff's recommendation to charge Smith Barney had prevailed by a 3 to 2 vote.

For their part, Lawyer, Lapidus, and their staff back in San Francisco had little doubt that Shad had tried to quash charges against Merrill Lynch, and as they arrived at SEC headquarters for the climactic meeting, they wondered whether Fedders, too, would be against them. Feelings about the case ran high in the San Francisco office—they had put years of work into it; they had come to know Matl's disgruntled customers well and shared their anger about the money they had lost. Fedders's attitude was more clinical. After urging Lawyer to "be reasonable" and perhaps revise the memo's recommendations about charging Merrill Lynch, the enforcement chief had taken a neutral stance, it seemed to some of the staff in San Francisco. They viewed Fedders as an ambitious wisp who would drift wherever the winds from Chairman Shad's office blew. Lawyer had told his staff that he was going to fight this case without Fedders's help. When the matter was taken off the calendar, he telephoned the office of Commissioner Peters, a black woman and Democrat about whom Lawyer had heard favorable comments from staff in Washington. He urged Peters to pressure Shad about the case. After a series of calls from Peters's office to Shad's, the matter had been restored to the closed calendar for a vote. Originally, Lawyer hadn't been planning to fly to Washington for the argument—in routine cases it wasn't necessary. But after all the back-channel lobbying, he and Lapidus decided it was essential that they go.

I don't understand how a firm the size of Merrill Lynch—one with tens of thousands of employees and offices all around the world—can be held responsible for the actions of one rogue account executive in San Francisco, Shad declared when the debate began. Shad was convinced there were a thousand other situations that were handled properly by the firm. How could charging the firm be fair?

The facts show that there were serious violations over a period of years, Lawyer argued.

Formal and restrained, Lawyer sat stiffly at the table. His manner contrasted sharply with the way he usually conducted SEC depositions, where he liked to put his feet up on the table and didn't mind addressing a witness with a simple assertion such as "That's bullshit." There was none of his usual bravado, and certainly no profanity, as he responded to Shad.

"This wasn't a systemic breakdown," the chairman said.

Lawyer fired back. Merrill Lynch had only one system for compliance with the securities laws. And in this case, that system hadn't worked. The failure *was* systemic.

The San Francisco staff had assumed coming into the meeting that Shad was against them, while commissioners Peters and Treadway would probably support their position. But they had no idea which way commissioners Marinaccio and Cox would go. Cox initially was seen by liberal staff lawyers as a lackey of Chairman Shad, who had engineered his appointment to the commission. (The views of many early critics of Cox changed over time, and he earned respect as an independent commissioner.) If Lawyer and Lapidus were to prevail, they needed one vote from either Cox or Marinaccio.

"You've got three votes," Fedders said to Bobby Lawyer some ten or fifteen minutes into the meeting, after Cox made a comment indicating that he was in favor of naming Merrill Lynch as a defendant. It was clear to Lawyer and his supporters in the room that Fedders, too, was behind him. The tension among the staff lawyers eased.

The final vote was 4 to 1; an attorney present recalled Shad acknowledging at one point that he was beginning to "feel a little bit lonely on this." When the tally was called, no attempt was made to distinguish between the question of whether to charge Merrill Lynch with fraud or whether to name three of its employees—the discharged Matl, and San Francisco officials Louis Trujillo and Robert Fisher—as defendants. It seemed from his comments that Shad had no objection to filing charges against the individuals, but since he didn't make that clear when he voiced his vote, he cast his ballot technically against filing the entire case. In a later interview, Shad clarified his vote, saying, "I have a basic visceral reaction to sanctioning the firm for one bad account executive," but adding that any individual stockbroker who abused his customers "should be prosecuted to the full extent of the law."*

---

* On September 11, 1985, Merrill Lynch settled proceedings with the SEC by accepting a public censure without admitting or denying wrongdoing. Robert Fisher, chief of the firm's San Francisco office, accepted a two-month suspension from the securities business, also without admitting or denying wrongdoing.

A second manager in the San Francisco office, Louis Trujillo, chose to fight SEC charges in an administrative proceeding. The Trujillo case showed that the commission's internal process for conducting civil trials was slow and sometimes ineffectual. The lawsuit lasted more than three years, consuming thousands of man-hours and tens of thousands of dollars in fees and expenses. In early, confidential settlement negotiations with the SEC, Merrill Lynch insisted that Trujillo deserved no more than a public censure. SEC lawyers initially held out for a suspension, but then agreed to recommend a censure to the full commission. At a closed SEC meeting attended by Shad, Peters, and Cox, the latter two commissioners toed a hard line, insisting that Trujillo deserved a suspension, not the censure recommended by staff. Shad supported a censure but was outvoted, 2 to 1. After a drawn-out trial, an SEC administrative judge ruled, in April 1987, that Trujillo deserved a censure. Trujillo appealed to the full commission, of which Cox was still a member. At a closed meeting in 1989, the SEC voted to exonerate Trujillo entirely.

Victor Matl settled SEC charges without admitting or denying wrongdoing and was barred permanently from the regulated securities business.

Merrill Lynch said in a statement that it was "committed to the highest standards of professional and personal ethical conduct," that its systems of employee supervision are "second to none" and that Matl's productivity as a salesman did not influence how the company handled the complaints against him. The firm added that "while the Matl situation was a unique one, we believe our firm acted

Some of the commission attorneys who supported Lawyer's fight for charges against Merrill Lynch considered his victory Pyrrhic. To them, it was absurd that so much energy had to be expended arguing about a case where the facts seemed so strong, the violations so egregious. It wasn't a question of whether Merrill Lynch's top executives had consciously engaged in fraud—the evidence showed they had not. The point was, if those executives were not held publicly accountable for serious breakdowns in discipline within their firms, what message would that send to Wall Street about the SEC's attitude toward fraud and misconduct? If it had taken that much effort for Bobby Lawyer to prevail against Shad in a case where the facts were mostly undisputed and relatively easy to prove in court, what would happen to all the other cases against Wall Street firms where the evidence was convincing but less clear-cut?

Still, for Bobby Lawyer and his supporters in the enforcement division, the victory at the table was a moment to savor and a boost to morale. For as 1985 began, the enforcement division became embroiled in a distracting and demoralizing scandal that would attract far more attention than the Merrill Lynch case.

Some of the SEC's own unsavory secrets were soon to be exposed.

---

reasonably and responsibly in dealing with it based on what was known at the time."

Smith Barney settled SEC proceedings on March 5, 1985, accepting a public censure without admitting or denying wrongdoing in connection with the Rhinelander naked options case. Denny Herrmann and his boss in Rhinelander, Robert Heck, also settled cases against them and accepted brief suspensions. Herrmann was fired by Smith Barney, and as the 1980s closed, he was working as a stockbroker with another firm in northern Wisconsin. He said in an interview that he believed he had been treated unfairly by his former employer. Smith Barney officials declined to make any comment about the case.

14

Testing a Friendship

On the wintry morning in 1985 when the story broke, the reporters gathered like a pack of hounds in the lobby of the commission's headquarters, television cameras slung over their shoulders, wires snaking outside to vans parked along Fifth Street, microphones poised to jab and thrust at any SEC official who tried to run the gauntlet. Shad happened by at one point, and they pounced. The chairman muttered that he would not comment on John Fedders's personal life, that he had not asked for Fedders's resignation, nor had the enforcement chief volunteered to quit.

John Fedders has done "an outstanding job" at the commission and had assembled "an excellent staff" to prosecute securities fraud cases, especially those involving insider trading, Shad told the reporters.

Upstairs, on the fourth floor, Fedders—visibly engulfed by emotional pain—moved between his office and those of his senior colleagues in the enforcement division, talking about the story in that morning's *Wall Street Journal*. His secret was exposed. His career and all it meant to him seemed about to collapse.

Several of the enforcement lawyers who had worked with him closely since 1981—including Gary Lynch, the associate director, Bill McLucas, an assistant director, and Michael Mann, a young attorney who had worked side-by-side with Fedders during the Swiss-bank secrecy negotiations and related insider trading cases—sympathized with Fedders's anguish. To one degree or another, and especially in recent days, they had heard about Fedders's troubled marriage, including the report that he had physically beaten Charlotte at least half a dozen times. They did not condone what Fedders had done, but they knew that he regretted it, that his relationship with Charlotte was complex, that he had been separated from her for more than a year, and that his performance at the SEC had seemed unaffected by the secrets he kept at home. To Fedders and some of his friends and colleagues at the commission, the story about his tenure as enforcement chief and his marital problems in the *Wall Street Journal* that Monday, February 25, 1985, seemed brutal and unfair. And they did not understand why virtually every media outlet in the capital had been stirred into a frenzy by disclosure of details about Fedders's private life.

"The path through the capital's revolving door—whirling into government service for a while and then back into the private sector at a big salary—is a heavily traveled one," began the story on the front page of the *Journal*, which has the largest daily circulation of any national newspaper in the country. "But it has turned into a bumpy road for John Fedders. . . ." The story, authored by investigative reporter Brooks Jackson, then listed in specially indented paragraphs four "troubles" that had placed Fedders at the "storm center." The news that Fedders beat his wife was buried beneath the disclosure that he was "strapped for cash and can't meet expenses," and above a description of Fedders's previously reported role as a lawyer in a criminal corporate-bribery case that predated his arrival at the SEC, a case in which he was never charged with any wrongdoing. It was as if the *Journal*'s editors had been sufficiently uncomfortable with the raw disclosure of Fedders's marital violence that they had found it necessary to create a larger context in which to report their startling scoop. (Newspaper reporters and editors frequently wrestle with whether to report the personal problems of public officials, guided in part by how the problems relate to on-the-job performance.) And yet, predictably, that Monday it was the news that John Fedders had beaten his wife while working as the top cop at the SEC that galvanized the *Journal*'s competitors and caused a sometimes-unruly pack of print and television reporters to assemble in the commission's headquarters lobby.

Up on the fourth floor, some of Fedders's senior colleagues in the enforcement division were asking a question about the *Journal*'s story: Was it, in part, an act of institutional retribution against the SEC for the insider trading prosecution the commission had recently mounted against R. Foster Winans, a fired *Journal* reporter?

Fedders thought this was possible. Winans had been the author of the *Journal*'s widely read "Heard on the Street" column about the stock market. Over a period of months, he had leaked advance word of his column's contents to a stockbroker at the Wall Street firm Kidder, Peabody & Company, and had profited from stock trading the broker handled. When Winans was about to write favorably about a company, they bought the company's stock before his column was published. After Winans was caught, the SEC and the Manhattan U.S. attorney's office launched investigations that caused embarrassment at the *Wall Street Journal*.

The notion that the Winans case had led the *Journal* to take revenge on Fedders by digging up the details of his marital violence was appealing to some of the senior enforcement staff, but it illustrated that they, like Jack Shad earlier, seemed unable to comprehend the central anomaly of Fedders's secret. The leading law enforcement officer at the commission, a six-foot ten-inch disciplinarian and the arbiter of right and wrong on Wall Street, committed battery against his wife in the privacy of his Potomac home. It was outrage about that contradiction and the power of such an anomaly to become sensational news that lay behind the *Journal*'s story and the ferocious scramble of other newspapers and the television networks that Monday to catch up.

Fedders wasn't sure what would happen. No decision about his future had been made by Shad or the White House that day. Fedders had talked about his marriage with Shad and White House counsel Fred Fielding earlier that February, after two days of testimony in his divorce trial in a small courtroom in suburban Rockville, Maryland. On the witness stand, Fedders had admitted in open court that he struck his wife during their marriage and said that he felt "tremendous remorse." The *Journal*'s Jackson had attended the trial and identified himself as a reporter, so Fedders knew a story was likely. In the several weeks it took Jackson to prepare his piece, Fedders's personal lawyer had negotiated with the *Journal*'s managing editor, Norman Pearlstein, in an attempt to forestall publication. On Sunday night, Fedders learned that the effort had failed, although he had no inkling until Monday morning of the length and prominence and details of the story. Shad, too, knew a story was coming, but not that it would be long and graphically detailed.

Fedders wanted to go home that Monday night to the apartment he had rented on Massachusetts Avenue after the separation from Charlotte, but he didn't want to push his way through the reporters in the lobby. Many of the enforcement lawyers on the fourth floor that evening were angry at the media. One or two reporters had snuck around commission security and tried to prowl the hallways, looking for Fedders. The enforcement staff thought this was outrageous and unprofessional. They felt besieged. Lynch, Mann, McLucas, and other enforcement staff told Fedders they wanted to help, and they said they had a plan.

Fedders had parked his car in a garage across the street from the SEC. Mann took the keys and went to retrieve it. Another staff lawyer escorted Fedders onto the elevator, rode with him to the commission garage below the lobby, and helped him into a different car. They slipped unnoticed out of the driveway and met Mann at a prearranged rendezvous several blocks from the commission.

For most of the evening, Fedders stayed at Gary Lynch's house in Chevy Chase, Maryland, just over the district line, talking with Lynch and Lynch's wife about Charlotte and his sons and his future. Around 11:00 P.M., he said he wanted to go home, and he drove off. As he neared his apartment building, SEC staff lawyers who had been waiting for him flagged his car down. The press had staked out his apartment lobby, Fedders was told. The gangly enforcement chief clambered out, walked down the block, and snuck into his building through the garage while the enforcement lawyers parked his car out on the street.

The next day it ended. Fedders managed to duck into SEC headquarters in the morning. He spoke with Shad.

Everyone has concluded that it would be best if you resigned, Shad said.

By that, it was clear, the chairman was referring to the Reagan White House.

I've come to the same conclusion myself, Fedders replied.

Others in the Reagan administration had been suspected of wife-beating and had not resigned. But the difference in Fedders's case, Shad agreed, was that the enforcement chief had admitted the violence in open court.

In his office, Fedders drafted a letter.

"Dear Mr. Chairman," he wrote to Shad. "Newspaper reports of yesterday and today have focused on my marriage and my pending divorce trial in Maryland. Those reports have exaggerated allegations in the divorce trial and have unfairly described occasionally highly regrettable episodes in our marriage. On seven occasions during more than 18 years of marriage, marital disputes between us resulted in violence, for which I feel, and have expressed, great remorse. Those isolated events do not, however, justify the extreme characterizations made in the press.

"Although I am thoroughly satisfied that my private difficulties have in no way affected the execution of my duties as director of the division of enforcement of the Securities and Exchange Commission and would not do so in the future if I remained in office, the glare of publicity on my private life threatens to undermine the effectiveness of the division and of the Commission. . . . I must now regretfully tender my resignation as of the close of business today."

At 5:30 P.M., the SEC announced officially that John Fedders had quit.

Shortly thereafter, on the CBS evening news, Washington reporter Leslie Stahl said, "White House officials insist that there was no pressure on Mr. Fedders to resign, although they admit that, given President Reagan's emphasis on family values, the Fedders case, if allowed to linger on, could have been politically damaging."

*   *   *

The fall of John Fedders set the stage for a quiet change inside the commission that would contribute, just a year later, to the biggest crackdown on Wall Street corruption in SEC history: Gary Lynch came to power as enforcement chief.

In those first weeks, he wanted more than anything to avoid making a serious, public mistake. Lynch was one of Fedders's closest friends and he felt bad about what had happened, but there was no question, either, that he wanted the job of enforcement chief now that Fedders was gone. Among the commissioners and the senior staff, there was little doubt that if Shad decided to hire from within, Lynch would be selected—he had no serious rivals among his colleagues at senior levels of the division. The question, though, was whether Shad would go outside to hire from among his former associates on Wall Street, in an effort, perhaps, to restore the enforcement division's credibility by attracting a well-known leader of the securities bar. On the Monday following Fedders's resignation, Shad named Lynch as the interim enforcement chief, but Lynch knew the chairman was continuing to talk with prominent lawyers in private practice about the job.

Fedders's abrupt resignation and Lynch's uncertain status left its mark on the enforcement division. Wall Street raced ahead—extravagant and seemingly abusive takeover deals sprang up, led by a wild fight for Phillips Petroleum involving Ivan Boesky, Boone Pickens, and Michael Milken; insider trading in advance of merger announcements grew; stock prices were buffeted by new, computerized trading strategies—and the SEC's vaunted enforcement division seemed uncharacteristically weak. Crises erupted one after the next. Less than a month after Fedders's resignation and the chaos that attended it, an official of the Federal Reserve Board, which monitored interest rates and helped to ensure the safety and soundness of the banking system, telephoned Lynch at home.

We've got a problem here, the official said ominously.

A little-known firm called Bevill Bresler that traded big batches of government securities, including U.S. Treasury bonds, was collapsing because an egregious fraud scheme had been exposed.

The firm's failure could threaten the integrity of the country's financial system, the Fed believed. Lynch was told to fly to Newark, New Jersey, on Easter Sunday, to attend a meeting about how to handle the fiasco.

It was weeks before Lynch could focus much time or attention on any enforcement matters other than the government-securities crisis. And there were other distractions. That spring, Shad was called several times to testify before Congress, not only about the Bevill Bresler scandal, but also about enforcement and the budget and the attempt to install a new, computerized filing system at the SEC. Late into the night, Lynch sat with Shad in the chairman's office, drafting testimony, rehearsing questions and answers, cramming facts and figures. Other senior staff were acquainted with the cycle of anxiety and intense preparation Shad went through before each appearance on Capitol Hill, but for Lynch it was mostly new, and it came just as the chairman was deciding whether to appoint him as the commission's permanent enforcement chief.

Shad was impressed by Lynch—especially the way he handled himself under pressure—but one had to be somewhat wary of his youth. The thirty-four-year-old Lynch was a lean six foot one weighing 185 pounds, with a sober intensity about him. He was energetic, yet often seemed unemotional and very serious. To some at the commission he seemed distant, though not aloof. Thick, dark hair parted in the middle draped his head; his eyebrows, which slanted in toward the top of his nose, suggested unusual intelligence. He had a brilliant command of securities laws, but what impressed people most about him was the way in which he accomplished so much in such a low-key, rational manner. Virtually all of Lynch's short career in law had been spent at the SEC. By working closely and successfully with Fedders, Lynch had proved that he shared the enforcement priorities of his Republican superiors, especially their emphasis on prosecutions of insider trading. But he was no ideologue, and he had no lengthy experience in the private sector, where Shad and Fedders each had developed the suspicion of bureaucracy that shaped their approach to enforcement policy.

Raised on farmland near New Hampton, New York, not far from the Delaware River in the foothills of the Catskill Mountains, Gary Lynch had known little of the wealth and sophistication of Wall Street, though the skyscrapers of the financial district were only seventy miles from his rural home. His father had an eighth-grade education and owned a small trucking business, hauling dairy products and onions into New York City and its environs. The Lynches lived beside a small farm that had been in the family for generations, and in the summers, until college, he worked in the onion fields and at the local onion processing plant. (Perhaps that explained Lynch's fondness while at the SEC for thick, pungent cigars.) He was no bumpkin. He knew that he wasn't going to grow up to be an onion farmer or a trucker, and in fact Lynch not only was the first member of his family to graduate from college, he also was Phi Beta Kappa at Syracuse University, where he focused on political philosophy. During law school at Duke University, an early marriage to his hometown sweetheart fell apart. After graduating and working a brief stint at a Washington law firm, Lynch drifted around the country for a while, landing finally at the SEC's enforcement division partly because it suited the sense he had of himself as someone on the side of the under-dog. Growing up, Lynch identified closely with his father's struggle as a small businessman against institutional forces more powerful than he was. The Teamsters Union tried to organize the drivers at his father's trucking company, and they threw rocks through truck windows when his father resisted. Lynch was young at the time, but he said later that it bothered him that the Teamsters didn't seem to care whom they hurt, even if their efforts produced the greatest hardship for the organizers' friends and neighbors.

Inside the enforcement division, Lynch was seen by a number of his colleagues as a rising star, a talented lawyer who had built a close working and personal relationship with Fedders, and was not tainted by involvement with the controversies over Stanley Sporkin's views and methods. When he reached the top of the division, first as associate director and then as Fedders's interim successor, Lynch's cool manner and the personal distance he kept made him seem sometimes unapproachable. There were those down at the workaday, staff-lawyer level of the division who saw Lynch as part of an exclusive, macho boys' club within enforcement, a club that included assistant director Bill McLucas, his friend Bruce Hiler, and other senior attorneys. These people, many of them women, felt that the SEC brass—including Fedders, Lynch, and even Chairman Shad—was insensitive to what they felt was their second tier, outsider status in the enforcement division, notwithstanding Shad's promotion of many women in other divisions of the SEC. But in the uncertain weeks after Fedders's resignation, when Lynch jockeyed to be named as the permanent enforcement director, most of his colleagues were rooting for him. The feeling inside the division was that despite some frustration over the failure to mount credible prosecutions of major Wall Street figures like Boesky and Milken, the commission was doing the best job it could to police corruption and insider trading in the markets. There were few voices inside or outside the commission clamoring for a change in direction or policy—all of the hullabaloo that February and March concerning Fedders focused on his secret personal life, not on the question of whether the SEC's enforcement program had succeeded or failed while he was in charge. Moreover, in the aftermath of emotional policy battles with Shad over cases such as Merrill Lynch and Smith Barney, Lynch's appointment would signal that the chairman supported continuity within the bureaucracy's most important division.

As he awaited Shad's decision, Lynch watched the newspapers. Stories in the leading papers about who was in contention and who was being interviewed for key government positions served in Washington as a kind of community bulletin board of rumor, akin to whispered stories in the bazaars and courts of ancient capitals. One newspaper story reported that Lynch was not Shad's first choice, that the chairman was anxious to find a prestigious attorney from Wall Street to take Fedders's place. Lynch could only grit his teeth and wait.

In April, Shad finally called.

I would be pleased if you would accept the position of enforcement director permanently, the chairman said.

Lynch answered that he would be honored.

The stories about your not being my first choice weren't true, Shad later told him. I talked to some people on the outside, but I decided that you could do the best job.

Lynch thanked him. Afterward, he wondered whether Shad had offered that disclaimer only to be gracious. But Lynch chose to believe that the chairman meant what he said.

That month Gary Lynch moved his personal belongings—his framed law degrees from Syracuse and Duke, his personal files, the art deco print on his office wall, the hundred or so law books and legal conference materials he had collected—two doors down the hall to Fedders's fourth-floor corner office. Lynch felt relieved and pleased to finally get the job, though it meant moving into his friend's domain, the office with the big desk, the old Western Union teletype machine in the corner, and the view of the American and SEC flags that fluttered just outside the window. He had no idea that what was soon to unfold on Wall Street and at the SEC would cause him to attain the fame and public prominence that Fedders had so desperately coveted.

15

A Tale of Two Buildings

In 1984, in the prime of middle age, Irving Einhorn loaded a bundle of his belongings into his silver Honda Prelude and headed west across the interstate highways from Washington to Los Angeles. He went west for the reason millions had gone west before him: It was time for a change.

He was not the picture of a frontiersman. Einhorn was a spirited, jocular man who liked to kibbitz; his belly suggested he enjoyed a good meal as well. He was bald, bearded, and just five-feet five-inches tall. He insisted that everyone call him Irv, including those who worked for him at the SEC.

For twelve years he had toiled as a trial lawyer at the commission, first at the regional office in Chicago and then at headquarters in Washington. He had done well, but no one had ever suggested Einhorn was on the fast track. Throughout his career, and throughout his life, Einhorn had been in no great hurry, a quality some of those around him found attractive and even charming. It was a quality that contrasted sharply, however, with the obsessive attitudes toward time and ambition exhibited by Michael Milken, the financier who was to become Einhorn's legal opponent in 1985, and whose junk bond department in Drexel Burnham's Beverly Hills office was by far the most important financial operation in Einhorn's new jurisdiction.

Einhorn had a general idea about who Milken was and how

junk bonds worked from a few articles he had read in newspapers and magazines. Beyond that, Einhorn would teach himself what he needed to know when the time came. He had always done it that way. The son of a Philadelphia cabdriver, Einhorn had enrolled at Temple University when Dwight D. Eisenhower was in the White House, and graduated when Richard Nixon was elected. The intervening nine years he spent in the leisurely pursuit of life's pleasures. The prospect of selling cars in Philadelphia persuaded him to complete his education, and after college he enrolled at Villanova University law school. He promptly transferred to a smaller school, losing academic credit in the process, mainly because he wanted to get away from his new mother-in-law. Working as an attorney at the SEC provided a safe geographical buffer for more than a decade, but it did not hold his marriage together. At forty-two, following his divorce, Einhorn spoke with Jack Shad about becoming the chief of the commission's sizable regional office in Los Angeles. It seemed a good time to move on.

Einhorn never boasted that he was a legal scholar, but Shad was impressed with him nonetheless. He had extensive litigation experience, he took a commonsense approach to enforcement cases, he got along reasonably well with his superiors, and he didn't take himself too seriously, as Shad thought some SEC lawyers did. That, and a solid interview with the chairman, were enough to win Einhorn the job.

The commission's Los Angeles office—staffed by dozens of attorneys responsible for policing securities fraud in an enormous region of the Far West and the Pacific, including Guam and Hawaii—was in an embarrassing state of disarray when Einhorn was appointed its administrator and prepared to move from Washington. It was hard to know whether Shad understood; he rarely visited the far-flung offices and didn't express much interest in their work. Yet in Los Angeles, the problems common to many of the commission's regional branches were especially acute. And since Drexel's junk bond department, arguably the most important profit-making financial institution in the country during the mid-1980s, was situated just blocks from the SEC's L.A. branch, the troubles at the commission had potentially grave implications.

When Einhorn finally arrived, it was hard at first for him to worry too much about Drexel and Milken—he had too many of his own problems. The office had been without a regional administrator for six months, saddling the senior attorneys with an almost unmanageable workload and depressing morale down through the ranks. Moreover, there was no senior enforcement lawyer managing the office's ongoing campaign against securities fraud. Turnover among the younger lawyers was high. The L.A. office was far from glamorous, its work garnered little attention or publicity, and the salaries it offered were outstripped by both private law firms and southern California's high cost of living. Many attorneys who stayed with the commission in Los Angeles weren't talented or energetic enough to find a better job.

Into this quagmire bounced Einhorn, snapping his fingers, trying to reinvigorate the place. He tried to sort out some of the lingering administrative problems by making fast decisions, and he brought in an outside lawyer to run the office's enforcement program, a move which further depressed morale. Some among the L.A. staff weren't quite sure what to make of him.

This much was clear soon after Einhorn took charge: If the office was ever to recover from its demoralizing disarray, it would do so by successfully prosecuting major securities-fraud cases. Success in prominent cases had built up morale in the enforcement division at SEC headquarters in Washington, and had contributed to a culture of achievement that attracted talented lawyers despite the commission's modest salaries. And if there was one case that could rocket the L.A. office to prominence faster than any other, it was the SEC's lingering and desultory investigation of Milken's junk bond department in Beverly Hills. Einhorn had an obvious opportunity. When Jack Hewitt's long investigation of alleged market manipulation by Milken had been closed by SEC headquarters staff in Washington, the files had been transferred to Los Angeles. In the year or so since Hewitt's probe was closed, staff lawyers in the L.A. office had opened a related and similar probe of suspicious trading by Milken and Drexel in the bonds of Caesars World, the gaming and casino company. Though he had no crackerjack investigators to assign to the matter, if Einhorn could make a case against Drexel, he might well turn things around.

Caesars was a prototypical Milken client, since the company's gambling business was too unsavory to attract many of Wall Street's prestigious, mainstream investment banks. An irony of the L.A regional office's investigation was that during his Wall Street career it had been SEC Chairman Jack Shad, then at E. F. Hutton, who had defied Street tradition and completed the first underwriting of a casino company by a major investment bank— the company was Caesars World Resorts. During the 1980s, Milken extended Shad's breakthrough into an enormously profitable business. Drexel's junk bonds financed the growth of nearly every casino in Las Vegas and Atlantic City. The investigation approved by Einhorn concerned a series of large and suspicious trades in which Caesars World bonds had been shuffled between Milken's personal account, a Drexel junk-bond-department account, and various Drexel customer accounts. There were questions about insider trading, manipulation, and conflict of interest—the same sorts of questions Hewitt and the headquarters staff had pursued to a dead end in 1982 and 1983. Einhorn hoped to succeed where headquarters had failed.

The trouble was that neither Irving Einhorn nor anyone else in the SEC's Los Angeles regional office seemed to know what to do about Milken and Drexel. They subpoenaed records, they prepared to take testimony from Milken and others, they followed all the rules of SEC investigative strategy. But never—not once—did a staff member from the L.A. office set foot inside the junk bond department to stage an inspection or watch Milken work as he directed his employees or his customers. The commission had the right to inspect and audit the books and records of its registered broker dealers, of which Drexel was one, to examine stock-and-bond-trading practices in detail, and to check that employees received proper training and supervision. But even in 1985, when Drexel began to engineer the wildest and most controversial corporate takeovers on record—financing billion-dollar merger bids with little but moxie and fee-producing promises about financing—the SEC lawyers kept to their offices down the block, poring slowly and methodically through their mounds of trading records, occasionally inviting a Drexel employee in for testimony, but never deviating from the narrow mandate of their Caesars World bond-trading investigation.

The Drexel and SEC offices may have been on the same street—Drexel was at 9560 Wilshire Boulevard, amid the exclusive boutiques and neatly groomed palm trees of downtown Beverly Hills, while the SEC was at 5757 Wilshire, in a seedier strip south of old Hollywood—but they might as well have been on different planets.

Milken and some of his business partners owned the choice property at the corner of Wilshire Boulevard and Rodeo Drive, and Milken profited by renting most of the office space in the building to Drexel. It was symbolic of his overall relationship with his New York–based employer; Milken was the landlord and Drexel was the tenant. Though he held no seat on the firm's board of directors, Milken called the shots, profiting from a wide range of special financial deals with Drexel—deals which Shad's old protégé Fred Joseph and the other top firm officials in New York permitted in part because they lived in fear of losing their biggest producer. Milken had the words DREXEL BURNHAM LAMBERT affixed in big gold letters high on his building's facade, prominently facing the Beverly Hills shopping strip. (In contrast to this conspicuous location, a passerby on Wilshire would not have known the SEC was hidden inside an office building alongside other anonymous tenants.) Milken and his traders and salesmen arrived for work in the predawn darkness; they passed by a flower and sculpture garden; entered through a private door in the rear of the building; crossed a sleek, cool lobby of black marble and gold trim; and rode finally up to the sprawling and brightly lit trading floor. Their workdays were dominated by transactions of dizzying complexity, with opportunities for incomprehensible wealth. By 1985, Milken's employees were almost certainly the highest paid in the history of American finance, with some junk bond salesmen—mostly young men in their twenties and early thirties—earning $20 million or $30 million a year, and Milken himself being paid $135 million by Drexel that year. Those numbers didn't include the millions of dollars a year in additional earnings available from special personal trading opportunities in the junk bond and stock markets, including the sort of trades under investigation in the Caesars World probe.

The salesmen and traders who worked closely with Milken, kids who became instant millionaires by their proximity to him, alternated between feelings of awe at their success and impulses of greed over what they did not yet have. Though they all earned tremendous sums, some of the most successful traders and salesmen became obsessed by how much their colleagues made, and there was widespread disgruntlement on the trading floor over the way Milken managed the employee-trading partnerships he organized—there was a feeling that while Milken doled out $1 million monthly paychecks, that wasn't enough, because his iron control of the private-trading accounts cheated them all of millions more. Perspectives about money and value and purpose had been distorted by the sheer scale of the operation in Milken's building that 1985, as if the junk bond department had been constructed in some new dimension where all the numbers automatically had extra zeros attached.

Irving Einhorn walked to work at the SEC. Milken was chauffeured to his office from his comfortable Encino home in a Mercedes Benz limousine. His traders and salesmen, almost all of them young white males, arrived in the modern equivalent of golden chariots. In the Drexel building, they traded bonds and talked about luxury sports cars with the enthusiasm of boys at a birthday party. Had an SEC investigator wandered through the parking lot at 9560, he would at one time or another have seen about thirty Porsches; a Testarossa; the BMW 750i that belonged to thirty-one-year-old top salesman Jim Dahl; the chauffeured Rolls-Royce in which Warren Trepp, the chief bond trader, commuted daily; the Mercedes 560sec belonging to salesman Roy Johnson; the Mercedes 560sec owned by assistant trader Lorraine Spurge; the Lotus Turbo Esprit belonging to salesman Terren Peizer, then about twenty-six years old; the Ferrari 328 driven by salesman Karl Deremer; the 700 series BMW driven by deal man Peter Ackerman; the pair of Jaguar XJ-S's owned by bond specialist Bill Tobey and takeover maven Josh Friedman; and either a Cadillac or a Corvette convertible driven by Bill Frymer, depending on his mood that day. More than a hundred of them belonged to a service called the Ultimate Motor Car Concept—for $1,000 a year per auto, the cars were washed and waxed regularly right in the Drexel parking lot, while their owners sat upstairs working the telephones, selling and selling and selling Milken's bonds.

There were two important rules: show up to work by 5:30 A.M., and make money. Registered brokerage and investment firms such as Drexel were expected to comply with a host of SEC rules governing trading practices, dealings with customers, capital rules, and other matters. But there was little emphasis on compliance with SEC rules in the Beverly Hills office, no formal orientation for new employees, no instructions about what practices in the bond and stock markets were legal and what were not. Milken was the boss, but beyond that there were no clear lines of authority, and in any event, what Milken wanted was work and profit. "I would say there is no second in command," Milken told Einhorn's investigators. "You could say on some days there's a hundred seventy people that are second in command, and other days, you know, there's ten. It depends on what's happening, what the situation is. People have responsibilities rather than a formal organizational chart."

Milken's people were expected to remain in the office until mid- or late afternoon, unless they were out visiting a client. On Saturday morning, there sometimes was a mandatory 6:00 A.M. junk-bond-department staff meeting, which was well attended. If a major deal was under way, it was expected that nobody would check their watches even if it meant working around the clock. At about 11:00 A.M. each morning, lunch was wheeled onto the trading floor so that work would be interrupted for the least possible time. Assistants were assigned to each of the salesmen and traders to take care of distracting, time-consuming personal business ranging from paying home electric bills to getting their precious cars repaired. The sometimes uncomfortable truth was that by 1985, the junk bond department at Drexel had become a kind of cult, revolving around loyalty to Milken and intense devotion to work. Turnover was very low, for Milken's salesmen and traders, many of whom had never sold or dealt a bond in their lives before he hired and trained them, could not have earned comparable salaries at any other firm on Wall Street.

Family, as a metaphor and in blood ties, was invoked to build loyalty. There was Mike's brother, Lowell Milken, who spent much of his time in an office off the trading floor, investing the Milkens' family money. There was Mike's brother-in-law, former dentist Alan Flans, a man who was said to take occasional naps in his car while others covered his junk-bond-sales accounts. One of the games the traders in the Drexel office liked to play was to "wake up Flans" by calling him on his car phone. He drove a Ford Thunderbird and had the curious habit some days of taking large amounts of food off the bond trading floor at midmorning, when the cold cuts arrived. Then Flans would head home and enjoy a hearty lunch with his own family, something it was felt Milken would not have allowed others to do. Even Milken's tenants at 9560 Wilshire had close ties; in addition to Drexel, there were clients, accountants, and lawyers close to the junk bond visionary who rented space.

Though controlled in public, on the trading floor Milken could be a screamer, a frantic obsessive. He sat at the center of a giant X-shaped desk, directly across from his blond protégé, Jim Dahl, juggling telephones and shouting the results of his trades to nearby aides. He handled call after call like a blindfolded man on a circus high-wire. "I sometimes don't even listen on the phone to people that are talking to me," he explained to the SEC during his day-long interrogation at the L.A. regional office a few miles east on Wilshire. "So, all I've got is the guy's name and his phone number. I don't even remember what company he was from, or what he wanted to do. . . . I might do as much as five hundred trades in one day. The normal procedure is, I turn around and in a loud voice, scream the trade I've done to any one of three to five people sitting behind me."

To the degree they thought about the Securities and Exchange Commission at all, Milken's top employees considered the chief regulatory agency responsible for oversight of their work to be a joke, a nuisance that cropped up from time to time and was easily dismissed. There was no panic when SEC subpoenas or requests for testimony arrived. Later, some of those who glided down to Einhorn's office for interrogations would say that they knew of widespread securities law violations and systematic corruption inside Milken's building, but none of them worried in 1985 that the commission would find out. Testimony was regarded as a necessity best handled as expediently as possible. At the time, nobody close to Milken believed the commission could touch him, although some said later that they worried in 1985 that practices on the junk bond trading floor were spinning dangerously out of control.

In addition to the pioneering, legal sales tactics the persuasive Milken used to peddle junk bonds, there were flagrant violations of the law that served Milken and his customers well. The violations gave the junk bond department a critical edge, enabling it to produce extraordinary profits and to build unusual loyalty from results-oriented customers who recognized that Drexel could perform feats of financial magic for them that other firms could not. Ivan Boesky was just such a customer, a trader of takeover stocks who often sought to avoid detection of his illegal activities and needed an accommodating broker on the other end of the phone to help him hide stock positions, rig takeovers, and purchase more shares than he had the money to buy. Milken obliged, personally approving of Drexel's purchase of millions of dollars of shares from Boesky with the oral understanding that Boesky would buy them back later and reimburse Drexel for any losses. That sort of "stock parking" scheme, which Einhorn and his SEC investigators knew nothing about and which was reflected in a secret set of records that a Milken employee maintained, allowed Boesky to continue loading up on the stocks of takeover targets even after he exceeded legal limits on borrowing to finance those purchases.

Boesky wasn't the only customer for whom Milken and his traders were willing to break the rules. When the casino company Golden Nugget, controlled by one of Milken's loyal clients and friends Steve Wynn, wanted to sell a big block of MCA entertainment company stock for the highest possible price, Wynn turned to Milken, who did not disappoint him. A traditional broker might have sought bids for the stock from other Wall Street houses, a move which could have depressed the value of the shares by signaling that a large amount of MCA stock was for sale. Even if it meant breaking the law, Milken wanted to attain the highest possible price and keep Golden Nugget's identity as a seller a secret, so he called upon his increasingly convenient relationship with Boesky. Milken arranged for Boesky to purchase the MCA stock in a series of trades that disguised what was going on by secretly promising that if Boesky bought the shares up front for a high price, Milken would reimburse him later for any losses, after Boesky had sold the shares into the marketplace over time to unwitting investors who ran the risk of seeing their holdings plummet after it became known that Golden Nugget had sold its MCA shares. Rather than depressing the MCA stock price, the illusion created by the sale of the shares to Boesky was one of additional demand for the stock.

Then, too, there was the loyalty Milken commanded from money managers at insurance companies, savings and loans, and mutual funds around the country who bought billions of dollars of his new junk bonds every year. Other Wall Street firms found it difficult to break into the junk market, and one reason was that Milken did illegal personal financial favors for some of the money managers. For one of his best clients, David Solomon of Solomon Asset Management Company Inc., Milken made it especially appealing: While Solomon bought Milken's junk bonds with the client funds that he managed, Milken helped Solomon cheat on his personal income taxes by engaging in a series of sham trades that generated paper losses that reduced Solomon's tax bill. Milken told Solomon he would arrange a series of transactions so that Solomon would suffer no real financial losses in the scheme. To conceal the true nature of the trades and to avoid detection of the fraud, Milken carefully and purposefully used seldom-traded securities so that he could set the prices where he wanted them in order to help Solomon lower his personal tax bill. While some of the Drexel employees who sat on the trading floor near Milken were aware of the Solomon trades and other violations of the law committed in the name of client service and Drexel profits, nobody down the road in Einhorn's SEC office had a clue. They either didn't ask the right people the right questions, or, when they did, Milken and the others dodged them, just as Milken had done when Hewitt had asked him a few years earlier about his trading with the Boesky firm. That the SEC investigators lacked the creativity and tenacity of their rivals only added to the impression on the Drexel trading floor that government investigators were easily brushed off.

The Drexel traders were not alone in their lack of respect for the commission's investigators, and it was widely believed in the enforcement division that people frequently lied to the SEC. One favorite during the 1980s was the "airplane defense." Time after time, when SEC attorneys asked people who had traded in a stock in advance of the announcement of a takeover bid how they had learned about it, they said they overheard people talking about the stock on an airplane. While it is illegal to trade on inside information about a corporate takeover bid, it is legal to trade on information about a stock that one randomly overhears on an airplane flight. Even when the SEC did file insider trading cases, as it did against several people who traded in the stock of RCA Corporation just before the company was acquired by General Electric, commission investigators were able to make cases against only a fraction of those they suspected had broken the law.

The public had little indication that SEC officials felt many people were getting away with insider trading. Agency officials hailed the RCA case as a triumph for the SEC's enforcement program, and as an important vindication of Jack Shad's policies, including the ability to detect illegal trading through Swiss banks. Inside the commission's enforcement division though, RCA was a reminder that Shad's much ballyhooed campaign against insider trading often was ineffective, even when it gave the public appearance of succeeding. There were scores of people who traded RCA shares that the commission just couldn't mount cases against. One man who worked in Manhattan's garment district and purchased 10,000 shares just before the takeover was announced said he had been in a croissant shop in New York a few days before he made his purchases and heard two men discussing something in hushed tones. He said that they repeatedly mentioned RCA and that they sounded like they "had just found something." After discussing what he had heard with his son, the father and son purchased RCA shares through a relative who was a stockbroker at E. F. Hutton. When SEC investigators heard the tale, they found it laughable. Of course, the man may well have been telling the truth, and certainly no one at the SEC could prove otherwise. But his "croissant defense" sounded like so many others the enforcement attorneys heard.

Many of the people the SEC suspected of trading RCA stock with inside information also traded suspiciously in other takeover stocks, according to a confidential 1985 SEC memo. "It appears that certain members of this group received information about not only RCA but about General Foods, Union Carbide, and WCI (Warner Communications), and that there may be a common link to all or some of these companies," the memo said. "We do not have any direct evidence that any of these individuals possessed and/or traded on material, nonpublic information relating to RCA, but the trading activity, superficially weak stories, and assertions of the 5th Amendment suggest that certain of the above-described individuals may have traded in RCA securities while in possession of material nonpublic information." But after a series of depositions with witnesses around the country, the RCA case was dropped; those on the fringes traded safely beyond the SEC's reach. Although in theory if someone had lied to the commission they could be prosecuted criminally for perjury, the risk seemed small since the SEC had difficulty getting criminal prosecutors interested in bringing such cases.

To those investors and traders large and small who escaped SEC prosecution, Shad's commission seemed weak. In the Drexel case, the SEC failed to inspect scrupulously the junk bond operation; other enforcement investigations also seemed flaccid to some Drexel salesmen who later said they were aware of corruption. Jim Dahl, Milken's protégé who later became a government witness against him, testified twice before the SEC during the mid-1980s, each time at the L.A. regional office on Wilshire, each time without any concern that the commission's investigation would lead to serious trouble. One of the cases involved the accumulation of stock in an entertainment company by Centrust Savings, a Florida savings and loan built almost entirely on a portfolio of junk bonds. Einhorn's staff wondered whether stock bought by Drexel for its own account at the same time that its client Centrust was accumulating the entertainment concern's shares had been intended for use in forcing a takeover—if so, Drexel might have violated SEC disclosure rules. But Dahl denied that there was any such intent, and the investigation petered out.

In 1985, when he was questioned about legal matters by the commission, Milken was his usual confident self. "Common sense is that you don't operate on inside information, period," he declared bluntly one Saturday afternoon early in 1985, when it was his turn to visit with Einhorn's staff and answer questions about "LA-441," as the Caesars World investigation was captioned.

Later, salesman Dahl and Terren Peizer would tell federal prosecutors in New York that Milken routinely acted on the basis of inside information about the deals he engineered—indeed, so convoluted was the web of corporate, personal, and client accounts that Milken controlled that it was difficult to imagine how he could avoid such a transgression. But at that Saturday's interrogation in the midst of Einhorn's investigation, Milken repeated the same blunt, sometimes contemptuous, denials he had made to Hewitt more than two years before: He was too busy to remember many specifics, but he never violated the federal securities laws. What else did the SEC want to know?

Not much, as it turned out. The handful of staff lawyers assigned by Einhorn to handle the Caesars investigation tried to assemble a case the commission could bring to court, but after Milken denied during his interrogation that he knew of anything improper about the bond trades, they were stymied. To a degree, because market manipulation and insider trading were crimes that depended on the perpetrator's motives, his state of mind, Einhorn's team was frustrated by the same problem that plagued the campaigns against insider trading run by Fedders and Lynch in Washington: Without a cooperating witness, the evidence was strictly circumstantial. That legitimate problem, however, didn't completely explain the failure of the L.A. staff to conduct on-site inspections of the Beverly Hills office or concoct creative approaches to investigation of Milken's systematic use of junk bonds, loyal clients, and personal and corporate trading accounts to shape and even determine the outcome of billion-dollar hostile takeovers.

In some respects, Einhorn and his troops failed to grasp the broader significance of what Milken did inside his building just a few miles away. That spring of 1985, for example, while Einhorn's staff was putting time and effort into the Caesars bond-trading investigation, Milken, Drexel, and Ivan Boesky engineered an unsolicited takeover of giant Phillips Petroleum that, on its face, raised questions about insider trading, conflict-of-interest, and market manipulation. Yet while Milken spent an entire Saturday in Einhorn's office being interrogated about his bond trades, remarkably he wasn't asked a single question about the Phillips deal, which was making headlines each day around the country.

Frustrated and worried that his staff couldn't break through the secrecy shrouding Milken's dealings in Caesars bonds, Einhorn finally called a meeting in his office. He and his senior staff sat around the conference table that doubled as a desk.

This investigation already has gone on six months longer than it should have, Einhorn told his staff. It is time to do something where we have a chance to make a case.

By that, Einhorn meant the smaller, simpler, more obvious insider trading and financial fraud cases that received too little attention in the office because there wasn't enough staff. Einhorn and his staff felt in their guts that Milken had violated the securities laws, but they had only circumstantial evidence. As a regional administrator, Einhorn's performance would be measured by Shad and the others in Washington largely in terms of the number of successful cases he filed in a given year. Far from providing a basis for a renewal of morale in Los Angeles, the Milken case was proving to be a debilitating drain.

The case has to be closed, Einhorn said. Let's forget about it and do something else.

John Shad liked to repeat over and over that trillions of dollars of stock changed hands in the United States each year and that most of the transactions depended on trust and honesty. In Caesars, RCA, and scores of other deals, the day-to-day experience of the enforcement division tended to undermine Shad's assumptions. The commission filed only about two-dozen insider trading cases a year, despite all the inquiries, all the charts and memos and phone calls from the stock exchanges alerting the SEC to suspicious trades. To some of the lawyers who worked so many months on investigations that yielded only memos for the file, the lesson seemed to be that only the bumblers got caught by the commission. That year it seemed that Shad understood—he surprised his colleagues at the SEC by suggesting that the agency should pay informants for information about insider trading. The enforcement lawyers who needed such help could almost write an Abbie Hoffman–like handbook about how to avoid detection by the SEC. If you were a lawyer or an investment banker, don't trade the stocks of companies involved in deals on which you worked. If you do, make sure you trade in a foreign account beyond the SEC's reach. If you don't work on Wall Street, but you have a pipeline to provide you with inside information every now and then, your chances of getting caught, especially if you trade in small quantities and can invent halfway plausible alibis, seem very slim. The demoralizing truth was that on both Wall Street and Main Street that 1985, the calculation of risk and reward was tilting against the commission—the risk of getting caught by the SEC seemed minuscule compared to the enormous profits available by trading the stocks of takeover targets on inside information.

John Shad was losing the war.

16

The Manipulation

If I find out who is leaking our positions," Boesky warned, "I'll kill."

He glared at them, so angry he seemed about to pop right out of his costume—the dark, vested suit with gold chain, the tailored white shirt, the worn loafers. There were moments like this when all of the props and trappings of legitimacy Boesky had so carefully arranged in his suite of offices high above Fifth Avenue seemed on the verge of collapse, like the rickety set of some off-Broadway play. (The Manhattan suite's previous occupant, fugitive commodities trader Marc Rich, had been forced to flee hurriedly to Switzerland when federal investigators came knocking one day, so while the office was opulently appointed, it did not reek of solidity or permanence.) Something about the way Boesky pronounced his threat—the way he said the word *kill*—both frightened and intrigued his gathered staff of researchers and traders.

It was just after New Year's Day, 1985, but Boesky wasn't feeling festive. The immediate cause of his distress was a newspaper report that the master speculator had suffered heavy losses in recent days when he was forced to dump millions of shares of Phillips Petroleum, the oil giant based in tiny Bartlesville, Oklahoma. Boesky had to sell because Boone Pickens, who had been pursuing a hostile takeover of Phillips, reached an unexpected

275

peace treaty with the company's management that caused the price of Phillips stock to fall below the price that Boesky had paid. The crisis had pushed Boesky into a kind of maniacal overdrive, a pace and fury even more exaggerated than his usual inhuman routine. He seemed to be shrinking into a haunted, almost skeletal figure. The embarrassment he felt over public disclosure of his financial loss apparently was the last straw.

No one in this office is to talk to anyone outside of this office about what I am doing or why I am doing it, Boesky declared.

The leak only added to Boesky's paranoia, driving him to keep secrets from his own staff by leaving certain stock positions off the daily list distributed in the office. Those among his small senior staff who had reason to suspect the real basis for Boesky's paranoia—illegal dealings—said nothing. They were well paid, and thus loyal, although perhaps more ambivalent about Boesky than the junk bond traders and salesmen in Beverly Hills were about Milken. (Boesky was not nearly so charismatic, and it was more difficult to think of him as an inspirational or innovative genius.) Many of them were young, in their twenties and thirties, although a few were a bit older and had been with Boesky since his early days on Wall Street. For all of them, these were good times. The business of speculating on the outcome of corporate takeovers had never been better.

In fact, that January of 1985, the political and economic forces steadily gathering over the previous three years had finally achieved a kind of critical mass. Chicago School–inspired deregulation at the SEC, the triumph of free market theory in the debate over takeover legislation in Congress, the accelerating and largely unexamined growth of Milken's junk bond operation, and the unrestrained use of capital for arbitrage speculation on Wall Street at last coincided in a frenzy of events. So much was happening at once. The deals piled one upon the other. But there was one deal—the contested, five-month battle for control of Phillips Petroleum—that seemed even in the midst of so much chaos to symbolize how much had changed.

In Washington, they thought of the Phillips deal as a model for the continuing debate about the theory of unregulated takeovers. In little Bartlesville, a company town where Phillips was the principal employer, a benevolent but sleepy management was under siege by corporate raiders who said they could make Phillips better, richer. Was this good or bad for the country? they asked in Congress and at the SEC. Senators from Oklahoma bellowed that the good people of Bartlesville were suffering an assault no less egregious than rape. Defenders of Chicago School theory in the Reagan administration answered that if Boone Pickens could squeeze more value from Phillips than its present management, then Bartlesville and the nation would benefit in the long run. Jack Shad, pressured by both sides, indicated that he saw little to be corrected. He had raised his questions about the dangers of debt in corporate takeovers the previous June, alarming his allies in the administration, and he would stir controversy no more. He instead retreated to his earlier position that battles such as this ought to be left to the free market's takeover warriors on Wall Street and in Corporate America, and that the ultimate arbiter of any contested takeover ought to be a company's stockholders, not the SEC.

Of course, it was what Jack Shad's SEC did not see, what it could not see, that actually drove the Phillips takeover toward completion. Partly because of its embarrassing courtroom defeat in the midst of the earlier Carter Hawley Hale fight and partly because the headquarters staff was distracted by Fedders's resignation, the commission didn't investigate the Phillips deal until it was over, and even then the probe was desultory and unsuccessful. What the SEC missed was an elaborate manipulation, in some aspects clearly illegal and in others merely abusive, that defined and exemplified the corruption prevalent in influential quarters of Wall Street during 1985.

At the core of the corruption was the intricate financial web that connected Ivan Boesky and Michael Milken. By the time of the Phillips deal in early 1985, they had grown accustomed to providing each other with favors, legal and otherwise, whenever the need arose.

The Phillips deal began in Amarillo, Texas, where Boone Pickens reported to work at his corporate park each day, late in 1984, to face a taxing challenge: how to spend the $500 million junk bond war chest raised for unspecified corporate purposes by Michael Milken.

That fall, Pickens began to buy shares in two oil companies—Los Angeles–based Unocal Corporation and Phillips—trying to decide which one he wanted to put into play first. By purchasing the shares through partnerships, Pickens was able legally to evade certain federal disclosure requirements, enabling him to conceal his intentions and accumulate shares at relatively low prices. But word about what Pickens was doing began to leak to Wall Street, as it nearly always did, and by December 4, when Pickens finally announced his intention to raid Phillips, saying in an SEC filing that he owned 5.8 percent of its stock, the news surprised few of the professionals involved in takeover speculation. If the deal followed the pattern of Pickens's previous bids, there would be a flurry of excitement and rumor and threats, and then Phillips would escape into the arms of a friendly merger suitor, a white knight, enriching Pickens and his allies with stock-trading profits but denying them their prize. In Bartlesville, the battle for Phillips was described as a mortal war over jobs and community and the future, but on Wall Street the truth was that Phillips was regarded as little more than a flickering green symbol on a Quotron trading machine, important because it was likely to vanish into electronic oblivion as soon as Pickens's hostile bid played out and made the speculators rich.

The terms of Pickens's bid suggested that he was too poor to actually pay for Phillips. But this was only an inconvenience, easily overcome. For example, Pickens's initial offer was to buy about 15 percent of Phillips for sixty dollars a share in cash. After that, he promised that somehow, he would buy the rest of the stock, worth billions of dollars. Pickens's imprecise plans for this multibillion dollar transaction didn't matter too much to speculators on Wall Street, since Pickens had never before actually bought the companies that he bid for. And if it did actually become necessary to pay for Phillips, Milken's junk bond department could probably raise the funds by selling a new issue of risky debt or convincing Phillips stockholders to exchange their shares for junk bonds. In another era, the SEC would almost certainly have raised immediate questions about the vague financing arrangements in Pickens's publicly filed takeover disclosures. When anybody asked Stanley Sporkin at the CIA about this sort of thing, he said that *he* would have ended the whole deal at the beginning by declaring that vague promises were not enough to start a takeover, that you actually had to have the money in place. But in late 1984 and early 1985, the commission's policy under Shad was that as long as you disclosed your poverty honestly to the public, then it was up to the free market, and not the government, to decide whether your takeover bid should be taken seriously.

Phillips took Pickens seriously—its management, led by chairman William Douce, was petrified. Douce attacked Pickens's offer in the press and in the courts, trumpeting the usual themes about preserving jobs and community and country, but in secret his advisers called Pickens on the phone and asked if Phillips could buy back his stock at a profit and make him go away.

Pickens was in a bind. He had promised publicly when he announced his bid that he wouldn't accept greenmail from Phillips. But Douce's offer was sweet. Moreover, the Organization of Petroleum Exporting Countries (OPEC), the international oil cartel, was having trouble propping up the price of oil, and Pickens feared that if he didn't sell out soon, he might take a bath as world oil prices tumbled. So he wrestled with his conscience and mulled his dilemma for a few days, and on December 23, agreed to sell out to Phillips and break his promise to Wall Street.

To relieved employees in Bartlesville, who had organized prayer vigils and donned BOONE BUSTER T-shirts to ward off the unwanted raider, Douce announced the deal: Pickens would renounce his takeover bid and sell his stock to Phillips for fifty-three dollars a share, handing the raider an $81 million profit for about two months' work. At the same time, to discourage other raiders from launching debt-driven hostile takeover bids and to preserve the power and perks of top management, Douce said the company would replace 38 percent of its stock with new debt, establish an employee stock plan controlled by management, and take other vaguely articulated steps to keep its stock price up. To finance this wall of defense, Douce said Phillips would have to sell off about $2 billion of its assets. The company would survive, but it wouldn't be the same. The plan was set for a stockholder vote in February 1985. As part of the deal, Pickens announced he would support mangement.

Ivan Boesky heard the news over a crackling telephone line in Barbados, where he had fled the Manhattan chill for a brief Christmas vacation at the beach with his family. Livid, he rushed to the airport and clambered aboard a jet bound for New York.

He was too late. By mid-December, Boesky's firm had gobbled up Phillips stock madly, purchasing about 5 million shares. Boesky didn't always have inside information about takeover deals, and sometimes he gambled heavily. This time, to buy so much Phillips stock, he had borrowed to the hilt. He had been comforted by Pickens's public declarations that he would never sell out to Phillips in a greenmail deal that would hurt other stockholders. Moreover, because of his secret arrangement with Milken, Boesky had a pipeline to Drexel for information about hostile takeover bids. But Drexel wasn't involved in Pickens's decision to sell out, and in any event, Boesky had no advance word of Pickens's decision to drop his takeover bid.

Phillips stock plunged in price more than ten dollars a share when Pickens's greenmail deal was disclosed on Christmas Eve. Those who had bought the oil company's stock anticipating that Pickens, as he had done in the past, would force a merger at an exhorbitant price, now rushed to dump their holdings. When Boesky, panicked and furious, returned to Fifth Avenue, he joined right in, selling as fast as he could. The loans he had taken to finance his stock purchases were coming due minute by minute as the fall in the price of Phillips shares reduced the value of his collateral. Between December 24 and December 28, Boesky sold 2.3 million Phillips shares, suffering a loss of more than $22 million.

He was angry—not only at his staff, for leaking the details of his calamity to the newspapers, but also at Pickens and Phillips and everyone else whom Boesky held responsible for his disaster. Among the tightly knit community of takeover speculators that had grown up so suddenly on Wall Street, there was a deeply emotional if utterly inconsistent code of conduct—basically, it was captured by the assertion, "He who causes me to lose money is morally wrong." That January, this conviction about Phillips was shared by a large number of bereft speculators on Wall Street, many of them clients of Michael Milken. Around New York and by telephone to Beverly Hills, they began to discuss the possibility of revenge: Why not find another takeover bidder, back him up with junk bond financing, and put the heat on Phillips again?

Milken and his salesmen and traders in Beverly Hills were intrigued. Virtually every takeover deal they put together, whether completed or not, generated tens of millions of dollars in advisory and financing fees. Because of the billions of dollars required to finance even a partial attempt for Phillips, the potential for fees in this deal was greater than usual. Then, too, because of the personal investment by Milken and his employees in Boesky's arbitrage partnerships, Milken had a personal interest in creating an opportunity for Boesky to recover his losses.

A series of meetings at Drexel's Wall Street headquarters and at 9560 Wilshire ensued. Initially, Drexel officials telephoned several oil companies and suggested that they bid for Phillips. But Drexel's relations with mainstream corporations were relatively weak, and in the fraternal oil industry, none of the major companies was willing to undertake an unwanted takeover.

No matter—Milken wasn't necessarily concerned about whether the bidder for Phillips knew anything about the oil business. Guts was just as important. Drexel flirted with the idea of backing Boesky, who seemed mad enough to make a run. But Boesky preferred to speculate on takeover deals rather than initiate them. For one thing, as a hostile bidder, he would be subjected to myriad lawsuits and private investigations that might expose the secret arrangements he had with Marty Siegel, Milken, and others—arrangements Boesky worked hard to protect. So Boesky demurred. Instead, he called up his friend Carl Icahn and encouraged him to make a bid for Phillips with Drexel's backing.

Icahn, a blunt-spoken former options trader from Queens, New York, who had a reputation for making greenmail takeover raids and conducting tough negotiations, didn't know the difference between an oil well and a fire hydrant. However, he knew a great deal about how to pressure a vulnerable corporate management team such as the one at Phillips. On Icahn's Manhattan office walls were framed annual reports of all the public companies he had threatened with takeovers, and in every deal he had profited either through greenmail or the arrival of a white knight to rescue his target. As Pickens had been when he first began to accumulate Phillips shares the previous fall, Icahn was flush with cash from a recent junk bond financing engineered by Milken.

On December 28, with Phillips's stock price sagging from all the hurried sales by speculators, Carl Icahn began to buy.

Shortly after he made his first purchases, Boesky called him up.

"I hear you are involved with Phillips," Boesky said.

Yes, I bought some stock, Icahn replied.

Boesky said he was angry at Phillips management, for reasons Icahn could appreciate. He suggested that Icahn join forces with him and launch a proxy fight at the meeting of Phillips shareholders scheduled for February, when the Pickens greenmail deal was to be put to a vote. In a proxy fight, Icahn and Boesky would attempt to win enough shareholder votes to defeat the greenmail plan.

The best way to run an effective proxy fight is to do it in conjunction with a takeover bid, Icahn told Boesky. That way you put more pressure on the company's management, which otherwise has unfair advantages in a proxy fight against outsiders.

Boesky thought that was an interesting idea. He began to call Icahn every day, urging him relentlessly to lead a fight against Phillips management. In those same conversations, Boesky pressed and needled and maneuvered to learn everything he could about Icahn's plans. The more he knew about what Icahn intended, the better off he would be when deciding whether to buy or sell Phillips shares.

As part of his campaign, Boesky invited Icahn to his huge Westchester estate early in January. He said that he wanted to discuss strategies the pair could undertake to drive up the price of Phillips stock.

Icahn arrived by car and settled in for a talk, surrounded by the

Renaissance art and eighteenth-century furniture and ancient sculpture Boesky had acquired so voraciously during the previous three years.

If we're going to make a joint takeover bid for Phillips, Icahn told Boesky, you're going to have to put up $100 million or $150 million in cash to help pay for it.

Boesky indicated that they could discuss financing in detail later if they chose to go down that road. The truth was that Boesky often borrowed aggressively because he was short of cash. In fact, Boesky was so strapped for money, and so heavily leveraged, that at one point during the Phillips fight he was as much as $50 million in violation of SEC rules governing how much cash a registered broker-dealer must keep on hand. Boesky had been able to evade detection, and buy more and more Phillips shares, because of his secret trading arrangement with Milken. When Boesky exceeded the limit of his allowable stock holdings, he just called upon his arrangement with Milken and asked to transfer some of his Phillips shares to Drexel's accounts, with the understanding that Boesky would buy them back at a fixed price and would protect Drexel against any losses it incurred while holding the shares. Moreover, Boesky agreed with Milken to split any profits made during the time Drexel held the shares. So even though he lacked the capital required by the SEC, Boesky kept borrowing and buying more. Given the importance of the upcoming shareholder vote at Phillips, it was like stuffing the ballot box to win the election. The more shares Boesky owned, the more power he could wield and the greater the likelihood he could shape, or help to rig, the outcome.

Not long after meeting with Boesky in Westchester, Icahn decided he was going to make a takeover bid for Phillips, or at least that he was going to give the appearance of making one. Icahn's bid would require about $8 billion in junk bonds, generating fees for Milken's operation that could easily exceed $100 million. Milken said that he was so confident about this deal that, in a break with precedent, there was no need for Icahn to seek even a dime from commercial banks. Milken wanted to finance the entire $8 billion with junk bonds.

All of them—Milken, Icahn, Boesky, the other Wall Street arbs who had bought large amounts of Phillips stock—understood that it was possible to make enormous sums of money just by threatening the takeover, even if it never was completed. The announced junk bond bid combined with an aggressive proxy fight would probably be enough to force Phillips into a "friendly" merger with another oil company or into sweetening the terms of its pending financial restructuring.

On January 28, Icahn bought 2.74 million Phillips shares from Boesky. For weeks, Boesky had been talking almost daily with Icahn about becoming his cobidder, and at the same time he had discussed selling his stock at a profit to assist Icahn's takeover plans. It was a technique for trading on confidential information similar to the one Boesky had used with Ted Forstmann in Dr Pepper, where Boesky gleaned inside information about Forstmann's takeover plans because of his access as an investor in Forstmann Little and then used the information to make stock-trading profits as an arbitrager. Icahn didn't mind. He needed Boesky's shares to make his threatened bid for Phillips more credible. Because there was no reporting system at the New York Stock Exchange or the SEC sophisticated enough to identify immediately the buyers and sellers in specific stock transactions, no one at the commission knew for certain that day that Boesky and Icahn had made such an enormous private trade.

Six days later Icahn announced a junk bond–backed, $55-a-share, $8 billion hostile-takeover bid for Phillips. He had relatively little cash to actually pay for the deal. Instead, Milken issued Icahn a letter saying Drexel was "highly confident" it could raise the money if called upon to do so. Icahn paid Drexel $1 million for the letter. Peppered with phone calls and other protests from Phillips headquarters in Oklahoma, the SEC voiced no objections.

For his part, Milken was eager to begin raising the funds by obtaining firm commitments from junk bond investors. But Icahn was reluctant to move so quickly, because if he did he would have to pay Drexel millions of dollars in "commitment fees" even if he never used the money Milken raised. Since the principal goal of Icahn's bid had all along been to drive up Phillips stock price, rather than to actually acquire and manage the oil company, it was unlikely the $8 billion in funds would ever be needed, and Icahn wanted to hold his costs down.

Milken saw that in exchange for a mere $1 million "highly confident" letter, Icahn was now in a position to reap huge trading profits without actually selling any junk bonds. So as part of his deal with Icahn, Milken extracted a concession: Icahn reluctantly agreed to give Drexel 20 percent of his stock-trading profits whether he succeeded with a takeover or not, and regardless of whether a single junk bond was sold. Drexel was now an investor in the takeover attempt, a partner of Icahn's rather than merely his investment banker or his agent.

About five days after Icahn announced his bid, he met with Boesky again, this time over dinner at Icahn's home north of Manhattan. Boesky wanted to discuss the Phillips situation.

I've purchased another four million Phillips shares, Boesky told him.

Icahn was pleased. Although Boesky's disclosure marked a turnabout from two weeks before, when Boesky had sold more than 2 million shares to Icahn, Boesky's new purchases provided Icahn with 4 million new votes for the upcoming proxy fight with Phillips management, scheduled for February 22 in Bartlesville. Icahn said plans were well under way for the proxy vote.

Meanwhile, Douce, the Phillips chairman, convened meetings daily that month in Bartlesville and sometimes in Manhattan, working with his own stable of Wall Street advisers to thwart Icahn, Boesky, and Milken, and in the process, preserve the jobs of Phillips management at all costs. (Douce's advisers, from the most blue-chip investment banks on Wall Street, charged Phillips millions of dollars in fees. They deplored Drexel's role in the deal, they said, but in truth the crumbs from Milken's table scattered far and wide.) With the pressure mounting early in February, Douce and his board of directors decided to greet Icahn with a blow to the ribs: They announced a "poison pill" antitakeover device designed to force Icahn to negotiate directly with Phillips management, compromising his right to take his offer directly to Phillips shareholders. The "pill" was a shareholder-rights plan that provided anyone who owned Phillips stock with the right to receive sixty-two dollars per share at the moment Carl Icahn bought 30 percent of the company's stock. Icahn and Boesky denounced the plan as a management abuse, since it was designed to take fundamental rights away from Phillips's stockholders and give them to the company's entrenched management.

The maneuverings grew so complex as the shareholder meeting approached that even Phillips's sophisticated institutional shareholders found the tactics difficult to understand. Their bewilderment was compounded by the blistering pace at which Phillips shares changed hands, due in part to the side agreements and private meetings among Milken, Boesky, and Icahn that drove the deal.

On Valentine's Day, Icahn and Boesky took the stage at a meeting at the University Club in Manhattan, called to explain the upcoming vote in Bartlesville. The 150 Wall Street professionals gathered before them, some of whom managed portfolios containing billions of dollars of stock, would decide with their ballots whether the scheme to pressure Phillips would succeed.

"I'm not telling you I'm Robin Hood," Icahn said, adding that he had agreed to pay Milken $7.5 million to line up the first $1.5 billion in financing. "I'm not doing it because I want to just save everybody. The trouble with corporations today is management. And the reason that management doesn't really function that well is because they are just not answerable. . . . A guy like me comes along and stands up to them."

Crowds formed around Icahn and Boesky in the lobby and out into the street when the meeting was over. The atmosphere was charged—that day, Harrison J. Goldin, the comptroller of the city of New York, had declared that he was forming a new group, the Council of Institutional Investors, to explore the issues Icahn and Boesky raised and to stand up for the rights of shareholders. The twenty-two public pension funds in Goldin's new group had more than $100 billion in pension assets at their disposal. Goldin alone controlled the enormous amounts of stock owned by New York City pension funds, and his declaration, following a meeting at City Hall with Icahn, Boesky, and Pickens, indicated that the raiders were winning powerful institutional allies. The buzz Goldin created at his press conference extended to the lobby of the University Club.

Somebody asked Boesky if he considered himself a pirate.

"That's a euphemism for people who seek a profit," Boesky replied. "By God, in America one of the great things about this nation is that we can seek profit. And I'm proud of that. And if you can gain profit, that's even better and that's not a dirty word."

When the day arrived, Bartlesville was alive with energy and crowds and bunting and banners. Employees carried picket signs and stood outside the auditorium where the shareholders would vote, urging that Icahn and Boesky and Milken be defeated. The lawyers and bankers poured past them in dark suits, many of them unsmiling. Only a few stopped to talk and hear what the pickets wanted to say.

Inside, one by one the shareholders waited to speak. Some, mainly the institutional investors who controlled large blocks of voting stock, spoke up for Icahn, denouncing Douce and describing his tactics as desperate. A few of the smaller shareholders and local citizens urged that something besides profit and loss should decide the election. "We are afraid ownership will change to people who don't care. And without care there is no community," said Joel R. Benbow, pastor of the town's Our Savior Lutheran Church.

That afternoon, Phillips announced it was suspending the meeting to allow the votes to be counted. Experts took the suspension as a sign that Icahn had prevailed and that Phillips management was going to explore a compromise settlement.

They were right. Icahn began to talk about a deal. He wanted Douce to improve the announced financial restructuring for all shareholders, including himself. He wanted Phillips to pay his $25 million in "expenses," helping cover his fees to Drexel, among other things. Douce and his advisers were willing to go along— giving Icahn a quick $50 million stock-trading profit—but they wanted a guarantee that there would be no third time, that after Pickens and Icahn, there would be no new raider on the horizon with Drexel's troops behind him. Phillips insisted that Drexel sign an unprecedented standstill agreement, saying it would not represent any other bidders for Phillips for a period of three years. Drexel, already well-compensated for its troubles, went along.

"Drexel is in one sense the most powerful financial institution in the country today," said Martin Lipton, the takeover attorney who had built his reputation protecting major corporations and who had advised Phillips on its takeover defense.

To extricate himself profitably from the deal Icahn had negotiated, Boesky still needed to do some private business with Drexel. The problem was that, because of the losses he incurred in December and the huge sums he borrowed afterward to buy Phillips shares, Boesky was in violation of SEC capital requirements governing how much cash he needed to maintain in his accounts. As a registered broker, arbitrager, and manager of funds, Boesky periodically was required to report his stock holdings to the commission. To conceal his capital problem before filing papers at the SEC, Boesky turned to his arrangement with Milken.

The pair mapped an elaborate series of transactions designed to make Boesky's books appear legitimate to the commission. Between March 7 and March 11, 1985, Boesky sold more than 4.1 million Phillips shares to Drexel, which in turn sold them to several of its most loyal clients, including Gibraltar Savings Association and Executive Life Insurance, and to private accounts in which Milken or his brother Lowell had an interest. Boesky agreed to protect Milken against any losses he incurred and to divide any profits. The arrangement allowed Boesky to reduce his net capital deficiency by tens of millions of dollars, and when he filed the required papers at the commission, he showed more than enough cash to be in compliance with SEC rules. The capital filings were a snapshot of Boesky's holdings, so once the filing date passed he was free to take back his Phillips stock from Drexel. (The SEC had the authority to inspect a firm like Boesky's between the filings, but it never inspected Boesky during the Phillips transaction, although newspaper reports suggested the arbitrager suffered heavy losses early in the deal.) On April 12, Boesky bought back 1 million Phillips shares from Drexel, and more shares the following week. He unloaded the stock in the open market over the next few months. Under the terms of his secret agreement with Milken, Boesky was later compensated for stock-trading profits made by Drexel and others during March and early April.

In the midst of these complex transactions and the preparation of his false filings for the SEC, a reporter asked Boesky what he thought about the success he and Icahn and Milken had enjoyed in the stockholder vote that forced Phillips management to capitulate.

"For the first time," he answered, "we see a clear recognition that big financial institutions and individual stockholders have expressed their view on what was fair."

17

A Big Fish

They sat around the conference table by the window in Gary Lynch's corner office on December 17, 1985, eight lawyers buttoned up in the uniform of their trade—crisp white shirts, dark or gray suits, suspenders, silk ties. Lined yellow legal pads were spread before them. The oldest wasn't yet forty-five, and most of the group were in their thirties. They knew each other well. Harvey Pitt, one of the two defense lawyers in attendance, had been SEC general counsel during the late 1970s, and now he made a handsome living defending banks and corporations and financiers who had trouble with the commission. Though Pitt was an aggressive adversary, there was a way in which he remained intensely loyal to the SEC and its rules even while in private practice. He accepted the sanctity of the commission's traditions and the gravity of its role. He was a "member of the club."

"We've been working with you guys, and it's taken a fair amount of time," Pitt was saying. He had asked for this meeting with Lynch, and the enforcement director had invited five other commission staff lawyers to hear what Pitt wanted. "We want to deal first with the things we feel we are ethically obliged to discuss. Then we'd like to engage in what I would refer to as an off-the-record discussion."

"What do you mean by off the record?" Lynch asked skeptically.

"Basically, you'll see when we get to that point."

Pitt kept talking. Bearded and rotund, he was regarded as a brilliant attorney, but he could also be quick-tempered and elliptical. He reveled in gamesmanship. As he spoke that morning, glancing at a legal pad that seemed to contain detailed, scripted notes, he kept referring to his ethical obligations and his desire to avoid a confrontation and to other things that seemed to make little sense under the circumstances. Pitt represented a Zurich-based Swiss bank named Bank Leu whose Nassau, Bahamas, branch was the subject of an SEC insider trading investigation. The commission knew that someone at the bank, or else the bank itself, had earned millions of dollars by trading stocks in advance of takeover announcements. For months, while negotiating to turn over some of the bank's documents to the commission, Pitt had told the enforcement staff that its investigation appeared to be a big mistake, that the trading of takeover stocks might look suspicious, but it actually was the product of sophisticated and systematic research by the bank's stock market professionals. All through the fall, Pitt had repeated this defense, but he had been slow about turning over any documents to back up his claims, and the SEC staff had grown angry over his procrastination. The investigation was like so many others—slow, frustrating, stymied by lawyers, bureaucracy, and in this case, Swiss banking-secrecy laws. Now, after so much time, Pitt had asked for an unusual meeting with Lynch. Yet he had again come to the commission without any of his client's records.

"Based upon our actual review of the documents and recent discussions with our clients, we are now obliged to tell the staff that you should not rely upon our prior factual representations," Pitt finally blurted out. All of the negotiations between the SEC and Bank Leu during the past five months, Pitt was saying, had been based on lies.

"What?" one of the enforcement lawyers shouted at him.

"That is why we are here."

Pitt said he now wanted to go "off the record." By this, he had earlier explained, he meant that while he couldn't "help your knowing what I've told you, once I've told it to you," he didn't want anybody at the SEC ever to claim that he had told them anything. "I don't want you to ever attribute what has been said here either to my client or to my client's lawyers. That is, you can use whatever I tell you for what you think it's worth." In short, Harvey Pitt—voluntarily, unsolicited by the SEC—was about to play the role of a confidential government informant.

Gary Lynch listened intently. It seemed clear from Pitt's bizarre and convoluted windup that a big pitch was coming—a major breakthrough for the SEC was about to be dropped onto Lynch's conference table. For Lynch, the gift was welcome. The truth was that before Harvey Pitt telephoned and asked to meet, Gary Lynch had begun to feel increasingly frustrated by the trend of his short tenure as chief of the SEC's enforcement division. The spring and summer had been awkward enough. First, he inherited a job he had long coveted from a friend, Fedders, who was beset by personal troubles. Then, annointed with "interim" status by Shad, he had been forced to compete and prove himself to win the permanent position, and he had felt acute pressure to avoid any mistake that might jeopardize his goal. Finally, Shad named him as director, but then in a sense Lynch had to begin all over again, building loyalty among his senior staff, familiarizing himself with cases he had not previously supervised, and attempting to resurrect the feeling of purpose and morale in the division, which had been shaken by the circumstances of Fedders's resignation. By the fall of 1985, Lynch was in command—but in command of what? Wild takeovers raged on Wall Street and stock prices of big companies like CBS and RCA zoomed up before merger events were announced, seemingly reflecting massive trading on inside information. On some days that autumn, takeover rumors and computer programs and new financial instruments seemed to turn the markets into a swirling kaleidoscope of speculation, fueled, Lynch suspected, by trading on inside information and market manipulation by professional arbitragers who bought shares and then profited after planting rumors about corporate takeovers. Yet there was little he could do about it. When, in November, he issued a bold and public warning that the SEC would crack down on arbitragers who manipulated stock prices, Wall Street's traders

and executives paid little attention. After such a long stretch of
desultory and ineffectual investigations of major players in the
markets, the commission's credibility was on the wane. Lynch felt
the SEC was doing everything it could, indeed that it had mounted
an effective deterrent to insider trading through its prosecutions
of individual wrongdoers away from Wall Street, but he was frustrated because he sensed that the commission was falling behind
and lacked respect from some of the most influential institutions
in American finance.

There had been no real reason to think that the meeting with
Harvey Pitt that December morning would offer any relief, though
Pitt had asked that the enforcement chief be present. The Bank
Leu insider trading case was a significant but routine investigation
handled by enforcement division attorneys beneath Lynch, and he
had not been intimately involved once it got off the ground. It had
been opened the previous June, when Robert Romano, the former
SEC trial lawyer now employed on Wall Street by Merrill Lynch,
telephoned Lynch in Washington. "I think we've got an offshore
bank that's hitting on every recent takeover," Romano had told
him. (One of the commission's biggest assets may have been that its
alumni in private practice still thought of themselves at times as
commission enforcement lawyers.) Romano explained that Merrill
Lynch had conducted an internal investigation of Bank Leu's stock
trading after an anonymous person sent in a roughly typed, one-
page letter from Caracas, Venezuela, accusing two brokers in its
Caracas office of trading on inside information about major takeovers in the United States. After looking into it, Romano told
Lynch, Merrill Lynch found that the employees trading in takeover
stocks were copying massive trades by the Nassau, Bahamas,
branch of Bank Leu. Intrigued, Gary Lynch had passed Romano's
tip down through the enforcement bureaucracy and asked Shad
and the other commissioners for a formal SEC investigative order.
Subpoenas were issued and negotiations with Pitt to obtain Bank
Leu's records had begun.

Pitt's presentation to Lynch and the other enforcement attorneys that December morning seemed confusing because he considered himself to be in an ethical bind. Just the week before,

during an exasperating trip to the Bahamas, Pitt and his law partner, Michael Rauch, had discovered that Bank Leu officials had systematically lied to them about the stock trading under investigation by the SEC. Pitt had persuaded the bank executive in charge that telling the truth to the commission was now the best course. But in doing so, Pitt didn't want to reveal all of what he knew about insider trading at Bank Leu before he secured a settlement deal with Lynch that was favorable to his client.

When he got around to it at last, Pitt proposed that Bank Leu and the SEC make an even trade: The bank would defy the traditions of Swiss and Bahamian bank secrecy and reveal the name of the customer orchestrating the illegal stock trades, but the commission would agree not to file fraud charges against the bank or its employees.

They went around the table for a while, arguing about whether the trade was fair. The obvious advantage to the commission was that Pitt had offered to help the SEC leapfrog over the arduous Swiss treaty process negotiated by John Fedders three years earlier—rather than waiting months or years by going through formal channels, the commission would have the name of the culprits trading through Bank Leu within weeks. The question, though, was whether the person or persons Pitt was prepared to hand over for prosecution were significant enough players on Wall Street to justify immunity for the bank and its employees, at least some of whom obviously had tried to cover up the illegal scheme. Lynch and his colleagues pressed Pitt for the identity of Bank Leu's customer, or at least some clue about his background, but Pitt gave little ground. At one point, Pitt called the customer a "status player" on Wall Street. Lynch, taciturn as always, asked Pitt and Rauch to leave the room for a minute. When they came back, Lynch said the deal was acceptable, so long as the details could be worked out over the next few weeks.

"Obviously, I can't commit the commission to this," Lynch told Pitt. "I'll have to talk to them. But I'll recommend we go for it."

The enforcement staff lawyers tried to press Pitt and Rauch again for the name of Bank Leu's customer, but all one of them would say was that the customer was a "big fish."

"For what you're asking," said John Sturc, the SEC's associate enforcement director who had supervised the Bank Leu investigation, "he'd damn well better be Moby Dick."

Three days later, in a cool interior conference room at Bank Leu's Nassau, Bahamas, branch, "Mr. Diamond," as he was known to the bank's employees, dramatically unfolded a piece of paper pulled from his pocket and displayed it to Richard Coulson and Bruno Pletscher, two of the bank's executives.

"It was sent to me," Dennis B. Levine said in his usual conspiratorial tone. "You must understand that for obvious reasons I have cut off my name. But it should give you comfort. The SEC doesn't have any suspicion I'm involved in this investigation. It has nothing to do with me. They haven't the slightest clue, or they wouldn't have sent me this letter."

Coulson and Pletscher looked the paper over. It was indeed a letter, written on Securities and Exchange Commission stationery and signed by SEC Chairman John Shad. Although "Mr. Diamond" had covered over his name, the letter thanked him warmly for accepting Shad's invitation and participating in the commission's November 26, 1985, roundtable discussion on whether takeovers should be more closely regulated by the SEC.

Perhaps Dennis Levine genuinely believed, as he refolded Shad's letter and returned it to his pocket, that he was still beyond the commission's reach. If he thought so, he had good reason. For more than five years Levine had been illegally trading stocks with ease and impunity, using the confidential information he gleaned as a Wall Street merger specialist to earn about $12 million in profits, nearly all of it still stashed in his secret Bank Leu account in the Bahamas. During that same five years, Levine had risen to the top of his profession. He had found it difficult at first to break into investment banking because he hadn't attended a top business school. But Smith Barney finally gave him his first job on Wall Street, and in 1985, Levine had finally ended up at the most aggressive firm on the Street, Drexel Burnham Lambert, where he was earning about $1 million annually in salary and bonus as a managing director in the firm's New York–based merger department. When Levine learned of a new takeover deal that Drexel had in the works, he merely stepped outside of the firm's towering headquarters at 60 Broad Street in Manhattan, wandered to a pay phone in the financial district, telephoned Bank Leu, identified himself as Mr. Diamond, and placed his order to buy large blocks of the takeover target's stock. It was astonishingly simple. From time to time, to withdraw cash or attend to the administration of his secret account, Levine excused himself from the office and flew round-trip to the Bahamas in a single day, not even telling his wife where he had gone, or so he later claimed.

As he piled up his offshore kitty, Levine had little fear of the SEC. During a commission interrogation in late 1984, Levine, then thirty-one, blithely lied to enforcement division lawyers about whether he had brokerage accounts and about his advance knowledge of a takeover bid for the giant Textron Incorporated conglomerate. The SEC was investigating insider trading in Textron stock, but it didn't know that Levine secretly had pocketed $200,000 trading Textron shares through his offshore account. At the deposition, an enforcement lawyer asked Levine whether he had used inside information to win investment-banking business for his firm. In truth, ever since his arrival on Wall Street, Levine had found that inside information about takeovers helped to attract new merger advisory clients. In the case of Textron, Levine had received a tip about an impending takeover from a coconspirator in his insider trading ring. But when the SEC asked how he learned about the Textron deal in advance, Levine spun an outrageous alibi.

I was sitting in the reception area at Drexel Burnham, one day in October 1984, when I overheard two men discussing a deal, Levine explained to the enforcement lawyers.

The men mentioned a wealthy Chicago businessman named Lester Crown and they also mentioned Skadden Arps, the law firm specializing in takeovers, and First Boston, Levine went on. And they said something about "fireworks in Rhode Island." The men were in their late thirties or early forties, "dressed in pinstripes, gray suits, just like all of us. They both had briefcases."

"Fireworks in Rhode Island" was the clue that gave it away,

Levine boasted, explaining that he knew the takeover target was Textron because the company had its headquarters in Providence.

The interrogation had ended inconsequentially and afterward Levine became convinced the SEC could never catch him. He grew bolder during 1985. Indeed, if there was one moment that defined the audacity and—who could deny the thrill of it?—the sheer, exhilarating success of Levine's fraud scheme, it was that November morning late that year, just a month before Pitt met with the enforcement staff in Lynch's office, when Dennis Levine flew down to Washington and strode into SEC headquarters on Fifth Street, possessed of an invitation for a roundtable discussion with Shad and others on how the commission might improve its scrutiny of corporate takeovers. "We do believe that these activities create wealth in the economy," Levine, who was pale and boyish-looking and overweight, told Shad profoundly. "There is clearly a flow of funds into the hands of shareholders and institutions which by and large is reinvested in the secondary market and many times invested in consumption and thereby stimulates spending and production."

Merger lawyer Martin Lipton, a great skeptic about Drexel and the takeovers it sponsored, had also been on the panel that day. At one point he turned to the SEC chairman and said that it would be "worth the commission's while to look at the trading in some of the more notorious takeovers of the past two years. Look at the trading pattern in the half dozen or so where there were no five percent filings but a series of rumors, very, very high trading in the securities of the company, and then the trading would drop off again and there would be another burst of trading and stories day after day that the company was a target. . . . Only the commission has the power to get at the facts behind this."

Levine had been impressed with Lipton's analysis, and he decided to contribute some additional advice to Shad. "If you look at some of the other major transactions that took place, Nabisco Brands, for instance, General Foods, both of which had significant run-ups in the stock, raiders presumably were not involved. It's [suspicious trading] an isolated pattern that develops from time to time with certain transactions not always precipitated by raiders."

What Shad didn't know was that Levine had made nearly $3 million trading Nabisco Brands stock on inside information.

As a boy growing up on a neatly manicured, middle-class block in Bayside, Queens, New York, they had called him Dennis the Menace, and in so many ways he was still the same—clever, precocious, mischievous, and utterly self-absorbed. He bragged of his ability to sell aluminum siding, his family's business. To sit in the SEC's hearing room and advise the chairman on how to improve the commission's investigations of insider trading was for Levine a seemingly transcendent achievement, proof not only that he was one of the most important investment bankers on Wall Street, but also that he was smarter and faster and more daring than all the rest of them. Later, there were journalists and pundits who wondered what system of values, what failure of family or education or community, could have led Dennis Levine—who obviously possessed certain charms and talents—to so thoroughly and unapologetically pursue a life of crime. Upon close examination, judging by what he actually said and did, it seemed clear that whatever the role of early traumas such as the death of Levine's sister and the unexpected passing of his mother, the banal, unexciting truth was that Levine was exceedingly greedy, and that during the course of his career as a Wall Street merger expert, he found that it was very easy to steal.

On that morning of December 20, 1985, in Nassau, when Levine showed his letter from Shad to the Bank Leu executives who managed his accounts, he argued that as long as the bank didn't break the sacred Swiss code of secrecy, there was no reason to believe that he would ever be caught. Coulson and Pletscher, the bank executives, knew that Harvey Pitt had cut a tentative deal in Washington three days before, all but ensuring that Bank Leu would eventually turn Levine over to the U.S. government. But when they examined Levine's letter, they only nodded their agreement that he was home free. They had been told by Pitt and others that it was essential Levine suspect nothing.

Levine kept flying down to the Bahamas, pressing to continue his stock trading, grilling the handful of Bank Leu officials with whom he dealt for information about the SEC's progress. Levine knew the bank had been subpoenaed by the commission—indeed, it was Levine who recommended Harvey Pitt as a skilled and politically connected attorney who could help respond to the government's demands—but he said that his only worry was that the SEC might inadvertently find a piece of paper that had his true name on it. When Levine returned to Nassau early in January to meet again with Pletscher, he said that he was concerned that somehow the commission would get hold of the handwritten cash withdrawal slips that Levine had signed, over the years, when visiting the bank.

"Hypothetically, couldn't the bank lose a file, a whole file, or part of a file?" Levine asked Pletscher.

"Theoretically, yes, we can lose a file."

"The withdrawal slips with my signature—I really feel that we should destroy them or lose them. They are the only remaining documents that could lead to me."

It was gray, wet, and cold in the capital on the February morning in 1986 when Ivan Boesky's limousine turned onto Fifth Street and glided to a halt before the commission's beige concrete headquarters. Boesky was late again. This time, in contrast to when he testified in the Dr Pepper investigation and argued with the enforcement staff about his inalienable right to smoke cigars, the arbitrager was an honored guest. He had been invited by the SEC chairman to appear at yet another of Shad's roundtable panels, this one convened to advise the commission on how to solve the problem of swirling takeover rumors in the stock market.

"Here is Mr. Boesky now," said Shad delightedly when the skeletal speculator pushed through the doors of the commission meeting room after the discussion had already begun. "Ivan, would you just identify yourself, please?"

"Ivan Boesky," he said.

He sat down at the panelists' table, alongside John Phelan, chairman of the New York Stock Exchange; William Schreyer, chairman of Merrill Lynch; Arthur Levitt, chairman of the American Stock Exchange; Boyd Jefferies, head of the Jefferies and Company brokerage, and Gary Lynch, director of the commission's enforcement division. The unacknowledged, unseen web of relationships around the table was as thick as glue: Lynch's enforcement division had been investigating Boesky for years; Boesky and Jefferies had embarked on a secret, illegal stock-trading agreement similar in some respects to the one between Boesky and Milken; Schreyer's firm, battered by takeover rumors, had initiated Lynch's investigation into "Moby Dick"; and Phelan's New York Stock Exchange had itself investigated Boesky in the past for illegal insider trading. It was as if Shad, oblivious, had invited to the same dinner party acquaintances who had been for years secretly entangled in love affairs and betrayals and revenge plots. Yet the dialogue was polite, mannered.

Shad asked Lynch to outline some of the legal issues slated for discussion by the experts.

Lynch understood that these roundtables were important to Shad. To the chairman, they seemed to represent all that was genuinely fun about government and power—the right to call up your friends, or people whom you wanted to be your friends, or people who were just smart and interesting, and have them fly to Washington and advise you and the public on decisive issues of the day. Virtually never did Shad act on the suggestions and ideas bandied about at these meetings, but he cherished them nonetheless. They served a political purpose because they created an impression that the SEC was grappling with issues such as takeovers, junk bonds, and computer-driven program trading. But mainly Shad seemed to like them because they were collegial, open, stimulating, and attended by prestigious experts. It would have been fair to observe that Lynch, anxious among other things about the progress of his Moby Dick investigation, perhaps had better things to do that morning than chat publicly with Wall Street titans about how to stop speculators from spreading false rumors in the stock market. But public appearances such as these shored up Lynch's relationship with Shad, enhancing the enforcement division's authority before the commission. And Lynch, too, benefited from his role as the commission's resident expert on securities law— these were the sorts of appearances that gave top SEC enforcement attorneys a public image on Wall Street and made them such hot properties when they moved into private practice.

The talk went round and round. Boesky and Jefferies argued vehemently that corporations regulated by the SEC should be required to disclose all of their secrets to the public. "To me it is a simple issue," Jefferies declared. "The absolute truth is what the marketplace is looking for."

"How do you begin to tear this all apart?" asked Boesky philosophically. ". . . The question is, what duty does that person have to disclose what is in his mind?" It was as if Boesky was asking that question at least in part about himself.

Shad joined in with eager questions, drawing from Boesky his opinions about a number of controversial issues. The pair seemed at times of one mind. Arguing against the idea of employing enforced halts to interrupt stock trading when takeover and other rumors in the market spin beyond control, Boesky echoed almost precisely Shad's oft-repeated thesis about the markets and the economy.

"Liquidity," Boesky said, "is something again that is one of the great elements of our stock market versus all other stock markets that I am aware of. The more of that there is, the better it is."

After lunch, Shad asked the panel whether it would be a good idea for the SEC, in order to improve its enforcement effort against insider trading and market manipulation, to adopt a bounty program similar to the one at the Internal Revenue Service, where citizen informants were paid in 1985 about $400,000 for tips about tax cheating. The idea was that if somebody on Wall Street knew of someone violating the securities laws, he could call up the SEC, and if his tip led to a prosecution, he would be paid for his information. Most of the experts thought this was a terrible idea. Dan Fischel, a free market economist from the University of Chicago and the only academic invited by Shad to the roundtable, said that no one had proven there was much market manipulation and insider trading to be concerned about.

Silent most of the day, Gary Lynch finally spoke up. He said it was hard to mount a major fraud prosecution without the help of an informant. "If you have ever tried to track a rumor to its source, I think you will know it is almost impossible to do that," he remarked. "As far as the insider trading area, I think we have

seen in a number of cases that informants can be extremely helpful to the case, and certainly it would be good to have an informant who could actually appear and testify at trial."

Ivan Boesky wasn't around to comment on Lynch's observation
about informants. He had been forced to leave the meeting early.
His schedule, he had explained, was pressing.

For Harvey Pitt and Michael Rauch, Bank Leu's attorneys, it
was a calculated risk. On an April afternoon in a conference room
at the London offices of Pitt's law firm, Fried, Frank, Shriver,
Harris & Jacobson, the bank's Bruno Pletscher was in the midst of
two weeks of interviews and SEC testimony about his dealings
with Dennis Levine. Because the settlement agreement outlined
by Pitt, Lynch, and the others at the SEC that past December
wasn't yet completed, Pletscher hadn't revealed Levine's name to
the SEC. He had agreed to testify—outside of the United States,
to protect Pletscher's own legal interests—but in telling his story,
he referred to Bank Leu's customer only as "Mr. X." Now,
Pletscher had reached the point in his narrative when Mr. X,
during his December visit to the Bahamas, had pulled a letter
from John Shad from his pocket and brandished it as evidence of
his intimate relations with the commission. If Pletscher told that
story, he would provide an easy clue to Mr. X's identity. Rauch,
however, couldn't resist. The story was priceless, and if the SEC
had any lingering doubts about its generous, pending settlement
deal with Bank Leu, the tale would surely wash those doubts away.

"Bruno," Rauch said. "Tell them about the letter."

Later that month, after the testimony in London was completed,
one of the enforcement lawyers working on the Moby Dick investigation asked a clerk to pull from the SEC's basement library the
agendas and guest lists from recent commission roundtables on
takeover issues. The enforcement staff assigned to the Moby Dick
case spent hour upon hour trying to guess or deduce who Mr. X
was, and one SEC attorney, Leo Wang, had begun to suspect
Levine for circumstantial reasons. Wang had harbored doubts
about Levine's honesty ever since he questioned him about the
Textron deal in 1984. When Levine's name showed up on the list

of investment bankers invited by Shad to attend the November 1985 roundtable on takeovers, the staff's suspicions hardened.

Still, they had no proof. One problem was that before Pitt would authorize Bank Leu to disclose Levine's name to the commission, he wanted the Bahamian government to exempt the bank from its secrecy rules. Largely because of the earlier efforts led by Fedders and SEC attorney Michael Mann, international banks and their regulators in Switzerland and certain other neutralist countries had grown increasingly willing to disclose the names of customers if incontrovertible proof of fraud was presented to them. In this case, the testimony of Bank Leu executive Bruno Pletscher and other investigative work by the SEC had established beyond almost any doubt that, whoever Mr. X was, he had earned more than $12 million in profits by trading illegally on inside information about takeovers in the United States. Early in May, Lynch and Mann flew to the Bahamas to meet with the country's attorney general. Mann argued that the Bank Leu case was exempt from Bahamian secrecy law because Mr. X had used the bank almost exclusively to trade securities and had not engaged in traditional banking practices. The attorney general agreed and granted unqualified permission for Bank Leu to turn over the name of its customer to the SEC.

Ecstatic, Lynch and Mann returned hurriedly to Washington. There were signs early that month that Bank Leu's customer had begun to panic and that he might try to move the millions in his account to Panama. Pitt still hadn't revealed Levine's name to Lynch—he said he needed an official letter from the Bahamas authorizing the disclosure.

Around noontime on Friday, May 9, 1986, Levine telephoned Bank Leu from New York and said that he was transmitting written instructions for his funds to be transferred out of the bank. Bank Leu's officials immediately called Pitt in Washington—they had to comply with Levine's written request, and even if they didn't, Levine's lawyers could quickly force them to in a Bahamian court. Pitt said he was still waiting for permission to turn over Levine's name to the SEC—then Lynch could rush into federal court in the United States and obtain a freeze on Levine's account pending court review of the SEC's insider trading charges.

Later that day, a messenger finally delivered to Bank Leu's Nassau offices the letter from the Bahamian government granting permission to reveal Levine's name. Around 5:30 P.M. that Friday, Harvey Pitt, the bank's attorney, called Gary Lynch.

Moby Dick is Dennis Levine, a managing director at Drexel Burnham Lambert, Harvey Pitt said. You're going to have to move fast. Levine is trying to transfer his money out of Bank Leu. The bank isn't going to voluntarily release any of his money, but the question could end up in a Bahamian court on Monday.

Levine transmitted his written order that Bank Leu transfer $10 million of his money to a new account in the Cayman Islands. The order arrived late enough that Friday so that the bank could plausibly refuse to act, saying it would take up the matter on Monday. At SEC headquarters in Washington, a team of enforcement lawyers led by Lynch drafted the voluminous papers necessary to obtain a freeze on Levine's account in U.S. federal court Monday morning.

There was no time to call a full commission meeting to obtain approval. All of the commissioners had been aware of the Moby Dick investigation since the previous July, and it had become a subject of increasing interest that spring. On Sunday, Lynch called Commissioner Aulana Peters at home and left a message on her answering machine, asking that she please come into work early the next morning. The commissioners rotated in the position of "duty officer," empowered by SEC rules to act for the full commission in emergencies. Peters picked up the message Sunday night, and early the next morning, she signed the papers authorizing securities fraud charges against Levine and the request for a court freeze of Levine's Bank Leu accounts. SEC attorney John Sturc flew to New York to argue the case before U.S. District Judge Richard Owen, who was reputed to be sympathetic to government prosecutors who appeared in his courtroom. In any event, Owen granted all of the SEC's requests promptly.

Levine didn't know what had happened. The previous Friday, he had attended an exclusive screening of the film *Top Gun* at the Gulf & Western building, which towered over the southwest corner of Manhattan's Central Park. He spent the weekend with his pregnant wife, Laurie, and his son, Adam, in their expansive upper Park Avenue cooperative apartment—Levine had recently spent $450,000 to redecorate the place, using money withdrawn from his Bank Leu account. (Levine was able to pay for the extra touches that can distinguish one investment banker's apartment from another: He paid $175,00 to his general contractor; $86,000 to an interior designer; $40,000 to an architect; $40,000 for cabinet work; $5,000 for marble work; $8,000 for a piano, and about $95,000 for miscellaneous items. Levine also owned a $90,000 Ferrari Testarossa.) On Monday, Levine was supposed to meet with Ronald Perelman, the corporate raider turned Revlon cosmetics executive whose acquisitions were financed by Drexel's junk bonds. But Levine never showed up. He had heard through the grapevine that the commission and the U.S. attorney in Manhattan were after him and that they were attempting to arrest him. Levine surrendered to U.S. marshals downtown and hired attorney Arthur Liman to represent him. He spent a night in jail before he was able to post bail.

The story of the SEC's insider trading charges against Levine, splashed across the front pages of every metropolitan newspaper in the country, dwarfed the attention paid to any previous event at the commission under John Shad, eclipsing the flood of negative publicity that surrounded the resignation of John Fedders. Though Shad seemed uncomfortable with the implications of the case, Lynch and Sturc and Mann and the other enforcement lawyers basked justifiably in the attention, even as they moved to fight Levine in court. "Let's just say it is not the end of our insider trading program," Lynch said.

The SEC's allegation that Levine had made more than $12 million in illegal profits made this the biggest insider trading case in history. The commission had moved swiftly enough to freeze his millions before they were transferred out of the Bahamas. But Lynch and his staff still had to reel Moby Dick in. Initially, Levine's lawyers boldly asserted their client's innocence, holding impromptu press conferences on the courthouse steps and promising to vanquish the government when Levine was brought to trial.

Levine himself reveled in the attention—far from collapsing into morose depression from the public humiliation of his arrest and downfall, he seemed at times to be genuinely excited by his notoriety. And why not? For six years Levine had directed a sophisticated ring of conspirators, brokering inside information about mergers to and from half a dozen other young lawyers and investment bankers. There was Robert Wilkis at the prestigious Wall Street firm of Lazard Frères, who had told him about Textron and many other deals; Ilan Reich, a highly regarded young partner and protégé of takeover critic Marty Lipton at the Wachtell Lipton law firm; Ira Sokolow, a vice president and rising star in the mergers and acquisitions department at Shearson Lehman Brothers; David Brown, an associate at Goldman, Sachs & Company; and Randall Cecola, a student at the Harvard Business School who had worked briefly at Lazard. Levine assured several of the members of his ring that everything would work out fine. He was still in charge.

On May 20, shortly after his arrest, Levine met Wilkis, with whom he had traded money and inside information for several years, at a garage in the seedy Hell's Kitchen neighborhood of Manhattan, near the Hudson River in midtown.

As they drove off in Wilkis's car, Levine exclaimed gleefully, "This is the biggest insider trading scandal in history and it's all because of me."

18

The Fall

There was hardly room for them all in the cramped, cluttered offices of the Manhattan U.S. attorney's securities fraud unit, situated in a bulding erected on cement stilts behind the city's towering and majestic federal courthouse. They were going to be here for hour after hour and day after day, so they had to get used to it. The unadorned environs seemed to suit perfectly the demeanor of Charles Carberry, the assistant U.S. attorney in charge of federal criminal securities-fraud cases in New York. Carberry was pale, at least seventy pounds overweight, balding, and utterly unflappable. Raised in Queens and graduated from Manhattan's Fordham University law school, he had never lived anywhere but New York, and he spoke with the marbled accent of the streets. A career prosecutor and lifelong bachelor, it was said that apart from an interest in attending college basketball games, Carberry had no social life. He did, however, enjoy his work.

Dennis Levine sat near Carberry, his brashness tempered by the presence of so many lawyers and the circumstances of the meeting. It was June 2, less than three weeks after his arrest.

It hadn't taken long for Levine, whose principal loyalty had always been to himself, to calculate that his best interest lay in cutting a deal with the government. The cooperation between the SEC and the Manhattan U.S. attorney's office—the commission had alerted the criminal prosecutors about their Moby Dick in-

309

vestigation earlier that spring—had squeezed Levine convinc-
ingly. He knew that if he pleaded guilty to insider trading, a
prison term was inevitable, but at least the government would
urge leniency because of his testimony against others. If he chose
to fight the case and was convicted following trial, a federal judge
might throw the book at him, particularly given the public hysteria about the collapse of Wall Street ethics, which had ensued
upon Levine's arrest. So Levine had decided to cut a deal and
provide testimony against his coconspirators. And his lawyers had
hinted that besides the several young Wall Street professionals
with whom he had traded tips, Levine would provide evidence
against one major financier whose importance dwarfed them all.

Before Levine was smuggled into the U.S. attorney's office that
Monday morning by his lawyers, Carberry and several SEC lawyers invited up from Washington to attend the debriefing didn't
know for sure who the coconspirators were in Levine's insider
trading ring, or the name of the fish who was purportedly bigger
than Moby Dick. That Monday morning in Carberry's office,
Levine dropped his bombshell.

I've leaked inside information about takeovers to Ivan Boesky
since February of last year, Levine said. As part of our deal,
Boesky promised he would pay me as much as five percent of
whatever stock trading profits he made. Although he never paid
me anything, in April we agreed that he owed me $2.4 million.

What stocks? the government lawyers wanted to know.

Many of the big ones, Levine answered—Nabisco, Houston Natural Gas, FMC, Union Carbide, General Foods, and others.

This might be it—after so many years, after so many false starts,
Dennis Levine appeared to be delivering to the SEC and the criminal prosecutors a potentially major fraud case against one of the
most influential stock traders on Wall Street. Lynch thought there
were gaping holes in Levine's story that might make his allegations difficult to prove in court, especially Levine's statement that
Boesky had never paid him anything. Boesky could just deny any
illicit arrangement with Levine and say that Levine made the story
up in return for lenient treatment. Still, this was as close as the
SEC had ever come to nailing Boesky, and the government attor-

neys grilled Levine over and over about Boesky that morning, and in about ten other sessions in Carberry's office extending over about a week's time in early June. They questioned Levine in minute detail, even asking him at one point to describe the interior of Boesky's limousine. At another session, Levine was presented with some of his own doodlings and was asked to interpret them. The prosecutors wanted to take advantage, as much as possible, of Levine's cooperation before his decision to plead guilty and turn state's evidence became known.

That same Monday night, June 2, using a tape-recorded telephone in the Manhattan U.S. attorney's office that was rigged to sound like a pay phone, replete with the chink of coins and the recorded voice of an operator, Dennis Levine began to telephone his friends and associates. He drew Robert Wilkis into a long and incriminating talk about their schemes. He telephoned others in his ring—attorney Ilan Reich and investment banker Ira Sokolow.

Then he called Boesky.

I'm in deep trouble, Levine told Boesky. I'm going to jail. If I don't give you up, what will you do for me?

Is there anything I can do for your family? Boesky asked, refusing to take the bait.

Although Levine had set a trap for Boesky, the arbitrager carefully avoided saying anything that would acknowledge their arrangement about inside information or cause him other legal problems.

The evidence Levine had provided about Boesky was good— but it was far from perfect. Levine said he was prepared to testify under oath that he had a deal to swap inside information about takeovers with Boesky in exchange for a percentage of Boesky's profits. But the trouble remained that Levine's deal with Boesky had never been fully consummated; they had exchanged only stock tips and promises about future compensation. And while a preliminary review of trading records and other documents provided by Levine tended to corroborate his claims about a secret relationship with Boesky, there was no "smoking gun" among Levine's files, principally because no money had ever changed hands.

At Drexel, Chief Executive Officer Fred Joseph did his best to minimize the damage from Levine's fall by granting interviews to major news organizations and speaking to employees throughout the firm. The controversial firm that had spearheaded the wave of junk-bond-backed hostile takeover bids found itself at the center of the storm over insider trading and ethics on Wall Street as speculation about the identity of Levine's coconspirators mounted.

There is no problem at Drexel Burnham, Joseph said. Dennis Levine was just a bad apple who happened to be working at our firm when he got caught.

Joseph did not mention that in the days after Levine's arrest, Drexel had been forced to pull thousands of its annual reports just as they came off the presses, in order to expunge a prominent photograph of Levine swaggering in his suit as one of Drexel's leading merger advisers. Joseph acknowledged that in the overheated corporate takeover game on Wall Street, standards had loosened at all firms in recent years. And he explained, too, that "as a statistical matter," Drexel, which had two other employees in addition to Levine with legal problems, was more likely than other firms to have difficulties because it had been the Street's fastest growing major firm. The truth was that Drexel was attracting a disproportionate share of criminals to its ranks because of its aggressive reputation and willingness to pay higher salaries. Included among those Drexel had hired in recent months was Kidder, Peabody investment banker Martin A. Siegel, who became co-head of the firm's merger department. At the time of Dennis Levine's arrest, Ivan Boesky thus had secret information/profit sharing arrangements with three Drexel employees: Michael Milken, Marty Siegel, and Dennis Levine. Even though Levine and Siegel worked in the same bank of offices in Drexel's lower Manhattan headquarters, neither man appeared to know anything about the other's secret relationship with Boesky.

Late in June, following Levine's debriefing, Gary Lynch began to work with key members of his senior SEC enforcement staff in Washington, attempting to devise a plan that would flush Ivan Boesky out.

Lynch feared that the SEC's new investigation of Boesky would collapse into what trial lawyers call a "one-on-one," a case where everything would turn on whether the jury believed Dennis Levine's testimony or Ivan Boesky's. With some additional work, the statements Levine had made in Carberry's office would certainly be enough for the commission to pursue public charges against Boesky, but if Boesky decided to fight, the ensuing litigation would likely absorb a large portion of the commission's resources for years. Lynch hoped to avoid a trial. He wanted to pressure Boesky into a settlement—that was the SEC's usual tactic.

Ever since Levine's arrest, Boesky had been under enormous pressure. While he had been investigated by the SEC before, the agency had never had a cooperating witness like Levine who could hurt him. The stakes had been raised in other ways, too. Boesky found himself facing the frightening prospect of both SEC civil charges and Justice Department criminal charges, which meant he could face jail time and banishment from the securities business. In addition to worrying that government investigators might find out about his illegal promise to pay Levine for inside information, Boesky had done something a few months earlier that the speculator now feared could turn out to be an even bigger legal problem: He had sent Drexel a $5.3 million check to settle accounts under his wide-ranging, illegal stock-trading arrangement with Milken.

Even when he made the payment in March 1986, Boesky had done so reluctantly. It wasn't just his usual aversion to parting with money; it was the check. Boesky hated the idea of writing a check to reconcile the balance due Milken, because it created a paper trail. He had always paid investment banker Marty Siegel in cash for inside information and had repaid Milken and Drexel for illegal favors through a series of rigged stock and bond trades. That was the clean and neat way Boesky liked to do business— virtually undetectable. But when Milken insisted on being paid the $5.3 million in March 1986, he had considerable leverage to persuade Boesky to go along. Milken had raised a whopping $660 million that March for Boesky to invest in takeover stocks, despite initial objections from Drexel's supervisory underwriting committee. (After the Drexel underwriting committee objected to the transaction, Drexel Chief Executive Joseph approved it, following discussions he had with Milken.) Combined with funds Boesky was raising at the same time, the Milken-raised funds would give the arbitrager the magic $1 billion to play with that Milken had promised him years ago, making Boesky by far the biggest and most powerful independent takeover stock speculator on the Street. Even though Drexel had charged princely fees of more than $20 million for raising the funds for Boesky, Milken refused to release any of the monies until Boesky paid him the $5.3 million and entered into certain compensating trades to settle accounts under their illegal agreement.

Boesky's fears about making the $5.3 million payment had been confirmed late in March when his outside accountants, who had descended on his firm to handle the final details of the $1 billion financing, started asking questions. The outside auditors' interest in the $5.3 million payment had been triggered by joking comments made by an in-house Boesky accountant who taunted them for scrutinizing small trading details while he struggled with how to account for the multimillion-dollar payment to Drexel. Was there an invoice from Drexel for the $5.3 million? they asked. What had Drexel done to earn that fee? Why had the accountants not been informed about the payment earlier?

After a flurry of phone calls between New York and Beverly Hills, the matter was resolved, at least temporarily. An aide to Milken sent Boesky an invoice dated March 21, 1986, which said Boesky owed Drexel $5.3 million, "FOR CONSULTING SERVICES AS AGREED UPON ON MARCH 21, 1986." With the invoice in hand, the accountants were satisfied, a check from Boesky to Drexel was cut, and Milken released the funds he had raised, giving Boesky the power to move markets with his new $1 billion war chest.

About two months after Levine's arrest, Boesky, still worried about the paper trail created by the $5.3 million check and invoice, traveled to California, where he discussed a range of issues with Milken beside the Drexel financier's San Fernando Valley swimming pool.

Milken cautioned that they needed to be more careful because of "the new environment." Among the items they discussed that day was a possible cover-up of the $5.3 million payment. The climate, Milken said, had changed. By that, Boesky thought Milken was referring to the increased risk of detection they faced following Levine's arrest and the general hysteria on Wall Street about where the SEC's insider trading probe was headed. Due to the new threat posed by the SEC–Justice Department law-enforcement efforts, they agreed to be more cautious and to limit their dealings. After he returned to New York, Boesky ordered his chief accountant, who had dutifully kept a tally of who owed how much under the Milken-Boesky arrangement, to destroy all documents describing it.

When Boesky and Milken met by the swimming pool, Levine's decision to plead guilty and cooperate with the government was publicly known. The disclosure had set off wild and nearly con-tinuous speculation on Wall Street about who would fall next, and already, Levine's younger accomplices in his insider trading ring—Wilkis, Reich, Sokolow—were dropping like birds from the sky. It seemed to Lynch and his enforcement division colleagues that the best way to approach the biggest fish, Boesky, was to convince him as quickly and dramatically as possible that Levine had told the government everything about their illegal dealings and that there was no use in fighting.

By striking at Boesky with force and precision, perhaps they could topple him quickly, Lynch thought.

The enforcement chief and his staff carefully drafted a series of subpoenas based largely on the information provided by Levine. Many of the subpoenas were addressed to different Boesky organizations—there were a number of units under the Boesky umbrella—and they asked for information about stocks and dates and names of people and other specific information calculated to convince Boesky that the evidence against him was overwhelming. One subpoena was delivered to Northview Corporation, the motel company in California through which Boesky conducted some of his stock trading; another went to IFB Managing Partners in New York; another was delivered to Seemala Corporation, the Boesky-controlled brokerage named after his wife, Seema. Although Lynch was hopeful that the barrage of subpoenas would unnerve

Boesky when they were served in early August, he thought the most likely outcome was months of arguments with Boesky's lawyers over the wide-ranging requests for information that the SEC had made.

Having completed successfully his legal representation of Bank Leu, which got the Swiss bank off the hook and led to the SEC's case against Levine, attorney Harvey Pitt had become involved once again, this time defending Boesky. Pitt's law firm, Fried, Frank, had long handled Boesky's legal work from its New York offices and Pitt had done some work for Boesky from time to time. When Boesky called to tell him about the SEC subpoenas and to ask him to represent him, Pitt explained, as he explained to all of his clients, that he would take the case under one condition: that Boesky tell him everything he had done wrong. Anything Boesky told him would, of course, be confidential, protected by the attorney-client privilege. And the ultimate answer to the most important question—whether to fight or settle with the SEC— would be up to Boesky. But first, Pitt wanted to know the truth. Boesky agreed to go along with Pitt's condition, and they held a series of confidential meetings in hotel rooms and other places in the ensuing days. Boesky shocked Pitt and his small team of defense lawyers from Fried, Frank and Wilmer, Cutler & Pickering by telling them about his insider trading arrangement with Levine and his illegal dealings with Milken and Drexel.

From the start, Pitt could tell that the SEC was playing hardball with Boesky. Normally, after subpoenas were issued to one of his clients, Pitt called SEC enforcement lawyers and asked to see the commission-approved "formal order of investigation" authorizing the probe. In it was valuable information not contained in the subpoenas that gave a sense of an investigation's scope and focus. In the past, the SEC had made a copy of the formal order available. But this time, SEC lawyers told Pitt they would not give him a copy. After some discussion, the commission staff agreed to let Pitt see the formal order at SEC headquarters, provided he did not make a copy of the document. Pitt responded to the offer by going over to SEC headquarters with two sharp-minded staff members from his law firm. Each of them memorized a portion of the formal order and then wrote it down as soon as they stepped out of the room where SEC officials allowed them to examine it.

Following his questioning of Boesky and many hours of tactical deliberations over how Boesky should respond to the commission, Pitt called Lynch, who was on vacation in Maine, to try to set up a meeting. Lynch's sister answered the telephone, and Pitt left a message. When he got the message, Lynch was certain that Pitt was calling to argue about the extensive information requests contained in the Boesky subpoenas, so when he returned the call, Lynch decided to get tough with Pitt for calling him on vacation about routine legal maneuverings.

"Hi, Harvey," Lynch said. "I hope you didn't call me here in Maine to negotiate a subpoena."

Pitt laughed.

"Gary, I want to come in and talk to you about this case," Pitt said, without naming Boesky. "I think we ought to get together."

"Harvey," Lynch replied, "I'm on vacation. If you're calling me back from vacation to argue about subpoenas, I'll be pissed."

"We ought to get together," Pitt said. "This is an important client, and I think it will be worth your while."

He had been skeptical, but Lynch trusted Pitt's judgment. Eight months earlier, at the "Moby Dick" meeting at commission headquarters, Pitt had taken the initial steps that led Lynch and his staff to the insider trading case against Levine. Although he enjoyed the time away with his family, Lynch knew, too, that timing was important. He decided to take Pitt up on his offer immediately.

Let's meet at the commission's Boston Regional Office, Lynch said.

I'll see you there, Pitt replied.

Around a government-issue conference table they met once again, the defense lawyers led by Pitt and the SEC attorneys headed by Lynch. To maintain confidentiality and explain why such a meeting of high-powered lawyers was taking place in the dog days of August, Lynch made up a plausible-sounding, but false, story for the agency's Boston regional administrator. Shad, too, knew nothing of the meeting's true nature, since Lynch felt it was within the normal course of enforcement division activities to hold preliminary discussions with defense counsel and to relay information to the chairman and the other commissioners when there was something more tangible to discuss.

As he always seemed to, for key meetings with SEC attorneys, Pitt showed up with carefully scripted notes, which he read from as he spoke.

"My client sees this as a matter that could go on forever, eat up his business, and be very distracting," Pitt said. "In this era of Levine and all the publicity, he thinks it is in his interest to get this behind him. He has authorized us to explore a possible settlement."

Lynch did his best to look stone-faced, as if to say, "So what else is new?" He had been expecting a fight over the details of subpoenas; instead, he suddenly heard Pitt talking about negotiating a settlement of the SEC's insider-trading case against Boesky. And that wasn't all.

"We could give you insight into practices on Wall Street that you're not aware of," Pitt said, offering an enticing carrot.

"This sounds like the outline of something we can talk about," Lynch replied.

There is enough there, Pitt added, that Boesky's cooperation could help to cleanse the securities world to such a degree that he should not have to plead guilty to any criminal charges. Boesky can't face jail, nor should he have to, Pitt said.

"The one thing I can't speak for is the U.S. Attorney's office," Lynch said, "but there is no way in the world there could be a deal without some kind of criminal plea. It is not my deal to cut, but I think you've gotta get real and that is not real."

Pitt knew that while it was important early in this minuet with government lawyers to be titillating, it also was important to "undersell," so he did not mention Milken's name as he hinted at the fruits of Boesky's potential cooperation. He did, however, reiterate that in return for becoming a government informant and settling the SEC case, Boesky wanted complete immunity from criminal charges, although he recognized there would be civil SEC charges and fines.

Both sides agreed on the need to maintain strict confidentiality; that would give them the best chance to reach an agreement and maximize the potential value of Boesky's cooperation. Although Pitt mentioned no names, he discussed with Lynch the nature of violations Boesky could help SEC investigators uncover.

"I need to think about it," Lynch finally said, dismissing those assembled. "We'll get back to you."

After Pitt and the other defense attorneys left the SEC's Boston office that day, Lynch broke into his widest grin since he had taken over the enforcement director's job from Fedders the prior year. Sure, there was work to be done and a settlement with Boesky was by no means certain. But it was clear that the stream of SEC subpoenas had shaken Boesky and that both sides wanted to enter into a major deal. In Lynch's experience, an investigation target in such a state of mind usually went ahead and agreed to a settlement after negotiations over the details. John Sturc and the other SEC attorneys gathered there with Lynch broke into a spontaneous celebration, with at least one person recalling that someone actually climbed onto the conference room table as they whooped it up. For the even-keeled Lynch, it was a great moment of rare elation.

By the third week in September, a secret deal involving Boesky, the SEC, and the Justice Department was close, including the understanding that Boesky would work as an undercover government informant, pretending to run his arbitrage firm and conduct business as usual while secretly telling the government all that he knew and wearing a device that tape-recorded conversations with his Wall Street compatriots.

Since the meeting in Boston, it had been an intense but productive several weeks. There were all-night negotiating sessions in Pitt's Washington office, after which a bleary-eyed Lynch stumbled into SEC headquarters, taking care not to miss work or give clues that anything unusual was taking place. Immediately after the Boston meeting, Lynch had called Carberry in the Manhattan U.S. Attorney's office to alert him to the talks and the possibility of settlement. Carberry had been adamant from the start that no matter how valuable Boesky's cooperation, he had to plead guilty to criminal charges. On the other side, Pitt had been firm about his client's desire to receive criminal immunity in return for his cooperation.

From the first time he heard Boesky tell of his fraud-riddled relationship with Milken and of the $5.3 million payment that Milken had demanded of him the prior March, Pitt thought Boesky should cooperate with the SEC while he still had something—Milken—left to trade. Pitt feared that if Boesky delayed, Milken might beat Boesky through Lynch's door, leaving the arbitrager facing a devastating array of witnesses. In that scenario, Boesky would become a professional defendant for the rest of his life, receive a gargantuan prison sentence if convicted, and probably see his business and his life destroyed. The ante had been raised for another reason, too, making this inquiry different from past SEC investigations of Boesky: The likelihood of criminal charges that carried a possible jail term seemed high. By settling the charges, it seemed, Boesky would be able to sell off his stock portfolio in an orderly fashion, receive leniency from a judge at sentencing for his cooperation, and then eventually try to put the matter behind him, after enduring years of pain and public humiliation brought on by his guilty plea, prison term, and his decision to snitch.

The scale of the settlement negotiations was unprecedented for Shad and the other SEC commissioners, but it was an especially high-risk strategy for a government employee like Lynch. If he cut a deal with Boesky, no matter what the deal, he was open to criticism that the SEC's director of enforcement was too soft. If he instead filed massive charges against Boesky, there was a risk the SEC would lose in court. But in that event, Lynch personally would not be subject to the same second-guessing. Despite the risk, Lynch preferred the certainty of a settlement. He thought that a settlement would eliminate years of litigation with Boesky and accelerate any possible SEC clean-up of Wall Street corruption—on Lynch's watch, and to Lynch's potential credit. Provided the commission received certain fundamental assurances from Boesky, Lynch preferred not to negotiate for months over all of the small details. It was more important to reach a settlement quickly so that Boesky could start taping a new set of targets, especially Milken.

To preserve secrecy as Lynch briefed the SEC commissioners during the negotiations, Shad and his colleagues met only in what were dubbed "super-executive sessions," meaning that only the commissioners themselves, none of their personal staff, and none of the SEC staff that normally was invited to closed meetings could attend. Normally, the commissioners kept the briefing papers prepared by the division of enforcement. But after these meetings, Lynch and a small band of trusted colleagues collected the briefing papers to diminish the risk of a leak. There were a hundred questions about the Boesky case. How much money would Boesky pay to the commission in disgorged illegal profits and fines? Would the commission allow him to sell off the millions of dollars in stock he owned? Would the SEC attempt to seize assets owned by Boesky's wife and children that may have been derived through his illegal activities? Who else would Boesky implicate? What about the link between SEC charges and his criminal plea bargain? Who had benefited from his massive insider trading over the years?

When he talked about the case and the negotiations with his fellow commissioners and with the few of Lynch's senior staff who were informed about what was at stake, Shad vacillated between shock and outrage. More than anything, he couldn't believe that Boesky would go through with the deal he was about to sign. Shad was afraid that Boesky would flee the country—given the scale of Boesky's fortune, it would be easy enough to arrange. And after all, Marc Rich, the indicted commodities trader who had occupied Boesky's suite of offices on Fifth Avenue in New York before fleeing to Switzerland, had managed to resurrect his career as a respected businessman and philanthropist who lived comfortably and seemingly happily near Zurich. With personal assets reportedly in excess of $100 million, wouldn't Boesky be tempted to do the same? Until Boesky actually turned over any money to the SEC, Shad was skeptical that the arbitrager would really do it. Given his interest in personal ethics, it was hard to imagine Shad trading on inside information or fleeing from the law if he were caught. But perhaps his fears about Boesky were based in part on a calculation about what he thought he would do if he were in Boesky's shoes.

Boesky, though, had been living such a grotesquely distorted life for so long—writing books and making speeches about the legitimacy of his success while systematically bribing Wall Street merger specialists for inside information—that it was hard for Shad and Lynch to know how he felt about the prospect of confession and maybe, in some way, it was a relief for him to disgorge his secrets and to feel that he could finally tell the truth about Wall Street and himself. In any event, there were no concrete signs that early autumn that Boesky, who only months before had appeared at an SEC roundtable and advised Shad, was preparing to flee the country. And he seemed to be following Pitt's advice that a settlement was in his best interest.

There was a way in which Boesky's exposure and the related cases shook the foundations of Shad's tenure at the SEC—his reliance on Chicago School theory; the push for liquidity and efficiency, liquidity and efficiency—even as it provided Shad with an enormous professional triumph. Shad found himself in a reflective mood that September as negotiations concluded with Boesky that would alter permanently and profoundly the public reputation of the SEC and its chairman. "In Washington, perceptions are too often given greater weight than reality," Shad wrote to a cousin in Utah that month. "New laws and regulations are frequently proposed in response to perceptions. It is not popular to attempt to disabuse misperceptions. It is easier to go with the flow—to address problems with flowery rhetoric, rather than facts. But then, I believe it was Mr. Churchill who said democracy is a very inefficient method of government, it is just the best man has devised. . . . It seems that life is dictated by emergency meetings— but I enjoy it."

The biggest question at the SEC that fall was how much Boesky would have to pay. After extensive negotiations back and forth involving Boesky's lawyers, Lynch and Carberry, the straight-talking Carberry finally blurted out, "Cut the crap. The number is one hundred million dollars." Soon thereafter, Boesky agreed to pay the agency the record $100 million, a figure the SEC commissioners approved following Lynch's recommendation. Although it was later explained by Shad, Lynch, and other SEC officials that Boesky made $50 million trading on the illegal insider tips from Levine and that the $100 million figure represented a return of that $50 million plus a one-time $50 million penalty, lawyers involved in the negotiations agreed that the $100 million figure was reached primarily for another reason: It was a nice round number that people would talk about for years to come and that would send a message to Wall Street and around the world that Shad's SEC had come down on insider trading with hobnail boots. So great was the figure in SEC terms that it approximated the agency's entire operating budget for 1986. Although Lynch did not require a detailed financial statement or endeavor to make any independent assessment of Boesky's assets, Pitt assured him that the $100 million payment would virtually wipe out Boesky's personal wealth. The SEC charges would relate only to tips Boesky received from Levine, but it would absolve him of liability for any other wrongdoing. As part of the settlement, the SEC also agreed to let Boesky sell off his huge holdings of takeover stocks before the public announcement of charges against him and agreed not to prosecute those investors who had made investments in Boesky's arbitrage fund. On the criminal side, Pitt and Carberry eventually reached a compromise. Boesky agreed to plead guilty to a single charge of filing false documents with the SEC, carrying a maximum five years in prison, in connection with the rigged 1984 takeover of Fischbach Corporation, a transaction that Boesky had helped Milken orchestrate.

At forty-nine, Boesky had effectively agreed to start a new career as a professional government witness. He secretly began taping conversations with investment bankers, traders, and the others whom he did business with on Wall Street. The better the tapes, the smaller the chance Boesky would have to testify publicly at trials of those he implicated, where the speculator would have to endure cross-examination from hostile defense lawyers. Wearing a wire that October, Boesky traveled to Beverly Hills, where he met with Milken in a room at the Beverly Hills Hotel. With rumors about Boesky's cooperation circulating on Wall Street,

Milken had been warned to stay away. But he went to meet Boesky anyway, cognizant of the need to be careful in what he said and did. Boesky hoped to tape the financier discussing the illegal $5.3 million payment and other, still unresolved financial aspects of their illegal arrangement. But Milken was circumspect, saying to a colleague before he met with Boesky that he would assume he was "speaking for the record." Milken seemed intent during the meeting on providing Boesky with a false explanation for the $5.3 million payment. The pair also assured one another that their employees would be reliable if confronted by government investigators. Shortly thereafter at the SEC, Shad and the other commissioners privately approved formal orders of investigation focusing on securities law violations committed by Milken, Siegel, and others whom Boesky had fingered.

As the day when Boesky's cooperation and settlement would be publicly announced neared, the spotlight turned on John Shad. It was his turn now to be a major player in Washington and in the national media. But the truth was that Shad had mixed feelings about the Boesky bombshell because of the shame it would bring on the industry where he had labored for so long.

The day before the SEC's case against Boesky was disclosed publicly, Shad called Federal Reserve Board Chairman Paul Volcker to clue him in.

The announcement about Boesky and the $100 million fine is going to be made after the stock market closes for trading on Friday afternoon, Shad said, but I wanted you to know about it in advance in case there are any problems with the banks.

The next morning—November 14, 1986, the day of the announcement—Shad called Congressman John Dingell and Senator Jake Garn, chairmen of the congressional committees that oversee the SEC. At 2:45 P.M., just hours before going public, Shad called Treasury Secretary James A. Baker III to inform him. He also called the White House chief of staff, Donald Regan.

Boesky was a major contributor to the Republican party, but the news of his demise was a "complete shock" to the White House.

On that Friday in November when the SEC prepared to tell the world that Ivan Boesky was a crook, rumors about the impending announcement had been circulating for much of the day through the enforcement division. It was about 3:00 P.M. when Gary Lynch finally called his staff together in an open hallway area outside his corner office. John Sturc stood beside him, along with the other attorneys who had worked on the case.

This is a very proud day for the SEC, Lynch told them. At 4:30 or 5:00 P.M., the commission is going to announce at a press conference downstairs that Ivan Boesky has agreed to pay $100 million in fines and disgorgement for insider trading.

Cacophonous cheers and applause erupted.

I want to apologize for the unusual secretiveness that has characterized this investigation, he went on. I will try in the weeks ahead to make an effort to get more people involved in the work that is yet to come.

At virtually the same moment, Ivan Boesky stood at the head of a marble conference table on the thirty-fourth floor of 650 Fifth Avenue in Manhattan and embraced his employees, one by one.

Moments before, drawn and somber, he had entered the crowded room to read a statement prepared by his lawyers. After apologizing and telling the dozens of gathered executives and support staff that what he was about to say was difficult, Boesky announced that he had settled insider trading charges by paying the government an unprecedented $100 million. He said that his firm ultimately would be closed, but that it would stay in business for the foreseeable future.

The government has given me eighteen months, or until early 1988, to sell off my stock portfolio, Boesky told them. I would like to have everyone's support.

I hope you will remember the whole Ivan Boesky, not just the bad part, he said.

There were questions and answers. At one point, Boesky was asked if he would be allowed to buy stock—purchasing stock while selling off his holdings would help Boesky disguise the unloading of his $1.2 billion portfolio.

"Well, we can still buy, but we won't be doing any hostile take-over deals," Boesky said.

Boesky also issued a public statement.

"The announcement this afternoon by the Securities and Exchange Commission and the U.S. Attorney justifiably holds me and not my business associates or business entities responsible for my actions," Boesky said. "I deeply regret my past mistakes, and know that I alone must bear the consequences of those actions. . . . My life will be forever changed, but I hope that something positive will ultimately come out of this situation. I know that in the wake of today's events, many will call for reform. If my mistakes launch a process of reexamination of the rules and practices of our financial marketplace, then perhaps some good will result."

Later that afternoon, when his employees had hugged him and dispersed, Boesky made telephone calls to investors in his arbitrage partnership and directors of the public companies he controlled. He told some of them that while his deal with the government would strip him of the right to ever again own a stock brokerage firm, he hoped that he would be able to work with them again some day, perhaps as an investor.

Some of those who heard him say such things thought that perhaps Ivan Boesky was being unrealistic.

Jim Dahl, the top salesman in Michael Milken's Beverly Hills junk bond department, was in Las Vegas that Friday, attending a friend's bachelor's party. His wife telephoned him in tears—she had heard the news about Boesky while at a health club with several other wives of Drexel traders, and she was afraid now that Milken and his employees were in trouble. Rumors about Levine and Drexel had been passing among the Drexel salesmen and traders for weeks, contributing at times to an atmosphere of paranoia.

Dahl told his wife not to worry. Nothing was going to happen.

He spoke with Milken, who told him to get back to Los Angeles immediately.

"The force in this country buying high-yield securities (junk bonds) has overpowered all regulation," the seemingly invincible Milken had declared in a speech just before Dennis Levine's arrest. But on Sunday morning, November 16, two days after Boesky's fall and the delivery of government subpoenas to Drexel and Milken, Dahl received a phone call from Milken who said he would like Dahl to come into the office to review some matters. Dahl wandered onto the junk bond trading floor and saw Milken, surrounded by boxes of documents and working with an assistant, sorting intently through his papers. Dahl, according to statements he later made to government lawyers, sat quietly for about two hours, waiting for Milken to finish. Finally, he grew a little impatient. If he wasn't needed, Dahl wanted to go home—it was a Sunday, after all.

"Mike, if there is something you want to talk to me about, let's do it, because I am out of here soon," Dahl said.

Milken said he wanted to talk. He motioned for Dahl to follow him. They circled off the junk bond trading floor and into the men's room. Milken checked the stalls to be sure that no one was inside. Then he walked over to the sink and turned on the faucet so that a crescendo of running water filled the room. If the room were bugged, the tape recording would have been engulfed by the sound of water.

Milken leaned down next to one of the sinks, motioning as if to wash his hands. Dahl leaned down to hear him.

"There haven't been any subpoenas issued and whatever you need to do, do it," Milken said.

19

A Generation of Giants

During the chaotic weeks of late November, the five SEC commissioners and their senior staff from the enforcement division gathered virtually every day in the sixth-floor meeting room to discuss the implications of Ivan Boesky's fall. There was an atmosphere of crisis. Moods shifted and passed like storm clouds racing across the horizon. At times, there was a feeling of feverish excitement as Shad, Charles Cox, Aulana Peters, Gary Lynch, and the others moved in and out of hastily called, highly secretive "super-executive sessions." Disclosure of Boesky's crimes and his decision to turn state's evidence had spawned a frenzy of rumor, speculation, and public outrage. Journalists from around the world deluged the SEC daily with telephone calls seeking information about Boesky's fraud and his settlement with the commission. Stock prices on Wall Street initially plummeted amid widespread fear that Boesky's exposure and his testimony against others would quash the takeover game once and for all. There was a sense, within the SEC and without, that the financial world had been turned upside down.

It might have been a period of unqualified celebration and triumph inside John Shad's commission. For nearly five years, John Dingell and his Democratic allies in Congress had attacked and ridiculed Shad's public commitment to the Reagan austerity program, saying that with Wall Street growing rapidly he could

329

not possibly achieve the SEC's mandate to protect investors without expanding the agency. The enforcement program crafted by Shad and Fedders, with its emphasis on insider trading, had been criticized as soft, ineffectual, and incomplete. Stanley Sporkin had repeatedly and publicly questioned his former agency, implying that the commission had gone downhill since his departure. And now, finally, with the stunning and unprecedented capture of Boesky, Shad's SEC had seemingly been vindicated. Already Boesky's $100 million settlement was being hailed as the most significant Wall Street corruption case since the 1920s.

Yet so often on those November afternoons when they took their chairs around the oval meeting table on the sixth floor, Shad and Gary Lynch wore expressions of exasperation, perplexity, and frustration. They could not understand why the Boesky case had turned against them. They could not understand how so much could have gone wrong so quickly. To Lynch, the triumphant Boston meeting about Boesky a few months earlier seemed a distant memory, replaced by a Kafkaesque nightmare. With the Boesky case in hand before it was announced, Lynch thought he might deliver Wall Street from an era of corruption to an era of cleansing. Now that the news about Boesky was out, he found that people were viewing him and his team of lawyers in the SEC's enforcement division as if they were criminals themselves.

The trouble had begun within hours of the SEC's Boesky press conference on Friday, November 14, presided over by Shad at the commission's Washington headquarters. As traders, money managers, and arbitragers prepared for Monday's reopening of the shocked stock market, three rumors—all of which turned out to be true—made the rounds on Wall Street. The first was that Boesky had been working as a government informant for months, wearing a wire to secretly tape record incriminating conversations with his coconspirators and other financiers. The second was that Boesky had provided damaging testimony and evidence to the government about Michael Milken and Drexel Burnham, which was in the midst that fall of financing several large takeover bids with junk bonds. And the third—the one that seemed the most incredible, almost impossible to fathom or accept—was that

Boesky, in order to preserve the fortune he had accumulated, had been able, with the SEC's apparent acquiescence, to secretly sell off hundreds of millions of dollars of stocks prior to the public announcement of his fraud and guilty plea.

So deep and pervasive was the bitterness about Boesky that it was hard in those first days to sort out exactly why everyone on Wall Street was so furious about him. There were some who seemed angry because Boesky—by allowing himself to be exposed, not merely as a crook, but as an outrageous liar who had advised Shad on takeover issues and had even written a book promoting his alleged genius—had generated an immediate public backlash that threatened to ruin the profitable pastime of takeover speculation for everyone else. There were many others who said they were mad because Boesky, once confronted with Levine's allegations, had chosen to rat on his friends rather than continue to lie and fight the government at a trial.

Scores of senior officials on Wall Street rushed to explain to reporters and to one another that Boesky was an aberration, that he was a crazed and maniacal outsider who in no way represented the trend of American finance. In these defensive and insistent voices it was possible to detect the tenuous denial of an overwhelming fear: that there were other Boeskys soon to be exposed.

During that first week, the fury on Wall Street about Boesky's confessed crimes became mixed and blended with anger and outrage directed at John Shad's SEC. It began with the arbitragers, generally a volatile lot by temperament and occupation. Dozens of arbs lost millions of dollars in the stock market as prices of takeover stocks fell in reaction to the SEC's announcement about Boesky. When the newspapers confirmed that Boesky was already out of the market himself, that he had been allowed to sell off shares before the disclosure of his own demise, the arbs reacted with unbridled rage. How could the SEC have allowed Boesky to trade on advance knowledge of his own plea bargain with the government? It appeared that he had been allowed to engage in one last series of insider trades, profiting on inside information about his impending fall and his work as a stool pigeon. It wasn't immediately clear whether Boesky had pulled a fast one on the regulators or executed the trades with the commission's explicit permission. But to the angry mob on Wall Street, it didn't really matter—John Shad and the SEC were responsible.

Inside the commission's locked sixth floor meeting room late that November, Shad, Lynch, and the others didn't so much debate whether their critics on Wall Street were right as console one another with rationalizations about their decision.

What Boesky did by selling his shares was not illegal, Shad declared at the table during one meeting. The criticism we are getting is unfair. The media coverage has been outrageous. The press just doesn't understand why we did what we did.

Lynch agreed. We can't tell the whole story yet without blowing our continuing investigations, the enforcement chief argued.

If Boesky had been forced to sell immediately after the announcement, he might have had to dump $1 billion of stock, causing a financial panic. How would the SEC have looked then? Shad wondered.

But inside the meeting room, Shad was preaching to the converted. They convinced themselves that they were right and that they had no choice but to keep quiet and conduct their work in total secrecy. The newspapers were full of stories attacking the commission for allowing Boesky to profit while others suffered financially. Still, in those crucial days when public opinion was formed on Wall Street and in Congress, Shad and the SEC remained silent.

It was characteristic of Shad, who had lurched from one public relations snafu to another since arriving in Washington, that he did not anticipate the political and public reaction to the Boesky settlement. Yet the truth was that no one else at the SEC had thought in advance, either, about the implications of Boesky being permitted to sell off stock before public disclosure of his plea bargain. In the midst of harried meetings and negotiations with Boesky's lawyers and the federal prosecutors in New York earlier that fall, the commissioners and enforcement staff had been concerned about other issues. Shad feared that Boesky would flee the country. Lynch worried about preserving secrecy so that Boesky's undercover work wouldn't be blown. All of them were distracted by the myriad technical and investigative issues raised by Boesky's deal—how his money would be turned over to the government; what arrangements would be made to supervise Boesky's existing business affairs; how the enforcement staff would pursue the influential financiers against whom Boesky had provided evidence, including Milken and Drexel merger-specialist Marty Siegel. During all of that time, during so many meetings at SEC headquarters and in New York, no one in power had argued against allowing Boesky to sell off his stock before the November announcement.

Not only had Shad, Lynch, and the others not doubted their decision to allow Boesky to sell, they hadn't even talked about whether it would be smart to disclose the sales publicly along with the terms of Boesky's plea bargain. In that respect, they were victims of their own obsession with secrecy. The belief that the SEC should conduct nearly all of its important business in private had become deeply entrenched among the commissioners and senior staff. This was true despite the fact that a foundation of SEC regulatory policy had for years been that public corporations should disclose the facts about their business, even if disclosure of the facts might be damaging. Had the commission disclosed up front, at the November 14 press conference, that Boesky had been permitted to sell off shares in advance in order to prevent a potential financial panic, questions about the SEC's judgment no doubt would have been raised, but the commission would have controlled the debate and been on the offensive from the start. Instead, after doing a superb job keeping the Boesky case secret, Shad and the others had put their backs to the wall.

On the sixth floor, questions about how much secrecy was really necessary to preserve the fruits of Boesky's confessions provoked bickering between Shad and his colleagues. Before the Boesky announcement, the commissioners had met with Lynch and a handful of top enforcement officials in "super-executive sessions," meetings that were off-limits even to the commissioners' own legal advisers. In the days after Boesky's crimes were announced and his undercover work was reported in the newspapers, Shad and Lynch told their colleagues that they were still inclined to exclude high-level staff, other than those with an absolute "need to know," from closed meetings. But Commissioner Aulana Peters argued with Shad, and after a sometimes awkward debate, the exiled staff lawyers were allowed back into the meeting room. Amid the internal disagreement over which SEC officials should be permitted to critique and debate the issues surrounding the Boesky settlement, the commissioners never considered opening the substance of their discussions to the outside world. Thus the decision to allow Boesky to sell had leaked to the public through rumor, speculation, and aggressive newspaper reporting. When Shad's spokeswoman in Washington finally issued an official statement on Friday, November 21 (one long week after the Boesky case was announced) in an attempt to revive the commission's public image, it sounded flat and defensive.

"Prior to the announcement, the commission and staff were concerned about a large number of important considerations including the fact that substantial margin debt [owed by Boesky] could force precipitous and uncontrollable liquidations of securities that would have had a very serious adverse affect on the market. The orderly reduction of these loans has avoided such consequences. . . . Throughout this matter, the commission has and will continue to exercise its best judgment to serve the public interest with minimum adverse impact on the market. The commission cannot comment further at this time because of the necessity to preserve the confidentiality of its continuing investigations."*

* The SEC's statement said additionally that Boesky's stock sales had not included "any of his personal holdings." In making this assertion, Shad and the commission attempted to respond to public criticism that the SEC had left Boesky a wealthy man after the $100 million settlement. The SEC settlement was based only on the estimated $50 million in illegal trading profits Boesky earned on tips from Dennis Levine plus a $50 million penalty under the Insider Trading Sanctions Act. Boesky earned more than $30 million in additional illegal trading profits based on tips from merger specialist Marty Siegel and pocketed additional money from other illegal schemes. There were those who believed the SEC left Boesky and his wife and children—to whom he had already passed certain of his assets—with considerable wealth from illegal trading.

Questions also were raised about whether the $100 million settlement was really worth $100 million. The assets transferred to the SEC by Boesky actually consisted of $50 million in cash and an estimated $50 million in stock. A problem

The SEC statement came too late to alter public perceptions. Two days later, on Sunday morning, Shad rode to the studios of ABC News just off Connecticut Avenue to appear on the television talk show "This Week with David Brinkley" and explain the commission's handling of the Boesky case publicly. Soon after the lights on the set went up, the vociferous correspondent Sam Donaldson began to arch his knifelike eyebrows and needle Shad about the stock sales.

"What is more insider than the knowledge that Boesky's about to take a fall?" Donaldson demanded loudly. "Why didn't you make that available to everyone who has stock in the market who could buy or sell based on the same information?"

"Because it would have blown the case, the ongoing investigations, and would have had a drastic effect on the market, that's why," Shad responded.

"So millions may have to lose profits, or lose in their stock, in order to preserve this case," Donaldson said. "Was it worth it?"

The answer clearly depended on what Ivan Boesky had delivered to the government in exchange for his plea bargain. In their tightly guarded executive sessions that fall, Lynch and the commissioners had mapped out a kind of investigative blitzkrieg designed to topple the financiers implicated by the government's new star witness. At the same time that Boesky's settlement was announced, SEC investigators in New York and Los Angeles fanned out to deliver dozens of subpoenas seeking trading records, accounting records, office diaries, and other documents concerning some of the best-known corporate takeovers of the 1980s. The biggest batches of subpoenas landed at the Beverly Hills office of Drexel Burnham Lambert and at the firm's headquarters at 60 Broad Street in lower Manhattan. (The subpoenas

---

arose later when the SEC found it could not obtain $50 million if it sold the stock. Nonetheless, Shad and others at the commission continued to insist the deal was worth $100 million. Enforcement chief Gary Lynch said the $100 million represented what the cash and shares were worth to Boesky when he gave them up, rather than what they were later worth to the SEC, and his view prevailed upon the media and the public consciousness. In some ways, it was a rare public relations victory for the SEC.

were delivered just at the time of the SEC's Boesky announcement so that anyone at Drexel who responded by destroying documents could be prosecuted for obstruction of justice. The delivery took place two days before Milken told Jim Dahl in the men's room that no subpoenas had arrived.) The subpoenas contained the names of two of the country's most celebrated financiers: Martin Siegel, the handsome young merger specialist, and Michael Milken, maestro of the junk bond economy. When some of the names on the subpoenas were reported in the newspapers, an angry and nervous consensus emerged on Wall Street: to justify its extraordinary deal with Ivan Boesky, the federal government would do everything within its power to bring down Milken and end his grip on the $100 billion junk bond market.

Though Shad's commission had angered and frightened Wall Street, it had failed to impress Congress. This, too, an increasingly shaken Shad could not fully comprehend. On December 11, about a month after the Boesky announcement, he was summoned over to Dingell's hearing room to testify about the implications of Wall Street's scandal. After all of the partisan abuse he had suffered at Dingell's hands, after five years of contentious debate over the commission's budget, its regulatory programs, and its enforcement priorities, Shad hoped that Dingell and his Democratic colleagues would at last acknowledge the righteousness of his reign at the SEC. But when the lights went up and Dingell rapped his gavel menacingly, it became clear that far from being impressed by the SEC's prosecution of Boesky, the Democrats wondered why so much corruption on Wall Street had flourished undetected for so long.

"The hearing today is about just the kind of events which can destroy public trust and confidence," Dingell began. ". . . In many ways, these are the same questions the House Commerce Committee was asking fifty years ago when it created the Securities and Exchange Commission. . . . At that time, the public was shocked by the revelations of stock manipulations, pools, insider trading, and a host of other abuses. Now, we are facing what appears to be the biggest series of stock market abuses since the 1929 crash."

"The Boesky and Levine cases demonstrate how much someone

can get away with before the system catches up to them," chimed in Congressman Ron Wyden, an Oregon Democrat.

"The system did not catch them; it was freak tips from outside," added Ohio Democrat Dennis Eckart, referring to the anonymous letter from Caracas, Venezuela, to Merrill Lynch that led the SEC first to Levine and finally to Boesky.

"I thought we were here for a Tony Award," Shad lamented.

As he observed the congressional proceedings, Lynch grew cynical. He had anticipated that the momentum that had developed as the enforcement division pursued Levine and Boesky would continue as the SEC bulldozed right through the 60 Broad Street headquarters of Drexel Burnham Lambert. He felt members of Congress, in their pursuit of the limelight, were giving aid and comfort to the enemy by criticizing the commission and complicating the ongoing investigations that grew out of Boesky's cooperation.

All through the Reagan years, Dingell had said that the SEC needed more money to fulfill its mandate. But in budget debate after budget debate, Shad had been loyal to the administration's streamlined approach, arguing that the commission's productivity had more than kept pace with Wall Street's explosive growth because of efficiencies achieved through the application of cost-benefit analysis. In fact, late in 1986, the SEC employed slightly fewer people than it had when Shad arrived in 1981, even though trading volume in the financial markets had grown exponentially and the number of registered stockbrokers in the country had almost doubled. In a reversal after the Boesky bomb hit, Shad revealed that he intended to seek the biggest increase ever in the SEC's budget—a 27 percent jump that would take the agency to about $145 million annually and enable it to beef up its enforcement ranks.* Shad never suggested that his past resistance to

---

* At another hearing, Shad pointed out that salary—the major SEC recruiting and retention problem—also needed addressing through a reevaluation of ceilings on individual salary levels. "People leave the SEC and get 100 percent to 200 percent salary increases," Shad said. "My daughter graduated from law school a year ago. She makes more than I do." Shad's salary as SEC chairman was $82,500.

budget increases had been a mistake, but his sudden enthusiasm for increased government spending seemed a public sign that despite his unrelenting rhetoric about the health of the nation's markets and the essential integrity of Wall Street, Shad, too, was disturbed by the revelations of Ivan Boesky.

Dingell pounced on this anomaly. "We are delighted to observe the SEC chairman is willing to ask for additional funds," he said, his tone dripping with sarcasm. "I intend to see to it, whether you like it or not, that you have the resources you need."

All across the capital that December, there was a giddy sense among Democrats that finally, after virtually two terms of Ronald Reagan's political magic, the spell had been broken. The Boesky case was seen as just one aspect of the Democrats' antidote. Just five days after John Shad's November 14 press conference at the SEC, Attorney General Edwin Meese had appeared before television cameras at the White House to announce an incredible discovery: The United States had sold weapons to the government of Iran's Ayatollah Khomeini in an apparent effort to free American hostages held by Iranian sympathizers, and proceeds from these sales were diverted to support U.S.-backed rebels in Nicaragua. So shocking were Meese's revelations that news of the burgeoning Iran-contra scandal quickly engulfed coverage of the continuing Boesky affair, but in some ways the two scandals complemented one another. Underpinnings of the Reagan political mandate—prosperity on Wall Street and Main Street, consistency and strength in foreign policy, efficiency in government—suddenly and simultaneously were called into question. There was a sense, manifested as glee among Democrats and dread among Republicans, that the politics of the Reagan era were coming unraveled at the seams.

Among John Shad's senior staff at the commission, chief economist Gregg Jarrell was committed more than anyone to the philosophy of the Reagan movement, and he was the first to see that the intellectual insurgency he had joined was no longer tenable. Jarrell was certain enough of his Chicago School ideology to be untroubled by Boesky's exposure—a crook is a crook, Jarrell thought—but he was smart enough to see quickly that Boesky's crimes had political as well as legal implications. Even if he had failed to recognize this immediately, the Democrats in Congress would have brought it home to him: by December of 1986, Jarrell had acquired enough of a reputation as an influential free market theorist at the SEC that Reagan's political opponents began to single him out for attack. Soon after the Boesky announcement, Democratic Senator William Proxmire, chairman of the powerful Senate Banking Committee, was quoted in the newspaper calling Jarrell a biased economist who churned out propaganda for the free-market movement. An aide to Proxmire called Jarrell soon thereafter and demanded that he send over all of the studies he had done for the commission. Jarrell began to lose sleep. He decided that he had done what he could in government, and that he should leave before the Democrats took him down the way they had taken down so many other radical conservatives who refused to accept the terms of conventional political debate in Washington. He managed to have one last iconoclastic study released. "Stock Trading Before the Announcement of Tender Offers: Insider Trading or Market Anticipation?" was the title. While everyone else buzzed about widespread corruption on Wall Street, Jarrell concluded that press reports and legal stock purchases were responsible for much of the suspicious movement of stock prices in advance of takeover announcements.

Jarrell was buoyed by his self-confidence and youth, but for Shad the implications of Ivan Boesky's fall were far more troubling. As the new details of the scandal came to light late in 1986 and early in 1987, Shad often defended Wall Street rather than relishing the victory over Boesky along with Gary Lynch and his comrades in the enforcement division. So much was happening after Shad had decided it was time to move on. Early in 1987—after Reagan had indicated he would nominate Shad to another term as SEC chairman—Shad had begun to press the White House for a change of assignment. He was anxious for a change of scenery besides, so he had put his name forward to become the next U.S. ambassador to the Netherlands. It was clear that he would win the post, but the nomination and Senate confirmation took time. Now, in what amounted to a period of professional limbo, an unprecedented scandal had erupted publicly. For Shad, one of the many difficult questions it raised was whether fraud and insider trading had grown into an epidemic on Wall Street while he chaired the SEC, or whether the scandal was a temporary problem detected and effectively expunged by the commission's enforcement program. Did the Boesky case and the continuing investigations of Drexel and others indicate that "the system" he supervised had worked, or had it failed?

It was the evidence Boesky provided to Shad and the SEC about Michael Milken and Drexel that seemed the most troubling. If Boesky was to be believed—and Lynch and others at the commission certainly believed him—Milken had systematically violated the securities laws to rig corporate takeovers, earn illegal trading profits, help select clients, evade taxes, manipulate stock prices, and push around some of its corporate clients. Not only had Drexel harbored Milken's scheme, it had employed at least two other senior investment bankers, Dennis Levine and Martin Siegel, who brazenly leaked inside information about takeovers to Boesky, partly because such leaks made it easier to complete takeover deals. Yet when presented with this evidence at closed meetings on the sixth floor, Shad openly rejected the idea that Drexel's spectacular growth during the 1980s had been founded on systemic corruption. Nor did he believe that Milken's alleged crimes had played a major role in the junk bond financier's success. Intellectually, objectively, Shad's position about Drexel was defensible, even if it wasn't widely shared inside the SEC. But some of those who listened to Shad talk about the massive Milken investigation in late 1986 and early 1987 understood that the chairman's view of the case had a deeply personal aspect. If Shad decided that Drexel and Milken were fundamentally corrupt, then his world view and some of his closest friendships would be called into question.

Drexel Chief Executive Fred Joseph had been Shad's friend for years. While working together at E. F. Hutton they had shared not only a common approach to investment banking but also a personal affinity. "You sure don't look like an investment banker to me," Joseph once kidded his overweight mentor. Their relationship was captured by an anecdote friends repeated about a cab ride the pair once had taken to LaGuardia Airport in New York. Impatient and demanding, Shad had told the cabdriver to move first into the right lane, then into the left lane, and then demanded that he take an exit and get back on the highway at the next entrance. The driver slammed on the brakes, got out of the car, and as a mortified Joseph looked on, opened Shad's door. "If you can drive better than me, sir, you drive," the cabdriver said. So Shad took the wheel and chauffeured Joseph and the stunned cabbie to the airport. Ever since, Joseph had in some ways followed Shad's lead. Even when Drexel's troubles grew while Shad was at the commission, Joseph relied on approaches to management and investment banking he had learned while working for Shad. Joseph thought so highly of Shad that he had framed a 1965 memo from Shad and hung it on his office wall high above Broad Street in the Manhattan financial district—it was still there late in 1986 when the SEC investigators came calling with their subpoenas. It was precisely because Shad knew and trusted Joseph on a personal level that he could not believe any problems at Drexel were pervasive, even after Boesky provided his evidence to the commission. From the arrest of Dennis Levine onward, Joseph maintained a high public profile, immediately issuing bold statements defending the integrity of the firm and its employees. He had learned from Shad years before not to tarry, and to act aggressively; now he was outmaneuvering his teacher on the public relations front. When news leaked that Milken was a focus of the SEC's investigation, Joseph declared categorically that he knew of no wrongdoing by Drexel or any of its employees. If the public had known that Drexel paid Milken an astounding $550 million in 1987, more than ten times his 1983 compensation of $45.7 million and more than the firm itself earned that year, after paying salaries and bonuses and taxes, Joseph would have been far less convincing. Even among big producers, no one in the history of Wall Street had ever been paid a salary approaching that figure. (At the same time, the firm paid Milken's brother, Lowell—who spent much of his time overseeing investment partnerships that made hundreds of millions of dollars for the Milkens and select Drexel employees—nearly $50 million. The salaries reflected the enormous clout Michael Milken had at Drexel to act independently, even when it came to setting salaries.) But the public had no clue, and Joseph's combative attitude gave pause to those in Congress and the press who assumed that Milken and his firm would topple like dominoes as Levine, Boesky, and the others had before. Joseph's attitude also helped to convince Shad that the increasingly harsh allegations about Drexel bandied about on Wall Street and in Washington did not tell the whole story about the firm or its lucrative junk bond business.

But the more Shad resisted, the more his assumptions about Wall Street seemed to crumble. During the second week of February 1987, all of the Street was jolted when federal marshals entered the trading floors of two prestigious firms and arrested Robert Freeman, the chief arbitrager at Goldman, Sachs & Company and Richard Wigton, a top trader at Kidder, Peabody, charging them with criminal insider trading. (While the initial charges against both men were dropped, Freeman later entered a guilty plea to one count of insider trading and Wigton was exonerated.)* The highly public arrests quickly moved the Boesky scandal to the heart of old Wall Street, to the world of clubs and handshake deals John Shad inhabited before he left to chair the SEC. The arrests were made because of information provided by Marty Siegel, the Drexel merger specialist who decided to plead guilty to two criminal counts soon after he received subpoenas indicating that Boesky had turned him in. Siegel resigned from Drexel in disgrace, acknowledging that he had accepted suitcases full of hundreds of thousands of dollars in cash from Boesky in exchange for insider tips. Later that same month, Dennis Levine was sentenced to two years in prison. But it was the spectacle of

---

* While declaring that the government's investigation would continue, U.S. Attorney Rudolph Giuliani acknowledged that the high-profile arrests of Goldman's Robert Freeman and Kidder's Wigton had been a mistake. Separately, Kidder, Peabody paid the SEC more than $25 million to settle civil insider-trading charges arising from some of the allegations originally made against Freeman and Wigton.

top traders at venerable firms like Goldman and Kidder being hauled away in handcuffs like common criminals that mortified traders and executives across Wall Street. If it could happen to these guys, the feeling was, it could happen to anybody.

To the public and to his colleagues on the sixth floor, Shad vacillated between boasts about the SEC's success and assertions that the scandal really wasn't such a big deal after all. "We came out in 1981 and said we'd come down on insider trading with hobnail boots," Shad told the Congress in early 1987. "Now you're seeing the boots hit the sidewalk."* But it was obvious to those close to him inside the commission that Shad was distraught. Congressional criticism that the SEC's settlement with Boesky was too lenient upset him terribly, leading some inside the commission to ask whether there were other sanctions the SEC could impose on Boesky. (Lynch resisted such pressure, saying the agency had to live up to its promises to Boesky. Boesky was sentenced to three years in prison in early 1988, a sentence Judge Morris Lasker said would have been more severe had it not been for the arbitrager's extraordinary cooperation with prosecutors.) Shad also seemed uncomfortable in his role as the chief Wall Street watchdog at a time of great scandal, and he seemed genuinely disappointed in the Street and shocked at the magnitude of the crimes uncovered. Yet even in closed meetings with only his senior staff and fellow commissioners present, Shad repeated his favorite aphorisms about the integrity of the stock market. One difference from the past, though, was that his staff began to challenge him.

Let's not forget that by the highest conjecture, the level of securities fraud is a fraction of one percent of overall stock market activity, Shad said during one closed meeting during this period. America has today by far the best securities markets the world has ever known—the broadest, the most active, efficient, and the fairest.

---

* To commemorate Shad's sixth anniversary at the commission in 1987— making him the longest-serving chairman in SEC history—members of his senior staff presented him with a pair of big, black hobnail boots. They were inscribed on the toe with Shad's famous 1981 pledge to "come down on insider trading with hobnail boots."

I don't buy the one-bad-apple theory, Lynch countered from across the table. I think we have found at least one bad apple in every firm at this point.

Through his actions more than his words, Shad seemed to acknowledge that Lynch was right. An active alumnus, he was in touch regularly with the Harvard Business School, and that winter he began to talk with school officials about an extraordinary gift—Shad said that he wanted to donate most of his personal fortune, approximately $20 million, to establish a new and unprecedented program to teach business ethics.* Harvard, naturally, was delighted, though some professors at the school were skeptical about teaching ethics. The school announced the donation in March 1987, just a month after Freeman and Wigton were arrested on their Wall Street trading floors. It was the single largest gift in the history of the Harvard Business School. Shad described the gesture—and the time he would devote to developing the ethics program while continuing his government work—as a consummation of his grandmother's adage that a person should spend one third of his life learning, one third earning, and one third serving. There were those who saw the gift as an attempt by Shad to secure his public legacy and to outdo the other members of the famed Harvard Business School Class of 1949. Others wondered whether it was intended in part to expiate some abstract guilt Shad felt about the corruption his commission had uncovered in the industry where he had labored. There was some questioning around the SEC about throwing money at a problem that money helped to create, and skepticism about whether integrating ethics into the business-school curriculum would make any difference. But most people accepted Shad's philanthropy at face value and lauded him for his extraordinary generosity. By any measure, he had come a long way from Brigham City, Utah.

If there was one thing that steeled and encouraged John Shad throughout the trying early months of 1987 as he prepared for his posting in the Netherlands, it was the stock market. The num-

* The $10-million-plus fortune Shad brought with him to Washington in 1981 was invested heavily in stocks and had grown with the bull market. The funds were in a blind trust, with investment decisions made by Morgan Stanley.

bers in the financial markets, on which he had always relied for an empirical measurement of success and failure, seemed to him unequivocal. They kept going up. Defying the insider trading scandal, the great Reagan bull stock market raced ahead. The Dow Jones Industrial Average had soared 400 points between 1985 and early 1987, reaching an unprecedented 2,300 points. The Dow had more than doubled since May 6, 1981, the day George Bush had sworn Shad in as the twenty-second chairman of the SEC. Shad's policies had clearly played a role in the Dow's rise. Five years of continuous economic growth was a major factor driving prices higher. But at the same time, the wave of corporate takeovers Shad encouraged had removed billions of dollars of stock from the public markets, driving up the price of those stocks and the remaining shares. Even more than the rise in stock prices, the growth in daily trading figures seemed to Shad a testament to his push for liquidity in the marketplace and the economy. Daily trading volume at the New York Stock Exchange had increased nearly fourfold since 1981 to about 175 million shares. While the stock market boomed, Shad developed tables in the SEC's 1986 annual report showing across-the-board productivity increases at the agency during his tenure. The number of insider trading cases was up, the number of corporate financial filings reviewed by the commission was up, and the fees collected by the agency from new issues of stocks and bonds were up. To Shad, these were hard and satisfying facts. These were the numbers that mattered.

But Shad found that there were many in Congress and even on Wall Street who were less impressed by the numbers than he was. As had been true on Capitol Hill after the Boesky announcement, those who had been his opponents for the previous six years remained skeptical of his achievements. New York Stock Exchange chairman, John Phelan, broke publicly from Shad and warned in the spring of 1987 of the potential for a "financial meltdown" caused by the buildup of computerized program trading in the stock and futures markets. Phelan found a receptive ear in Congress, where Democrats expressed concerns about the violently volatile short-term moves in stock prices apparently caused by program trading. Though there were many variations, at its core the program trading that raised concerns was an outgrowth of Shad's SEC-CFTC accord. Whenever stock futures in Chicago were offered for sale at one price, and the underlying stocks were offered in New York for another price, aggressive traders using computers could earn arbitrage profits by simultaneously buying one and selling the other. On the day every three months when stock futures expired and the prices in Chicago and New York converged, massive buying or selling of stocks was necessary to lock in these profits. On one such day, January 23, 1987, the Dow had whipped up and down 115 points in about an hour and stock market volume had zoomed above 300 million shares, a record.

Program trading was a game played exclusively by and for large institutional investors, who by early 1987 had begun to dominate the action in the stock market. Pension fund assets, insurance company funds, Wall Street brokerage monies, and other institutional assets comprised an estimated half of the $3 trillion of public stocks owned in the United States and more than three-fourths of the daily trading volume. By 1987, the competition among money managers had led many of them to look in every nook and cranny of Wall Street for any short-term edge they could find to beef up their performance numbers. Program trading gave them just what they needed: by pouring millions of dollars into and out of the market with the help of computers, the managers could lock in "sure" profits and bolster their short-term performance. Some corporate executives complained loudly that the trading games drove their own companies' stock prices up and down without regard for corporate financial performance. Yet these same executives hired money managers for their corporate pension funds who played the very program-trading games that roiled the markets. One reason they did was that the edge in short-term performance delivered by program trading created excess cash in the pension funds, which corporations could then tap for other business purposes. The truth was that everybody wanted an edge—the institutions, the managers who controlled their money, the Wall Street firms that sold program-trading services, and with the exception of Phelan at the NYSE, the financial markets themselves, which profited from the increased trading volume.

"When people talk about . . . the possibility of a market melt-down because of this telescoping and that you get everybody coming through the door at the same time. . . . Is it feasible for that kind of thing to happen, in your view?" John Shad was asked on May 13, 1987, while appearing before a Senate subcommittee to testify about the stock market. The questioner was Senator Donald Riegle, a skeptical Democrat from Michigan.

"I think there's an enormous panoply of reasons why something comparable to 1929 is incredibly improbable to occur under the present economic and regulatory environment," Shad predicted boldly. "Nothing is impossible [but] I think that there are an awful lot of reasons why that is highly, highly improbable. As for the meltdown theory, I just don't think that's likely."

"Some have argued that given the number of market devices that are now being used . . . that you could conceivably get a combination of events where, in the name of volatility, you might see the market in a given day not go up or down 150 or 200 points but maybe 500 points. Is that also beyond the realm of realistic possibility in your view?" Riegle asked.

"In terms of probabilities of a one-day break of 500 points of the Dow Jones average? I would say I think it's highly remote, very remote," Shad answered. "But I don't want to say anything is impossible."

It was the last major market prognostication Shad made before Congress, as his six-year tenure as SEC chairman—the longest in commission history—drew to a close.

They came to the basement on Fifth Street to say good-bye at his official farewell party, even some of those who had fought him and criticized his policies and warned that potential disaster lay ahead: Congressman John Dingell, New York Stock Exchange Chairman John Phelan, and former SEC enforcement chief Stanley Sporkin. In the crowd were Federal Reserve Board Chairman Paul Volcker as well as several former SEC commissioners and advisers to Shad. And there was a large group of current staff and commissioners.

Standing at the head of the room, mumbling as he spoke, Shad tried to get off a few jokes, pausing rhythmically for them all to laugh. "The first two years were pretty rocky," he said. "In fact, yesterday wasn't too great. . . . At my initial luncheon with John Dingell, there were just the two of us and our food tasters. Partisan politics aside—in the trenches, I want 'Rambo' Dingell on my side."

Shad had never completely adjusted to Washington—he still lived in a hotel room and heated his bowl of Campbell's soup for dinner just as he had ever since his wife's stroke quashed their plans to buy a house—but he clearly had been at home inside the commission for some time. When his first grandchild was born just before he left the SEC, he had received hearty congratulations from his colleagues at the commission; none of his family was in Washington to share his joy. He had pushed the agency away from its focus on the "public good" and toward a concentration on shareholders' interests. Now there was a new public interest group being formed in Washington—the United Shareholders Association led by T. Boone Pickens—to fight for stockholders, Shad's favorite cause, even after the chairman had gone, a symbol of how much had changed in Washington during the Reagan years. As he bid them an official farewell, Shad thanked his staff and colleagues on the commission, and then he reeled off a series of points, ranging from the SEC-CFTC accord, creating stock futures, to the insider trading crackdown, which he said reflected the highlights of his tenure.

"My only regret," Shad concluded, "is that I will be a distant observer of the exciting events that are unfolding before this great institution."

On a sweltering afternoon in early summer, John Shad sat in the conference room of his large corner suite at the SEC and answered questions under oath while movers in the adjoining office gathered up his personal belongings to haul them out of the building. It was Friday, June 12, 1987, the last day of the chairman's last full week at the helm of the commission.

He had spent a lot of time in the last six months answering questions—from the press, from Congress, and from his own staff. It had been a long and reflective farewell. But this session was different from all the rest. For one thing, there were no hot television lights bathing him or microphones jabbed toward his face or reporters pressing in around him. Shad, in his last hours of power, was being interrogated aggressively behind closed doors by a former SEC enforcement lawyer.

Seated across from him was Cathy Broderick, the former Washington Regional Office (WRO) attorney who had filed a lawsuit against the SEC and against Shad as chairman of the commission. In her suit, Broderick alleged sexual harassment by her supervisors at the WRO across the Potomac River in Arlington, Virginia, saying she had been forced to labor for five years in a "hostile work environment" poisoned by open sexual liaisons, afternoon drinking parties, and favoritism toward women employees who slept with their bosses. Broderick had never before met Shad. She had come to the deposition so she could look him in the eye before he departed from the SEC.

His predicament as a witness that afternoon was in some ways of Shad's own making. There had been a chance to close off the Broderick matter privately a year before, around the time when the Dennis Levine case broke. Broderick's lawyer, Beville May, who had worked for two years in the commission's enforcement division before entering private practice, had made overtures to Shad and the other commissioners about a settlement of the case. May felt strongly about the case and had mixed feelings about her own experience as a female attorney in John Fedders's enforcement division. When May returned to private practice, she was frustrated with the SEC bureaucracy, unimpressed by Shad, and disillusioned with her own treatment by other enforcement division attorneys. Shad had reviewed May's settlement proposal and the detailed allegations made by Broderick, but he hadn't studied the case in depth. At a closed meeting on the sixth floor that spring, Shad indicated he thought a settlement was worth considering if for no other reason than to avoid the negative publicity of an open trial in federal court, where Broderick's complaint was destined to be heard if the commission didn't take care of it privately. But Shad, always a tough negotiator, wanted to press for better settlement terms from Broderick. Two of Shad's senior staff lawyers, Dan Goelzer and Linda Fienberg, recommended at the meeting that the case should be settled because the risk of losing at trial and the possibilities for adverse publicity were too great. But another commission lawyer, Ben Greenspoon, who had investigated the matter thoroughly and would represent the SEC if the case went to court, wanted to go to trial. He said that Cathy Broderick, who was under the care of a psychiatrist and sometimes given to emotional outbursts, would make a flaky witness and that no one would believe her. A report prepared by EEO Manager Ernie Miller's office confirmed Broderick's allegations about the trysts and drinking, but said no EEO violations had occurred.

In the end, the commissioners had voted 5 to 0 not to settle the matter. Broderick had sued, and now Shad found himself seated across from Broderick and her lawyer, a witness in the drama that had dominated Broderick's life for more than five years.

"You are the chairman of the commission, though, Mr. Shad, are you not?" Beville May asked him.

"Yes."

"And as chairman you head the agency?"

"That's your definition."

"What is my definition?"

"That I head the agency. I'm not sure I have ever seen it in writing that I head the agency."

"Frankly," May said, "I didn't expect to get into this much trouble over this kind of question." She went on to another subject and then came back to ask him whether, as chairman of the Securities and Exchange Commission, he found the allegations of discrimination and harassment made by Cathy Broderick to be "of a serious nature."

"The terminology is serious, but whether it has any merit is another matter," Shad said. ". . . The matter of a sexual harassment case is so rare and doesn't rise to the same significance as the major ongoing responsibilities of the executive director and the division directors and the heads of other major offices. . . . There are established procedures for handling this type of matter and they do not involve bringing them to the attention of the chairman of the SEC, who has an awful lot of other more serious responsibilities."

"You will be confronted with subtle temptations, close calls, conflicts of interest, difficult decisions—but if it would not read well on the front [page of a newspaper], don't do it," Shad pronounced into the microphone. A sea of students, their graduation gowns and hats billowing, was spread before him.

He had flown to Rochester, New York, shortly after completing his deposition in the Broderick case, to deliver a commencement speech to the graduating class at the University of Rochester on Sunday, June 14. Gregg Jarrell had become a member of the Rochester faculty after his hasty retirement from the SEC, and he had arranged for Shad to deliver the address and to receive an honorary doctorate degree. It was fitting, given the power Shad had granted to the SEC's chief economist, that Jarrell had helped to plan the event on Shad's last weekend as SEC chairman. Flattered and intrigued by the university's invitation, Shad had drafted a sweeping speech about ethics, business, free market ideology, and the condition of American finance.

"A recent Harris poll indicates that 82 percent of Americans believe business is primarily motivated by greed," Shad advised the graduates. "By contrast, a recent study by Johnson & Johnson indicates that 30 companies presumed to have above-average ethical standards have significantly outperformed the stock market. . . . $30,000 invested in the Dow Jones average 30 years ago would be worth about $150,000 today, a fivefold increase. However, $1,000 invested in each of the [ethical] 30 companies would be worth about $700,000, a 23-fold increase. . . . There are at least strong clues and opinions that the marketplace does indeed reward quality, integrity, and ethical conduct—that it is smart to be ethical."

Having quantified the value of business ethics, John Shad then defended the integrity of Wall Street, espousing the themes that had guided him throughout his tenure as chairman of the SEC.

"Wall Street has long been a favorite target, and yet Wall Street's

ethics compare favorably with other professions and occupa-
tions. . . . Business management still suffers from the image of the
robber barons, caricatured as fat, greedy old men with gout. The
few robber barons who existed were born over a century ago and
buried in the debris of the 1929 crash. Today the bulk of American industry and finance are managed by a generation of giants.
They are well-read and educated, widely-traveled, honest, sensitive and attractive human beings."

He paused.

"Like you and me."

20

A Form of Service

His bedroom window at the rear of the embassy residence looked over a garden of riotous color. Rows of tulips stood like sentries beside the lawn and when the sun came out, as it did occasionally, the shrubs and ancient trees threw off sculptured shadows in the thin North European light. But for the clip, clip, clip of the gardener's shears or the muffled rumble of a passing delivery van, the place was silent, tranquil. And John Shad, too much of the time, was bored.

Often Shad cloistered himself in the ground-floor room near the kitchen where friends had installed an arcade-size Pac-Man video-game machine. There he stood bent over the six-foot contraption—a glass of milk resting nearby, a cigarette burning in an ashtray—jabbing his joystick this way and that to a loud and demonic rhythm. Amplifiers at the base of the machine blared as Shad's yellow Pac-Man gobbled across the video screen. At the top of the screen, where the score was tallied, the numbers rolled higher and higher each time the Pac-Man swallowed one of its electronic enemies. Shad glanced up occasionally to check his score. The numbers still mattered, just as they had during his thirty years on Wall Street and his six years as SEC chairman.

The embassy residence resembled in some ways a museum depicting the scale and character of Shad's successful career. When he arrived in The Hague during the summer of 1987, following his appointment by President Reagan as the new U.S. ambassador to the Netherlands, Shad brought with him boxes of memorabilia that now lined the bedroom hallway and covered the bookshelves and walls of two sitting rooms. There were diplomas—one from the Harvard Business School, another from the New York University School of Law—as well as alumni achievement awards. There were framed magazine covers on which Shad had been featured. There was a molded plastic seal of the Securities and Exchange Commission that hung slightly crooked. (The sharp-eyed federal eagle at the center of this ubiquitous symbol had inspired the SEC's in-house documentary "Eagle on the Street." But during Shad's reign the movie had grown obsolete because no monies were appropriated to update it.) Along the walls hung posed and candid photographs, many of them inscribed, from his six years in Washington: Shad with George and Barbara Bush; Shad with former Treasury Secretary and White House Chief of Staff Donald T. Regan; Shad with Federal Reserve Board Chairman Paul Volcker; Shad with Defense Secretary Casper Weinberger; Shad with former White House Chief of Staff James A. Baker III; and Shad with Ronald Reagan. On one side of the bedroom hallway, there was a framed June 17, 1987, letter from Reagan praising Shad for his work as Wall Street's chief regulator at the SEC. The president's words had the ring of 1980s truth—liquidity and efficiency, liquidity and efficiency—and they sounded more like John Shad than Ronald Reagan.

"Under your stewardship, our capital markets have experienced phenomenal growth and today are the largest, most liquid and efficient in the world," the letter from Reagan said. "Through automation, paperwork reduction and regulatory simplification, you have increased the commission's productivity to help keep pace with the market's expansion. All the while you have achieved remarkable success in rooting out fraud and abuse in the securities industry. When you became chairman you promised to come down on insider traders with 'hobnailed boots' and you can be proud of your record on that score. I know that in the future you can look back with pride on all you have achieved at the Commission and take satisfaction that you did so without increasing the size of the staff."

Shad did feel proud about what he had done. Yet by the time he celebrated his sixty-fifth birthday, in June of 1988, one year after he left the SEC for The Hague, it was becoming increasingly obvious that his legacy at the commission was not yet settled. In October of 1987, the high-flying stock market had crashed, provoking widespread questioning about government regulation of the financial markets during the 1980s. Already weakened by criminal charges, the E. F. Hutton brokerage, Shad's longtime employer on the Street, had been obliterated by the market crash. A sex scandal dating to the era of Shad's SEC tenure was in the headlines. In New York, Shad's understudy Fred Joseph and his Drexel firm faced devastating criminal and civil charges amid the biggest Wall Street–corruption probe ever—an investigation launched by the SEC under Shad.

Shad faced personal problems, too. Already suffering from paralysis due to her 1981 stroke, his wife, Pat, was now dying of throat cancer. Shad appeared as phlegmatic as ever even as he carried flowers to her hospital bedside. Pat spent considerable time in a hospital in the Dutch town of Leiden, not far from The Hague. Shad often was alone in the cavernous embassy residence. Given all of these setbacks and the relative lack of satisfaction he felt professionally as ambassador—a job he had sought out as a new challenge—it was, for Shad, an altogether uncomfortable time.

The crash was a particular sore point, not least because Shad had boldly and publicly proclaimed before Congress in the spring of 1987 that a 500-point drop in the Dow Jones Industrial Average was virtually unthinkable. Between the time of Shad's pronouncement and the 508-point, single-day plummet of the Dow on October 19, 1987, the stock index had risen by several hundred points, making a steep fall more likely than it had been in the spring. Shad pointed this out anytime his prediction before Congress was mentioned, and he suggested that if he had been asked the same question in August 1987, when the Dow peaked at more than 2,700 points, he wouldn't have said that a crash was so unlikely. Shad's revisionism helped to obscure the point that the issue before Congress in the spring hadn't been the SEC chairman's skills as a prognosticator, but his effectiveness as a regulator. During 1988, as the stock market returned to a semblance of normalcy and studies poured forth about what had gone wrong in the October crash, few people blamed Shad explicitly. To assign responsibility for such a complex and chaotic event to a single person or even a single institution would be absurd. Yet it was hardly lost on Shad that analyses of the crash by academics, financial exchanges, and even the bipartisan study commission appointed by President Reagan focused on many of the regulatory and political issues that had dominated his tenure as chairman of the SEC.

Shad understood from the day it happened that one cause of the chaos on Black Monday, 1987, was the growth of massive speculation in the Chicago stock-futures pits, the markets Shad had helped to create when he first arrived in Washington. Isolated in The Hague when the panic struck, Shad could do little more than read the news reports of catastrophe on Wall Street. He wanted to get involved. Shad thought the regulators in Washington should raise the small down payments required to trade millions of dollars of stock futures, a move he hoped would quell speculation and dampen volatility caused by computer-driven trading. From his office in the embassy, Shad dispatched telegrams to White House Chief of Staff Howard Baker and to his successor as SEC chairman, former Northwestern University law school dean David Ruder.

"Action is needed now," Shad urged.

While serving as SEC chairman, Shad from time to time had expressed concern about the growth of speculation in the Chicago futures markets, yet neither he nor any other regulator in Washington had done anything about it. Many of those who examined the crash blamed uncoordinated and, at times, speculative stock futures trading in Chicago for contributing to the shock and steepness of the October 19 "market break," as the crash was euphemistically called by the SEC. President Reagan's Brady Commission report said that between 1982 and 1987 the rise of computer-driven, mathematical, speculative trading in Chicago had caused the stock exchanges in New York and the futures and options pits in Chicago to blend into a single, bubbling, volatile marketplace—and that one determined regulator was needed to bring it under control. The split in regulatory jurisdiction that left the SEC in charge of stocks and the Commodity Futures Trading Commission in charge of stock futures—the split devised by Shad and CFTC Chairman Johnson in 1981—had to be repaired immediately to "reduce the possibility of destructive market breaks," the Brady report said. But the White House distanced itself from the recommendation. Shad seemed to agree that given the political opposition fueled by the well-heeled Chicago markets, this idea was too extreme a form of government intervention to be feasible.

The SEC had been ineffective on Black Monday in part because its authority was truncated by the existence of the CFTC but also because its new chairman, David Ruder, lacked Shad's intuitive feel for the financial markets. To Shad's credit, during those long and sometimes difficult months of 1988 when so many of his convictions and accomplishments seemed threatened by events on Wall Street that he could not control, he never gloated over Ruder's missteps to those who visited him in Holland. Shad's friends and former colleagues were not so discreet. They said that if Shad had been at the commission when the panic hit, he would have taken charge and stemmed the hemorrhaging.

But even those who were closest and most loyal to Shad could not pretend to ignore the overarching implications of the crash: that the great bull market of the 1980s, the Reagan market, had been driven to a large degree by feverish speculation, whether on options or futures or the boom in corporate takeovers. It was axiomatic to economists of every ideological stripe that stock prices plummeted in October 1987 because investors in their collective, if suddenly reversed, wisdom thought prices were too high and decided to sell. But why? Only a few months before Black Monday, no less a bastion of cautious, corporate establishment thinking than *Fortune*—John Shad's favorite business magazine—had queried on its cover, "Are Stocks Too High?" Inside, the magazine offered the "surprising answers" of some experts that various old rules of thumb, which indicated stocks were excessively valued, no longer applied and that stock prices were destined only to go up.

That a balloon so inflated would burst two months later was, looking back on it, not such a perplexing mystery. Yet the pin that pricked it seemed to reveal a great deal about the culture that had grown up on Wall Street during Shad's reign at the SEC. As the stock market began to buckle, early in October, the fall was led by shares whose prices were inflated by speculation about takeovers. During the week before the crash, the same sort of volatile, high-profile takeover stocks that had led the market up during the 1980s suddenly plunged in value. Some takeover speculators feared that a new bill introduced in the House Ways and Means Committee—a bill that wasn't close to becoming law—might eliminate certain tax benefits associated with takeovers. In the aftermath of the Boesky scandal, mere consideration of such an initiative was apparently enough to spook the arbitragers on Wall Street, who promptly dumped their shares. To what extent the early collapse of takeover stocks was a significant factor in the Black Monday debacle was widely debated during 1988, but the discussion itself pointed up how fragile the relationship between Wall Street speculation and Washington regulation had become.

For a while after the crash, it was widely feared that 1987 augured a repeat of 1929, that the stock market collapse, in which $1 trillion in paper value was wiped out from August through October, would plunge the country into a depression. Shad worried aloud that negative publicity in the aftermath of the crash would dampen consumer and business spending, pushing the nation into a dangerous economic and psychological tailspin that could be difficult to reverse. But the U.S. banking and credit system, which had collapsed during the 1930s, held firm, mainly because the regulators in Washington who controlled the money supply had absorbed important lessons from the Great Depression. By loosening credit supplies and publicly indicating its intention to pump funds into the banking system where needed, the Federal Reserve made sure, late in 1987, that there was enough cash coarsing through the economy—enough of Shad's cherished liquidity—to soothe those banks wounded by losses in the crash. The New York Stock Exchange and its biggest member firms voluntarily curbed the most egregious forms of computerized program trading in an effort to quell volatility, restore investor confidence, and perhaps most importantly, stave off legislative fixes from Washington. The securities industry also went to work on expanding and improving its trading systems, which had been overwhelmed by the extraordinary October volume, leaving many small investors unable to execute trades as the value of their once hot takeover stocks and other holdings vaporized amid the panic. (Had Rip van Winkle dozed off at the beginning of 1987 and glanced at the Dow Jones Industrial Average when he woke at year end, he would have wondered what all the fuss was about. Though it peaked in August at 2,722 and hit bottom nearly 1,000 points lower on October 19, the Dow opened the year slightly below 1,900 and closed the year slightly above, at 1,938.) By the summer of 1988, the markets had steadied and the economy was chugging along. The Republican party, John Shad included, breathed a collective sigh of relief. And yet, because he had unleashed the forces that overwhelmed the market system, Shad's reputation had been tarnished somewhat.

Shad and his tenure at the SEC had come under scrutiny for other reasons, too. In May of 1988, the long-simmering sex-discrimination lawsuit filed by SEC attorney Catherine Broderick finally erupted into public view. Following a trial in open court in Washington, federal Judge John H. Pratt ruled in Broderick's favor, against the SEC, and ordered that she receive overdue promotions and compensation and be restored to a job of her choosing because the sexual harassment in the commission's Washington Regional Office (WRO) "was so pervasive . . . that it created a hostile or offensive work environment which affected the motivation and work performance of those who found such conduct repugnant and offensive." Pratt said he found the testimony of some SEC officials to be "less than forthright." None of the men was sanctioned by the SEC; one of them had been promoted by Shad before the trial.

Judge Pratt was unimpressed by Shad's role in the Broderick case. The judge asserted that even though Shad and other high-level SEC officials knew of the problems in the nearby Washington Regional Office for years, they "made no serious effort to enforce the guidelines prohibiting sex discrimination." (Shad had testified that he only became aware of Broderick's allegations years after the events in question, on the eve of her lawsuit. His supporters also pointed out that, during the 1980s, the SEC increased the number of women in senior executive positions from 2 percent to 24 percent.) When contacted in the Netherlands for comment at the time of Judge Pratt's ruling, Shad referred back to the internal investigation that SEC staff lawyers had conducted. "They advised the commission that no conduct rule violations had occurred," he said.

For many of the senior bureaucrats at the SEC, the embarrassment of Judge Pratt's ruling in 1988 was obviated in part by the continuing success of the commission's enforcement division. Shad, though, appeared to take little solace in the commission's revelation that corruption and insider trading had been widespread on Wall Street during the 1980s. In fact, during his informal talks at the dinner table in Holland, it was often clear that Shad didn't believe the ongoing, massive SEC investigation of Drexel was as serious a matter as the U.S. press made it out to be. Despite what he knew of the evidence about Michael Milken's illegal conduct, which Ivan Boesky had provided confidentially to the SEC, Shad continued to admire Milken and his work deeply. Milken should be punished if he had broken the law, Shad believed, but that didn't change his feeling that Milken was a genius who had accomplished much that was praiseworthy. Moreover, Shad thought that if Milken had cut any corners while running his powerful junk bond operation in Beverly Hills, his illegal conduct had been incidental to Drexel's success.

Shad's decision to give away his fortune to the Harvard Business School to establish a program on ethics suggested that he believed American finance was beset by serious problems. And yet at the same time, privately and publicly, he continued to insist that things really were not so bad, and that certainly there was no need for the government or the SEC to change its approach. It wasn't clear whether Shad said this so often because he believed it was correct or because he wanted to convince himself that it was true. None of the events that had so shaken Wall Street and the country after his departure from the SEC—the stock market crash of Oc-

tober 1987; the spread of the Wall Street corruption scandal to
nearly every major investment bank; the shattering, at least temporarily, of investor confidence in the fairness and integrity of the
financial markets—deterred Shad from repeating his rhetorical
speeches at the dinner table in The Hague during 1988. He told
his visitors that the raging hysteria over the crash and the corruption cases was overblown, exaggerated, that the United States still
possessed the "richest and fairest and most efficient financial markets in the world." To those who had heard him before, Shad
sounded like a broken telephone answering machine that repeated the same message over and over without ever stopping to
listen. Some thought his soliloquies in the Netherlands were a
coping device, that he simply could not acknowledge how he actually felt.

In any event, it became clear during 1988 that neither the Justice Department nor the SEC shared Shad's beneficent view of
Drexel and Milken. In September, following nearly two years of
active investigation—and long after two earlier SEC probes of
Milken led by Jack Hewitt and Irving Einhorn had been
dropped—the SEC filed a massive lawsuit accusing Drexel and its
junk bond chief of rigging corporate takeovers, trading on inside
information, evading taxes, manipulating stock prices, and bullying clients. True to form, Milken and Drexel vowed to fight the
SEC and to continue serving clients and making money.

"For the past 22 months I have been the subject of a shadow
trial of systematic leaks and innuendo based upon false accusations," Milken said in a statement released the same day as the
SEC charges. "Drexel Burnham and I have a record of ethical
dealings with thousands of community leaders, customers and
clients of which I am proud. . . . When the truth is substituted for
false accusations, I am confident that I and my colleagues will be
fully vindicated."

Drexel Chief Executive Officer Joseph joined Milken, aggressively attacking the SEC's case in a letter to clients. "We believe,
based on information available to us, that the charges filed by the
SEC are wrong," the letter from Joseph said. "After an examination of 1.5 million pages of documentation and interviews of

scores of Drexel Burnham employees, we continue to believe that neither Drexel Burnham nor any of our employees named in this matter have engaged in any wrongdoing. We expect to be vindicated."

Though the commission faced vigorous opposition from Milken and Drexel, the filing of the charges was a testament to the prowess of the SEC's enforcement division under Gary Lynch. With the crucial help of Boesky and other cooperating witnesses, the division of enforcement finally had succeeded in mounting the type of case it had failed to make twice before when the earlier Milken probes were dropped inconclusively. Yet the case also highlighted flaws in the SEC's regulatory and enforcement efforts during the 1980s, especially the way in which the agency's various divisions under Shad had worked at cross-purposes when it came to takeovers. Shad had sounded warnings about debt-driven takeovers in his 1984 "Leveraging of America" speech, but neither he nor anyone else at the commission had acted upon those words. While state court judges became increasingly active—occasionally acting to block the most abusive hostile takeovers—the SEC's role as a serious takeover regulator in the 1980s diminished, in large part reflecting Shad's view that takeovers were good for shareholders. One effect of the commission's hands-off attitude was to encourage investment bankers, corporate raiders, and arbitragers to employ increasingly aggressive takeover tactics. Had there been somewhat more balanced regulation of takeover financing, disclosure, and trading practices by the SEC's divisions of Corporate Finance and Market Regulation in the early 1980s, there would have been less police work for the agency's enforcement division to do later. Even the most successful enforcement division prosecutions could not undo the damage done years before when companies were acquired in rigged takeovers.

Whatever the limitations and obstacles, Lynch and his team in the agency's division of enforcement seemed more determined than ever to nail Milken and his employer. They worked closely with criminal prosecutors in pursuit of that goal. On the same day the SEC charged Drexel, the Manhattan U.S. Attorney's office sent "target letters" to Milken, his brother, and other Drexel employees in Beverly Hills, informing them it was likely that they would be charged with criminal fraud under the powerful federal racketeering statute known as RICO. To many it seemed that prosecutors were using the threat of RICO, a law originally enacted to attack organized crime and that permitted the freezing of a target's property even before a trial was held, as a sledgehammer and unfairly attempting to coerce guilty pleas out of Drexel and Milken. But the government argued the threat was justified given the scale and systematic nature of Drexel's crimes. On Wall Street and in Corporate America, some of Drexel's competitors and targets privately enjoyed the confrontation. After all of the hardball tactics that Drexel and Milken had employed in pursuit of investment banking and junk-bond-trading fees, they seemed to be getting a taste of their own medicine. Within weeks, James Dahl, the junk bond salesman who had sat across from Milken for nearly a decade in the Beverly Hills office, was granted immunity from criminal prosecution in exchange for his testimony about Milken and Drexel. In addition to corroborating aspects of Boesky's story about Milken's fraud, Dahl's testimony provided the government with new descriptions and allegations about illegal practices at Drexel. Rushing to avoid criminal charges, other key employees from Drexel's Beverly Hills office lined up against Milken and Drexel and became witnesses for the government. Milken and Joseph reacted to the swelling tide against them by making claims of innocence and charges of prosecutorial abuse even more stridently than before.

When he finally caved in late in 1988, Joseph went down defiantly, scrapping like the boxer he had once been. Saying that he had finally seen hard evidence from government prosecutors that there had been serious wrongdoing at Drexel, Joseph cut a plea bargain on Drexel's behalf with Manhattan U.S. Attorney Rudolph W. Giuliani. Drexel agreed to plead guilty to criminal charges, forfeit $650 million and cooperate with the government in its prosecution of Milken. Joseph hardly sounded contrite. He said a big factor in the decision to plead was the potentially catastrophic financial consequences of racketeering charges. He implied that but for the threat of RICO property seizures, Drexel would have stood firm against the prosecutors.

After teaming up with Milken for so long, Joseph's decision to cut a plea bargain was controversial within the firm because it seemed to betray Drexel's most important money-maker, leaving him on his own to fight SEC and criminal charges. After negotiating the deal and ensuring there were enough votes on the Drexel board to approve it, Joseph cast a symbolic vote against the plea bargain at the climactic board meeting in New York. It was an effort, transparent and duplicitous to some, to appease the factions in the firm that remained loyal to Milken.

Joseph next turned his attention to making peace with the SEC and to bolstering Drexel's future prospects. What he needed, his top advisers said, was someone the SEC would trust, a "white hat" who could serve as Drexel's chairman and restore the firm's credibility in Washington and elsewhere—someone who could make corporations feel comfortable about hiring a brokerage that was now an admitted felon.

From his distant perch, Shad admired the way his former protégé Joseph handled himself. Though there were serious questions about Joseph's apparent naïveté and his failure to supervise Milken and the others in Beverly Hills, no one had accused him of intentional wrongdoing, and he had deftly preserved his power at the helm of the firm, reassuring employees regularly in pep talks over an internal communications network and publicly asserting Drexel's innocence—at least until the plea bargain, when he shifted to talking brightly about the firm's postcriminal future.

That Joseph had managed to postpone for two years a public admission of Drexel's problems—a strategy that permitted Drexel to continue doing deals and earning huge fees—didn't seem to bother Shad, who accepted Joseph's explanation that he had seen no hard evidence of wrongdoing until the end of 1988, more than two years after Ivan Boesky first leveled his allegations. When Joseph finally admitted Drexel's guilt, after making so many public denials and mailing out thousands of letters indicating the firm had done nothing wrong, Shad only admired Joseph's composure and tenacity.

And Shad was restless that wintry season in the Netherlands. His wife, Pat, had died in the fall, ending a terrible ordeal for both of them. Shad found in those melancholy months that he missed the hectic pace of the SEC. Although he had worked at staying busy as ambassador, it had been a slow period for diplomacy in the low countries. "I miss the stress," he often said. Never a man to appreciate form over substance, Shad slipped in and out of the nightly cocktail parties in The Hague, refining his ability to shake the right hands and make a clean getaway in minutes. So little of the job, it seemed, involved the sort of tangible accomplishments Shad liked to record on his mental scorecard. He described his frustration this way to several visitors:

When I was on Wall Street, I could get $100 million financings done with a few telephone calls. At the SEC, it took months or years to get things done but there was progress. Here in Europe the issues are global and there are no decisions at all. You can't get things done the same way.

By the time Irwin Schneiderman telephoned him in January 1989, it was clear to Shad that the ascendant Bush administration would have no place for him in government, or at least no station of cabinet or equivalent rank. The previous March, during a ride from the Old Executive Office Building beside the White House to Andrews Air Force Base, Shad had talked with then Vice President George Bush about resigning as ambassador and coming to work in his presidential campaign. Although they discussed the possibility of Shad becoming a spokesman on ethics, Bush already had his fund-raising under control and apparently didn't feel a need to add Shad to the team—he never called to follow up.

After Bush won the presidency, it seemed to Shad and those friends who talked with him about it that if Bush were elected, only a cabinet post—at Commerce or Treasury or perhaps as the president's chief trade representative—would be appropriate for someone of his stature and experience. Anything else might seem an embarrassing slight, a step down. Bush and his advisers, though, kept saying that they wanted to find new blood, new approaches for their administration. In the field of economic and financial regulation, they seemed distrustful of the more radical adherents to Chicago School free market theory. And in Shad's case, there was the not insignificant matter of the 1987 stock market crash. Still, from The Hague, Shad made some overtures about returning to Washington to join the Bush team. After the election, Bush's chief campaign strategist, James Baker, called Shad and said, "I hope you'll stay with the new administration." But the call from the White House for the right job never came.

Instead, that January of 1989, Irwin Schneiderman telephoned from Wall Street—in his dual role as friend of Shad and counsel to Drexel—to urge Shad's acceptance of a stunning proposition.

"It would be very helpful to Fred and Drexel if you came," Schneiderman said. Shad would be the new chairman of Drexel Burnham Lambert, Incorporated, technically superior to chief executive Joseph but absolved of day-to-day mangement responsibility.

Initially, Shad was lukewarm, having had no intention of returning to Wall Street and the money business. He had been only too aware as salaries escalated on Wall Street during the 1980s of the financial sacrifice he had made as SEC chairman. But when he left E. F. Hutton to become chairman of the SEC in 1981, Shad had self-consciously entered the third phase of his life. He had lived by his Mormon grandmother's credo; at sixty-five, this was the time for serving, which he had always thought meant government duty, teaching, or charitable work, something other than pursuing wealth. Schneiderman suggested to Shad that if he were encouraged to take the Drexel chairmanship by SEC and Justice Department officials, and if he donated his salary to charity, it would not be purely a job situation. When nothing materialized in the Bush administration, Shad had thought briefly that charitable foundation work at a top institution would be appealing, but nothing suitable had come through in that field, either. Shad's daughter, Leslie, urged that he consider slowing the pace of his life, that he perhaps learn how to take it easy. He did have offers to become an outside director of some large and prestigious corporations. But that didn't seem enough to feed his need for stress. With Pat gone, Shad found the prospect of returning to Manhattan—to sit idly in his quiet Park Avenue apartment—utterly uninviting.

I'll have to think it over, Shad told Schneiderman. And I would have to be sure in advance that any decision checks out with the ethics people.

On the weekend of January 7, 1989, Fred Joseph boarded an airplane in New York bound for The Hague. He met with Shad at the embassy residence and their talk was simple and direct, a negotiation between old and trusted friends. Nearly two decades before, Joseph had backed Shad in an unsuccessful bid for the top job at E. F. Hutton. Now, they scratched on a single piece of paper the outline of a proposed deal that would make Shad Drexel's chairman and reunite them as a team. It would have been possible with no one else besides Joseph. Shad had trained him years before and had complete confidence in his candor. The prospect of their being together again—with side-by-side offices in the heart of Wall Street's financial district—was appealing to Shad in many ways.

But there were issues to consider. Shad said he couldn't join the firm before Drexel reached a legal settlement with the SEC. He also said that, if he accepted, he didn't want to be a figurehead recruited solely for his good name or as a stock-market cop. He wanted to be an active chairman of the board. "The best defense," of Drexel's soiled reputation, he believed, "was a good offense within the rules." Shad told Joseph that he had to know more about the circumstances surrounding Drexel's guilty plea and about the financial health of the firm. And he said again that he would have to consult with the ethics people at the SEC. What would SEC officials think of the longest-serving chairman in SEC history—and the one who presided over the initiation of the Drexel probe in the first place—taking over as chairman of an outlaw investment bank? What would his friends say about his apparent abrogation of the oft-repeated pledge to spend the final one-third of his life serving?

Shad began a telephone campaign to ask friends and associates on Wall Street what they thought. Shad told them that he didn't feel Drexel should be put out of business and he kept reminding people that the economy had produced eighteen million new jobs since 1982, most of them in the kind of small and medium size companies that Drexel and Milken had financed with junk bonds. He didn't mind the newspaper leaks mentioning that he was considering the job—he wanted desperately to hear reactions. Some of his friends urged him to stay away from Drexel, arguing that the risk of another scandal at the firm was too great and that the firm had unsavory clients. Others told Shad that he ought to concentrate on developing the ethics program at Harvard and other eleemosynary pursuits. Still others said that whatever wrongdoing Drexel had engaged in, the firm had done much good through its pioneering work to finance takeovers and growing companies with junk bonds. It was important for stockholders, and therefore for the nation, that the firm survive, these friends and acquaintances said. These were the friends to whom Shad listened.

Ever the investment banker, Shad wanted to perform due diligence before giving Joseph his final okay. He hired Perrin Long, the prominent Wall Street analyst, to advise him on the firm's financial situation. He met with scores of employees in Drexel's headquarters and in the firm's Beverly Hills office, to learn more about its business and to ascertain whether he would be able to ensure high ethical standards. He talked for hours with Fred Joseph about how he would play the dual role of chairman of the firm and chairman of a special oversight committee that would keep a close eye on Drexel's compliance with securities laws.

All in all, Shad was impressed. It seemed to him that with more than $1 billion in capital, the Drexel brokerage was in strong financial shape. There seemed to be a hefty backlog of business in the pipeline. Despite the years of legal turmoil, the guilty plea and the split within the firm over Joseph's decision to cut off Milken, it appeared to Shad that key employees and clients appeared to be sticking with the firm. Still, Shad knew his reputation for integrity and effectiveness could be put at risk. The more conservative Wall Street where he had worked was gone. Drexel seemed willing to take enormous financial risks in return for holding on to 100 percent of a deal and its fees. Joining Drexel would be something of a gamble, but he had prided himself throughout his career on taking intelligent risks and felt that his willingness to do so had been one of the major factors responsible for his success.

Shad wanted the support of government prosecutors. He didn't want to take the job and then be attacked by the Justice Department or the SEC as someone who once had prosecuted a renegade firm and now was going to help it prosper. He received a boost when U.S. Attorney Rudolph W. Giuliani called and urged him to take the job. Shad asked him to make his endorsement public and Giuliani did, declaring in a television interview that it would be a good thing if Shad joined Drexel. The government wasn't trying to put Drexel out of business, Giuliani said, and Shad could play a constructive role in making sure the firm avoided misdeeds in the future.

One last issue worried Shad, a question neither Joseph nor anyone at Drexel or in the government could address. Would Michael Milken—now at legal odds with Drexel after the firm had agreed to cooperate with the government in his prosecution— take revenge against the firm either by using his clout with key clients to wreck its business or by encouraging his loyalists within the firm to turn on Joseph? On the one hand, Shad thought, if Milken continued to fight and were acquitted, that opened up all kinds of possibilities for Drexel's business in the future. On the other hand, if the defiant Milken perceived that he was going to be nailed by prosecutors as a result of Drexel's decision to coop- erate in the probe, would he try to take down the firm and Joseph with him?

"I know it takes guts for me to come from New York and ask you to turn the other cheek, but I believe it is in your best inter- est," Shad said, as he gazed into Michael Milken's eyes.

Struggling to make up his mind about the Drexel chairman- ship, Shad had made the pilgrimage to California in March 1989, to seek Milken's counsel. They met at Milken's home in Encino. The financier was playing basketball with one of his sons when Shad pulled up. Shad's motivation was self-interest; he had come to size Milken up for himself, to attempt to determine whether Milken was likely to make life difficult for Drexel in the months ahead. In a sense, Shad was also seeking Milken's blessing before accepting the chairman's job. Considering the magnitude of fi- nancial crimes the SEC had charged Milken with, it was remark- able that a former SEC chairman would consider such a meeting. But Shad was far less convinced of Milken's venality than Gary

Lynch and others at the SEC, and he was more convinced of the merits of Milken's junk bonds.

"You have been instrumental in building Drexel," Shad told Milken, stroking his ego. Milken often stated that he saw himself as a builder and that too many people in Washington were interested in tearing down rather than building up.

I have been asked to help Drexel along in the future, Shad said. I want to talk with you about the future, not the past.

They met for five hours, adjourning at one point to a nearby restaurant. Shad came away impressed and reassured. Milken seemed to him a man of conviction who, like Shad, made rational rather than emotional decisions. Before their meeting, Shad had thought Milken's pronouncements on such public-spirited matters as helping Latin America's faltering economy were nothing more than public relations rhetoric from a man in deep trouble. But after hearing Milken discuss his ideas about restructuring outstanding Latin American debt and financing businesses in the region, Shad thought Milken truly cared about the region and had highly developed theories that made business sense and could someday be put into practice. After dinner with Milken and his wife, Lori, Shad left feeling confident that Milken was not a man who would take steps that would hurt the Drexel firm.

Soon after Shad's private meeting with Milken on March 29, 1989, and following the breakdown of settlement talks between lawyers for the financier and government officials, the Manhattan U.S. Attorney filed a ninety-eight-count criminal racketeering indictment charging Milken, his brother, Lowell, and others with manipulating stock and bond prices, bullying clients, insider trading, rigging takeovers, and numerous other securities law violations. Added to the SEC charges that had been filed against Milken the previous September, the former Drexel junk bond king now faced the most devastating array of charges ever filed against a major Wall Street figure. He stood accused of the most sweeping set of financial crimes leveled by the U.S. government since the 1920s. Upon the filing of charges, much of the attention was focused on Milken's salary, including the $550 million he drew in 1987, which was listed by prosecutors in the opening

pages of the indictment. Milken, once again, proclaimed his innocence and predicted he would be vindicated at trial.

Two weeks later, on April 13, SEC enforcement chief Gary
Lynch announced that the commission had reached a settlement
of the agency's civil charges against Drexel that included an array
of unprecedented monitoring techniques designed to prevent
fraud at the firm in the future. Lynch said that despite the breadth
of Drexel's violations and its belligerent attitude, the decision had
been made not to strip it of its license to do business. The SEC's
financial sanctions against Drexel were included in the settlement
that had been reached between Drexel and the Justice Department, in which the firm agreed to pay $650 million, about half to
be set aside for claims of those injured by its fraudulent activities.
The SEC filed no charges against Fred Joseph or anyone else at
Drexel for failing to properly supervise Milken and the junk bond
operation, a decision that Lynch said had something to do with
technical aspects of the case and that the commission would review.

On the same day in Manhattan, Drexel announced that former
SEC chairman John Shad would become its chairman. Shad said
he wanted to help save the firm and enable it to continue financing American industry. He had been away from the Street
for a decade and now he had a sense of purpose as he returned.
Lynch called Shad "a great choice" that would give SEC officials
"comfort."

Shad received phone calls from Lynch and SEC Chairman
David Ruder congratulating him on the decision. Michael Milken
also phoned.

Shad felt the need to reconcile publicly how his decision to
return to Wall Street fit with his grandmother's credo to spend the
final one third of his life serving. Unwilling to face up to what was
clearly an abrogation of that pledge, Shad found a way to package
it for himself and for public consumption. His solution was replete with irony; Shad indicated that he would donate his entire
multimillion-dollar salary as chairman of Wall Street's most notorious investment bank to the Harvard Business School ethics program he had funded.

In a statement released by Drexel upon Shad's acceptance of the chairmanship of that profit-making enterprise, the firm said, "The bulk of Mr. Shad's present and future resources are dedicated to charitable activities."

Nobody challenged the words.

"I look on it," Shad declared that day, "as a form of service."

Epilogue

Michael Milken was sentenced to ten years in prison on November 21, 1990. He had pleaded guilty to six felony counts of securities fraud, market manipulation, and tax fraud the previous spring, ending nearly four years of shrill defiance of the SEC and federal prosecutors. Standing in the august courtroom of New York federal Judge Kimba Wood, the forty-four-year-old Milken seemed a broken man. He wept at public court proceedings. In addition to confessing that he was a felon, Milken said he had violated his own values and standards of morality. Still, Milken's offer of contrition struck some as halfhearted, since his lawyers continued to insist that his crimes were technical and small relative to the sum of Milken's business and philanthropic accomplishments.

Judge Wood said to the two hundred raptly attentive spectators in her chambers that in sentencing Milken, she did not want to hand down "a verdict on a decade of greed." Instead, she wanted only to punish an individual who had admitted to serious crimes. Despite Wood's disclaimer, Milken's sentencing had become the essential public postmortem on the 1980s, a decade neatly memorialized in newspaper columns as a period of excess and avarice. The sentence she meted out was by far the stiffest punishment given to any defendant in the Wall Street scandals uncovered by John Shad's SEC. Some former clients of Milken and lawyers

involved in the investigations that led to his guilty plea denounced
Judge Wood's sentence as grossly excessive. Others called it a
welcome and just deterrent against Wall Street fraud. The debate
grew voluble and the sentencing became a kind of democratic
catharsis, with every bystander in the street asked to opine on how
many years Milken should spend in the slammer. Their answers
were a measure of public judgment on what had gone wrong in
America during the Reagan years.

On the evening that Milken was sentenced to a decade behind
bars, Luis Baston, a thirty-six-year-old nursing student from
Brooklyn, stood on a windy Wall Street corner, wearing the uniform of the Salvation Army, ringing a bell beside his charity's
collection can. "I think they should lynch him," Baston answered
when asked about Milken's ten-year term. "These people always
get away with the white-collar crimes. Ten years should be the
minimum, but when he serves, they should put him in with the
regular prison population."

But what about the hundreds of millions of dollars that he had
contributed to charities from his junk bond profits? "I'm helping
charities also," Baston answered. "But I'm not putting my hand in
the pot."

Inside SEC headquarters, where senior enforcement division
officials had taken a straw vote on the sentence just days before
Judge Wood ruled, they were pleased with Milken's full sentence:
a ten-year prison term, plus three years of community service,
plus the $600 million he had agreed to pay the government. The
ten-year sentence for Milken on the day before Thanksgiving was
only slightly more than most of them had expected.

Shad viewed Milken's sentence as a shrewd trade by Judge
Wood. When Milken cut his plea bargain, he refused to answer
questions from investigators before his sentencing. Judge Wood
said in determining his sentence that she would not give him any
credit for possible future cooperation. To the contrary, the judge
said there were signs Milken had encouraged others to destroy
incriminating documents during the probe in subtle ways that
allowed him to maintain some deniability. Wood also said Milken
deserved harsh punishment because many of his crimes showed a

pattern of just stepping over to the "wrong side of the law" in an apparent effort to get some of the benefits without running a substantial risk of being caught. In contrast, Ivan Boesky and Marty Siegel committed more blatant crimes—exchanging cash in briefcases for inside information—but received lesser sentences than Milken because of their swift and thorough cooperation with prosecutors. At his sentencing, Milken received neither the benefits of his years of fighting nor of his guilty plea, a dismal outcome for a man who had made his fortune achieving optimal returns. The one thing Milken did achieve in his plea bargain was criminal immunity for his brother, Lowell. He also avoided the stigma that goes with ratting on colleagues and clients. Judge Wood said that if government prosecutors later asked her to reduce Milken's ten-year term—after his reluctant but legally mandated post-sentencing cooperation—she would consider shortening it.* Shad felt Judge Wood had found a clever way to maintain leverage over the fallen financier.

Intellectuals saw in Milken's predicament confirmation of their own ideologies. The editorial writers at the *Wall Street Journal,* strident but eloquent adherents of the Chicago School economic theories who had cheered Milken and Drexel lustily during the 1980s, described the harsh sentence as a harbinger of economic bad times. "Michael Milken has often been depicted as the symbol of the 1980s, the Master of the Universe presiding (with Ronald Reagan) over the decade of greed," they wrote. "We fear he is becoming the symbol of the 1990s, the decade of vengeful destruction. . . . The sentence is best understood as penance for the heretic. Michael Milken was a threat—to entrenched corporate managers, to Wall Street competitors, to regulators who prefer their markets neat and pretty. It was his bad fortune to serve as

---

* In early 1991, before prosecutors asked her to reduce Milken's sentence, Judge Wood recommended that Milken serve a term of thirty-six to forty months before being eligible for parole. She made the statement at a hearing in connection with her recommendation to the U.S. Parole Commission. The judge said she reached this conclusion after calculating that Milken's six admitted crimes cost investors only $318,000, much less than prosecutors had estimated. Judge Wood said those losses, tied only to Milken's admitted crimes, didn't reflect the overall damage he had caused for financial markets and investors.

the symbol of this era that many people apparently want to lock away forever in some deep dark cave. . . . It matters only in a perverse sense that the decade of the 1980s was a period of unparalleled economic growth, surely far better than the malaise of the 1970s. And better, we fear, than the 1990s are likely to be if current humors prevail."

Perhaps the overwrought tone of the *Journal*'s editorial writers reflected a recognition that at the turn of the decade, Michael Milken's America (and Ronald Reagan's, too) no longer existed. Unemployment was rising and recession taking hold. Hard times had come again to Wall Street. Many of the big securities firms that profited from the 1980s boom were hurting badly, as takeovers and trading volume dried up. Thousands of young Wall Street traders, investment bankers, salesmen, lawyers, and clerks were out of work. (This made it easier for the SEC to hire and retain top legal talent.) As the economy slowed, scores of junk bond–financed companies that once were clients of Milken's declared bankruptcy or teetered on the edge under the weight of junk bond debt. Investors suffered staggering losses in junk bonds, and Merrill Lynch issued a study refuting Milken's thesis— and primary sales pitch—that a diversified portfolio of junk bonds produced superior financial returns. As takeovers soured and real estate values fell, the stability of the nation's banking system was threatened. Bankruptcies in the savings and loan industry (S&Ls), including the collapse of several large thrifts that had staked their profitability on Milken's junk bond market, had precipitated political scandals and a taxpayer cleanup expected to cost more than $500 billion. Savings and loan regulators sued Drexel, seeking the recovery of billions of dollars, claiming that the entire junk bond market had been a fraud and a sham. Stock prices were weak, and there was a sense on the Street that it would be years before individual investors, burned by the 1987 stock market crash, would return to the market. Consumer confidence, as measured by surveys and spending patterns, was at its lowest point in a decade. The biggest growth industry in the legal and financial world was bankruptcy law.

Brokerage houses that had raced into the arbitrage business disbanded these stock trading units as the losses from busted takeovers mounted. The image of Ivan Boesky, the fit-looking arbitrager in his three-piece suit with gold pocket watch, had been replaced by that of a freakish, decaying Boesky, who appeared with long hair and a scraggly beard on the front page of the *New York Post*. While Boesky's three-year prison sentence at Lompoc had changed his appearance, it apparently had not changed everything else.

"Now, Mr. Boesky," he was asked under oath, as he testified in one of many trials that resulted from his cooperation with the SEC, "under your cooperation agreement with the United States government, you agreed not to break any laws of the United States or of any state. Is that correct?"

"That is correct."

"While you were at Lompoc prison, did you break any laws of the United States?"

"I think I did."

"And tell us what you did."

"Well, there were a couple of chaps who did laundry there. And I gave them a few quarters and they did my laundry."

"And that was a violation of the law of the United States. Isn't that right?"

"I think it was."

The outlaw investment bank that had financed Boesky when he was at his peak also would not survive.

Ten months to the day after John Shad joined the firm as its chairman, it was all over. Hammered by collapsing confidence in the junk bond market, pinched by new laws restricting how many junk bonds a savings and loan could own, and unable to overcome the financial and legal costs of its plea bargain with the government, Drexel filed for protection from its creditors under the federal bankruptcy laws on February 13, 1990. It was the largest Wall Street firm ever to fail.

Shad felt depressed. He had bet wrongly about Drexel, and his return to Wall Street had been a colossal personal and professional mistake. When he left the SEC in 1987, he had felt like a hero, celebrated for coming down on insider trading with hobnail boots, and for removing regulatory burdens that had unduly hampered the financial markets. But like Drexel's junk bonds, the perceived value of some of Shad's accomplishments had proved fleeting. Since his departure from the commission, the stock market had crashed, E. F. Hutton had fallen, Milken had admitted his guilt, and Drexel had collapsed into insolvency while Shad held the chairmanship. Shad could not help but feel that he deserved better.

Inside Drexel, the firm's rapid demise came as a surprise. Shad and Joseph said they had no idea deteriorating conditions in the junk bond market would lead to an abrupt loss of confidence in the firm's creditworthiness. Without the ability to borrow, Drexel could not stay in business. Toward the end, Shad and Joseph tried and failed to convince anyone to extend credit to prolong Drexel's life. But after years of running roughshod over Wall Street firms, commercial banks, and industrial companies, Drexel had no allies in the establishment or in government willing to lend a hand. When it was over, Shad blamed Congress for Drexel's bankruptcy, saying its ill-conceived rules barring S&Ls from owning junk bonds had killed the firm.

In the aftermath, Shad wrestled with his legacy. The morning after Drexel filed for bankruptcy, he was troubled to see a report in the *New York Times* that said he had joined Drexel to help repair the firm's image. It bothered Shad that anyone would think he had been hired for public relations value. As always, he calculated his own value in hard numbers, and by his reckoning he had carried his weight at Drexel. His annual pretax compensation was $3.175 million and during his ten months at the firm, he figured he had brought in business that paid for much of his salary. Stung by what he saw as the negative implications of the *Times*'s report, Shad seized on an idea: He would write a letter to the newspaper praising himself, and then ask his protégé Joseph to sign it and send it along.

Joseph didn't think this was a very good plan. It would be obvious to anyone paying attention that immediately after the bankruptcy, he wasn't going to be spending his time writing letters to defend Shad's honor, which hadn't really even been attacked. But Shad was a stubborn man. He drafted his letter anyway, and Joseph, willing to make his friend happy, signed.

"Your February 14th report that John Shad joined Drexel to help repair the firm's image is an understatement," the letter signed by Joseph said. "First, he accepted the chairmanship last April only after being encouraged to do so by the Justice Department and approved by the Securities and Exchange Commission—and he is contributing his after-tax Drexel compensation to the Harvard Business School. He was invited to become chairman because of his demonstrated ability to manage the firm, based upon his outstanding record and reputation as an investment banker, top executive, corporate director, and chairman of the SEC. During the past 10 months, he has exceeded our expectations . . . [producing] well over a million dollars in investment banking fees and [he] has important transactions in progress."

The *Times* never published the letter, but Shad made sure it was distributed to members of the press.

While serving as chairman of Drexel, Shad made his mark in Cambridge one other way: He made another charitable bequest to Harvard Business School. The school wasn't sure what to do with all of the $20 million Shad had donated for a program in business ethics. So in the time-honored tradition of academic fund-raising, it asked Shad for more. The business school dean indicated that Harvard would name a building after Shad if he came up with additional funds. Shad liked the idea of bricks and mortar, took out his checkbook once more, and soon a new Harvard Business School athletic center was dedicated in his name. It was quickly dubbed "Shad's Shed" by faculty and students.

When he resigned as Drexel chairman in the summer of 1990, Shad remained firmly convinced of virtually all of the deregulatory precepts he had carried with him from Wall Street to the SEC a decade earlier. But the SEC he left behind was by now a very different place. Gone was the enthusiasm for Chicago School economic theory and quantitative cost-benefit analysis. First under law professor David Ruder and especially under the chairmanship of Richard Breeden, an attorney and a political intimate of President George Bush, the commission had moved away from the narrow interpretation of its powers under Shad to the more regulatory, expansionist, moralist mode it had projected during

Stanley Sporkin's time and during certain other periods in its
history. The commission's approach to regulatory and enforcement issues under Breeden became openly interventionist and
more aggressive. Breeden, who had superb White House and
congressional contacts, obtained new powers to regulate the trading and finances of Wall Street brokerages, new authority to close
the markets in an emergency, and new enforcement tools. He
unsuccessfully sought to gain regulatory control for the SEC over
stock index futures. Inside the agency, he shifted enforcement
priorities, putting stockbrokers on notice that the commission
would watch out for small investors more closely and setting up a
special unit to scrutinize banks and other financial institutions.
Criticism of Breeden echoed the 1970s complaints against Sporkin and his colleagues—it was said that he was too tough, too
arrogant, too much a regulator.

If Shad had emphasized the stockholder's interest and market
liquidity, Breeden focused on the public interest and market stability. On the February night that Joseph had been meeting with
bankers seeking emergency funding for Drexel, he received a
late-night telephone call in his office from Chairman Breeden of
the SEC and a senior official of the Federal Reserve. (Shad had
already gone home.) They told Joseph, who had not yet obtained
financing, that for the sake of market stability, Drexel should file
for bankruptcy and make its intentions known the next morning
before markets opened for trading. Breeden threatened to take
action unless Joseph did. The next morning, the resilient American financial markets absorbed the news of Drexel's voluntary
bankruptcy with barely a ripple.

As Breeden sought to reshape the commission in his image, the
reputation of Shad's Securities and Exchange Commission and its
historic insider-trading prosecutions loomed large. Fictionalized
incarnations of its vigilant officers omnisciently apprehending
anyone who even considered trading on inside information were
depicted in Hollywood films and popular television shows. The
corporate raider was now an archetype of popular American culture, villified for selfish amorality and celebrated for swashbuck-
ling verve. Depicted in dramatic fantasies in the latter half of the

1980s—the raider usually got his comeuppance in the last act. The door would open and a handful of glum men in dark suits would enter the raider's swank office or home. The intruders announced stiffly and sternly that they had come from the SEC, and the antihero would be led away. He always knew, the expression on his face suggested, that he would be caught.

The reality that many insider traders got away scot-free during the 1980s was lost in the excitement about Milken, Drexel, Boesky, and the rest. The compelling argument that the SEC, through its abdication of serious junk bond and takeover regulation during John Shad's tenure, had helped to create some of the very problems it was later credited with solving, was never discussed.

Instead, the image of a strong and righteous commission had retained its place in the national consciousness, and the agency's public service mission seemed likely to endure well into the next century.

A Note on Sources

This book is based primarily on thousands of hours of interviews with more than 250 people. Most of the interviews were conducted between 1987 and 1990 on a "background" basis, meaning that people agreed to talk with us only if we agreed not to identify them. The desire of Securities and Exchange Commission employees and alumni for anonymity seemed to grow out of loyalty to the agency's long tradition of secrecy. In some cases, sources cited the need to protect client and business relationships in their requests that they not be named. The ultimate willingness of so many people to talk with us seemed a function of many factors, including strong feelings about the importance of the SEC's work and a desire to shape our views.

In addition to present and former SEC officials, we interviewed people who served in the White House, Congress, the Justice Department, the Federal Reserve, the Treasury Department, the Commodity Futures Trading Commission, and the Office of Management and Budget. We talked with officials from the major stock and futures exchanges in New York and Chicago, and finance industry lobbyists. We did much of the reporting in Washington and New York. But our work took us throughout the United States to sites ranging from Drexel Burnham Lambert's Beverly Hills office to SEC Chairman John Shad's birthplace in Brigham City, Utah, to courthouse basements in Milwaukee and Madison, Wisconsin. We interviewed scores of people who know Shad, including relatives, classmates at Harvard Business School, and executives on Wall Street and elsewhere who have had dealings with him over the years. We interviewed subjects of SEC investigations, witnesses, and their lawyers.

We talked with investment bankers, traders, money managers, arbitragers, and attorneys who work at the highest levels of global finance. We also talked with ordinary investors.

We are aware of the pitfalls presented by any attempt to reconstruct events after the fact. Wherever possible, we relied on transcripts, contemporaneous notes, Congressional records, court papers, and other documents that, unlike memories, do not change with the passage of time. We relied on confidential SEC memos and other documents in some instances. In other cases, we gained access to commission records, including testimony by Michael Milken in enforcement division investigations, by making requests under the Freedom of Information Act. We reviewed voluminous public records, ranging from SEC enforcement cases to financial disclosure forms filed by Shad and other commissioners. In two instances—the Citicorp and Mobil cases of the early 1980s—transcripts of closed commission meetings were available from public sources.

We were aided enormously in our research by the work of other journalists and authors. A few of these works were notable for being ahead of their time or unusual in their depth. These include Allan Sloan and Howard Rudnitsky's 1984 *Forbes* magazine cover story, "Mike Milken's Marvelous Money Machine," and a variety of reporting by James B. Stewart and Daniel Hertzberg of the *Wall Street Journal*, including their Pulitzer Prize–winning account of Ivan Boesky's relationship with investment banker Marty Siegel in February 1987. Two articles in 1985, "The Roaring Eighties," by Steven Brill, in *The American Lawyer*, and "The Casino Society," by Anthony Bianco, in *Business Week*, explained early on how takeovers, corporate raiders, and arbitragers fueled speculation in the financial system. Our work benefited, too, from James Sterngold's *New York Times* reporting on the fallout from the 1987 stock market crash, particularly the collapse of Shad's old firm, E. F. Hutton. A series of articles spanning several decades in *Fortune* magazine on the Harvard Business School class of 1949, including "The Class the Dollars Fell On," by Marilyn Wellmemeyer in 1974, enhanced our understanding of Shad and his peers.

Other articles and books helped us in specific areas covered by our narrative. John Brooks's "Once in Golconda," Joel Seligman's *The Transformation of Wall Street: A History of the SEC*, former SEC secretary John Wheeler's review of the Seligman book in the *Yale Law Journal*, and "Regulation by Prosecution," by former SEC commissioner Roberta Karmel, all provided important background about the commission's formation and development. Articles about Bohemian Grove in *Psychology Today* in 1975 and by Jack Anderson in 1981 provided details about that summer camp for the rich and powerful that we otherwise would not have known. *Off the Books: Citibank and the World's Biggest Money Game*, by Robert Hutchison, provided insight into the SEC case against Citicorp. Investigative reporting on the Citicorp matter and Shad's finances by Jeff Gerth in the *New York Times* revealed the tension between Shad and Congress. We relied on *Three Plus One Equals Billions: The Bendix–Martin Marietta War*, by Allan Sloan, for details on that takeover fight. *Boone*, an autobiography by oilman T. Boone Pickens, Jr., provided extensive information on takeover battles in which he was involved.

Connie Bruck's 1984 article in the *Atlantic Monthly*, "My Master Is My Purse," on Ivan Boesky, and her later book about Michael Milken, *The Predator's Ball: The Junk Bond Raiders and the Man Who Staked Them*, told us a great deal about two of the most important financiers of the era. Brooks Jackson's *Wall Street Journal* scoop on John Fedders's marital problems and divorce trial, and *Shattered Dreams*, by Charlotte Fedders and Laura Elliot, provided us with much information about the violence in the Fedders' home. Sharon Walsh's account of the Catherine Broderick sexual harassment case against the SEC in the *Washington Post* opened our eyes to new avenues of inquiry about Shad's commission. Douglas Frantz's 1987 book, *Levine & Co: Wall Street's Insider Trading Scandal*, provided much helpful background on Dennis Levine, including the December 1985 SEC meeting concerning the case and the encounter involving Levine and his partner-in-crime Robert Wilkis, when they discovered Levine's notoriety at a newsstand in Manhattan's Hell's Kitchen neighborhood. Reporting by Laurie Goodstein of the *Washington Post* in 1990 provided us with reaction on the streets of New York to Michael Milken's ten-year prison sentence.

If we have inadvertently failed to cite any published works from which we have benefited, we apologize in advance.

Acknowledgments

This book is the result of the generosity of our sources—the more than 250 people who agreed, despite busy schedules and wariness of reporters, to help us understand and explain the relationship between the Securities and Exchange Commission and Wall Street during the 1980s. Many of these sources sat for long and repeated sessions, enduring persistent and personal questions without any guarantee that they would like the result in print. We thank them for their trust, patience, guidance, and time. Of course, they are not responsible for our errors and opinions.

From the beginning of our interest in this subject, the *Washington Post* unfailingly trusted our instincts and provided us with the resources to pursue them. Four unusually talented editors—Peter Behr, Tom Dimond, Bob Woodward, and Steve Luxenberg—supervised the newspaper series "The Man from Wall Street: John Shad's Reign at the SEC," from which this book is drawn and for which we received the 1990 Pulitzer Prize. We could not have done it without them. They protected us from distractions, taught us a great deal, and helped to craft the final articles. Behr, the *Post*'s assistant managing editor for business coverage, allowed us to pull back from daily reporting while we pursued our newspaper series. We cannot thank him enough. Later, Behr, executive editor Ben Bradlee, managing editor Leonard Downie, Jr., and assistant managing editor Michael Getler gave us the support and time we needed to research and write our book, reminding us again why the *Post* is such a wonderful place for journalists to work.

In addition to his considerable contribution to our newspaper series, Luxenberg provided valuable editorial advice and criticism that helped shape the book. We are grateful to him for being so unselfish with his time and ideas.

Olwen Price at the *Post* cheerfully and accurately transcribed hours and hours of tapes from our interviews with sources. Staff researcher Melissa Mathis contributed immensely to our reporting. Among other things, she assembled the labyrinthine charts of past and present SEC employees that served as important maps for our reporting.

Melanie Jackson, our literary agent, worked relentlessly and loyally to make this book happen. At Scribners, publisher Barbara Grossman brought enthusiasm and a talented eye to the manuscript. Her assistant Hamilton Cain was also a great help.

Our wives, Lori Vise and Susan Coll, provided us the love and support we needed to write this book as well as the judgment and wisdom that helped us see it to the end.

Index

ABC television, 335
Ackerman, Peter, 264
Aetna Life & Casualty Co., 113–15, 147
Agee, William, 102, 103, 104, 105
Allied Corporation, 103, 104, 183
American Airlines, 12
American Financial Corporation, 90, 134
Anheuser-Busch, 183
AT&T, 146, 157

Baker, Howard, 356
Baker, James, 199, 324, 354, 366
Banca Della Svizzera, 54–58
Bank Leu, 292–306, 316
Barron's, 192
Baston, Luis, 374
Batterymarch Financial Management, 148
Bear, Stearns & Company, 214
Belvedere Securities, 97–98
Benbow, Joel R., 287
Bendix Corporation, 102, 103–4, 105–7, 118, 146, 147
Bergen, Edgar, 22
Bergquist, Judith, 155
Bevill Bresler, 254–55

Biggs, Barton, 75
Black, Eli, 4
Blackburn, Robert, 53–55, 58
Boesky, Ivan, 98, 99, 105–6, 182, 210–20, 254, 257, 267, 268, 269, 272, 275–77, 280–89, 300–303, 310–26, 360, 362, 364, 375, 376–77
  in Dr Pepper case, 207–10, 220–23
  impact of Boesky's fall, 329–43, 358
Boesky, Seema, 213–14, 315
Bohemian Grove, 21–22, 23
Brady, Nicholas F., 109–10
Breeden, Richard, 379–80
British Oxygen Corporation, 219
Broderick, Catherine, 229–31, 349–51, 359–60
Brown, David, 307
Bruns, John J., 233–34, 238
Buffett, Warren, 118–19, 126
Burke, James E., 38
Bush, Barbara, 354
Bush, George, 22, 23, 26, 185, 345, 354, 365–66, 379
Business Roundtable, 186, 188, 189
Butler, "Doctor Tom," 155, 157

389

Caesars World Resorts, 33, 261–64, 271–73

Califano, Joseph, 78, 110

Campbell, Tom, 199

Carberry, Charles, 309–11, 313, 319–20, 322, 323

Carr, Fred, 96

Carter, Jimmy, 6, 7, 8, 28, 123, 164

Carter Hawley Hale, 203–4, 277

Casey, William, 13, 14

CBS, 37, 253, 293

Cecola, Randall, 307

Central Intelligence Agency (CIA), 2–3, 13, 16, 72

Centrust Savings, 271

Cheek, Dwayne, 132

Chevron Corporation, 181

Chicago options exchange case, 127–28

Christensen, Max, 234–35

Citicorp case, 1, 5–6, 59–72, 78, 79–80, 86–88, 105, 239

Cities Service Co., 153, 154, 155, 158, 159–60, 165–69

Clements, Bill, 154

Cohen, Manuel F., 16

Commodity Futures Trading Commission (CFTC), 39–41, 63, 109, 121, 123, 125, 357

Connally, John, 23

Conner, William, 53

Connolly, Joseph, 180, 202, 203

Cook, G. Bradford, 11

Coulson, Richard, 296, 299

Council of Institutional Investors, 286

Cox, Charles, 107–9, 116, 171, 173–74, 184, 186, 199, 202, 226, 244, 246, 247, 329

Credit Suisse, 53, 55, 56–58

Crown, Lester, 297

Cunningham, Mary, 102

Curnin, Thomas, 93, 96, 138

Dahl, Jim, 264, 266, 270–71, 326–27, 336, 363

D'Amato, Alfonse, 78

Davis, Polk and Wardwell, 208

DeMuth, Christopher, 199, 201

Deremer, Karl, 264

Dillon, Read, 109

Dingell, John, 73–76, 77, 78, 80–81, 82–88, 105, 109–10, 112, 114, 191, 205, 324, 329, 336–38, 347–48

Doherty, David, 1, 5–6, 16–20, 59, 62, 63, 64–69, 70, 72, 86, 87, 88

Donaldson, Sam, 335

Douce, William, 279–80, 285, 287

Douglas, William O., 10

Drexel Burnham Lambert, 33, 89, 90, 92, 96, 97, 98, 131–37, 140–41, 143–46, 179, 181, 182, 187, 211, 216, 241, 259, 260–69, 270–72, 280, 281, 283, 284, 285, 287–89, 296–97, 298, 305, 306, 312, 313–14, 326–27, 330, 333, 335–36, 337, 340–42, 355, 360, 361–64, 376, 380, 381. *See also* Milken, Michael

Shad's chairmanship of, 366–372, 377–79, 380

Dr Pepper, 209–10, 220–23, 284, 300

Drucker, Peter F., 217

E. F. Hutton, 15, 22, 24, 25, 26, 32–33, 34, 35, 75, 77, 101, 109, 142, 144, 227, 242, 262, 270, 340, 355, 366, 367, 377

Eckart, Dennis, 337

Edwards, David, 65, 66

Edwards & Hanly, 218

Einhorn, Irving, 259–63, 264, 267, 271–73, 361

Eisenhower, Dwight, 260

Evans, John, 69–70, 71, 226

Executive Life Insurance, 288

Exxon Corporation, 157

Fedders, Charlotte, 111–13, 115, 250, 252

Fedders, John, 43–44, 85, 86–88, 90, 94, 99, 109, 115, 129, 138, 139, 141, 147, 203, 209, 218, 219, 223, 225, 226, 228, 232, 239, 243–46, 254, 255, 256, 257, 258, 271, 293, 295, 304, 306, 319, 330, 349
  choice and appointment as SEC enforcement chief, 44–47
  in Citicorp case, 60–63, 67–68, 69, 72
  insider trading, focus on, 49–60, 52–58
  marital problems of, 111–13, 115, 249–52
  priorities of, 47–50
  resignation of, 253
  and Swiss-bank secrecy, 53–58, 106
Fielding, Fred, 251
Fienberg, Linda, 350
First Boston Corporation, 103, 297
Fischel, Dan, 302
Fisher, Robert, 233, 236, 238, 243, 247
Flans, Alan, 266
Flom, Joe, 114–15, 147
Fomon, Robert, 35
Ford, Gerald, 79
Ford Motor Company, 74, 310
Foreign Corrupt Practices Act, 25, 49
Forstmann, Ted, 220–23, 284
Forstmann Little & Company, 220–22
Fortune magazine, 49, 357
Frankfurter, Felix, 10
Freeman, Robert, 342, 344
Fried, Frank, Harris, Shriver & Jacobson, 316
Friedman, Josh, 265
Friedman, Milton, 122–24, 194, 195
Frymer, Bill, 265
futures trading revolution, 118–26

Gable, Clark, 92
Garn, Jake, 25, 200, 324
Geisinger, Ethel, 81, 83
General Electric, 269

General Foods, 270, 298, 310
Gerth, Jeff, 76–78, 79, 86
Gibraltar Savings Association, 288
Gibson Greeting Card Company, 146
Ginsburg, Douglas, 199, 201–2
Giuliani, Rudolph, 232, 342, 363, 369
Goelzer, Dan, 41, 226, 245, 350
Goldberg, Arthur, 148
Golden Nugget, 267–68
Goldin, Harrison J., 286–87
Goldman, Sachs & Co., 145, 214, 307, 342, 343
Goldsmith, James, 177
Graf, Larry, 155–57, 159, 160, 165, 168
Greene, Ed, 41, 44
Greenspoon, Ben, 350
Grundfest, Joseph, 199
Gulf Oil Corporation, 12, 159, 160, 178–83
Gut, Rainer, 56–58

Hackel, Lori Anne. *See* Milken, Lori.
Hammerman, Stephen, 238
Haraszthy, Jan, 236
Hart, Gary, 172–73
Harvard Business School, 26, 31–32, 38, 101, 102, 144, 230, 307, 344, 354, 378, 379
Heck, Robert, 167, 245, 248
Herrmann, Denny, 155–58, 160–61, 165–70, 239, 245, 248
Hewitt, Jack, 89–99, 106–7, 109, 131–41, 143, 212, 241, 261, 269, 271, 361
Hiler, Bruce, 257
Hoffman, Abbie, 273
Houston Natural Gas, 310
Huber, John, 180, 202

Iaccarino, Albert, 235
IBM, 157
Icahn, Carl, 281–89
IFB Managing Partners, 315
Iran-contra scandal, 338
Iran hostages, 7–8

Jackson, Andrew, 6
Jackson, Brooks, 250
Jackson, Michael, 199
James, E. Pendleton, 24
Jarrell, Gregg, 149–51, 175–76, 184, 186, 189, 338–39, 351
　leaks and private campaign within SEC, 191–206
Jefferies, Boyd, 300–302
Johnson, Philip, 39–41, 63, 80, 109, 118, 125, 357
Johnson, Roy, 264
Johnson & Johnson, 38, 351
Joseph, Fred, 32–33, 35, 144–46, 179, 263, 312, 340–42, 355, 361–64, 366–69, 371, 378, 380
junk bonds, 143–46. *See also* Milken, Michael

Karmel, Roberta, 5
Kennedy, John F., 6, 11
Kennedy, Joseph P., 10, 27
Ketchum, Rick, 226
Khomeini, Ayatollah, 338
Kidder, Peabody & Co., 104, 106, 251, 312, 342, 343
King, Henry, 208, 210
Knauf, Wayne, 154–59, 168
Kohlberg Kravis Roberts & Company, 182
Kopel, Jared, 131–33, 136–37, 139–40
Kuenzli, David, 155, 159, 160–65, 166, 168

Landis, James M., 10
Lapidus, Cary, 234, 236–37, 239, 242–43, 244–46
Lasker, Morris, 343
Lawyer, Bobby, 225–26, 228–29, 231–33, 236, 237–39, 242–48
Lazard Frères, 103, 104, 307
LeBaron, Dean, 148
Lehman Brothers, 103
Levin, Theodore, 208–9
Levine, Dennis, 296–300, 303–7, 308–13, 314, 315, 316, 317, 318, 326, 331, 334, 340, 341, 342, 349
Levine, Ted, 5, 15–16, 20, 47, 90, 131, 133, 136–37, 139–40, 203
Levitt, Arthur, 300
Levy, Gus, 214
Lewis, Salim B., 214
Liman, Arthur, 306
Limited, The, 203
Lindner, Carl, 90, 134, 137, 181
Lipton, Martin, 24, 147, 186, 189, 205, 217, 288, 298, 307
Lockheed Corporation, 4
Lombardi, Vince, 94
Long, Perrin, 368
Longstreth, Bevis, 69, 70–71, 72, 82, 86, 226–28
Loomis, Phil, 18, 69
LTV Corporation, 183
Lynch, Gary, 203–4, 209–10, 249, 252, 254–58, 271, 300–303, 310, 329, 330, 332, 333, 335, 337, 339, 362, 369–70, 371
　in Boesky case, 312–13, 317–23, 325
　in Levine case, 291–96, 304–6

Mann, Michael, 249, 252, 304, 306
Marinaccio, Charles, 226, 244, 246
Martin Marietta Corporation, 102–4, 105–7, 118, 146, 147
Matl, Victor, 233–39, 243–44, 245–48
May, Beville, 349–50
MCA Corporation, 267–68
MCI Communications, 145–46
McLucas, Bill, 249, 252, 257
Meese, Edwin, 338
Melamed, Leo, 121–24
Merrick, David, 218
Merrill Lynch, 23, 225, 233–48, 257, 294, 300–301, 337, 376
Mesa Petroleum Company, 154, 178
Metromedia, 182
Metzenbaum, Howard, 172, 175
Milken, Lori (Hackel), 92, 370

Milken, Lowell, 96, 98, 266, 341–42, 362–63, 370, 375
Milken, Michael, 89–99, 104, 106–7, 109, 130, 131–41, 143–46, 178–79, 181–82, 185, 187, 188, 211–12, 217, 223, 241, 254, 257, 259, 261–69, 271–72, 276, 278, 281, 283–89, 312, 313–15, 316, 320, 321, 323–24, 326–27, 330, 333, 336, 340–42, 360, 361–64, 367, 369–71, 377, 381
sentencing and aftermath, 373–76
Miller, Ernie, 350
Mitchell, Steven, 50, 52
Mobil Oil Corporation, 1, 5–6, 16–20, 36, 76, 172
Mondale, Walter, 172–73
Monocle, the, 38–39, 40, 80, 81, 109, 157
Morgan, J. P., 95
Morgan Stanley & Co., 75, 76–77, 145

Nabisco Brands, 298, 310
Nader, Ralph, 4, 41, 103, 241
New York Financial Writers Association, 186–88
New York Post, 132, 376
New York Times, 53, 76–78, 378, 379
Nixon, Richard, 11, 12, 13, 69, 79, 260
Northrop Corporation, 12
Northview Corporation, 315

Occidental Petroleum, 182
Owen, Richard, 305

Paine Webber, 220
Pearce, Ira, 2
Pearlstein, Norman, 252
Pecaro, Susan, 166–69, 239, 245
Pecora hearings, 94–95
Peizer, Terren, 264, 271
Perella, Joe, 103
Perelman, Ronald, 306

Peters, Aulana, 226, 244, 245, 246, 247, 305, 329, 334
Phelan, John, 300–301, 345, 346, 347
Philadelphia options exchange case, 127–28
Phillips Petroleum, 254, 272, 275–89
Pickens, Boone, 153–54, 158, 159, 172, 177–84, 185, 187, 188, 193, 221, 254, 275–76, 277–80, 282, 286, 287, 348
Pitt, Harvey, 291–96, 300, 303–5, 316–20, 322, 323
Pletscher, Bruno, 296, 299, 300, 303–4
Pollack, Irv, 243–44
Pollack, Milton, 54–55
Pownall, Thomas, 102–4
Pratt, John H., 359–60
Proxmire, William, 339

Quinn, Linda, 175–76, 226

Rauch, Michael, 295, 303
RCA Corporation, 146, 269–70, 273, 293
Reagan, Nancy, 8
Reagan, Ronald, 1, 2–3, 5, 13, 15, 18, 40, 45, 75, 80, 82, 108, 109, 110, 116, 123, 145, 153–54, 158, 159, 172–74, 176, 177, 185, 194, 195, 206, 210, 227, 253, 329, 338–39, 348, 354, 374, 375, 376
arrival in Washington, 6–8
Shad and, 21–26, 110, 339
Rees, Sarah Johnson, 26, 29
Reeves, Robert, 235–36
Regan, Donald, 23, 24, 199, 200, 205–6, 324, 354
Reich, Ilan, 307, 311, 315
Reliance Group, 96–97, 135–36
Revlon Corporation, 306
Rich, Marc, 275, 321
Riegle, Donald, 347
Romano, Robert, 243–44, 294
Roosevelt, Franklin D., 27

Ruder, David, 356, 357, 371, 379
Ryan, Robert, 62, 68

St. Joe Minerals Corporation, 53, 54
St. Regis Corporation, 177
Salomon Brothers, 102, 104, 144–45
Sampson, Clarence, 193
Sampson, Gary, 50–52, 53, 56, 58
Santa Fe International, 50–53, 58
Savage, Phil, 107, 231
Scalise, Rose, 235
Scarff, Doug, 44, 126
Schneiderman, Irwin, 45, 46, 147,
    365, 366
Schreyer, William, 300–301
SEC policy. *See* Shad, John; Sporkin,
    Stanley
Seemala Corporation, 98, 315
Shad, John, 1, 3, 5, 14–16, 18–20,
    49–50, 53, 73, 102, 104, 111–
    13, 124, 136, 137, 163, 170,
    199–200, 210, 219, 249, 251,
    252, 253, 254, 255, 257–58,
    260, 262, 269, 270, 272, 273,
    293, 296, 298, 299, 300–302,
    303, 306, 317–18, 320, 321–
    22, 323, 324
  and advisory committee on merg-
    ers, 147–51
  and Aetna case, 113–15
  as ambassador to Netherlands,
    353–61, 364–69
  on arbitrage and Boesky, 216–18
  Boesky case, trouble from, 329–44
  budget increase for SEC, seeking,
    337–38
  childhood and youth, 29–32
  and Citicorp case, 59–72, 79–80,
    86
  on computer surveillance system,
    128
  confirmation as SEC chairman, 25–
    26
  departure from SEC, 339–40, 347–
    49
  Dingell committee, troubles with,
    74–88, 105, 109–10, 336–38

  Drexel chairmanship for, 366–72,
    377–79, 380
  ethical focus and contradictions of,
    113–19, 120, 344, 351–52,
    360–61, 371–72, 378–79
  and Fedders apointment, 44–47
  first days at SEC, 26–29, 38–41
  free market view of, 106–9, 116–
    19, 125–30, 141–44, 145, 230
  futures/options deal with Johnson
    of CFTC, 39–41, 63, 109, 118,
    125, 157, 357
  golden parachute policy, 177
  greenmail policy, 177
  on insider trading, 49–50, 53, 182–
    183, 219, 273, 334–35
  and Jarrell's private campaign
    within SEC, 191–206
  junk bonds, view of, 143–46
  "Leveraging of America" speech,
    184–89
    reactions to, 191–92, 200–202,
    204–6
  and Merrill Lynch case, 239–42,
    244–48
  Reagan and, 21–26, 110, 339
  resentments within SEC, 226, 228–
    31, 242
  on sexual discrimination case
    (SEC), 230–31, 349–51, 359–
    60
  on stock market crash, 344–47,
    355–59
  takeovers, policy toward, 106–9,
    147–51, 171–77, 206, 277, 279
  reassessment speech, 184–89
  Wall Street career of, 32–35, 99–
    102, 366–72, 377–79, 380
  wife's stroke, 36–38
Shad, Leslie Anne, 34, 37, 230
Shad, Lillie Mae, 29, 30
Shad, Patricia Pratt, 32, 34, 35–38,
    41, 70, 185, 355
  death of, 364–65
Shad, Rees, 34
Shearson, Hamill & Company, 32
Shearson Lehman Brothers, 307

Sherman & Sterling, 65–66, 68

Shinkle, Jack, 66

Siegel, Martin, 102–3, 104, 105–6, 182, 210–11, 223, 281, 312, 313, 324, 333, 334, 336, 340, 342, 375

Silberstein, Ben, 213–14

Simon, William, 146

Skadden, Arps, Slate, Meagher & Flom, 297

Smith Barney, 154–59, 160, 161, 165–70, 233, 239, 242, 245, 248, 257, 296

Sokolow, Ira, 307, 311, 315

Solomon, David, 268

Sommer, A. A., 186

Sorkin, Ira Lee, 228

Speakes, Larry, 172

Spencer, Lee, 19

Sporkin, Stanley, 16, 17, 18, 20, 44, 46, 47, 61, 66, 69, 72, 86, 87, 94, 239, 243, 245, 256, 347, 379, 380

  activist nature of, 3–5, 11, 12–13, 27–28, 41

  departure from SEC, 1–6, 13–16

  disclosure theories of, 12–13

Spurge, Lorraine, 264

Stahl, Leslie, 253

Steinberg, Saul, 96, 135, 182

Stigler, George J., 194, 195

Stillwell, Robert, 159

Stockman, David, 26

Sturc, John, 296, 305, 306, 319, 325

Sullivan & Cromwell, 176

Superior Oil, 172

Swiss banks, 53–58, 106, 292, 294–97, 299–300, 303, 304–6, 316

Tashima, A. Wallace, 204

Tavoulareas, Peter, 17

Tavoulareas, William, 17, 18

Teamsters Union, 256

Tet Offensive, 91

Textron Incorporated, 297–98, 303, 307

Thayer, Paul, 183

Thomas, Barbara, 18–20, 63, 82, 226

Tisch, Laurence A., 24, 37

Tobey, Bill, 265

Tome, Giuseppe, 58

Treadway, James, 171, 173, 174, 244, 246

Trepp, Warren, 264

Trujillo, Louis, 233, 237–38, 243, 244, 247

Twentieth Century Fox, 218

Union Carbide, 270, 310

United Brands, 4

United Jewish Appeal, 213

United Technologies Corporation, 103, 219

Vietnam War, 91–92, 129, 199

Volcker, Paul, 125, 205, 324, 347, 354

von Stein, Thomas, 62, 72, 86

Wachtell, Lipton, Rosen & Katz, 307

Wall Street Journal, 79, 93, 154, 157, 165, 193–94, 222, 249–52, 375

Walt Disney Company, 182

Wang, Leo, 303

Warner Communications, 270

Washington Post, 18, 76

Wasserstein, Bruce, 103, 104, 147

Watergate scandal, 12, 65

Wharton School, 92

Wheeler, John, 128–29

Whittaker, Bob, 87–88

Wick, Charles, 8

Wigton, Richard, 342, 344

Wilkis, Robert, 307, 311, 315

Williams, Harold, 3, 28, 66, 245

Williams Act, 11

Wilmer, Cutler & Pickering, 316

Winans, R. Foster, 251

Wirth, Tim, 82

Wood, Kimba, 373–75

Wyden, Ron, 337

Wynn, Steve, 267–68

ABOUT THE AUTHORS

DAVID A. VISE was a Wall Street investment banker with Goldman, Sachs & Co. Previously a financial reporter for *The Washington Post,* he is currently the paper's deputy financial editor. He lives in Bethesda, Maryland.

STEVE COLL, New Delhi bureau chief of *The Washington Post,* is the author of *The Deal of the Century* and *The Taking of Getty Oil.*